OXFORD THEOLOGICAL MONOGRAPHS

OXFORD THEOLOGICAL MONOGRAPHS

Karl Rahner and Ignatian Spirituality

PHILIP ENDEAN

OXFORD
UNIVERSITY PRESS

*This book has been printed digitally and produced in a standard specification
in order to ensure its continuing availability*

OXFORD
UNIVERSITY PRESS

Great Clarendon Street, Oxford OX2 6DP

Oxford University Press is a department of the University of Oxford.
It furthers the University's objective of excellence in research, scholarship,
and education by publishing worldwide in

Oxford New York

Auckland Bangkok Buenos Aires Cape Town Chennai
Dar es Salaam Delhi Hong Kong Istanbul Karachi Kolkata
Kuala Lumpur Madrid Melbourne Mexico City Mumbai Nairobi
São Paulo Shanghai Taipei Tokyo Toronto

Oxford is a registered trade mark of Oxford University Press
in the UK and in certain other countries

Published in the United States
by Oxford University Press Inc., New York

ISBN 0-19- 827028-3

Acknowledgements

This book is a heavily revised version of a doctoral thesis, submitted an embarrassingly long time ago in the University of Oxford. I would like to record my gratitude to Rowan Williams, my supervisor—now Archbishop of Wales—for his constant encouragement and support of the dissertation, as well as for many helpful suggestions as to how it should proceed. I must also thank Edward Yarnold for additional help in an official capacity as representative of the Theology Faculty of the University of Oxford, and my examiners, Nicholas Lash and John Macquarrie. I remember, too, the teachers at Heythrop College, University of London, with whom I first studied Rahner—Joseph Laishley, John O'Donnell, and Michael Simpson—as well as Edward Vacek, at Weston Jesuit School of Theology, Cambridge, Massachusetts, in whose 1985 seminar, 'Emotions in the Christian Life', the idea of this study first crystallized. Later, in Innsbruck, I learnt much (though certainly not enough) from Otto Muck on Rahner's metaphysics, and from Karl Heinz Neufeld on the historical and institutional contexts in which Rahner worked.

Rahner's unpublished writings are cited by kind permission of the Upper German (South German) Province of the Society of Jesus. For permission to use the resources of the Karl-Rahner-Archiv in the Jesuitenkolleg, Innsbruck, I thank Walter Kern and Karl Heinz Neufeld, successively directors of the archive, and heads of the Fundamental Theology department in the Theology Faculty of the University of Innsbruck. I must also note the unfailing kindness of Roman Siebenrock, the Rahner archivist, not only in making materials available to me as I needed them, but also in many other ways. I am grateful, too, to Peter Knauer for his permission to use a 1959 exchange of letters between himself and Rahner, to Bruno Niederbacher for obtaining German materials for me during the final stage of editing, and to Joseph Munitiz, who in many and diverse ways supported this project, before, during, and after his time as Master of Campion Hall.

Campion Hall is only one of the religious communities which have welcomed and supported this project. I remember with gratitude also the Jesuitenkolleg in Innsbruck, where I was allowed to live and work very contentedly for more than a year; my present home community in Harlesden, north-west London; St Beuno's Ignatian Spirituality Centre, where I spent three happy sabbatical months in the spring of 1997; and the Ignatiushaus in Munich, where I experienced a patience and hospitality during the summer of 1987 that greatly alleviated the pain of learning German. For financial support, I am grateful to the British Academy, to the British Province of the Society of Jesus, and to the Karl-Rahner-Stiftung, Munich.

It was Robert Morgan who, as chair of the Oxford Theological Monographs committee, invited me to submit this project, and Paul Fiddes who read two versions of the text with a care and critical sympathy that were quite extraordinary. I am most grateful to both, especially for their patience with my dilatoriness. I should also acknowledge help from Diarmaid MacCulloch, as a later chair of the monographs committee, and from the staff of the Oxford University Press. Many friends have discussed Rahner with me over the years. I think particularly of Richard Lennan, now on the faculty at the Catholic Institute of Sydney, a companion both in Oxford and in Innsbruck, and also of Sarah Boss, Michael Kirwan, John Moffatt, Stephan Rothlin, and Martin Maier. I should add that the latter was responsible for drawing my attention to the Rahner–Knauer exchange.

To recall such kindnesses is an experience at once delightful and humbling. I hope that what follows is worthy of the commitment shown to it by so many people.

P. E., SJ

Contents

Abbreviations

Aut	Ignatius's *Autobiography*.
Const	*The Constitutions of the Society of Jesus.*
Diary	Ignatius's *Spiritual Diary*.
Dir	The *Directories* to the *Spiritual Exercises*.
Exx	Ignatius's *Spiritual Exercises*.
KRA	Karl-Rahner-Archiv, University of Innsbruck.
KRSW	*Karl Rahner Sämtliche Werke.*
LTK	*Lexikon für Theologie und Kirche*, 2nd edn., 10 vols. and 3 supp. vols. (Freiburg: Herder, 1957–65).
MHSJ	Monumenta historica Societatis Jesu
MHSJ *EI*	*Sancti Ignatii de Loyola epistulae et instructiones*, 12 vols., edd. M. Lecina, V. Agusti, F. Cervós, and D. Restrepo (Madrid: 1903–11).
MHSJ *Exx* (1969)	*Sancti Ignatii de Loyola Exercitia Spiritualia*, edd. José Calveras and Cándido de Dalmases (Rome, 1969).
MHSJ *FN*	*Fontes Narrativi de S. Ignatio de Loyola et de Societatis Jesu initiis*, edd. D. Fernández Zápico, C. de Dalmases, and P. Leturia, 4 vols. (Rome, 1943–60).
MHSJ *MN*	*Epistolae (Monumenta) P. Hieronymi Nadal*, edd. F. Cervós and Miguel Nicolau, 6 vols. (Madrid and Rome, 1898–1964).
SM	*Sacramentum mundi*, ed. with A. Darlap, trans. C. Ernst and K. Smyth, 6 vols. (New York: Herder, 1968–70). German version in 4 vols. (Freiburg: Herder, 1967–9).
SzT	*Schriften zur Theologie*, 16 vols. (Einsiedeln: Benzinger, 1954–84).
TI	*Theological Investigations*, 23 vols. (London: Darton, Longman and Todd, 1961–92).

Conventions Regarding References

Many of the sources, both primary and secondary, for this study were originally written in languages other than English. Where an English translation is available, I have, when possible, compared it with the original, and given a double page reference: roman type to the translation and *italics* to the original. An asterisk after the roman-type number (e.g. 453*) indicates that the published translation is seriously unreliable; lighter amendments—for example shifts in emphasis or the removal of gender-specific pronouns—have been made tacitly.

For Ignatian primary materials (apart from the letters), I have followed the internationally standardized paragraph and verse numbering. I have adopted a standard English convention regarding the term 'Spiritual Exercises': *italicized* it refers to the text as such, in roman type to the lived process which the text aims to foster. When referring to the *Constitutions*, I have referred first to the part, chapter, and paragraph from which the citation is taken, and then to the running paragraph numbers that have become common in modern editions (e.g. *Const*, VI. i. 1 [547]).

References in a date or date-and-letter format—e.g. 1936, 1954/5, 1956*a*—refer to Rahner's major writings on Ignatian topics, narrowly conceived, listed in the first part of the bibliography.

1

Fragments, Foundations, and Bearings

In November 1936, Karl Rahner was in Innsbruck. Some months previously he had submitted in Freiburg his doctoral thesis in philosophy—what we now know as *Spirit in the World* (*Geist in Welt*). Its failure was soon to become public, but this event was not to disturb Rahner too much. His superiors had in any case changed their minds: he was to teach not philosophy but dogmatic theology, and he had already in that same year submitted a second doctoral dissertation, this time to the Innsbruck theology faculty. Now he was assembling material for his habilitation, a task that would be completed by the following summer, as a final preparation for his career as a teacher.[1] Rahner's life was thus in transition, between the life of a student and that of a teacher, and between philosophy and theology. At this point he received what now appears a significant invitation. Would he like to write on the dogmatic theology of Ignatius Loyola's *Spiritual Exercises*?

The request is to be found in a folder among Rahner's unpublished papers.[2] It came on a postcard from Emmerich Raitz von Frentz (1889–1968). Frentz had been on the staff at Valkenburg, the German Jesuit faculty just across the Dutch border, while Rahner was doing his ordination theology studies there. He had led seminar groups on the Ignatian Exercises, and, from 1932, had been responsible for successive revisions of what was then the standard German translation of the text, first produced by Alfred Feder in 1922. In 1936, Frentz's intention was to bring out a fuller edition than had

---

[1] It is well known that Rahner's superiors originally intended him to teach philosophy at the faculty in Pullach, on the outskirts of Munich. It is far less clear why and how that plan changed. But Rahner's doctorate in theology, and indeed his move to Innsbruck, were planned before it was known that his philosophy thesis had been rejected. For testimony from the elderly Rahner, see *Faith in a Wintry Season*, 44, 53; for the biographical issues, see Neufeld, *Die Brüder Rahner*, 121–3, 130–3, and the discussion by Albert Raffelt in *KRSW*, vol. ii, pp. xxiii–xxix. Rahner's theological dissertation, '*E latere Christi*', a study in patristic ecclesiology, was to pass unproblematically in December 1936.

[2] See Bibliography, part I, under 1936.

been available hitherto, supported by a critical commentary. He himself would contribute textual and exegetical notes, while a psychologist and a canon lawyer would each write chapters from their own professional standpoints. To Rahner, Frentz wrote, 'since even back then (i.e. in Valkenburg) you were already of the view that we still basically lack a systematic theology of the Exercises, I should like to ask you to undertake one or more chapters on the subject'. The same archive folder contains two tantalizing scraps of paper with scribbled notes in Rahner's own hand. One appears to sketch out a possible table of contents. Not surprisingly, given the author, it begins with the understanding of the human person presupposed in the *Exercises*, and seems to envisage a contrast between modern and medieval models. Then we move through various theological themes: the image of God (with a note to the effect that Ignatius echoes Luther and Calvin); the encounter with God; sin; nature and grace; the theology of meditation on the life of Christ; the theology of vocational choice; and finally the theology of mysticism. The second sheet is less systematic, giving simply a wide-ranging list of people and ideas—among others, modern science, the Renaissance, Descartes, the Enlightenment, and individualism. At the bottom, more suggestively, Rahner has written, 'instead of Catholic dogma, personal relationship to Christ—a theology of the religious event itself'.[3]

There is also a notebook in the folder. On the outside we find an imposing inscription, in Rahner's own Gothic hand: *Dogmatik der Exerzitien*. But inside, there is nothing whatever to be found. Raitz von Frentz's initiative, at least as far as Rahner was concerned, came to nothing.[4]

Or did it? The scribblings and the empty notebook just described are to be found amid a large collection of Rahner's manuscript juvenilia. Not many are worth the formidable effort required to decipher them; many are simply transcriptions of his teachers' lectures. However, the tiny holding connected with Frentz's invitation

---

[3] '*statt katholischem Dogma—persönliches Verhältnis zu Christus—Theologie des religiösen Vorgangs selbst*'. Batlogg reads '*Drama*' instead of my '*Dogma*'—given Rahner's handwriting, the precise reading can only be a matter of opinion.

[4] Frentz may, however, have managed something along the lines he was planning. In 1939, the Feder translation was taken over from G. J. Manz by the Herder Verlag, and from 1940 onwards it was available in two forms. The larger of these contained an appendix with a substantial essay by Frentz and a bibliography.

appears, in retrospect, particularly significant. Rahner did not produce, back in the 1930s, the chapters Frentz wanted. But perhaps this was not just a matter of laziness, overcommitment, or accident. Perhaps the very emptiness of the notebook indicates an unconscious intuition on Rahner's part, a sense that a classical *Dogmatik* of the Exercises was a contradiction in terms. Ignatius's spiritual pedagogy demanded more than a mere theological commentary. If the *Spiritual Exercises* were to be read with the seriousness they deserved, they implied a thoroughgoing renewal of the whole theological enterprise: fundamental and practical as well as dogmatic. To that renewal Rahner was to devote his whole professional life.

Sage Reminiscences

Such a reading of these 1936 fragments—a few scribblings and an empty notebook—is obviously fantasy. But many statements from Rahner's last years encourage it. By the 1970s, Rahner had become an international celebrity, and was constantly being interviewed. In the institutional upheaval following Vatican II, Rahner seemed to offer reassurance and encouragement, and was regularly asked his opinion on a wide range of topics. In such contexts, Rahner began to articulate his sense of how Jesuit tradition had fed him. Rahner saw Ignatius Loyola (1491?–1556) as an original genius. Previous Jesuit theologians had simply failed to articulate key Ignatian insights; by contrast, Rahner's own creativity had been linked quite decisively with a rediscovery and retrieval of these ideas. Thus, for example, Rahner referred disparagingly during an interview in 1976 to retreats he had made under Augustin Bea (1881–1968), the provincial who had received him into the Society of Jesus, and who, at the end of his life, became a cardinal with considerable influence at Vatican II. Rahner's strictures extended also to retreats given by his own moral theology teacher, Franz Hürth (1880–1963), whom we will meet again later in this study. Their approach was 'disappointingly traditional', whereas 'the spirituality of Ignatius himself, which we picked up through the regular practice of prayer and a religious formation, has probably been more significant for me than any learned philosophy or theology, whether inside or outside the Society'.[5]

[5] *Karl Rahner in Dialogue*, 191, ii. 51.

The theme recurred at a celebration of Rahner's eightieth birthday in his home town, Freiburg, a few weeks before his death at the end of March 1984. Rahner structured the main body of his speech around four key aspects of his theology. The third of these was what he owed to his membership of the Society of Jesus. Self-evidently, contemporary theology was too complex and pluralist for different religious orders to generate their own distinctive schools in the way they once had:

> But this, however obvious it is, is very far from meaning that the theology of a religious has nothing to do with his or her order's distinctive form of life and spirituality. I hope, for example, that the great father of my Society, Ignatius of Loyola, will allow that a tiny bit of his spirit and of the spirituality distinctive to him is discernible in my theology. I hope so, at least!

Rahner then went further, comparing what he had tried to do with the Jesuit theological tradition he had inherited:

> Indeed, I am of the somewhat immodest opinion that on some individual points I stand closer to Ignatius than did the great Jesuit theology of the baroque period. This theology—admittedly not always but nevertheless on some not unimportant points—did not do sufficient justice to what in Ignatius is a legitimate existentialism (if one can speak in such terms).

He spoke of one key moment in the Ignatian Exercises, where Ignatius sets the idea of freedom before the Augustinian triad of memory, understanding, and will: 'Take, Lord, and receive all my liberty, my memory, my understanding and all my will.'

> I do not believe that this is just a coincidence in the choice of words and in the rhetoric; but I also do not believe that the traditional Jesuit theology has actually taken this seriously. I don't know if it's really any better in my theology, but nevertheless I have tried to do it a bit.[6]

It seems, however, to have been only in the 1970s that Rahner became so consciously convinced of how Ignatius had influenced him. His biographer speaks of 'a perceptible, explicit turn by the older Rahner to his Society and its spirituality' in this period.[7] As late as 1972, Rahner could write a very personal piece, 'Why am I a Christian today?', without making any explicit reference to

---

[6] 'Erfahrungen eines katholischen Theologen', 142–4. See *Exx*, n. 234.4, and also, for a foreshadowing of the point about Ignatian liberty and the Augustinian triad, 1954/5, 272, 272.

[7] Neufeld, *Die Brüder Rahner*, 360.

Ignatius. In the same year, however, he also published an essay speculating on how the Exercises were of hitherto unacknowledged significance for fundamental theology.[8] Two Ignatian essays from 1974 bring out links between Ignatius and Christian existence as such. The Ignatian process does not merely presuppose Christian belief, but is rather, 'a putting into practice, so to speak, in real life' of the relationship with God that 'amounts to the basic substance of Christianity'.[9] The dynamics of Ignatian choice reflect and continue the theological pattern articulated by the Chalcedonian definition.[10] Then in 1978, Rahner wrote a passionate piece in which he adopted the persona of Ignatius Loyola speaking to a contemporary Jesuit. Subsequently he named this his spiritual testament—'if one may speak in such sentimental terms'—and said that it summed up the whole of his theology.[11]

Why was it that only in his last years Rahner became aware of Ignatius's importance for him? One answer may lie in the effect of retirement on a productive man, prompting him to think back on what his whole life had been about. Another answer might be connected with the collapse in the 1960s and 1970s of many ideological and institutional structures within Roman Catholicism. Vatican II stimulated Roman Catholics to *ressourcement*, a renewal of their faith at its roots and sources. Conscientious believers were seeking a new and richer foundation for their faith. But one must also reckon with the beginnings of large-scale secondary literature on Rahner. An important essay by Rahner's former assistant, Karl Lehmann, first published in 1970, had speculated on how 'the experience of grace' might be the theme integrating Rahner's bewilderingly diverse theological work. In 1974, Klaus Peter Fischer, an Oratorian, had published a seminal doctoral thesis in which he had taken up Lehmann's claim and specified it. 'Obviously', claimed Fischer, 'this experience of grace first became available—and probably nameable also—for Rahner within the framework and through the method of Ignatian spirituality, in particular through the Exercises.'[12]

---

[8] 1972, partly anticipated in 1968.

[9] 1974*b*, 100, *96*: '*Sie setzen also voraus und üben existentiell zugleich ein, was zur Grundsubstanz des Christentums gehört: daß der lebendige, unbegreifliche Gott ist, daß wir ein personales Verhältnis zu ihm haben.*'

[10] 1974*c*.   [11] 1978*b*; *Bekenntnisse*, 58; *Faith in a Wintry Season*, 104, *128*.

[12] Fischer, *Der Mensch als Geheimnis*, 20; Lehmann's essay, in revised form, introduces the Rahnerian anthology, *The Content of Faith*; see esp. 27–33.

Fischer seems to have published this claim before Rahner made any public statements confirming the central role of Ignatian themes in his thought; perhaps perceptive interpretation had a decisive effect on the elderly Rahner's self-understanding. If so, it is fitting that a key statement about Ignatius's influence on Rahner was in fact drafted for Rahner by another important commentator, Karl Heinz Neufeld. The passage comes in the preface to the twelfth German volume of Rahner's collected essays, his *Schriften zur Theologie*. The subtitle of this volume was *Theologie aus Erfahrung des Geistes*, 'theology from an experience of the Spirit', and the preface claimed that this subtitle pointed to a theme, 'or, better, indicated a basic starting-point (*Grundlage*), which is of crucial importance, beyond the particular texts brought together here, for the author's whole theological activity'. This was not, however, simply to repeat the truism that all Christian theology presupposes the action of the Holy Spirit. Rather, in any genuine Christian theology, 'there should be indicated that quite specific experience in which Ignatius Loyola, through his retreat programme, his *Spiritual Exercises*, wanted to school people, and towards which he wanted to lead them'.[13]

The Way Forward

If Rahner himself is to be believed, then, his theology depends less on systematic writers such as Maréchal or Heidegger than on the terse text—written in an idiom that is 'a downright provocation to theological pride'[14]—we know as the *Spiritual Exercises* of Ignatius Loyola. What are these Exercises? Ignatius's book is a manual for retreat-givers, equipping them to lead others through a process of prayer—or set of Exercises—which lasts, in its full form, around a month. The aim of the Exercises is to help people order their everyday lives according to God's will, and thus truly to 'find God in all things'. The process involves a structured programme of imaginative prayer. In the first part, one deepens one's awareness of being a forgiven sinner, and then one spends up to three weeks contemplating the life, death, and resurrection of Christ. During the process,

[13] *TI*, vol. xvi, p. viii (*SzT*, xii. 8). Information from an interview with Fr Neufeld, February 1990.
[14] 1956a, 88, 77.

one may arrive at decisions about one's own life and conduct, of greater or lesser import.[15] The explicit theology in the text is often archaic, and embarrassingly naive. But, as Rahner once pointed out, the practical instructions Ignatius gives are also of major speculative significance. These may seem 'merely matters of how-to-do-it and psychology', but there is often 'a whole theology' hidden within them, and therefore a commentary on them is 'a properly theological task'.[16]

This study explores the relationship between Karl Rahner's theology and the Ignatian[17] spiritual tradition. It presents the theology, both explicit and implicit, in Karl Rahner's interpretation of the Exercises, and thus explores what he might have meant when he claimed that Ignatius was the most important influence on him. Moreover, by claiming that Rahner's achievement is ultimately rooted in his spirituality, this study relativizes the importance of his early philosophical works, and confirms how unhelpful it is to see Rahner's theological achievement as merely the outgrowth of *Spirit in the World*.[18] Less directly, the present study also contributes to some current theological discussions regarding experience. How dependent is our experience, sacred or secular, on the languages and cultures into which we are born? Given that people claim to know God through their experience, what is the status of such claims over against the authority—mediated in various forms—of Christian tradition? How, in short, should we understand the vexed relationship between 'theology' and 'spirituality'?

Rahner's Ignatian writings are diverse, both in content and genre, and they come from all stages in his career. His earliest extant

[15] *Personal Writings* is a convenient collection of Ignatius's texts. For up-to-date introductions, see Lonsdale, *Eyes to See, Ears to Hear*; O'Malley, *The First Jesuits*, 23–50; Zahlauer, *Karl Rahner und sein 'produktives Vorbild'*, 21–85. Lonsdale's is the first book of its kind to exploit the new freedoms in Catholic theology after Vatican II and to draw on the experience of the contemporary Ignatian renewal. Zahlauer's account is closely oriented to his reading of Rahner.

[16] 1974*b*, 103, *100*.

[17] I differentiate between 'Jesuit' and 'Ignatian'. 'Jesuit' will refer to things specific to the Society of Jesus; 'Ignatian' will be a broader term, indicating the particular way of appropriating the gospel embodied in the *Exercises*.

[18] A sympathetic example of such a presentation would be the collection of essays edited by Leo J. O'Donovan, *A World of Grace: An Introduction to the Themes and Foundations of Karl Rahner's Theology* (New York: Crossroad, 1981), which follows the structure of *Foundations of Christian Faith*. For von Balthasar and his followers, Rahner's theology is dependent on philosophy in such a way as to make it irredeemably rationalist. See, for example, Rowan Williams, 'Balthasar and Rahner'.

writing is a school essay on the Jesuit novitiate, while his first published essay has clear Ignatian resonances.[19] Similarly, when he
died, he left on his desk an open letter about the charismatic movement in the light of Ignatian tradition.[20] The genres are of three
broad types. Some are homiletic in character: most obviously the
two collections of conferences for an eight-day retreat,[21] and the
piece in which Rahner imagines Ignatius speaking from heaven to a
contemporary Jesuit.[22] Others are short pieces, mostly written as
forewords or afterwords for books, or for some kind of tribute to
Jesuit figures. Finally, there are various essays on individual themes
in Ignatian spirituality: on how Ignatius reconciles mysticism with a
commitment to the world;[23] on the relationship between Ignatian
spirituality and devotion to the Sacred Heart;[24] on the logical and
theological claims implicit in the Ignatian rules for decision-
making;[25] on the Ignatian motto 'for the greater glory of God';[26] on
how the Ignatian process might help resolve old problems about the
grounding of Christian faith without prejudice to the gratuity of
revelation;[27] and on the relationships between Ignatian spirituality
and commitment to the institutional Church.[28]

The diversity of this material requires us to take a threefold
approach: expository, critical, and constructive. The next four
chapters will be expository. They will show how Rahner's work in
dogmatic, fundamental, and practical theology can be traced back
to three key Ignatian convictions. Conveniently, we find all three of
these set out in a letter written by Ignatius to Francis Borgia, Duke
of Gandía, dated 20 September 1548.[29] Borgia had become, at least
in some sense, a Jesuit two years previously, but the fact needed to
remain secret while he was extricating himself from family and state
commitments. The situation for Ignatius was a delicate one: Borgia

---

[19] 'Im Jesuitennoviziat des Jahres 1919'; 'Warum uns das Beten nottut', as analysed by
Zahlauer, *Karl Rahner und sein 'produktives Vorbild'*), 86–95 (see end of Chapter 2 below). Karl
Rahner's notes from the two full thirty-day retreats he made in his novitiate and tertianship
have survived, as well as another set made from the retreat given to the group behind him
while he was a second-year novice (KRA, IV. A. 40–1). The notes, however, are only skeletal.
Rahner seems simply to have taken down material dictated, while not confiding any of his
own reactions to paper.

[20] 1984.   [21] 1954/5; 1961.   [22] 1978*b*.   [23] 1937.
[24] 1955.   [25] 1956*a*.   [26] 1959.   [27] 1972.   [28] 1968.

[29] MHSJ *EI*, ii. 233–7 (*Personal Writings*, 204–7). The original letter is lost; this text is an
office copy, with corrections in Ignatius's own hand, here indicated by italics. On Borgia, see
Cándido de Dalmases, *Francis Borgia: Grandee of Spain, Jesuit, Saint*, trans. Cornelius Michael
Buckley (St Louis: Institute of Jesuit Sources, 1991 [orig. 1983]).

needed restraining, but he was a high court official. Ignatius made some tactful and deferential suggestions about how Borgia should moderate his asceticism, and in so doing articulated some of his own central spiritual convictions.

For our purposes, the first and most central of these comes towards the end of the letter. Ignatius believes that a person can, in some sense, experience God's self-gift.

Instead of drawing blood, and somehow trying to force it out in some way, you should seek more directly the Lord of all, i.e. the holiest of his gifts . . . By these I mean those gifts which are not in our *very own* power to summon *when we wish*, but which are purely gifts from the One who gives all that is good, and can do all that is good, gifts such as the following (always understood as being directed and aimed at His Divine Majesty): intensity of faith, of hope, and of love; *spiritual rejoicing and repose*; tears; intense consolation; the raising up of the mind; impressions or illuminations from God; and all the other spiritual relishings and intuitions that lead to such gifts.

The next two chapters, therefore, will deal with the theme of grace as an experiential reality, one that is in principle open widely, indeed universally. Chapter 2 will explore the concept of 'the immediate experience of God' that is so central to the 1978 testament, and trace its roots in Rahner's early work on historical theology. Chapter 3 will then bring out how this idea shapes Rahner's distinctive theology of grace.

At the outset of the letter, Ignatius had told Borgia that the experience of God is not a reality confined to special moments, but rather emerges from ordinary, everyday activities. Borgia should halve the time spent in formal prayer, and use the time gained for study, administrative work, and 'spiritual conversations':

You should always take care to maintain your soul in peace, in quiet, and in readiness for whatever Our Lord might wish to do within it. There is no doubt that it is a greater virtue in the soul, and a greater grace, for it to be able to relish its Lord in a variety of duties and in a variety of places, rather than simply in one.

This Ignatian understanding of the experience of God contrasts with the views prevalent in the Roman Catholic theology that Rahner inherited, and Chapter 4, 'The Rahner Brothers and the Discovery of Jerónimo Nadal', will explore the differences. According to standard 'ascetical and mystical theology', the experience of God, if it occurred at all, was an extraordinary event. Moreover, closeness to God implied disengagement from created realities. Against such accounts, Rahner drew on Ignatius to insist that business and activity did not exclude contemplation. The title of his 1937 Ignatian essay, 'The Ignatian Mysticism of Joy in the World (*Weltfreudigkeit*)', was intended as a provocative paradox.

Ignatius also tells Borgia about how such experience of grace can guide our actions, our choices. The self-giving God,

sees and knows what is better for a person; and God, knowing everything, shows the person the way forward. And for our part, to find that way, through the medium of His divine grace, it is very helpful to search about and make many kinds of experiments so that we can follow the route that is *most clearly declared to us*, the happiest and most blessed one in this life, completely governed and directed towards that other life which is without end, and that we be enfolded in and united to such *holiest of* gifts.

Ignatius's addition, 'most clearly declared to us', foreshadows a key conviction of Rahner's moral theology. Following the law, whether natural or ecclesiastical, is not enough: there are also individual obligations, which God reveals—or 'declares'—through a person's experience. The function of the Ignatian Exercises is to help us discover such duties. Chapter 5, 'Transcendence Becoming Thematic', explores Rahner's writings on Ignatian discernment, above all the major essay he published in 1956, 'The Logic of Concrete Individual Knowledge in Ignatius Loyola'. Within the limits set by generally valid principles, whether of reason or revelation, God can reveal, through a person's experience, individual directives. If this is so, then moral theology and spirituality must inform each other in ways unknown to what Rahner called *die durchschnittliche Schultheologie*—'conventional academic theology' or 'the average theology of the schools'.

By the end of these expository chapters, it will be clear that Rahner's interpretation of Ignatius, when not plain wrong, nearly always needs adapting and clarifying. Chapter 6, 'Immediacy, Mediation, and Grounding', will be critical in its thrust, bringing out the major problems. Rahner is not precise about the sense in which our experience of God yields certitude, and he does not clarify the relationship between our ongoing experience and the traditions we inherit. The chapter also proposes a procedure for handling these issues. Though there certainly are some faults in Rahner's arguments, one must also allow for the impressionistic, occasional nature of his Ignatian texts. These writings generally address specific, limited questions, and their formulations often need to be linked with what Rahner says elsewhere, in ways which Rahner left to subsequent commentators.

Following such a constructive procedure, Chapter 7, 'First Principles', seeks to clarify what Rahner says about the certainty of God's presence in our experience. Then Chapter 8, 'The Standard of Christ', attempts to link Rahner's statements about human experience of God with his commitment to Christ, to historical revelation, and to ecclesial tradition. The positions developed in these two chapters lead to Chapter 9, 'Decisions and Discipleship', which sets out an integral Rahnerian theology of Ignatian choice, and to Chapter 10, 'The Decision of Faith', which clarifies a further claim of Rahner's: namely, that Ignatius's process also illustrates how faith in Christian revelation can be grounded.

On this basis, we will be able to specify and evaluate the continuities between Rahner's theology and the spirituality of the Ignatian Exercises. The final chapter, 'Ignatius, Rahner, and Theology', begins by bringing out how Rahner follows Ignatius in developing a distinctive and creative approach to the relationship between dogma and experience. Fischer and his followers have often rather assumed that any spiritual motif in a Jesuit's writings must somehow be Ignatian, and sometimes indeed to write as though Ignatius is the only source of sensible ideas about the spiritual life. While avoiding such misconceptions, this study argues that there are nevertheless significant continuties between Ignatius's spiritual heritage and Karl Rahner's theological achievement. The study ends with a brief look at some wider implications regarding the relationships between experience, tradition, and theology.

2

The Immediate Experience of God

In 1978 Rahner gave an interview about the Ignatian Exercises. At the outset he distinguished the Exercises in the full sense from two other styles of Christian formation—styles often associated with the Exercises and easily confused with them. The first of these Rahner termed 'a course of theological instruction'. Ironically, perhaps ruefully, Rahner made a disclaimer: 'perhaps all the books I wrote about the Ignatian Exercises are, on the whole, not Ignatian Exercises in the full sense of the word, but theological treatises'. Rahner also distinguished the Exercises from 'practices of a meditative type, particularly in the style of Eastern meditation', in which 'it is a matter of becoming tranquil, of a certain silencing of purposeful thoughts, of quiet, perhaps also of a certain openness towards deeper existential layers of the human person'. In the Exercises, something different was at stake:

> In contrast to exercises in self-awareness (so far as this is possible), and in contrast to a verbal theological indoctrination, however important this latter can be, the Exercises are concerned with something else. It is a matter here . . . of letting the Creator and the creature, as Ignatius says, deal immediately with each other . . . It is nothing other than this experience to which Ignatius in the Exercises wants to lead a person.

Quite evidently, the elderly Rahner associates Ignatius with 'the immediate experience of God'—*unmittelbare Gotteserfahrung*. This kind of experience is deeper and more radical than the encounter with God fostered by liturgical prayer or mediated through Church structures. In a secularized, pluralist society, the survival of Christian commitment will depend on such an 'ultimate, immediate encounter of the individual with God'.[1]

This chapter and the next focus on Rahner's conviction that God can be 'immediately' experienced, a conviction which he articulated

---

[1] 1978*c*, 175–6, *32–4*; *Exx*, n. 15.6.

most explicitly in his late writing on the Exercises. Our central source will inevitably be the 1978 testament, 'Ignatius of Loyola Speaks to a Modern Jesuit'. This chapter discusses how 'the immediate experience of God' functions in the rhetoric of that text, and traces the sources of the idea in Rahner's reading of earlier tradition: not only of Ignatius, but also of Evagrius, Gregory of Nyssa, and Bonaventure. The next chapter explores the theological use Rahner made of the idea, normally without naming it. Though Rahner learnt the concept from 'spiritual theology', he used it to renew the theology of grace, the Christian understanding of humanity in general.

Rahner's Spiritual Testament

Speaking to his modern disciple, Rahner's Ignatius begins by evoking the novelty of his ministry, and claims that this creativity depends on his *experience* of the truth which Christianity proclaims:

I thought—and this opinion was true—that I could say what was old in a new way. Why? I was convinced that I had encountered God, at first incipiently during my sickness at Loyola and then decisively during my retreat time at Manresa; and I wanted to mediate such experience to others in so far as this was possible.[2]

Moreover, for Rahner's Ignatius, this experience relativizes any verbal and institutional expression of Christianity. When referring to the experience, he draws primarily on apophatic idioms and traditions:

I say simply: I experienced God, the nameless and unfathomable one, silent and yet near, in the triuneness of his turning to me (*in der Dreifaltigkeit seiner Zuwendung zu mir*) . . . From Manresa onwards I experienced in increasing measure and ever more purely the modeless incomprehensibility of God (*die weiselose Unbegreiflichkeit Gottes*).[3]

[2] 1978*b*, 11, *373–4*. Ignatius's conversion is conventionally said to have begun at home in Loyola during his convalescence from a battle wound. He then set off for the Holy Land, but was delayed in Manresa, a small town north-west of Barcelona, where he had a range of powerful experiences. See the appropriate sections of his *Autobiography* or *Reminiscences*, e.g. in Ignatius, *Personal Writings*, 12–28, or of any Ignatian biography, such as Philip Caraman, *Ignatius Loyola* (London: Collins, 1990).
[3] 1978*b*, 11, *374*; 12, *375*. *Weiselos* is a term taken from the medieval German mystics. 'In a special theological and mystical sense, *wise* in middle high German denotes human being

Rahner's spiritual testament is not a well-written piece. Its argument rambles; its expression is often tortuous and purple; it would have benefited from a good editor. In at least three ways, moreover, it is a paradoxical text. Firstly, though Rahner can describe it as summing up the whole of his theology, much of the latter part deals with topics immediately relevant only to Jesuits; the title, 'Ignatius of Loyola Speaks to a Modern Jesuit', is largely accurate. Secondly, this spiritual testament of a theologian at least seems to relativize theology to experience. When Rahner's Ignatius claims to have experienced God immediately, this 'does not need to be tied up with a theological lecture on the essence of such immediate experience with God'; moreover, he reminds his modern disciple that he was already giving the Exercises 'before I had studied your theology and had managed with some effort (I laugh) a masters degree from Paris'.[4] Finally, and most importantly, the references to Ignatius's own texts, even as Rahner adopts the persona of Ignatius, are few, fleeting, and indirect. Indeed, Rahner's heavenly Ignatius looks back on the texts he wrote in his lifetime and finds them 'touchingly childlike'. Sceptical though he is about some modern proposals regarding 'improvements' to his texts, he is well aware of the need for adaptation.[5]

In a 1974 Christmas homily on the Exercises, Rahner had suggested that the Ignatian experience of God showed up the parallels between Chalcedonian Christology and a more general Christian anthropology. If we live by Ignatius's teaching, 'we find God in the low-key banality of the everyday without becoming a slave to it'. In us too there can grow a unity of the divine and the human 'without confusion and without separation'.[6] In and through the physical, the finite—or, to use Rahner's jargon, the categorical—we experience ourselves as transcendent, as open to God. Nevertheless, in these late Ignatian writings, it is the transcendental aspect which Rahner stresses. Words like 'nameless' and 'modeless' reinforce an insistence that the experience of God eludes categorization: 'I experienced

insofar as it is activity, action, expression of the higher and lower powers of the soul and of the senses (*modus essendi*), as opposed to the *wiselos* state of being opened into the ground of the soul in the *unio mystica* and towards the pure being of God' (Grimm, *Deutsches Wörterbuch*, XIV. i. i. 1050: '*im Gegensatz zum* wiselosen *Zustand des Aufgegangenseins in den Seelengrund bei der unio mystica und zum reinen Sein Gottes*').

[4] 1978*b*, 11, *374*; 13, *376*.   [5] 1978*b*, 12, *375*; 14–15, *378*.   [6] 1974*c*, 7, *333*.

God . . . above all as beyond any pictorial imagining'.[7] The experience of God is not the same as words about God—'God's own self I experienced, not human words about God'—and the strength of conviction it brings renders not only theology but even Scripture superfluous.[8] When one gives the Exercises one is not mediating the word of the Church as such, but 'giving facilitation from a distance'[9] while the immediate encounter between God and the human person takes place. Though Ignatius takes ecclesial Christianity for granted, he is concerned with a radical immediacy of God's presence that is deeper, and that 'ultimately sustains and contains everything Christian and ecclesial'.[10]

This experience of God also leads to a detachment from one's own survival. Even if one continues to live in a biological sense, the experience anticipates death; Jesus serves as an example of death in Godforsakenness, enabling Rahner's Ignatius to find God 'without turning God into a figment of my own uncommitted speculation'. One only gets beyond such speculation 'if one dies a real death all the way through life; but this death is died well only if, with Jesus, one calmly accepts the Godforsakenness it includes, which is the ultimate modeless mysticism'.[11]

There is a further sense in which this experience is subversive. What is at stake is a miracle of grace overshooting our expectations:

God is able and willing to deal immediately with his creature; the fact that this occurs is something that human beings can experience happening; they can apprehend the sovereign disposing of God's freedom over their lives and take this up—a disposing that can no longer be predicted through objective argument 'from below' as a law of human reason (be that philosophical, theological or experiential).[12]

Talk of human beings experiencing God may sound conventional 'in your pious trade, working as it does with the most exalted words possible—but it is basically outrageous'.[13] Such experience is a strictly theological reality, dependent on the mystery of God's *self*-gift.

In an article written in the same year, 1978, for the Austrian Jesuit spirituality review *Entschluß*, Rahner linked 'the immediate experience of God' with his theology of nature and grace. In normal

---

[7] 1978*b*, 11, *374*.   [8] 1978*b*, 12, *374*.   [9] 1978*b*, 13*, *376*.
[10] 1975*b*, 9.   [11] 1978*b*, 12–13, *375*; 20–1, *385*.   [12] 1978*b*, 13, *376*.
[13] 1978*b*, 12, *374*.

everyday living our 'transcendental experience' is simply 'the condition of possibility for categorical being-in-the-world, for dealings with everyday things and with the concept of God'. In a mystical life-history, by contrast, it acquires a significance in itself. Moreover, whatever might be the case in a hypothetical world of pure nature,

this experience of transcendence is always in practice sustained by the self-communication of God. Through what we call the Holy Spirit, grace, the supernatural virtues of faith, hope, and love, this transcendence is radicalized to the point of being a real capacity to approach God as such. Through grace human transcendentality is no longer merely a condition of possibility for concrete dealings with the world, and is also no longer directed merely to an asymptotic, never reachable point (called God). Rather, the promise is made by God's own self to this transcendentality— in gracious, Spirit-filled (*pneumatischen*) self-communication—that it also can actually *reach* this point. And wherever a human person—this is fundamentally something quite incredible—as a wretched creature can dare to talk with God's own self, tap God as it were on the shoulder, and expect that one can actually get there, they are affirming their transcendentality as a transcendentality *radicalized* by prevenient grace from God, always given and existing, at least in the mode of an offer to our freedom. And in this grace—'from within'—God is experienced, imagelessly (*bildlos*).[14]

The grace of God may be amazing grace, transcending our expectations, but it nevertheless builds on, rather than abolishes, nature and the transcendence already given therein. For Rahner it can be proved philosophically that ordinary human experience in any possible world presupposes a distant, creator God; but the world in which we actually live is a graced world, shaped by a miracle 'that overshoots all your metaphysics',[15] the miracle of a self-communicating God. In the economy of grace and salvation, God's transcendent reality becomes identified with the creation, albeit in a strictly qualified sense.[16] And this miracle is something we can experience.

Rahner is passionate about the immediate experience of God, about its transcendence of particular realities, and on the need for people to have such experience:

[14] 1978*d*, 21–2.   [15] 1978*b*, 19, *384*.

[16] The unity referred to here is a deficient mode of that which grounds the interchange of predicates in classical Christology, a unity which Rahner describes as 'a unique unity, not otherwise to be found and remaining deeply mysterious, between really different realities, infinitely distant from each other' (*Foundations of Christian Faith*, 290, *284* [*KRSW*, xxvi. 276–7]).

But it remains true: human beings can experience God's own self. And your pastoral care must have this goal in sight always, at every step, remorselessly. If you fill up the storehouses of people's consciousnesses only with your theology, however learned and up-to-date it is, in a way that ultimately engenders nothing but a fearful torrent of words; if you train people only for devotion to the Church, as enthusiastic subjects of the ecclesiastical establishment; if you make the people in the Church no more than obedient subjects of a distant God represented by an ecclesiastical hierarchy; if you don't help people get beyond all this; if you don't help them finally to abandon all tangible assurances and isolated insights and go with confidence into that incomprehensibility where there are no more paths, if you don't help them manage this both in life's situations of ultimate, inescapable terror, in a love and a joy that do not admit of measurement, and then, radically and ultimately, also in death, with Jesus dying in Godforsakenness—if you don't help people in *this* way, then, in what you call your pastoral care and missionary vocation, you'll have either forgotten or betrayed my 'spirituality'.[17]

For Rahner's Ignatius, the activities of his modern disciples must centre on the giving of the Exercises—not through organized courses given *en masse*, but rather,

a mystagogical help for others not to repress the immediacy of God, but to experience it clearly and accept it. Not as though each of you can and should give Exercises in this sense; there's no need for every one of you to imagine you can do this. Nor is it any disparagement of all the other pastoral, scholarly and socio-political undertakings which in the course of your history you have thought you ought to try. But the proper way in which you should see all this other business is as preparation for or consequence of this ultimate task, which should remain yours in the future: helping people towards the immediate experience of God, in which people realise that the mystery past all grasp that we call God is near, can be spoken to, and blessedly protects us in person precisely when we do not try to subject it to ourselves, but rather make ourselves over to it unconditionally.[18]

Ignatius and Transcendental Experience

What were Rahner's sources for these ideas? In the 1978 testament, close reference to Ignatian texts is conspicuous by its absence. But the *Entschluß* piece brings out some of the connections in Rahner's

[17] 1978*b*, 14, *377*.   [18] 1978*b*, 16, *380*.

mind between the Ignatian heritage and 'the immediate experience of God'.

Firstly, in common with a number of Rahner's Ignatian writings, the *Entschluß* piece links Rahner's 'transcendental experience', and hence the immediate experience of God, with the Ignatian concept of 'indifference'. In 1975, Rahner wrote of how 'immediacy to God takes place for Ignatius in an indifference given by God and lived out concretely in "poverty"'.[19] The term 'indifference' originates from an adjective, *indiferente*, used by Ignatius in the *Spiritual Exercises* to denote an attitude of detachment. If one is making a choice in the third of the ways indicated by Ignatius, one should be free from 'any inordinate propensity', free to focus on 'the end for which I am created'—namely, the praise of God and the salvation of my soul—and thus 'to find myself indifferent, without any inordinate propensity, so that I be not more inclined or disposed to take the thing proposed than to leave it, nor more to leave it than to take it, but find myself as in the middle of a balance'. In such a state one can then 'ask of God our Lord to be pleased to move my will and put in my soul what I ought to do regarding the thing proposed, so as to promote more his praise and glory'.[20] The term also appears in the summary statement which Ignatius places at the beginning of the Exercises proper. Humanity is created for the praise, reverence, and service of God—and the rest of creation is there to help humanity in this. 'Other things' are to be used only in so far and in such ways as they further this end:

> For this it is necessary to make ourselves indifferent to all created things in all that is allowed to the choice of our free will and is not prohibited to it; in such a way that, on our part, we want not health rather than sickness, riches rather than poverty, honour rather than dishonour, long rather than short life, and so in all the rest; desiring and choosing only what is most conducive for us to the end for which we are created.[21]

In Ignatius the focus is on the affective hold of attachments, and on the struggle not to be simply determined by any particular attachment. Rahner arguably goes beyond Ignatius in making indifference a category in his metaphysics of mind. He suggests that we can experience a transcendence of all particular objects, and that our ability to do so, our capacity for 'indifference', belongs 'to the essential structure of mental life':

---

[19] 1978*d*, 19–21; 1975*d*, 9.   [20] *Exx*, nn. 179.2–180.1.   [21] *Exx*, n. 23.5–7.

If the human person is always the one who grasps the finite, individual thing in their knowledge and freedom in a fundamental movement directed towards absolute reality, towards absolute truth and goodness, then . . . they are always transcending the individual thing, distinguishing themselves from it, placing the finite individual thing against a broader horizon, rising above it, making themselves independent of it: they are 'indifferent' in regard to the individual thing.[22]

The immediate experience of God is in one sense an experience without object, in which this transcendence becomes the focus of our awareness.

There is, however, a passage in the *Entschluß* article—or transcribed table-talk[23]—which is uniquely revealing of the connections in Rahner's mind between Ignatius and 'the immediate experience of God'. Rahner is discussing the role of imaginative visions in Christian mysticism, and citing Ignatius as one who, though richly gifted with such visions, regarded them as secondary:

I'd like to refer to two things. Nadal, one of his most trusted friends . . . says expressly that Ignatius in his mysticism has passed beyond the imaginative and, as Nadal puts it, *versatur in pure intellectualibus* ('he is taken up with what is purely intellectual'). And secondly—perhaps much more importantly— Ignatius himself expressly testifies at the end of his *Autobiography* that his devotion had always been increasing when he says that his ease in entering into communication with God was now greater than at any time in his life. Always and at any hour that he wanted to find God, he could find him. That's one point. But even at this point he was still often granted appearances, particularly of the kind that had been described earlier in the text, namely those in which he saw Christ as the sun. He had often experienced this, especially when he had difficult questions to settle, and thus these appearances came to him by way of confirmation. While celebrating Mass he had this vision, and just as often while he was working on the *Constitutions*.

With Ignatius we have something remarkable. On the one hand, he cultivates an imaginative mysticism based on visions. On the other, he says that he could find God at any time and at all times. He did not mean by that—this is for me more than obvious—that he could at any time summon up a sun as a vision of Jesus. No: he had an immediate experience of God, which became more and more straightforwardly available to him

[22] 1961, 30, *41–2*.
[23] No typescript or manuscript exists for this relatively late piece. The preface to the book edition, on page 7, speaks of how the essays in the collection 'arose not at the desk but in conversation'.

the older he became—and which therefore cannot be that imaginative reality which he often has and is happy to accept as a confirmation. There has to be here an encounter with God which '*versatur in pure intellectualibus*'. Now, it must be said also that this is an awkward and easily misunderstood expression of Nadal's: today it can easily be misinterpreted along the lines of an Enlightenment intellectualism or rationalism. But all it refers to is how this experience of God was imageless.[24]

Rahner is drawing here on two Ignatian sources. The first of these is a diary entry written probably in 1545 by Jerónimo Nadal, who was reporting how Diego Laínez, one of Ignatius's first companions and his successor as general superior of the Society, described Ignatius at that stage of his life:

Ignatius is, in a very singular way, on the most familiar of terms with God. For he has gone beyond all visions, whether real (such as seeing Christ or the Virgin etc. as present) or based on images and likenesses, and he is now taken up with what is purely intellectual, with the unity of God.[25]

The second source is the Epilogue to the *Autobiography*. Ignatius is making a formal declaration to his scribe, Luis Gonçalves da Câmara, confirming the authenticity of his narrative. Though he had committed many offences since his conversion, he had never given consent to a mortal sin. He was,

on the contrary, always growing in devotion, i.e. in facility in finding God, and now more than ever in his whole life. And every time and hour he wanted to find God, he found him. And . . . now too he had visions often, especially those which have been talked about above, when he saw Christ like a sun. This often used to happen as he was going along talking about important things, and that would make him arrive at assurance. When he was saying Mass, he would have many visions too, and when he was producing the *Constitutions* he had them too, very often.[26]

For Rahner, both these texts bear witness to an immediate experience of God coexisting with experiences of particular things,

---

[24] 1978*d*, 18–19.

[25] MHSJ *MN*, vi. 33: '*Est Deo familiarissimus selectissime. Nam visiones omnes tum reales, ut videre praesentem Christum, Virginem etc., tum per species et representationes iam transgressus, versatur nunc in pure intellectualibus, in unitate Dei.*' This reference to Nadal in 1978*d* clarifies a reference to him in 1978*b*, 12, *375*, as one who formulated Ignatius's convictions about the experience of God 'in a more philosophical way'. The passage is cited also in 1937, 280, *333*, and in an essay of Hugo Rahner's which, as we shall see, significantly influenced Karl's reading of Ignatius: *The Vision of St. Ignatius in the Chapel of La Storta*, 104.

[26] *Aut*, nn. 99.6–100.1 (*Personal Writings*, 63).

yet distinct from them—associated with the categorical, yet superior to it. In neither case, however, is the textual evidence conclusive. Nadal's note is too brief to be taken as serious theological evidence; moreover, Ignatius's dealings with the Trinity do involve the ability to make particular distinctions. Nadal continues:

Later I came to understand from the same Fr Ignatius that he was taken up with the divine persons, and that he could find different and distinct gifts from the distinct persons, as if the Father was imparting his grace through the Son as a channel. But in this contemplation he found greater gifts in the person of the Holy Spirit.

Again, Ignatius's finding '*Esse* itself and God whenever he gives himself to prayer' seems, despite what Rahner says, to be co-ordinated with the statement that this can occur in different ways, including meditation. Nadal goes on to say that no set rule is to be kept: on the contrary, 'prayer is to be exercised in various ways, and God to be sought by various meditations'.[27] As for the passage from the *Autobiography*, there is simply no evidence in the text as to whether Ignatius's regular facility in finding God was or was not distinct from his frequent visions. When Rahner claims this to be self-evident, his grounds lie outside the text itself.

When, therefore, Rahner adduces strictly Ignatian sources for his late rhetoric of 'the immediate experience of God', his arguments are shaky. The origins lie elsewhere: in Rahner's own theology and in other positive sources. Though 'the immediate experience of God' had never been an explicitly central concept in Rahner's systematic work, it had featured large in his early writing on patristic and medieval spirituality. As an old man he was retrieving a theme which had long lain buried, as if to recognize a significance in his juvenilia hitherto unacknowledged. To understand what is at stake in the late Rahner's Ignatian writings, we need to consider what

---

[27] '*Intellexi postea ego ab eodem P. Ignatio versari ipsum in personis divinis, ac invenire varia dona et distincta a diversis personis, quasi si Pater per Filium, ut per canalem gratiam suam communicaret. Sed in hac contemplatione, maiora dona invenit in persona Spiritus Sancti; tum etiam intellexi ab eodem P. Ignatio in contemplatione ipsum Esse et Deum invenire quoties se dat orationi, nec certam regulam et ordinem servandum, sed varie exercendam orationem, et variis meditationibus quaerendus Deus. Si quis vero ex proxima gratia in oratione habita inchoat, non damnavit; sed dixit esse incipientium.*' Particularly given the obscurities of the last sentence, it could be that Ignatius's ability *ipsum Esse et Deum invenire* denotes a special privilege, to which the various ways of prayer and meditation, though legitimate for the kind of beginner Nadal was in 1545, *cannot* be expected to lead. But the text is simply too short and isolated to be used as a theological source.

Rahner has said about 'the immediate experience of God' in the
Greek fathers and in Bonaventure.

Gregory of Nyssa and Evagrius

Thus, at this highest level of mysticism, we are dealing with an immediate
experience of God. . . . Gregory calls this immediate experience—knowing through unknowing—'knowledge', 'vision' etc. But however naturally
these expressions come to the Greek mind, Gregory is equally aware of
how inadequately they describe the mystery. The reality is the event, the
nocturnal experience, of the bridegroom 'being here' even when he does
not 'appear', an 'apprehension of his presence' in which the soul is
swathed in the divine night. We are dealing less with a knowledge than
with an ecstasy.[28]

The topic is Gregory of Nyssa's *Life of Moses*. In 1939, Rahner published a German edition of a French work: Marcel Viller's history of
early Christian spirituality. He added extensive bibliographies and
footnotes to the original, and also revised and updated some passages, notably on Evagrius and on Gregory.[29] It is from one of the
latter that the above quotation is taken.

Central to Rahner's additions are two themes: the immediate
knowledge of God, and ecstasy. Even at a less exalted stage, where
Gregory is speaking of God's reflection in the purified soul and the
soul's consequent striving in love for God, Rahner can see this as
implying that the creature 'knows of this movement without discursive reasoning'. For Rahner, Gregory believes that even at this stage
the knowledge of God has moved beyond 'inferential mediation'.[30]
It is in this sense that it is 'immediate'.

Evagrius, too, talks of humanity attaining a vision of God in
'formless light'. What makes this possible, says Rahner,

[28] *Aszese und Mystik in der Väterzeit*, 142 (*KRSW*, iii. 247), quoting from Gregory of Nyssa's
Life of Moses, Homilies on the Song of Songs, and *On Virginity*.

[29] For information on this work, see Neufeld's introduction to the 1989 edition, or *Die
Brüder Rahner*, 133–6. On the thought of Evagrius and Gregory, good introductions are: *The
Mind's Long Journey to the Holy Trinity: The* Ad Monachos *of Evagrius Ponticus*, ed. and trans.
Jeremy Driscoll (Collegeville: Liturgical Press, 1993), 1–30; Anthony Meredith, *The Cappado-
cians* (London: Geoffrey Chapman, 1995), 52–101.

[30] *Aszese und Mystik in der Väterzeit*, 138–9 (*KRSW*, iii. 244): '*weiß er auch ohne Schluß von dem Ziel
dieser Bewegung. So versteht man vielleicht, wie Gregor in dieser Erkenntnis die schlußfolgernde Mittelbarkeit
der gewöhnlichen Erkenntnis überwunden glauben konnte.*'

is not that a species of knowledge is formed as a copy of this essential knowledge, this spiritual sea without boundaries or differences. That would no longer be a vision: it would mean seeing the essential light through another light. . . . Thus this vision of God is quite free and distanced from any kind of material basis that might be thought to be a medium through which the holy Trinity could be known. It is 'a state beyond all images': the spirit is quite simple and identical with itself. . . . It is a state of being overwhelmed by the boundlessness of the infinite.[31]

Rahner had published an earlier version of this material on Evagrius in an article in 1933. There he equated these Evagrian ideas as anticipating the teaching both of Denys and of John of the Cross: this version of ecstasy involved some kind of rupture.[32] In the meantime, however, Irénée Hausherr had published his edition of Evagrius's treatise on prayer together with an important article. These led Rahner to reformulate the matter, and to see in Evagrius an alternative form of ecstasy:

However, one cannot identify straight off this 'boundless unknowing' with the 'divine darkness' in the mysticism of pseudo-Denys. For in Denys ecstasy is what makes the intellect, faced with the incomprehensibility of God and its own darkness, give itself up into the intoxication of love. In Evagrius 'unknowing' is merely the exclusion of all discrete and conceptually separable acts of knowledge related to finite things. For Evagrius, God's own self is only light and the human *nous* is where the light shines; hence for Evagrius there was no question of humanity's innermost essence moving out in ecstasy from its intellectuality.[33]

In retrospect, the shift between Rahner's two accounts of Evagrius appears significant. The earlier account shows a Rahner fascinated with how God's own self can be apprehended in darkness: the apophatic idioms stress how this knowledge differs from our

[31] *Aszese und Mystik in der Väterzeit*, 104–5 (*KRSW*, iii. 216), quoting from a range of Evagrian texts: *Centuries*, letters, *On Prayer*.
[32] 'Die geistliche Lehre des Evagrius Pontikus', 36–7. At the beginning, Rahner describes this article as little more 'than a free German rendering' of Viller's work on Evagrius, and it may have served as a preliminary sketch for the broader project. However, as far as Evagrius is concerned, Rahner is being disingenuous here: in this earlier piece he expands Viller's text even more than he does in *Aszese und Mystik in der Väterzeit*.
[33] *Aszese und Mystik in der Väterzeit*, 105 (*KRSW*, iii. 216–17). Hausherr's work is now available as *Les Leçons d'un contemplatif: Le Traité de l'oraison d'Evagre le Pontique* (Paris: Beauchesne, 1960). An English version of the text can be found in Evagrius Ponticus, *The Praktikos and Chapters on Prayer*, ed. and trans. John Eudes Bamberger (Kalamazoo: Cistercian Publications, 1972). Rahner cites in particular n. 117, as also an article by Hausherr, 'Ignorance infinie', *Orientalia Christiana Periodica*, 2 (1936), 351–62.

everyday awareness of finite objects. The later account begins to converge with the philosophy of mind and of God which Rahner had developed in *Spirit in the World*. For now, Rahner is seeing the encounter with God and knowledge of the finite, for all their distinctness, as inseparable. He is beginning to develop his own account of the 'mystical': one that would, as we shall see, articulate what he and other Jesuits were discovering as they explored the newly published Ignatian sources.

Bonaventure and Spiritual Touch

In a footnote to the first passage quoted above on Gregory, Rahner alludes, slightly inaccurately, to a sentence in Bonaventure's *Commentary on John*: '*et tunc magis sentiunt quam cognoscant*—and then they feel rather than know'. In so doing, he points us to a fuller account of ecstasy and the immediate experience of God: his account of spiritual touch in Bonaventure.[34] This account comes within a broader history of a spiritual motif: the five spiritual senses. The latter's earliest form is as an essay in a *Festschrift* presented by Hugo and Karl Rahner to their father for his sixtieth birthday in 1928. Karl later expanded the essay into two articles, which were published in French in 1932 and 1933; the latter of these included the Bonaventure material. A fuller version of the material on ecstasy and spiritual touch then appeared the following year in German.[35]

---

[34] Since the publication of *Schriften zur Theologie*, xii, in 1975, a number of Rahner's commentators have made telling use of this material. See in particular Schwerdtfeger, *Gnade und Welt*; Miggelbrink, *Ekstatische Gottesliebe im tätigen Weltbezug*. For introductory material on Bonaventure, see Paul D. Rout, *Francis and Bonaventure* (London: Fount Paperbacks, 1996). Rahner's interpretation of Bonaventure may be exegetically questionable. For early criticism, see S. Grünewald, 'Zur Mystik des hl. Bonaventura', *Zeitschrift für Aszese und Mystik*, 9 (1934), 124–42, 219–32; for an interpretation much more in line with Rahner's subsequent development, see McIntosh, *Mystical Theology*, 76–8.

[35] The first version is entitled 'Geschichte der Lehre von den fünf geistlichen Sinnen', and will occasionally be cited in what follows because of its biographical significance and its comparative clarity. The Bonaventure material appeared in 'La Doctrine des "sens spirituels" au moyen-âge' and in 'Der Begriff der Ecstasis bei Bonaventura'. The German typescript underlying the French text is lost. The version translated in *Theological Investigations*, 'The Doctrine of the "Spiritual Senses"', is an editorial construction by Neufeld drawing mainly on the 1933 French text, but the section on ecstasy includes material from the German article (which expands one part of the argument). As the original text in what follows, I am working from the two 1930s' versions, with preference, where possible, for the German.

Towards the beginning of his account of spiritual touch in Bonaventure, Rahner quotes the tag just mentioned in context:

One can know God in God's own self or in God's effect. To know God through God's effect: this is to see through a mirror, and in two ways— either through a clear mirror and eye (so the first human being saw before the fall), or through an obscured mirror, which is how we see. . . . In another way, God is known in God's self, and this in two ways: either clearly, a way only for the Son and for the blessed, or in darkness, as blessed Denys says in the *Mystical Theology*. And this is how Moses saw, and those who contemplate sublimely. In their regarding there is no image formed of a creature. And then, in truth, they feel rather than know.[36]

The contemplative experience of spiritual touch is a middle term between, on the one hand, the beatific vision, and, on the other, an inferential knowledge of God based on God's effects. The longer version of Rahner's account of spiritual touch begins with an allusion both to earlier discussions about Bonaventure's epistemology and to what were, in the 1930s, live conflicts about his mystical teaching. Just as it was a mistake to read Bonaventure's epistemology as either Thomist or ontologist (i.e. claiming that human knowledge was rooted in a direct intuition of God), so also 'research into Bonaventure's doctrine of mystical knowledge must get away from limiting Bonaventure to the choice between the proposed solutions around which today's struggles in the theory of mysticism revolve'.[37]

Rahner is here alluding to a lively controversy, chiefly among French-speaking theologians, regarding exalted prayer states. The limit-positions had been set out by Auguste Saudreau, in *Les degrés de la vie spirituelle* (1896), and Augustin-François Poulain, in *Des grâces d'oraison* (1901). The former, though affirming that all Christians were called to mystical prayer, interpreted mysticism less extravagantly than others, and denied that human beings in this life could experientially apprehend God unless God intervened in a quasi-miraculous way. By contrast, Poulain held that the mystical state, which was granted only to some, could involve a direct perception of God's presence. Though Poulain's own approach was descriptive rather than theological, there were theologians who took his

[36] *Commentarius in Joannem*, i. 43, in Bonaventure, *Opera omnia*, vi. 255*b*–256*a*, quoted in 'The Doctrine of the "Spiritual Senses"', xvi. 119 ('Der Begriff', 6): '*Et sic vidit Moyses et sublimiter contemplantes, in quorum aspectu nulla figitur imago creaturae. Et tunc revera magis sentiunt quam cognoscant.*'
[37] 'Der Begriff', 1–2.

findings seriously. Rahner's essay takes its place within the variety of intermediate positions canvassed in the discussions.[38] Though the young Rahner is writing in the idiom of manualist spiritual theology, we can, with hindsight, see him beginning to chafe at its restrictions. He reads Bonaventure as teaching that contemplation is in continuum with the life of grace, the spontaneous activity of a perfectly restored soul. The term *sensus spirituales* refers not to a new and distinct set of faculties, but to acts of the self renewed under grace—not so much spiritual senses as spiritual sensings.[39] Moreover, Rahner damns with faint praise passages where Bonaventure enumerates the five spiritual senses, even though it is only at this point, if anywhere, that there is a link between Bonaventure and the Ignatian tradition.[40] For Rahner, the idea of five spiritual senses is contrived, and it is not surprising that the doctrine in this conventional form has died out. Bonaventure's achievement, that of developing and enriching the tradition of the

---

[38] I depend here on Joseph Maréchal, 'Sur les cimes d'oraison', *Nouvelle revue théologique*, 56 (1929), 107–27, 177–206, esp. 107–14; on Cuthbert Butler, *Western Mysticism: The Teaching of SS. Augustine, Gregory, and Bernard on Contemplation and the Contemplative Life*, 2nd edn. (London: Constable, 1926 [1922]), ix–lviii; and on various contributions to the *Dictionnaire de Spiritualité*, notably by Pierre Adnès on the theory of mysticism in the nineteenth and twentieth centuries (x. 1936–7), by Henri de Gensac on Poulain (xii. 2025–7), and Irénée Noye on Saudreau (xiv. 359–60). These sources provide abundant further references. In 'Geschichte der Lehre', 2, Rahner refers explicitly to 'the more recent disputes on the essence of Catholic mysticism, which centre chiefly round the names of Poulain and Saudreau'. There are English translations of the two works named here: A. Saudreau, *The Degrees of the Spiritual Life: A Method of Directing Souls according to their Progress in Virtue*, trans. Bede Camm, 2 vols. (London: Washbourne, 1907); Aug. Poulain, *The Graces of Interior Prayer*, trans. from 6th edn. Leonora L. Yorke Smith (London: Kegan Paul, 1910).

[39] 'The Doctrine of the "Spiritual Senses"', 110 ('La Doctrine', 269). Rahner's published statement of this position is a refutation of a study by J. Bonnefoy, *Le Saint-Esprit et ses dons selon Saint Bonaventure* (Paris: Vrin, 1929), and becomes very tortuous. 'Geschichte der Lehre' is clearer, e.g. on p. 20: the spiritual senses 'do not represent any new mental capacities or a new *habitus*, but rather the actual mental perceptions which directly ensue from this state of perfection of the soul (*die sich aus diesem Vollendungszustand der Seele unmittelbar ergebenden aktuellen, geistigen Wahrnehmungen*)'.

[40] Rahner refers to the *Breviloquium*, v. vi. 5, and to *The Soul's Journey into God*, iv. 3. In the published version of his essay, Rahner asserts that these passages are forced, and do not do justice to the full richness of Bonaventure's teaching. For that, one has to look elsewhere, but in such places Bonaventure only deals with three of the five senses ('The Doctrine of the "Spiritual Senses"',115 ['La Doctrine', 276]). However, there are allusions to Bonaventure's teaching on the five senses in some early Jesuit documents: *Dir*, xx. 60, xxxi. 96; the Nadal text translated by the Rahner brothers in 1935 (German, 407; Spanish, 677–8; English, 290). See 'The Doctrine of the "Spiritual Senses"', 130–1 ('La Doctrine', 294–5) for Rahner's discussion of such passages. Rahner also mentions texts from the spiritual journal of Pierre Favre, but these seem only tenuously linked to Bonaventure.

spiritual senses in such a way that it comes to express 'the mystical reality of immediate experience', depends on his having effectively abandoned the fivefold scheme.[41]

Rahner reads Bonaventure's texts on spiritual touch, therefore, as both transcending what he said within the conventional schema of the five spiritual senses, and as a middle position in the then current discussions about 'elevated' states of prayer. For Rahner's Bonaventure, spiritual touch is equivalent to 'ecstasy'.[42] It falls between two other kinds of conceivable state. On the one hand it is not the same as *raptus*, 'an immediate and clear vision of God through the intellect' anticipating the beatific vision—*raptus* is a privilege given only in the rarest of cases.[43] But equally it must also be distinguished from even the highest 'intellectual' experience. Even when such experiences are mystical, they depend on a created effect of God in the one beholding. Thus Bonaventure's spiritual sight depends on an infused species, and his spiritual taste on a created 'sweetness'. But spiritual touch is different,

because it is an immediate experience of God, immediate in the proper ontological sense, not merely in the sense that the experience of God's created effects of grace (which are, as created effects, known in an intellectual sense) allows God too to be known, almost immediately (on the model of a medium through which they occur), as their ultimate cause.[44]

There is a middle position between a clear vision and an inferential knowledge of God: a dark but immediate touch, accessible to the will but not to the intellect, apprehended not through knowledge but through love. 'In ecstasy what is happening is an act of union in love, which does not occur in the intellect at all.'[45] The passage antedates the distinction Rahner later made between Dionysian and Evagrian ecstasy: though Bonaventure cites the parallel with Denys, his position sounds closer to what Rahner found in Evagrius.[46]

[41] 'Geschichte der Lehre', 29; 'The Doctrine of the "Spiritual Senses"', 127 ('La Doctrine', 291).

[42] 'The Doctrine of the "Spiritual Senses"', 117 ('La Doctrine', 279).

[43] Ibid. ('Der Begriff', 2).

[44] Ibid., 118 ('Der Begriff', 4–5). 'Ontological' here probably does not have the technical nuance it acquires in Rahner's mature writing, where it is contrasted with 'ontic'. Here it should simply be understood as 'real' or 'literal'.

[45] Ibid., 123 ('Der Begriff', 15).

[46] See 'The Doctrine of the "Spiritual Senses"', 125 ('Der Begriff', 18): 'Certainly, the influence of Ps. Denys is evident here. But the manner in which this idea is taken up, in which

The question arises: how does this doctrine of an immediate experience of God through love, excluding the intellectual faculty, square with the maxim *Nil volitum nisi cognitum*, the principle that nothing can be willed unless it is known?[47] In the early version of his study, Rahner wrote of Bonaventure's conviction that we can know an object 'simply through the fact that it is present, in its own self, in the soul': such objects were known 'through their essence—not through a *species* nor through a likeness but through their presence'. This can be applied to the soul's knowledge of itself, of love, and of God, who is the self's 'creative essence'.[48] In the published text, Rahner's account is more cautious and less clear: he denies that Bonaventure clarified the issue, and takes himself to be importing ideas which Bonaventure developed in other contexts. Drawing on a monograph by Bonifaz Luyckx, Rahner writes:

> an object of awareness can under certain conditions be known without the forming of a mental representation of this object within the faculty apprehending—simply because the object in question is present in its own self in the faculty which knows.[49]

In Bonaventure, this principle applies to the intellect's awareness of itself. Rahner takes it further, applying it not to the intellect as such, nor indeed to the will, but to a reality in the human person deeper than either of these faculties: what Bonaventure calls the *apex affectus*. From here both intellect and will both proceed, even if the will is somehow closer; here God's presence is located. 'If God touches this deepest point of the soul from within, informing it as it were,' Rahner concludes, 'the *apex affectus* will be able to have an awareness of this immediate union of love, without the intellect thereby becoming active.' At the deepest level of the self, deeper than intellect or will, there is God.

The youthful Rahner may also have associated the idea of

---

this darkness of mystical experience is explained metaphysically in a way foreign to Ps. Denys, shows nevertheless that this night motif in Bonaventure's mystical theology is more than a piece of mere tradition.'

[47] Ibid. 'Der Begriff', 18.
[48] 'Geschichte der Lehre', 23, quoting *The Soul's Journey into God*, vii. 5.
[49] This paragraph draws on 'The Doctrine of the "Spiritual Senses"', 124–5 ('Der Begriff', 15–17), esp. n. 95* (orig. n. 60). See also Bonifaz Anton Luyckx, *Die Erkenntnislehre Bonaventuras* (Münster: Aschendorff, 1923), 82–3. Rahner's assertion that the principle 'can be extended' from the intellect to the experience of God in the *apex affectus* seems in some tension with Luyckx's insistence that it applies only to the 'faculty of knowledge', not to the 'soul' itself.

spiritual touch with Ignatius. The first piece he published was on our need for prayer, and referred to how prayer makes us capable of 'touching our Creator and Lord'. In the margin of his manuscript, Rahner wrote 'Ex. Spir.'. The reference indicates that Rahner is drawing on a passage in the 1548 Latin version of the *Exercises*, where Ignatius—or his translator—speaks of how a retreatant can become better placed 'for seeking and touching their Creator and Lord'. Moreover, as Zahlauer suggests, Rahner's omission of 'seeking' may be significant; it is the reality of spiritual touch, and its implication that no seeking is necessary, which fascinate him.[50] The idea may also recur in the 1978 testament. In so far as the divine reality is united to the conscious self in spiritual touch, God becomes both subject and object of this dark experience. The language may be convoluted, but its passion is unmistakable:

But whatever happens, you must not today fall into the temptation of believing that the silent and modeless past-all-graspness, which we call God, would be doing something impossible or something against some law if it turned itself towards you in free love, in order to be itself—if it took you by surprise, in order that it itself might empower you, from your most intimate centre in which it is present, to address this nameless one as person to person. This is a miracle beyond comprehension and which overshoots all your metaphysics; the fact that it *can* happen is understood only if its reality has been risked.[51]

God's Touch in Darkness and the Everyday

This account of Rahner's sources has been complex, but it yields two substantive conclusions of importance for this study. The first concerns the nature of Rahner's *unmittelbare Gotteserfahrung*. This phrase indicates something dark and often tacit, more a matter of feeling than of knowing. *Erfahrung* is contrasted with *Erkenntnis* (knowledge).[52] This finding is important, given that 'immediate

[50] 'Warum uns das Beten nottut', 79: '*Dann nahen wir uns Gott und werden fähig "ad attingendum Creatorem ac Dominum nostrum, unseren Schöpfer und Herrn zu berühren"*.' Cf. the manuscript (KRA, I. A. 2); *Exx.* n. 20.9; MHSJ *Exx* (1969), 162. For information about the manuscript, I am indebted to Dr Roman Siebenrock and to Zahlauer, *Karl Rahner und sein 'produktives Vorbild'*, 86–8.
[51] 1978*b*, 19, *383–4*.
[52] 'The Doctrine of the "Spiritual Senses"', 120 ('Der Begriff', 7).

experience' in ordinary English suggests clarity, distinctness, and a lack of ambiguity. Rahner's phrase, however, refers to an immediate contact between the self and God—a contact to which our conscious awareness has some access, but normally of an obscure and oblique kind. There is, indeed, some convergence with the teaching of John of the Cross on his version of contemplation:

> In this loving awareness the soul receives God's communications passively, just as a person, without doing anything but keeping their eyes open, receives light passively. This reception of the light infused supernaturally into the soul is a passive knowing. It is affirmed that the person does nothing, not because they fail to understand, but because they understand by dint of no effort other than the reception of what is bestowed.[53]

The second concerns the continuities between Rahner and Ignatius. In a late interview Rahner spoke of how Ignatius's 'simple, profoundly deep theology in the Exercises' had brought home to him that there is such a thing as the experience of grace—a point which many earlier Jesuit theologians had denied. Thus, Rahner saw Ignatius as standing 'alongside Luther and Calvin as one of the great figures at the beginning of Christian modernity', as 'one of those great people who see the actual basis of Christian existence in a mystical experience of God'.[54] The stress in this last sentence must fall on the phrase 'actual basis'—*das eigentliche Fundament*. Rahner did not need Ignatius to tell him that an experience of grace was possible. When he did invoke Ignatius in this regard his readings were highly questionable; moreover, even if they were acceptable, what Rahner takes from them would need much further development before it could give us an adequate theology of the experience of grace. The continuity must lie in a conviction that people's ongoing experience of God is *central* to Christianity. Both Rahner and Ignatius take it as axiomatic that theology's claims about reality must also be claims about the human subject who can affirm such claims—or at least find them meaningful. A consequence is that the reality of revelation is still in process; its detailed realizations are unpredictable. God's self-gift to human beings must be as chaotic in appearance, and pluralist in form, as we are.

In Rahner's studies of Bonaventure, Evagrius, and Gregory of Nyssa, 'the immediate experience of God' is a rare, privileged

---

[53] *The Ascent of Mount Carmel*, II. xv. 2.
[54] *Glaube in winterlicher Zeit*, 29 (not translated in *Faith in a Wintry Season*).

event. The earliest version of the Bonaventure material did contain the tag, '*contemplatio fit per gratiam*—contemplation occurs through grace',[55] and Rahner stressed the continuities between the spiritual senses and the life of grace. Nevertheless, spiritual touch occurred only in the perfect. In Rahner's late spiritual testament, however, the languages of mysticism and grace are virtually interchangeable. The immediate experience of God is 'not a special privilege of a person chosen for an elite'. Instead it is something 'not in principle denied to anyone'. The grace which grounds it is present in all human beings.[56] Rahner's 1978 testament is original and distinctive in its transposition of mystical concepts to a general Christian theology of the human person. If Rahner is right in claiming that Ignatius decisively influenced him, it is this which is the chief point of continuity. The next chapter explores this transposition more systematically.

[55] 'Geschichte der Lehre', 23.
[56] 1978*b*, 13, *375*.

3

The Mystical and the Gracious

'On his account, all knowledge of God is more or less mystical.' The young Rahner may have been writing this sentence about Origen,[1] but he was also, more or less consciously, expressing one of his own central convictions. When Rahner's professional interests broadened from the history of spirituality into speculative theology, he continued to take seriously what he had learnt from Bonaventure and Evagrius. His contribution was to take their account of 'the immediate knowledge of God' out of the intellectual ghetto called 'ascetical and mystical theology', and to use it for the renewal of Christian theology in general.

One commentator makes a suggestive comparison between how Kant reacted to Hume and how Rahner responded to the witness of spiritual texts:

Just as Kant was convinced *that* the Newtonian physics of his day could be relied on . . . but, intellectually shaken by Hume's analysis of causality, was unable to be satisfied *how* such knowledge was possible until he made the 'Copernican revolution' of focusing his attention on . . . the knowing subject . . . so . . . Rahner—convinced that Ignatius and other mystical writers had truly experienced God—began to examine the 'conditions for the very possibility' of such experience. He did so first in an apparently only historical way . . . and then in a more systematic and explicitly transcendental way.[2]

If 'the immediate experience of God' occurs at all, it must be a human possibility; the potential for it must be present in the human as such. Thus the study of such experience, of spirituality, is not a marginal subdiscipline, but rather a central theological task.

Moreover, the theology of grace and the study of spirituality become, in this perspective, co-extensive. In the 1978 testament,

---

[1] 'The "Spiritual Senses" according to Origen', 96*, *134*. Cf. *Aszese und Mystik in der Väterzeit*, 79.

[2] Wiseman, ' "I Have Experienced God" ', 28.

'the immediate experience of God' is also the acceptance of the reality of grace, inescapably present in the human person—grace, in which 'God's own self is there, immediately'.[3] Again, in the *Concise Theological Dictionary*, Rahner and Vorgrimler describe 'religious experience' (*Erfahrung*) as the 'self-testimony within of supernatural reality (grace)'.[4] Conversely, the reality of mysticism is identical with Christianity as such: 'initiation into Christianity is basically initiation into mysticism—in biblical terms (for example Galatians), into the experience of the Spirit of God'.[5]

In his late Ignatian writings, Rahner is attributing to Ignatius, and perhaps finally making explicit, a set of theological moves he had already accomplished by the end of the 1930s. One prayer in *Encounters with Silence*, first published in 1937, takes up a mystical idiom:

Thanks be to your mercy, you infinite God, that I don't just know about you with concepts and words, but have experienced you, lived you, suffered you. Because the first and last experience of my life is you. Yes, really you yourself, not the concept of you, not your name which we give you . . . you have spoken your word through my being, through and through, the word which was before all things, more real than they, and in which all reality and all life stays in being. This word, in which alone there is life, has become, through your action, God of grace, my experience.[6]

Yet the ground of this claim is neither experiential testimony nor a lifetime's struggle for holiness, but rather the routine ritual of infant baptism. Rahner retains from his study of Bonaventure the idea that the experience of God in spiritual touch excludes the intellect, but he transposes it. Spiritual touch occurs, not only on a rarefied height, but also at the inarticulate beginnings of human existence. When Rahner was an infant,

there was nothing that I thought out or excogitated about you. Then my reason with its flip cleverness was still silent. Then you became, without asking me, the fate of my heart. You took hold of me—it wasn't that I 'comprehended' you (*Du hast mich ergriffen, nicht ich habe dich 'begriffen'*).

In several interviews, Rahner said that his theological innovations centred on one conviction: grace was a matter of experience. Often he articulated this conviction in terms of his having recovered a

[3] 1978*b*, 15, *378*.   [4] *Concise Theological Dictionary*, 165, *108*.
[5] 1978*d*, 24.   [6] 'God of Knowledge', in *Encounters with Silence*, 30–1*, *44–6*.

central Ignatian insight, and thereby having corrected imbalances in earlier Jesuit theology. The first main section of this chapter, therefore, will look at how Rahner grounded his claims about grace and experience. If Rahner's claims are true, then the witness of the mystics, however idiosyncratically expressed, is a source for theology in general. Spiritual texts are not reports of unique and unusual experiences so much as interpretations of human existence at large, showing forth what all of us are called, under God's grace, to become. Thus we find important structural continuities between the theology of spiritual touch that Rahner finds in Bonaventure and two of Rahner's key insights in the theology of grace: the primacy of uncreated over created grace, and the supernatural existential.

If Rahner is right, then the contexts of 'the immediate experience of God' are far more varied than conventional spiritual theology assumed. If spiritual touch is central to grace, then it characterizes not just the highest stages of contemplative prayer, but rather the whole life of grace, even in its smallest beginnings. It must also be a more common phenomenon than conventional Catholic spiritual theology used to imply: indeed, if God wills all human beings to be saved (1 Tim. 2. 4), then spiritual touch must in some sense be universal. 'This light is never lacking to the soul', as John of the Cross had taught.

John continues, however, by reflecting on how the light nevertheless cannot be infused 'because of creature forms and veils weighing upon and covering it', and exhorts us, therefore, to 'pure nakedness and poverty of spirit'.[7] Here Rahner diverges from John, at least in tone. Since grace builds on nature, the theology of spiritual touch must also connect with what philosophy can tell us about human knowing and willing. And whereas John often writes as if an experience of God's own self must exclude an experience of anything created, a general theology of grace centred on spiritual touch must present that touch as compatible with other, all too mundane realities. Creator and creature may remain distinct, infinitely so, but they are not mutually exclusive. The latter half of the present chapter takes up these contrasts and explores them further.

[7] The Ascent of Mount Carmel, II. xv. 4. For fuller discussion of the relationship between Rahner and John of the Cross, see Denis Edwards, 'Experience of God and Explicit Faith: A Comparison of John of the Cross and Karl Rahner', *The Thomist*, 46 (1982), 33–74; Steven L. Payne, 'The Relationship between Public Revelation and Private Revelations in St John of the Cross', *Teresianum*, 43 (1992), 175–215.

Despite its centrality to his theology, Rahner never produced a full systematic treatise on grace. Some of the reasons for this are biographical; it would appear that he came to teach the topic through a series of accidents, and for his lectures he was content to use as a codex (or student guidebook) an amended version of one written by his own teacher.[8] There may also be a deeper explanation, however, organically linked to his central insight on grace: if grace is correlative with human experience, grace must be as unsystematic and diverse as human beings are. Whatever the reasons, Rahner's theology of grace is scattered over a wide range of writings. Any overall presentation requires the interpreter to supply a structure.[9]

Rahner's Ignatian writings will not often be treated directly in this chapter, for the concern here is not so much with these texts' content as with the interpretation they suggest of Rahner's whole achievement, namely, that this latter proceeds from a fusion, inspired by the Ignatian Exercises, of the idioms of mysticism and grace. Other interpretations are obviously possible, and this study makes no claim to discredit these wholesale. But it is Rahner's own suggestion that the Ignatian writings can be seen as the key to his whole work, and such an approach throws his achievement, both its strengths and its weaknesses, into particularly clear relief.

The Presence of Grace in Experience

As Rahner reminisced on the past during his last years, a recurring motif was the contrast between his own theology of grace and that of the Jesuit tradition he inherited, notably as this had been presented to him by his own teacher, Hermann Lange. When he died, Rahner left on his desk an open letter to a young Jesuit involved in the charismatic renewal. Rahner was obviously irritated by what he saw as the movement's lack of intellectual responsibility.

---

[8] *De gratia Christi*—I cite normally from the first of five editions (1938). According to the foreword, the text was hurriedly composed, and reproduces much material from the corresponding volume by Hermann Lange, Rahner's own teacher (who had, perhaps conveniently, died in 1936). A critical edition is forthcoming in *KRSW*, edited by Roman Siebenrock. For biographical information, see Neufeld, *Die Brüder Rahner*, 133.

[9] Note, however, that this present account parallels 'Nature and Grace' in starting from the fact that grace can be experienced.

Nevertheless, he also stressed that the Exercises were themselves charismatic. Ignatius wrote,

in the almost bizarre, but true faith that the true and authentic Spirit of God is able and willing to give a directive to the individual conscious creature, despite his or her narrowness and the hundredfold ways in which he or she is materially and mentally conditioned—a directive that cannot be attained by any rational or depth-psychological consideration on its own.

Jesuit tradition, however, had not reflected this conviction:

I am of the opinion—though this is not to be taken as definitive—that we Jesuits, down the history of our theology (and probably also of our praxis), have not been very Ignatian at all. Now I can't document this here. But take for example my highly respected teacher in the theology of grace, Hermann Lange. He was convinced that specifically supernatural grace is only an 'ontic' reality, totally beyond consciousness, and that whatever religious element there is in human consciousness arises *only* through indoctrination from without.[10]

Again, in an interview during his last months, Rahner spoke of how he had,

always drawn attention, against a certain baroque scholastic tradition in my own Society, to the fact that there is an experience of grace. My teacher in Valkenburg, Hermann Lange, S.J., radically opposed anything like this. Lange relentlessly defended a so-called 'sanctifying, entitative (*seinshafte*) grace'. But this grace was, in his opinion, absolutely beyond consciousness (*absolut bewußtseinsjenseitig*). According to this tradition, one could only know about this grace through external revelation, sacred Scripture. I insistently argued against this opinion with a set of concepts largely based on Maréchal. In my opinion there is something like 'an experience of grace', even if there is a real difficulty in interpreting this correctly. This too was what Ignatius suggested to me in his simple, but profoundly deep theology in the *Exercises*.[11]

Rahner also expressed the point more technically, in scholastic jargon. If grace is imparted, then human mental acts are directed

---

[10] 1984, 133–4, 3.

[11] *Glaube in winterlicher Zeit*, 29 (not translated in *Faith in a Wintry Season*). Cf. Lange, *De gratia*, n. 453g (p. 342). Here Lange cites the view that God can be present 'as an object (*objectum*) experientially knowable and relishable within the soul'. Lange concedes that this is the case in the beatific vision and perhaps in mystical union, 'when God is felt as present and as united to the soul by a certain substantial touch'. But his judgement is clear: 'this means cannot be used to explain the indwelling common to all the just'. Elsewhere in Lange's text, the topic is conspicuous by its absence.

towards, and sustained by, a distinctively supernatural *a priori* formal object. In yet another late interview, this time in 1982, Rahner claimed this belief made him a radical Thomist even when he went beyond Thomas Aquinas—'one has to learn some things from Thomas against Thomas'—and to part company with mainstream Jesuit tradition as represented by Suárez and Molina. This latter school had made too rigid a distinction between nature and grace— 'one of the original and mortal sins of Jesuit theology'. Even Dominicans such as Garrigou-Lagrange, who accepted some of Rahner's particular innovations, failed to recognize that Rahner's way of thinking was 'opposed to the basic framework of their theology'.[12]

Scholastic philosophy distinguished between the material and the formal object of knowledge: the object known, and the viewpoint taken by the knower. If I study psychology, the material object of my study is the human person, while the formal object is those aspects of the human on which, abstracting from others, psychology focuses. Transcendental philosophy, however, applies the term not only to what is known but also to the knower. If I can study psychology, there must be an orientation in me to psychological reality; if I know that a table is brown through looking at it, then there is an orientation in me to the visible in general and to colour in particular. The general principle was once set out by Emerich Coreth, one of Rahner's Jesuit colleagues in Innsbruck, in his standard textbook on transcendental Thomist metaphysics: the formal object (*Objekt*) is not merely a reality of what confronts us (*Gegenstand*), but also of the knower's 'outward look' (*Hinblick*).[13] Similarly, Rahner writes in 1960 of how the 'formal object' is neither 'something over against us in knowledge' nor something which we abstract from a range of individual objects that we encounter, but a reality of consciousness: 'the conscious, accompanying *a priori* horizon. Everything which is apprehended as an actual object over against the knower, through the apprehending of individual objects given *a posteriori*, is known under this horizon.'[14]

For Rahner, the formal object of the human mind, abstracting from grace, consists in its openness for *Sein*—'being' or 'reality'—as

---

[12] *Faith in a Wintry Season*, 48–9, 58–9.

[13] Coreth, *Metaphysik*, 165—cf. the corresponding passage in the abridged ET by Joseph Donceel (New York: Herder, 1968), 75. Another source of information on background philosophical issues is Brugger (ed.), *Philosophisches Wörterbuch*, a reference work sponsored by the Jesuit philosophy school in Munich.

[14] 'Nature and Grace', 178, 225.

such: a contradiction arises if human beings postulate the existence of a reality in principle beyond human knowing. Lange and his predecessors, says Rahner, had seen grace as merely an 'objective' transformation of the material object of knowledge, without carrying the point through to consideration of the knower. Grace was a reality in us, but not in our consciousness: it did not entail a divinization of our subjectivity. In the background was a defensiveness regarding the Reformation assurance of salvation, independent of ecclesial obedience. The most that would be conceded is that revelation can transform *a posteriori* our motivations for acting: .

If, for example, I learn or hear that God can be honoured by charity towards a poor person, and as a result give alms to a poor person, the formal object and motive of this deed is the ethical value of giving honour to God. Nevertheless, this kind of formal object is by the same token *a posteriori*. It is something added on to what is intrinsic, an extrinsic object like any other.

But Rahner was claiming something more: the existence of grace has implications for our understanding of our own identity. Just as the faculty of touch can in no way perceive the movement of the air as sound, so a 'purely natural' subjectivity could not apprehend grace. 'If we are talking about what, for clarity's sake, I want to call the *a priori* formal object, then this means the ordered structure under which objects coming from outside will be perceived. This kind of formal object is intrinsic to the faculty itself.'[15] The dry idiom belied the claim that Rahner was making: in grace, God's own self is the principle of human mental acts. What Christianity has regularly proclaimed about the divine presence in Jesus must also in some way apply to any graced creature.

In *De gratia Christi*, Rahner devotes far more space to describing what he means by 'the supernatural *a priori* formal object' than to defending his claim that the reality in fact obtains. However, at the end of his account, he gives four arguments.[16] Firstly, the traditional view, whereby the supernatural quality of a given act lay outside

[15] See *De gratia Christi*, 300, 297–8: '*Si vero sermo est de objecto formali, quod claritatis gratia vocare volumus aprioristicum, intelligitur ratio, sub qua objecta adventicia percipientur, talis, quae ipsi facultati ingenita est, sub qua a priori ad omnem ejus perceptionem vel volitionem omnia objecta possibilia aggreditur.*'

[16] In this paragraph, I follow *De gratia Christi*, 311–13, with reference to the fifth edition in order to clarify a misprint. Some of the argumentation can be found later in 'Current Problems in Christology', 168–71, *189–92*; in 'Nature and Grace', 178–9, *224–6*; and in 'Gnadenerfahrung'.

consciousness, involves a self-contradiction: on the one hand the act is specified by the intention underlying it, on the other by something lying in principle beyond human awareness. If grace makes a difference to a human act, then this change is manifest in consciousness, or else the difference does not count as intrinsic to the act.[17] Secondly, if reality and consciousness are correlated, then it makes no sense to postulate an action of grace which raises human activity to a higher level of reality while remaining beyond consciousness. Thirdly, only on such a hypothesis can one do proper justice to scriptural and patristic language regarding the influence of grace. Finally, the traditional arguments against this view, as collected by Lange, depend on a deficient philosophy of mind and epistemology. In particular, Rahner's opponents 'wrongly suppose that everything conscious can become, through reflection, an object objectively represented as such in itself'.[18]

This fourth argument is important, and takes up a motif from Rahner's account of Bonaventure.[19] Spiritual touch is dark: it is not a reality we can 'see'. Rahner in no way claims that we have clear reflective awareness of our life in grace, or that we can clearly distinguish our experience of grace from the 'purely natural'. Thus he continues to respect the traditional Tridentine teaching that we cannot normally be assured of our state of grace.[20] But there can be elements in consciousness (*Objekte*) other than the objects which appear over against it (*Gegenstände*).

Rahner's claims about the supernatural formal object, however dry the idiom, have momentous consequences, both within the rather narrow Catholic world in which he formulated them, and for the relationship between Catholic Christianity and the world at large. Three points may be indicated here, anticipating fuller subsequent discussion. Firstly, by insisting that grace was an experiential reality, Rahner subverted the then conventional way of distinguishing the study of mysticism from the study of grace. Karl Richstätter (1864–1949) lectured at Valkenburg on spirituality, or as

---

[17] *De gratia Christi*, 311: '*ubi habetur mutatio aliqua ontologica, aut se manifestat in conscientia, aut non pertinet ad talem actum.*'

[18] Ibid., 313: '*false supponunt omne id, quod est conscium, debere per reflexionem fieri posse objectum ut tale in se objective repraesentatum*'. Rahner refers to Lange, *De Gratia*, nn. 309–10.

[19] Wiseman, '"I Have Experienced God"', 50–4, uses Rahner's Ignatian writings to clarify Rahner's position, against critics who accuse Rahner of neo-ontologism.

[20] 'Decree on Justification', n. 9 (Tanner, *Decrees of the Ecumenical Councils*, 674).

he called it 'asceticism and mysticism'. Perhaps fortunately for his
subsequent reputation, he just missed having Rahner as a student.
His 1939 codex begins with some definitions. Up to the seventeenth
and eighteenth centuries, 'mysticism' had denoted the spiritual life
in general. Now, however, it was confined to the 'higher' reaches, to
'the life of grace which has reached awareness, the experientially
perceived life of grace'. The two terms were not to be confused:
'mysticism' should be reserved for a particular class of supernatural
acts.[21] On Rahner's account, by contrast, the mystical and the gracious are co-extensive. Any distinction between them is a matter of
empirical psychology, of no particular theological significance.

Secondly, Rahner's theory helps us move beyond the impasse of
the Reformation period regarding how believers can be conscious
or certain of grace. Trent, as has just been mentioned, rejected the
Reformers' belief that a person could be assured of salvation. We
could only hope for it. But, if this hope is placed in the graciousness
of God, what grounds can there be for doubting? Rahner's vision of
an immediate touch inaccessible to reflective awareness enables us
to interpret the tradition of assurance in terms of an absolute confidence *that* God's saving grace is present with us, while simultaneously asserting that an uncertainty remains regarding *how* this
grace is at work.

Thirdly, in claiming that divine revelation was always an event in
human consciousness, Rahner established that any theology focusing only on the official Word would be in principle incomplete, and
grounded a dynamic, generative view of tradition. God's grace is
always a free interaction between the external word and the
indwelling divine presence. Teachings and exhortations are useless
unless 'they meet up with the ultimate grace from within'.[22]
Rahner's Ignatius criticizes 'a large part' of Jesuit theology in terms
that will be by now familiar: Jesuit theologians should not, 'contrary
to the fundamental conviction of my Exercises, have shifted divine
grace as such to a realm beyond consciousness, believing that one
knew of this grace only through external indoctrination from the
Church, without an actual experience of it'. Nevertheless, Jesuit

[21] Karl Richstätter, 'Vorlesungen über Mystik' (unpublished lecture codex: Valkenburg,
1939), 1–2. For a subtler treatment of the distinction between asceticism and mysticism, more
sensitive to the pressures under which the distinction was coming, see de Guibert, *The Theology of the Spiritual Life*, pp. 1–8.
[22] 1978*b*, 16, *379*.

tradition also upheld an optimistic view of human nature, a view reflected in controversial and innovative mission strategies in China and India. All of this foreshadowed 'the kind of theological anthropology that must exist in a Church claiming to be the Church of the whole world and of all cultures, rather than to be selling European Christianity as an export article throughout the world'.[23]

Spiritual Touch and Formal Causality

By his claim that grace was a reality of human experience, Rahner was subverting conventional distinctions between the different branches of Catholic theology as practised in his time. He was reconceiving the theology of grace he inherited so that experiential, or mystical, categories became central. Implicitly, too, he was also reworking standard accounts of how Christian revelation related to the natural, to the human as such.

As we have already seen, Rahner was aware that the issues he was tackling in his discussion of Bonaventure's mysticism arose also in discussions of Bonaventure's epistemology. At the end of his account, he offers an overall judgement. Bonaventure's is,

a brilliant attempt to solve the problem of how to reconcile the distinctiveness of the mystical life of grace (which is not deducible from the events of the ordinary life of grace) with the fact that the direct vision of God is only the reward of heaven, not the lot of pilgrims. It is not the only conceivable solution to the problem as thus expressed, but probably the one which falls least into the mistake of suppressing the distinctiveness and sublimity of mystical experience.[24]

In this early work Rahner presents Bonaventure's theory as a middle position in the idiom of conventional mystical theology. Spiritual touch is the immediate, yet dark, experience of God, distinguished both from clear vision (as in rapture or in heaven) and from inferential knowledge, which is as such indirect. Rahner's subsequent writings on grace, as we have begun to see, subvert the conventions within which he develops his interpretation of Bonaventure. Nevertheless, in this early exegetical work, Rahner

[23] 1978*b*, 32, *399–400*.
[24] 'The Doctrine of the "Spiritual Senses" ', 125 ('Der Begriff', 18).

developed structures of argument that would recur, to telling effect, in other contexts.

In the Bonaventure essay Rahner is addressing a conflict. On the one hand, positive and experiential sources stress the immediacy of the human creature's contact with God. On the other, theological tradition stresses the gulf between creator and creature, between the all-holiness of God and the sinfulness of humanity. The essay thus touches onto a wider speculative issue. Christianity sees creator and creation as both united and distinct: how should Christian theology strike the balance between these two claims?

Rahner's general strategy is twofold. Firstly, he finds an alternative theological account of the difference between creator and creature. Subsequently, and on that basis, he develops a theology articulating with new boldness the union which the positive sources attest. In the Bonaventure essay, for example, he introduces the concept of loving contact through darkness, as opposed to the intellectual clarity of the beatific vision. No longer, then, need the evident distinction between creator and creature imply that creaturely knowledge of God is merely inferential, merely knowledge *about* God as the wholly other creator of the effects accessible to us. A similar move occurs in Rahner's much more famous essay of 1950, 'Concerning the Relationship between Nature and Grace'. Rahner here glosses the supernatural in terms of 'unexactedness', thereby avoiding conventional extrinsicism. On this basis, he can then affirm in a new way the continuity between human openness for God and 'humanity as it really is'.

In Rahner's theology of grace, 'spiritual touch' appears as uncreated grace, as God's own self, operative in us through quasi-formal causality. Without it, 'there does not exist even the beginning of a possibility of thinking of created grace'.[25] Once again, Rahner's argument starts from a claim that conventional theology fails to accommodate what positive sources say. On Rahner's reading of scripture and tradition, the primary referent of 'grace' is uncreated grace, God's immediate self-communication: 'the created gifts of grace are seen as a *consequence* of God's substantial communication to justified human beings'.[26] The standard scholastic theologies, by contrast, whatever their other differences, 'see God's indwelling and conjunction with the justified human being as exclusively

<hr/>

[25] 'Some Implications', 341, 370.   [26] Ibid., 322, 350–1.

grounded on created grace. God imparts himself to the soul and dwells in it on the basis of the fact that created grace is imparted to the soul.'[27]

There was, however, an anomaly in this position. For it was also generally accepted in scholastic theology that the beatific vision could serve as a model for the theology about grace here and now. The relationship between the two was not 'purely moral and juridical';[28] for all their difference, there was a theological continuum between them. Now, in the beatific vision, uncreated grace must be primary. There, 'God's essence itself takes the place of the *species* (*impressa*) in the created mind'.[29] Rahner is drawing here on Thomist epistemology, which holds that knowledge is caused by the object known impinging on the intellect, or mind, of the knower, and forming a *species*.[30] The knowledge of God's own self in the beatific vision cannot be grounded on a created reality within the human mind, 'for this could only reveal its object, God's infinite being, in the measure of its own entitative capacity as a finite determination of the knowing subject'.[31] In the beatific vision, therefore, God is somehow present as more than creator. Moreover, if there is a theological continuum between grace and the beatific vision, this more-than-creative presence of God must also apply at earlier stages in the life of grace.

Rahner thus exposes a contradiction. His solution—though he later acknowledged that Maurice de la Taille had anticipated him[32]—was to suggest that God's grace operated not only through

[27] Ibid., 324, *352*.   [28] Ibid., 326, *354*.
[29] Ibid., 327, *355*. Rahner's account bears comparison with Thomas Aquinas's, in *Summa theologiae*, I. xii. 5.
[30] Despite the etymology, *species intelligibilis* is for Rahner an austerely formal concept. See *Spirit in the World*, 311–13 (*KRSW*, ii. 233–4): 'The species of something can be anything determining the reality of a mind in such a way as to enable the mind concerned to know about this "something". In this formal talk . . . it remains completely open how the inner nature of this "determination of reality" in itself is to be understood' (pp. 311–12, *233*). Thus, for example, the kind of *species* through which God knows things is quite different from those operative in human knowing.
[31] 'Some Implications', 328, *356*.
[32] Ibid., 340 n. 2, *369 n. 1*. See Maurice de la Taille, 'Actuation créée par acte incréé', *Recherches de science religieuse*, 18 (1928), 253–68, and the general historical account in Trütsch, *SS. Trinitatis inhabitatio*. For an ET of de la Taille's essay, see *The Hypostatic Union and Created Action by Uncreated Act* (West Baden, 1952), 29–41. Rahner's claims to originality have recently come under thorough scrutiny in Simon F. Gaine, 'Indwelling Spirit and a New Creation: The Relationship between Uncreated Grace and Created Grace in Neo-Scholastic Catholic Theology', D.Phil. thesis (Oxford, 1994). Gaine shows convincingly that the innovations in

efficient causality, but also, and primarily, through formal causality. In grace, God's own self is the creature's principle of identity; God's relation to the creature is as form to matter in a substance.[33] Obscure, even outrageous, though the formulation may sound, it is only a translation into scholastic terminology of what Rahner found in Bonaventure's spiritual touch: God's own self informs the creature. Equally, the creature is not reflectively or objectively aware of this presence. Bonaventure's 'darkness' has become something more commonplace and prosaic: the fact that our reflective consciousness will never comprehend the full truth of our identity.

Again Rahner is renegotiating issues regarding the distinctions and unities between creator and creature. By invoking the scholastic contrast between outer (efficient) and inner (formal) causality, Rahner can articulate the distinction in terms of the latter and the union in terms of the former. God makes a creation distinct from God, so as to impart the divine self in love and grace. In a Christological context, Rahner wrote of 'an ontological ultimate which a merely rational ontology would perhaps never suspect':

> the absolute One has in the pure freedom of his infinite unrelatedness, which he always preserves, the possibility of himself becoming the other, the finite. He has the possibility, through his dispossessing *himself*, giving *himself* away, of *establishing* the other as his own reality.[34]

Rahner is here expressly dependent on revelation. As he was to put the matter on Ignatius's lips, he is articulating 'an incomprehensible miracle which overshoots all your metaphysics'.[35] Equally, however, it is not just a homiletic piety when Rahner's Ignatius says that God

---

Rahner's essay, though significant, are less radical than his tone suggests. Rahner is not being entirely fair to his predecessors.

[33] For clarification on the terminology, see Viktor Naumann, 'Ursache', in Brunner (ed.), *Philosophisches Wörterbuch*, 424–5: 'One distinguishes between *inner* and *outer* causes according to whether or not a cause is an inner formative principle (*inneres Aufbauprinzip*) of that which is caused. For all bodies, according to hylomorphism, the inner causes are *matter* and *form*. They constitute the whole being of the body in question by their mutual participation (*Mitteilung*): the matter, in so far as it takes up the form and bears it; the form, insofar as it determines the matter and thus endows the whole with its specific character.' It is only the Aristotelian outer causes (efficient and final), therefore, that correspond to the normal English sense of 'cause'. More accessibly, see Brian Davies, *The Thought of Thomas Aquinas* (Oxford: Clarendon Press, 1992), 46–9.

[34] *Foundations of Christian Faith*, 222, *220* (*KSRW*, xxvi. 213), taken from material first published in 1958.

[35] 'Some Implications', 329, *357*; 1978*b*, 19, *384*.

only allowed sin and guilt into the world 'because in Jesus he made it *his own*'.[36]

The technical term on which Rahner ultimately settles to describe God's action in grace is 'quasi-formal causality'.[37] The force of the 'quasi-' is twofold. On the one hand, it points to the difference between divine and creaturely causality. More specifically and importantly, the 'quasi-' expresses the difference between the hypostatic union and grace. In the former, the Logos through formal causality is the logical subject of Jesus's humanity. In the latter, there is a 'true, ontological communication' between the formal cause and the matter thus determined, 'but to the end and only to the end that (the formal cause) can become in virtue of this quasi-formal causality the object of immediate knowledge and love'. In his philosophy of mind, Rahner had, in substance if not in terminology, developed 'quasi-formal causality' as an explanation of how the object of knowledge can determine the human intellect without absorbing it totally.[38] Grace does not annul our distinctness from God: on the contrary, what is at stake is 'the highest degree of unity in the fullest distinction'.[39]

Rahner is of course not denying the existence of created grace, but merely asserting its dependence on God's own reality within the self: 'there is no actual possibility of conceiving created grace separated from uncreated grace'. Conversely, uncreated grace never exists except in and through created effects. Rahner takes himself merely to be correcting a distortion in the theological tradition he

---

[36] 1978*b*, 20, *385*, emphasis added.

[37] Zahlauer, *Karl Rahner und sein 'produktives Vorbild'*, 195, 89–90, attractively conjectures that this term can be traced back, through the Bonaventure material, to 'Warum uns das Beten nottut', 79. Here, the youthful Rahner speaks of God imparting himself to his creation, and filling *his* (emphasis original) soul with the power of grace. The 'his' indicates not just ownership but also ontological union. Zahlauer further links this very early Rahner text to the 1919 publication of the Autograph manuscript (so called because of some corrections by Ignatius himself) of the *Exercises*, now widely taken as normative. Whereas the 1548 Vulgate version of *Exx*, 15.6 had spoken of God communicating himself to 'the soul devoted to him', the Spanish spoke of '*la su ánima devota*—his devout soul'.

[38] See Schwerdtfeger, *Gnade in Welt*, 124–5; Mannermaa, '*Lumen fidei*', 26–31.

[39] 'Some Implications', 345, *374*; 336–7, *364–5*. See too 1954/5, 272, *272*, where Rahner implicitly links the idea with Augustinian Trinitarianism. Trütsch identifies this distinction as the point on which Rahner improved de la Taille's formulation (*SS. Trinitatis inhabitatio*, 105, 109–10). The material on grace and the hypostatic union is found in the section added to the essay for the 1954 publication. Later, Rahner handled the matter differently (e.g. *Foundations of Christian Faith*, 198–203, *198–202* [*KRSW*, xxvi. 191–6], taking over material from 1962); see my 'Rahner, Christology, and Grace', *Heythrop Journal*, 37 (1996), 284–97.

inherited. This had been shaped by Trent's concern to refute what it took to be the teaching of the Reformers; the stress was on how grace, as something really inherent, was fully proper to the justified, while the references to 'the promised Holy Spirit' were marginalized.[40] Rahner is re-establishing the balance between created and uncreated grace. God's own self and the graced creature are united, without confusion and without separation.

Grace and the Constitution of the Self

As we have seen, Rahner first discussed 'the immediate experience of God' in essays on mystical theology. Conventionally, the genre described exalted states, episodic or lasting, of privileged people. On Rahner's reading of Bonaventure, the spiritual senses come into play only after a person has passed through a differentiated process of growth to a state of perfection.[41] Matters are different in the 1978 testament. If one evokes 'the immediate experience of God' in another person, one is not indoctrinating them into something hitherto alien to their awareness. Rather, what is at stake is 'the coming more explicitly to the reality of the self, the free acceptance of a reality of the human constitution—a reality which is always there, mostly buried and repressed, but an inescapable fact'.[42]

'A reality of the human constitution': the gracious presence of God's own self and 'the immediate experience of God' now characterize the human condition in general; how far one accepts or articulates this reality is a secondary, though not unimportant, question. This universal aspect of grace was what Rahner dubbed 'the supernatural existential'. Rahner grounded this concept in a variety of ways. In 1950, as we have already seen, he presented it as providing

---

[40] 'Some Implications', 340–2, 369–71; Trent, *Decree on Justification*, n. 7 (Tanner, *Decrees of the Ecumenical Councils*, 673).

[41] 'The Doctrine of the "Spiritual Senses"', 111 ('La doctrine', 271). Stephen Fields, 'Balthasar and Rahner on the Spiritual Senses', *Theological Studies*, 57 (1996), 224–41, notes how Balthasar, in contrast to Rahner, reads the spiritual senses as characteristic of the second, illuminative stage of spiritual growth in Bonaventure. For Fields, this divergence points towards deeper differences between the two modern theologians in their approach to human knowledge of God. Fields's claim is worth pursuing, but his analysis must be qualified: the mature Rahner abandoned the elitism implicit in his early writings on the spiritual senses.

[42] 1978*b*, 15, *378*: '*das ausdrücklichere Zusichselberkommen und die freie Annahme einer Verfassung des Menschen*'.

the necessary middle course between intrinsicism and extrinsicism.[43] Biographically, Rahner seems first to have developed it as a corollary of the Incarnation, following the Greek Fathers' doctrine of recapitulation: 'God himself willed to become, in the supernatural order, a member and part of the human race as something total and in solidarity . . . Thus it appears that through the hypostatic union itself the human race has already, at its root, been redeemed, or rather called to the supernatural order.'[44] For our purposes, however, the most revealing text is Rahner's dictionary article on the systematic theology of grace for the *Lexikon für Theologie und Kirche* (1960), reworked for *Sacramentum mundi* (1968). In this text, where Rahner sets out most fully the relationship between his theology of grace and earlier tradition, he grounds the supernatural existential on the universal salvific will of God, a teaching implicit in the official condemnation of Jansenism and in Vatican I.[45] If God wills all to be saved, then all must have access to what was called a 'sufficient grace'.

Conventionally, this grace had been understood as an 'actual grace', as a *transiens auxilium*, a special divine impulse.[46] This impulse was contrasted with a 'habitual' grace, stably present within the justified. Such a distinction clearly shapes the narrative account of justification given in Trent's decree,[47] and was central to post-Tridentine Roman Catholic theology. The terminology, though arguably not the substance, derived from Thomas Aquinas. Rahner's account of created and uncreated grace had already subverted this framework radically. Even within it, however, Rahner argues against seeing this universally present grace as simply 'actual'. The grace in question, as Augustine would have taught, is something 'absolutely necessary for any saving act', not merely an aid for what we could, in principle, do anyway. Hence 'it does not consist merely in the outward circumstances shaped by God's providence which

---

[43] 'Concerning the Relationship between Nature and Grace'.

[44] *De gratia Christi*, 20–1. See Mannermaa, '*Lumen Fidei*', 80–9, for a survey of the biographical evidence, only partially taken up by Schwerdtfeger in *Gnade und Welt*, 164–9. As Mannermaa also points out, the treatment at this stage of God's universal salvific will is still conventional, in terms of actual grace (*De gratia Christi*, 1–10).

[45] Vatican I, *Dogmatic Constitution on the Catholic Faith*, n. 3 (Tanner, *Decrees of the Ecumenical Councils*, 807–8).

[46] Lange, *De gratia*, n. 12—with an emphasis on *transiens*.

[47] Council of Trent, *Decree on Justification*, nn. 4–7 (Tanner, *Decrees of the Ecumenical Councils*, 672–4).

favour humanity's religious action: it is also . . . "interior" grace in
the same sense as sanctifying grace'.[48] To structure the theology of
grace around the distinction between 'actual' and 'habitual' grace,
as post-Tridentine theology conventionally did, was 'very superfi-
cial and alien'. Such an approach does not do justice 'to the unity
and nature of the one grace divinizing the essence, capacities, and
self-realization of the human person'.[49] In his 1960 essay, 'Nature
and Grace', Rahner puts the matter more sharply:

> when a person is summoned by the message of faith given by the visible
> Church, what this summons meets is not a person coming thereby (and
> hence through conceptual knowledge) into mental (*geistige*) contact with
> the proclaimed truth for the first time. What the call does is to make
> reflectively available—in a way that is obviously necessary for a full and
> informed attitude about it—what was already there in the grace that was
> already encompassing them, inarticulately but really, as an element of
> their mental existence.

Grace always surrounds the human person, even the sinner and the
unbeliever, as an 'inescapable setting'.[50]

Conversion, therefore, is not to be seen as a transition from
grace's absence to grace's presence. Nor is it a graduation from
dependence on 'actual' grace to the stable possession of habitual
grace. Conversion consists in an acceptance of the grace already
and inescapably given. Even the person who rejects grace or finds
the concept meaningless nevertheless receives it as an offer shaping
their identity. Thus, given Rahner's correlations between the theologies of grace and mysticism, it is not just that 'the immediate
experience of God' is accessible to everyone: it is present at all stages
of everyone's life.

At the end of his *Der Mensch als Geheimnis*, Klaus Fischer reproduced an exchange of letters between himself and Rahner. Fischer
had asked why Rahner believed that the lowest steps of mysticism
were accessible to everyone. Rahner replied by saying that everyone
was a more or less latent mystic:

> in my opinion you can talk about different stages of this kind of experience
> (i.e. the experience of God's grace) only in one of two senses: either about
> different stages in the free acceptance of this experienced reality, or about

[48] 'Grace', 419, *459*. 'Sanctifying grace' is here equivalent to 'habitual grace'.
[49] Ibid., 420, *460*.   [50] 'Nature and Grace', 181, *228–9*.

different stages in the ability to reflect on this reality and to make it an object of one's verbalized, concrete awareness. But the experienced mental reality as such is permanently present in the human person.[51]

As a young man, Rahner discovered how for Bonaventure 'the whole mystical ascent was nothing more than a person's step-by-step return to what is most interior in them, a step-by-step ascent into the summit of the person's soul'.[52] In his old age, he could write to a depressive sixteen-year-old whom he had met while visiting a youth club:

We cannot choose our life according to our pleasure and the demands of our problematic wishes. We must accept ourselves as we are. But when we do this really honestly, courageously and hopefully, we accept God's own self.[53]

Two relatively early essays had at least pointed to the underlying theology. 'Reflections on the Problem of the Gradual Ascent to Christian Perfection' effectively argues for an interpretation of mystical ascent in terms of ever greater personal freedom in the exercise of the spiritual life, correlated with the life-cycle, and thereby also for a radical reworking of the concept of mysticism.[54] 'Reflections on the Experience of Grace', while recognizing that the experience of grace is not easily expressible, points towards various grim experiences—absolute loneliness, unjust treatment—as steps along the way. The underlying theory is not made explicit. However, given that Rahner here also acknowledges that God's grace is present in all things, the point may be that growth in grace and mysticism involves the gradual acceptance and appropriation of that presence. It is not masochism or mean-spiritedness which leads Rahner to focus on the bleak, but rather a recognition that dark experiences can have sacramental significance. In human experiences which, on other than Christian world-views, are null and meaningless, 'people of the Spirit and saints' can 'assure themselves' that they are really living authentic Christianity, and that 'the Spirit in them is not just the way in which they live a humane life'.[55]

---

[51] 'Ein Brief von P. Karl Rahner', 408.
[52] 'The Doctrine of the "Spiritual Senses"', 123 ('Der Begriff', 13).
[53] *Is Christian Life Possible Today?*, 65, 67.
[54] 'Reflections on the Problem', esp. 15–23, *24–34*.
[55] 'Reflections on the Experience of Grace', 88, *107–8*.

Mystical Grace and Human Nature

As has been said above, Rahner's theologies of grace and mysticism are unashamedly dependent on revelation. Nevertheless, grace builds on nature. Though an adequate Christian theology can never reduce to a philosophy, it does require one. If theological claims about uncreated grace and the immediate experience of God are to be credible, they need somehow to connect with a philosophical account of human knowledge and experience. We must find, somehow, a middle course between rationalism and fideism. In the opening chapters of *Hearer of the Word*, Rahner speaks of a 'twofold task'. On the one hand, we need to show that God can give a revelation which somehow transcends the conclusions of philosophy, and which amounts to 'more than the mere objectivation of humanity's subjective state':

On the other hand, we must show to what extent we possess an inner openness for such a revelation; we must make intelligible the fact that we can and must welcome it if it is proffered, and how we welcome it—without anticipating its content through our openness.[56]

It goes beyond the purpose of this study to explore in detail the arguments of *Spirit in the World* and *Hearer of the Word*.[57] My concern here is simply to point up the links between these philosophical works and what, if the late Ignatian writings are to be believed, was Rahner's central theological concept: 'the immediate experience of God'. This idea shaped not only Rahner's innovations in the theology of grace, but also his account of the human nature which this grace transforms.

The crucial point can be established relatively simply from a

---

[56] *Hearer of the Word*, 19, *38* (*KRSW*, iv. 44).
[57] There are no really satisfactory, easily available accounts of Rahner's philosophy. Thomas Sheehan, *Karl Rahner: The Philosophical Foundations* (Athens: Ohio University Press, 1987), is tendentious, although it helpfully refutes some frequent misconceptions. The recent general introductions to Rahner by William V. Dych (London: Geoffrey Chapman, 1992) and Karen Kilby (London: Fount Paperbacks, 1997) avoid the issue, on good pedagogical grounds. The most helpful secondary materials known to me are three essays by former colleagues marking the tenth anniversary of Rahner's death, essays which, unfortunately, are available only in German: Emerich Coreth, 'Philosophische Grundlagen der Theologie Karl Rahners', *Stimmen der Zeit*, 212 (1994), 525–36; Karl Lehmann, 'Philosophisches Denken im Werk Karl Rahners', in *Karl Rahner in Erinnerung*, ed. Albert Raffelt (Düsseldorf: Patmos, 1994), 10–27; Muck, 'Heidegger und Karl Rahner'. See too the biographical discussion in Raffelt and Verweyen, *Karl Rahner*, 17–40.

passage in *Hearer of the Word*. After the preambles, the book's argument proper opens with an observation about what distinguishes human conscious activity:

As human we can never stop, in our thought or in our activity, at this or that reality in isolation. We want to know what reality is all about, particularly in the previously established unity within which everything always meets us. We inquire about the ultimate foundations, about the one ground of all things. To the extent that we recognize every individual as something which is, we are asking about the *being* of the things which are. We are pursuing metaphysics.[58]

It is part of being human that we ask questions like ' "What does it *all* mean?" How is it that I am in a situation at all? Why is there Being at all and not rather nothing?'[59] Admittedly, even this latter, simpler formulation hardly corresponds with daily conversation on the Clapham omnibus. But Rahner's concern is not with what is said, but with what is implicit in the saying. Even a refusal to answer the question, or a denial that it is meaningful, even the idolizing of a particular reality—all these constitute nevertheless an answer to the question regarding 'being' or reality (*Sein*). Such evasive scepticism, or making a particular value 'our be-all and end-all', are the ways in which,

we say what we mean and wish to mean by reality (*Sein*). We are practising metaphysics. Therefore we necessarily pursue metaphysics, in that we are always doing it anyway. We necessarily ask what is the *Sein* of the things that are.[60]

Human consciousness necessarily involves some metaphysical commitment, however confused and however erroneous.

Rahner's epistemology is comparatively unconcerned with questions about the subject's reflective awareness, about how the individual deals with external reality. There are more fundamental issues at stake: questions about the connections between reality and knowledge, and about how the reality known can affect the knower. As Rahner puts it in the uncreated grace essay, Thomas Aquinas's

[58] *Hearer of the Word*, 24, *44* (*KRSW*, iv. 52): '*Der Mensch kann nie bloß bei diesem oder jenem allein denkend oder handelnd sich aufhalten. Er will wissen, was alles zumal in seiner Einheit, in der ihm alles schon immer begegnet, sei; er fragt nach den letzten Hintergründen, nach dem einen Grund aller Dinge, und insofern er alles einzelne als seiend erkennt, nach dem Sein alles Seienden; er treibt Metaphysik.*'
[59] See Cornelius Ernst's introduction to his seminal translation of *TI*, vol. i, p. xvi.
[60] *Hearer of the Word*, 25, *44–5* (*KRSW*, iv. 52–4).

species 'is primarily an ontological and only subsequently a gnoseo-logical concept'.[61] If, therefore, we necessarily ask the question about reality as a whole, then whatever counts as an answer to that question must somehow be in connection with our minds. But this 'ontological' approach to epistemology, while relativizing a more 'gnoseological' account, does not exclude it, and Rahner's point both can and should be transposed into a more 'gnoseological' idiom. Then it appears as how we always know enough, at least in principle, about the ultimate reality to be able to make meaningful, even false, statements about it.

Wittgenstein writes of the 'great deal of stage-setting' presup-posed in a language 'if the mere act of naming is to make sense'.[62] We can formulate Rahner's basic claim in the philosophy of religion as follows: the 'stage-setting' for the concept of God is present in any human language. In *Foundations of Christian Faith*, Rahner introduces the idea of God by pointing out how all human languages have a word confronting us with the single whole (*das eine Ganze*) of reality and with our own existence. A system of communication without any kind of resource for expressing a world-view would not be a human language at all.[63] Our statements about the absolute may well be mistaken, in dire and permanent need of development and correction; our ideas of God are no doubt frighteningly conditioned by all kinds of prejudices and projections. Hence Rahner's constant stress on Christian commitment as a surrender to mystery:

My Christianity, when it understands itself aright, is the act of letting myself go into the mystery past all grasp. My Christianity is therefore any-thing but an 'explanation' of the world and of my existence; it is rather the prohibition against regarding any experience, any understanding (how-ever good and illuminating they may be) as finally and definitively valid (*endgültig*), as completely intelligible in themselves.[64]

But we cannot claim that our concepts of the ultimate are completely and systematically illusory without falling into self-contradiction. 'One cannot ask about reality as a whole without thereby affirming the fundamental knowability of reality as a

[61] 'Some Implications', 328, *356*. The paragraph which this sentence ends gives a concise, and relatively clear, summary of the issues at stake.
[62] Wittgenstein, *Philosophical Investigations*, § 257.
[63] *Foundations of Christian Faith*, 47–8, *57–8*.
[64] 'Why am I a Christian Today?', 6–7, *30* (*KRSW*, xxvi. 491).

whole.'[65] In that sense, we are permanently in epistemic contact with the absolute.

When Rahner talks about human knowing and willing necessarily presupposing a *Vorgriff auf Gott*, or an unthematic knowledge of God, the point he is making is much less explicitly Christian, much less religious in the conventional sense, than it initially sounds. Philosophically, we must postulate that the ultimate ground of things (the only proper referent of 'God') lies in some way primordially present to consciousness, that it has somehow, as we say, impinged on us, although we cannot grasp it as we grasp particular objects. The affinity with Bonaventure's spiritual touch does not need to be laboured.

Once again, Rahner is renegotiating conventional ways of conceiving the relationship between Christianity and our other systems of knowledge, between grace and creation. Once again he is making bolder claims about grace than his teachers had presented as standard. Conventional Catholic theology had laboured under a 'natural knowledge of God' that seemed to constrict the possible content of revelation. Rahner, without denying a sense in which we can know by natural reason that God exists, presents this claim as secondary to a more general one: the primordial link between human minds and the ground of reality. It is at this link that he locates the continuities between nature and grace. Philosophy insists only on a correlation between reality and our knowledge of reality: the content of reality is left radically open to God's gracious freedom.

There are close affinities between Rahner's position on reason and revelation and the famous lines towards the end of Eliot's 'Little Gidding':

> With the drawing of this Love and the voice of this Calling

> We shall not cease from exploration
> And the end of all our exploring
> Will be to arrive where we started
> And know the place for the first time.[66]

The quatrain parallels Rahner's claim that metaphysics is simply the making explicit of what we know already, the making *erkannt* what is always previously *bekannt*.[67] The point is entirely formal. Just

---

[65] *Spirit in the World*, 68 (*KRSW*, ii. 62). In the second edition, Metz added 'indeed a certain *a priori* already-knownness'.

[66] *The Complete Poems and Plays of T. S. Eliot*, 197.

[67] *Hearer of the Word*, 28, 49 (*KRSW*, iv. 58).

nothing is said about the content of what we explore, or about how we are enabled to explore it. Thus nothing here excludes the conviction reflected in the quotation from Walter Hilton: that the whole process is enfolded in a rich mystery articulated only through the word of tradition—a mystery which Rahnerian philosophy, despite its cool, abstract tone, allows to be permanently subversive.

Grace, Mysticism, and Ongoing Discovery

'In this experience of the soul's direct union in love with God at the soul's summit, any activity of the intellect is excluded.'[68] This sentence comes from Rahner's Bonaventure essay, and Rahner is still in his dogmatic slumbers. Within conventional mystical theology, conscious union with God's own self excludes knowledge of a created reality, and vice versa. Even in this early essay, however, Rahner was beginning to subvert the conventions of the genre, and once 'the immediate experience of God' had been transferred to the theology of grace, then this immediacy clearly had to be compatible with everyday sensory experience. Thus, the 1978 testament at once asserts that mysticism is for all, and insists that it must, in some sense, be mediated in various ways: by the life of Jesus, by the institutional Church, by love of neighbour, and by the choice of particular life-options. Admittedly, the connections are often unclear—a point to which we shall return in subsequent chapters. In this expository phase, however, our task is simply to set out how Rahner's 'immediate experience of God', far from excluding engagement in messy historical reality, in fact depends on such engagement.

Once again, we need to refer to Rahner's work in the metaphysics of mind. The central conviction of *Spirit in the World* is that metaphysical knowledge cannot be based on a specific metaphysical intuition, 'self-contained, based on itself as self-generating, possessing a content independent of sensory experience'. Metaphysics had to stay connected 'with its basis in the *imaginatio*, as the one ground that made it possible': there was no 'self-authenticating metaphysical intuition'.[69] Rahner's claims about God, grace, and human experience depended on revelation, and were in no way

---

[68] 'The Doctrine of the "Spiritual Senses"', 123 ('Der Begriff', 13).
[69] *Spirit in the World*, 28, *13* (*KRSW*, ii. 33).

reducible to philosophy. Equally, they did require an account of how we human beings, limited as we are to the physical, can make any kind of metaphysical claims.

'Quasi-formal causality' is, as we have seen, a translation into metaphysical terminology of 'the immediate experience of God'. The Aristotelian terminology gives a clue to the crucial point. Forms do not subsist without matter. If God's self-gift 'quasi-formally' transforms our subjectivity, then we also have to speak of God's self-giving presence in the external realities we know under grace. When we hear the phrase 'the immediate knowledge of God', it all too easily suggests an experience of pure interiority, somehow bypassing the mediations of history. The objections to such a position were put powerfully by Rahner's student and friend, Johann Baptist Metz:

> The concept of experience developed in the transcendental theology of the subject does not have the structure of historical experience. It makes the social contradictions and conflicts, out of which historical experience achingly lives and in and through which the historical subject is constituted, disappear into the non-objectiveness (*Ungegenständlichkeit*) of a previously known 'transcendental experience', in which these contradictions are already undialectically reconciled.[70]

The issues Metz raises here are wide-ranging: some we must leave aside, others will be dealt with, indirectly, in the constructive phase of this study.[71] Here we need simply to note that when Rahner

[70] Metz, *Faith in History and Society*, 65*. Rahner once described Metz's criticism of his theology as the only one he took seriously, but he also thought that his positions could at least be developed to meet it. See his foreword to Bacik, *Apologetics and the Eclipse of Mystery*, pp. ix–x.

[71] On the differences between Rahner and Metz, see now Ashley, *Interruptions*. Ashley argues that Metz's differences from Rahner can be traced, not so much to 'concepts and themes' as to 'the different spiritualities that nourish their respective theologies' (pp. x, 175). This position arises partly from procedures of interpretation regarding Rahner that highlight Rahner's weaknesses more sharply than I do, but more importantly from a different understanding of 'spirituality'. This present study takes its lead from the theological tradition Rahner inherited, and understands 'spirituality' as the experiential aspect of grace; Ashley talks of 'a spirituality', as 'a classic constellation of practices which forms a mystagogy into a life of Christian discipleship' (p. 12). Comparative studies based on the former kind of account will tend to harmonize; those based on the latter kind will stress difference. Ashley differentiates Rahner and Metz partly in terms of the medieval traditions on which they draw, partly in terms of their highlighting different aspects of the Ignatian Exercises (pp. 177–82). I may differ from Ashley reading both Ignatius and Rahner as articulating, not one 'transcendental' spirituality (Ashley's definition) to which there are 'categorical' alternatives, but rather the general conditions, never met purely in isolation, which any Christian spirituality must satisfy.

describes the experience of God as *unmittelbar* (im-mediate), he is insisting only that there is a knowledge of God not mediated through inference. The crucial premise is that finite minds exist only in and through relationship with external reality. If this is so, and if God immediately touches our minds, then God's contact must embrace also the external realities which constitute us. In play, therefore, are two different senses of the term 'mediation'. Rahner's doctrine of 'the im-mediate experience of God' depends on one of them, but in such a way as not to exclude, indeed rather to require, created realities to act as mediations in the second sense.

The fullest documentation for these claims comes in Rahner's grace codex. Rahner begins his discussion of the supernatural formal object by making a philosophical claim: existence as such (*ens ut sic*) is the *a priori* formal object of the human understanding. Rahner glosses this as follows:

> It is not that there is some intuition into existence as such. For where could existence as such be seen, given that the only existents are individual, concrete realities? How would the concrete reality actually perceived, and existence as such thus 'intuitively' perceived, relate to each other? Rather, there is present a direct awareness (*conscientia directa*)—in no way intrinsically a reflective awareness—of the *a priori* transcendence of the particular which is proper to a faculty capable of intentional acts.[72]

Human knowledge is dependent on the external world. Built into human awareness is an ability to distinguish one object from another. On the one hand, this orientation transcends the particulars which we happen to meet here and now; it is open to any possible existent. On the other, this orientation has no existence whatever independently of the fact that concrete particulars do actually impinge upon the human mind:

> Moreover, this *a priori* tendency in the mind (abstracting from grace) that is not limited to a particular object cannot give itself, through itself, any concrete object. If such is to be given—and it is only in the knowing of such

---

[72] *De gratia Christi*, 308. Rahner goes on to make a qualification: '(Obviously on this basis, if reflection is possible, the fundamental conditionings—"transcendentals"—of the object corresponding to this faculty can be known *a priori*.)'. Orig. '*Non adest intuitus aliquis in ens ut sic (nam ubi tale quid ut tale videri posset, cum non existant nisi entia singularia et concreta et quomodo res concreta actu percepta et ens ut sic ita perceptum se haberent inter se?), sed adest conscientia directa (de se nullatenus reflexa) illimitationis aprioristicae propriae facultatis intentionalis (ex qua utique, si reflexio fieri potest, a priori cognosci possunt fundamentales determinationes ["transcendentalia"] objecti, quod huic facultati correspondet).*'

that this tendency itself becomes conscious—there has to be something affecting the mind from outside, some quasi-material cause, i.e. the sensory object, or at least a limited, created *species*. Then, given this being-affected, the *a priori* tendency will, at one and the same time (as if it were its quasi-form), constitute it as something actually—as opposed to potentially—knowable.[73]

The tendency only comes into being *in* the object known: as such, it is only a partial principle of cognition. Human consciousness is radically relational, radically receptive.

The principle applies also if God acts in us supernaturally:

God's own self is not placed in its very essence, whether clearly or obscurely, before the intuition of a supernatural act in this life. Rather, one has a direct awareness—and in no way a reflective awareness—of the tendency towards enjoying God in an eventual beatific vision. The supernatural understanding places in this horizon all particular supernatural objects which might cross its path. And even this *a priori* tendency is only a partial principle of cognition, and thus is not, of itself, a reality in awareness. If it is to become a reality in awareness, it requires the representation of some object (*indiget, ut conscia fiat, obiecto aliquo representato*).[74]

'The direct experience of God' is not a vision of God, but a 'spontaneous, obscure datum' underlying all our other, normal human acts.[75]

It follows, then, that the direct presence of God within our subjectivity correlates with God's gracious presence in an external reality. In his grace codex, Rahner writes of this object as follows:

Unless and until this object is God's own self, immediately seen in the beatific vision as such, an object of the kind required cannot but be created and finite.[76]

[73] Ibid.: '*Haec tendentia aprioristica obiective illimitata intellectualitatis naturalis insuper per se solam nullum potest sibi dare obiectum concretum. Ut tale detur (in quo cognito ipsa haec tendentia solum conscia fit), requiritur determinatio ab extra, causa aliqua quasi materialis, i.e. obiectum sensibile, seu saltem species creata limitata. Cum qua determinatione simul tendentia aprioristica (tamquam quasi-forma eius) intelligibile actu constituit.*'
[74] Ibid.
[75] Juan Alfaro, 'Formalobjekt, Übernatürliches', 208: '*Es handelt sich nicht um eine Anschauung Gottes; vielmehr um eine spontane und dunkle Gegebenheit einer aktiven Tendenz auf Gott hin.*' One can assume at least Rahnerian approval, if not active suggestion. For attempts to situate Alfaro within the complicated debates on nature and grace among Rahner's contemporaries, see Luis F. Ladaria, 'Naturaleza y gracia: Karl Rahner y Juan Alfaro', *Estudios eclesiásticos*, 64 (1989), 53–70; Stephen J. Duffy, *The Graced Horizon* (Collegeville: Liturgical Press, 1992), 137–44.
[76] *De gratia Christi*, 308–9.

Here Rahner makes a qualification, but his later work in eschatology was to imply its removal, for even in the beatific vision, the humanity of Jesus retains a mediating role.[77] The experience of God thus presupposes an external gracious reality. Our life in grace may be grounded in God's immediate contact, but we realize that life only in and through cumulative interaction.

To translate Rahner's *Erfahrung* as 'experience' is inevitable, but also problematic. In ordinary German there are at least two words corresponding to the English 'experience': *Erfahrung* and *Erlebnis*. The former derives from *fahren*—'to travel'. It is far more cognitive in tone than *Erlebnis*, and can connote, unlike the English 'experience', a process of gradual reflection. By contrast, most English uses of the word 'experience' as in 'religious experience' should be translated into German as *Erlebnis*.[78] In his *Easter in Ordinary*, Nicholas Lash points out how such a usage, focusing as it does on 'brief and isolated moments of heightened awareness or profound emotion, moments which occur unexpectedly', contrasts with our use of the term in other contexts. When we speak of an '"experienced" teacher, parent, or politician', we are designating people who have gone through a great deal and learnt from it. Rahner's 'immediate experience of God' has little to do with the paranormal: the focus is rather on our potential to grow in a God-sustained wisdom.[79]

In their *Concise Theological Dictionary*, Rahner and Herbert Vorgrimler present *Erfahrung* as the passive dimension of knowledge.

Erfahrung is a form of knowledge that arises from the direct reception of an impression from a reality (inner or outer) that is outside our free disposal. This is to be contrasted with that kind or aspect of knowledge in which the human person actively deals with the object, subjects it to his or her own points of view and methods, and examines it critically.[80]

In the Bonaventure essay, Rahner had contrasted intellect and love. Here he is making a similar contrast, but now between two kinds or

---

[77] See 'The Eternal Significance of the Humanity of Jesus'.

[78] Here, as everywhere, I depend on the *Collins-Klett German–English English–German Dictionary*, 2 vols. (London: Collins, 1983), esp. here, i. 369, 375; ii. 372.

[79] Lash, *Easter in Ordinary*, 91. Contrast Caroline Franks Davis, *The Evidential Force of Religious Experience* (Oxford: Clarendon Press, 1989), esp. 20 n. 33, illustrating the difference between a conventional Anglo-American approach and Rahner's: 'I have had to make a distinction between "episodic" and "accumulated" senses of "experience" which would have been obvious to a German speaker: "experience" here means *Erlebnis* rather than *Erfahrung*.'

[80] *Concise Theological Dictionary*, 164–5, 107–8.

aspects of knowledge. The knowledge from *Erfahrung* is different in kind, though also inseparable, from our active reflection:

> In so far as religious *Erfahrung* is the inner self-testimony of supernatural reality (grace), it is only in the context of an objectifying, conceptual reflection that it is possible for human beings, or for humanity as a whole in its faith-history.

Rahner's 'immediate experience of God', therefore, is not primarily a matter of report or testimony. It refers, rather, to an experiential realization, nourished by time and reflection, of God's abiding presence within human consciousness. Because human consciousness is essentially dependent on its situations and interactions, the process of discovering God must also involve external history, ultimately in its entirety. Such a vision shapes how Rahner's Ignatius sees spiritual growth:

> how a person can . . . meet God up to the unfolding of this experience, where God then meets a person in everything, and not just in special 'mystical' moments, and when everything, without getting submerged, becomes transparent towards him.[81]

Grace and Mysticism in Mutual Exchange

Rahner's late Ignatian writings, therefore, retrieve 'the immediate experience of God' from his earliest writings in the history of spirituality, and handle it in a radically transformed way. No longer does the term denote a particular, privileged state of mind and heart: it has, rather, become central to the theology of human experience as such, a reality present in anyone, at whatever level of holiness.

Rahner's 'spiritual testament' centres on an interchange between two theological idioms: those of grace and mysticism. It emerges from a background of vehement controversies about the mystical: was it a privileged state for chosen souls or a stage in normal faith-development? None of the participants, however, disputed that the *experience* of grace constituted only a *part* of the life of grace, or, conversely, that one could be in 'a state of grace' which was in no sense a reality of consciousness. Drawing on Maréchal's interpretation of Thomas Aquinas, Rahner rejected these fundamental

---

[81] 1978*b*, 14, *378*.

assumptions, and thus modified the conventional theology of grace he inherited. He interpreted the everyday life of the Christian in terms originating from the theology of privileged prayer states. Central to all grace, even the so-called sufficient grace available to the heathen, is the experienced presence of God's own self (uncreated grace) at the heart of human subjectivity. What is real is also, in principle, a reality of human knowledge and experience. Hence any theology or piety that depends on an absolute disjunction between the orders of being and knowing is incoherent. The economic and immanent Trinity—God's own self and God-for-us—are identical; similarly God's self-gift as such (grace) and God's self-gift as we experience it (mysticism) are one and the same.

We have seen how this insight led to innovations in the theology of grace; it also generated an approach to mysticism different from that of Rahner's predecessors. Rahner's treatment of these matters is scattered and sporadic,[82] but one key point can be isolated. Academic study may well identify regular psychological and physical patterns within religious commitment, and designate these as 'mystical', but such a categorization bears no special theological significance. The distinctions being made belong to the 'natural'. For Rahner, of course, the natural is suffused by grace. He is not saying that states identified by psychologists as mystical are of no significance in the life of grace. His claim, rather, is that their status as mystical does not, of itself, render them of greater theological significance than other mental states. What psychologists call a mystical state,

can of course always, as with any natural basis of acts raised to the supernatural (consciousness, freedom, reflectiveness etc.) be itself of great significance for salvation, to the extent that it enters the context of the whole mental living out of a graced person's life (*insofern sie auftritt in Zusammenhang mit dem ganzen geistigen Vollzug des begnadeten Menschen*), and is itself graced. It can be experienced as grace on account of its gratuity and the nature of the goal to which it is directed. It can let the supernatural act (of faith, of love etc.) take deeper root in the heart of the person concerned.[83]

[82] Besides 'Reflections on the Problem', see 'Ethik und Mystik'; 'Mystik'; 'Mystical Experience and Mystical Theology'; 'Zu einer Theologie der Mystik'; 1978d. For a magisterial general survey of contemporary scholarship on the issues, see Bernard McGinn, 'Theoretical Foundations: The Modern Study of Mysticism', in *The Foundations of Mysticism* (London: SCM, 1991), 265–441.
[83] 'Mystik', 744–5.

But the 'mystical'—in the psychological sense—is not *eo ipso* a privileged state of grace. In principle any human experience is shot through with God's self-gift. The mature Rahner does write often about the mystical as one particular kind of experience, but the distinction is empirical (between the mystical and other states of consciousness) rather than theological (between mysticism and 'normal' grace).

Rahner's 1944 essay on the ascent to Christian perfection ends simply by noting how the concept of 'mysticism' requires reworking; he does not explicitly attempt the task.[84] Similarly in 1978, Rahner's Ignatius is content to leave the ends untied:

Whether one calls such an experience 'mysticism' or something else is not, in this context, important; how one can make the very possibility of something like this in some way intelligible through human concepts is a matter on which your theologians might like to speculate.[85]

Effectively, however, Rahner has made a radical move. In his 1978 *Entschluß* article, he recalled the old controversy between Saudreau and Poulain, and aligned himself with the former:

People used to argue about whether mysticism was an extraordinary way to salvation, intended only for a few, or whether it was an unavoidably essential—though more or less reflected upon—element of Christian life and Christian perfection. Our Fr Poulain declared that it was something quite extraordinary, which normal mortals do not experience. Against this the Dominicans and various theologians were of another opinion on the subject. I think the only sensible option is to be against Poulain, on biblical grounds, because of the theology of grace, and because of the theology of faith. Mystics are not a step higher than believers at large; rather, mysticism in its authentic, theological root sense is an intrinsically essential aspect of faith, not the other way round.[86]

However, Rahner is not here, despite the reference to Poulain, simply taking up one side of the debate regarding the frequency or normality of mystical experience in the life of faith, but rather subverting the terms in which that debate was conducted. Both Poulain and Saudreau saw the mystical as a part of the gracious; their disagreement was about whether the life of 'ordinary' believers has mystical elements. Rahner may sound as though he is

[84] 'Reflections on the Problem', 22–3, 33–4.
[85] 1978*b*, 12, 374–5.   [86] 1978*d*, 23–4.

aligning himself with the less élitist side, but his position is based on a quite new account of grace and mysticism. For Rahner, the mystical and the gracious are materially equivalent. In so far as the language of mystical ascent is of intrinsic theological significance, it applies to the life of grace and faith as a whole—indeed, given Rahner's claims about grace's universality, to human life as such. Conversely, grace—which is always grounded on the uncreated presence of God in the heart—has necessarily an effect in experience, even if this is largely repressed and unarticulated.

Nicholas Lash expresses the substance of Rahner's position at the outset of his *Easter in Ordinary*. Lash is considering how a theologian should handle the concept of 'the religious' as it appears in the human sciences. His central claim is this:

> on the one hand . . . it is not the case that all experience of God is necessarily religious in form or content and, on the other hand, . . . not everything which it would be appropriate to characterize, on psychological or sociological grounds, as 'religious' experience . . . thereby necessarily constitute(s) experience of God.[87]

Lash's language here has the potential to mislead. Given the Rahnerian premises which Lash surely shares, all experience is experience of God; it would be better to make the contrast between 'religious experience' and 'experience of *growth in relation to* God'. But terminology is never stable in this area. Rahner at one point makes the contrast in terms of 'finding God' over against the 'mystical'. To designate 'mystical' phenomena in the empirical sense as 'natural' is not to devalue them theologically, because even in the 'natural' one can 'find God'. Rahner cites a saying of Eckhart's:

> One can, after all, find God imparting himself in the most direct way by selflessly letting a poor person have one's soup, and remaining hungry oneself.

Again, in a 1941 lecture, Rahner contrasts 'genuine religious experience' with the 'numinous'. He is considering a broad and untheological definition of 'mysticism', as 'any existential experience of the boundlessness of some realm of being, going beyond the everyday impression of reality', and in this context insists:

> Given this concept we can . . . at once add: but not every mysticism in this

---

[87] Lash, *Easter in Ordinary*, 7.

sense is automatically a genuine religious experience, not every experience of the numinous (to use for once the terminology of Rudolf Otto) . . . is, as such, religion.[88]

Whatever the terminology, two points are centrally important. Firstly, if 'mysticism' is understood in the sense standard in Roman Catholic theology, as denoting an experience of grace, then the mystical and the gracious are co-extensive. Secondly, the particular experiences of significance for theology are not to be contrasted with experiences in which God is supposedly absent. 'The experiences that matter most' are those where there is somehow a turning-point in the appropriation of a grace already present.[89]

'Tomorrow's devout person will either be a mystic—someone who has "experienced" something—or else they will no longer be devout at all.'[90] In this often quoted saying, Rahner is referring not to 'singular parapsychological phenomena' but to 'a genuine experience of God emerging from the very heart of our existence'. In context, this is primarily a sociological observation, a reaction to the demise of a culture in which mainstream institutional Christianity was conventional. In fact, however, the saying can and should be interpreted more radically. There is no such thing as a grace which is not experienced: the sentence points us to what 'in the last resort' is the wellspring of any Christian commitment.[91] Rahner often places Ignatius as the ecclesiastical counterpart to the great thinkers of Renaissance and Enlightenment rationality; Ignatius's 'immediate experience of God' marks the beginning of modernity (*der Neuzeit*) in the Church, 'and is perhaps rather closer to the basic experiences of Luther and Descartes than . . . Jesuits for centuries

[88] 'Ethik und Mystik', 7–8.
[89] Lash, *Easter in Ordinary*, 251: 'In denying that there are any particular districts, or places, or times, in which God is more likely to be met than in any others, I am not saying that anything that happens to us equally, or indiscriminately, facilitates relation with God . . . But the experiences that matter most . . . are at least as likely to have the character of responsibility acknowledged, or suffering endured, as they are to have the character of aesthetic satisfaction or heightened feeling. A Christian account of the "experiences that matter most" should be derived from a consideration of the ways in which Jesus came to bear the responsibility of his mission and, especially, of how it went with him in Gethsemane.'
[90] 'Christian Living Formerly and Today', 15, 22: '*der Fromme von morgen wird ein "Mystiker" sein, einer, der etwas "erfahren" hat, oder er wird nicht mehr sein*'. See Egan, '"The Devout Christian of Tomorrow will be a Mystic"'; Josef Sudbrack, 'Karl Rahners Wort vom Frommen, der ein Mystiker sein wird', in *Mystische Spuren: Auf der Suche nach der christlichen Lebensgestalt* (Würzburg: Echter, 1990), 50–76.
[91] 'The Spirituality of the Church of the Future', 149, 175–6.

have wanted to admit'.⁹² In Rahner's view, the Renaissance and the
Enlightenment period have brought Christianity to a new and
enriched level of self-awareness. Compelled to abandon a pre-
critical, naive realist metaphysics, Christian theology has had to
move—or move back—talk of the experience of God from the
periphery to the centre of theology.

To integrate 'spirituality' and theology in this way is not to surrender to anti-intellectualism in the name of piety, but rather to situate
the academic enterprise of theology within something greater: God's
ongoing self-revelation in human experience. Rahner's retrievals and
developments of the Christian speculative tradition are ultimately
attempts to articulate, through a kind of transcendental deduction,
what must be the case if it is true that we human beings can experience
God. If we can experience God, then God's own self must dwell
within us. If God's own self is with human beings, then the one-in-
threeness of human cognition and volition (subject–object–indefinite
horizon) must be reflected in the ontology of the godhead: hence a
doctrine of the Trinity. Given the ambiguities of our own experience,
there must be a point in human history where the presence of God
within us is somehow different, where our fragile life in God is seen as
guaranteed: the life, death, and resurrection of Jesus of Nazareth.
Further, our means of communication with the guarantee that is Jesus
Christ must themselves, derivatively, share his privileged status: hence
doctrines of Church, of the inerrancy of Scripture, of the sacraments,
of ordained ministry, and of the teaching authority within the Church.
Claims about experience imply theoretical commitments, whether
we are aware of these commitments or not, and whether we assent to
them or not. Rahner's theology attempts to ground the central
dogmas of Christianity by presenting them as transcendental principles, as what must be true if our experience of God is to be possible.

Only a small number of texts directly confirm the claim that
Rahner's fusion of grace and mysticism is central to his theology.
Even in the late Ignatian writings, the point is implied rather than
stated. The case has to be made more indirectly, by invoking how
such a claim enables a simple, overall view of Rahner's diverse
work. In particular, Rahner's option to take mystical experience as
normative for Christian anthropology explains what many have
seen as his weaknesses. If God's grace is determinative of human

⁹² 1978*b*, 13–14, *376–7*; cf. e.g. 1959, 39, *46*.

identity, then traditional statements about sin are attenuated: 'I do not think it forbidden for a Christian theologian to take the theme of human sinfulness and the forgiveness, in sheer grace, of guilt to be in a certain sense rather more secondary in comparison to the theme of the radical *self*-communication of God.'[93] It becomes simply impossible—despite what many a preacher has said—to cut oneself off definitively from divine grace: 'to live within the near past-all-graspness of God . . . is at once terrifying and blissful. But we have no choice. God is with us.'[94]

A similar point can be made about how Rahner characteristically understates the categorical. As we are about to see, Rahner's formative years as a Jesuit were marked by the publication of a range of Ignatian texts, transforming conventional images of a militarist, authoritarian Ignatius, and replacing them with a vision of Ignatius as 'mystic'.[95] More generally, the literary origin of Rahner's most original and creative theology lies in a genre of mystical writing where the categorical is ignored. This approach to mysticism correlated with an inadequate, sub-Platonist eschatology. The lingering influence of the latter may explain the indeterminacies in Rahner's work about the form of mysticism available to us in our everyday lives. Is it merely the lowest step in a progression that moves towards higher, more traditionally conceived stages, or does it constitute the only kind of mysticism there is?[96]

These are issues for later chapters: the point to note here is how these problems, as such, are generated by one of Rahner's key speculative options. When Karl Rahner first joined the Innsbruck faculty in the late 1930s, a number of its leading figures (including Hugo Rahner) were attempting to develop a 'theology of proclamation'. In 1961, Karl Rahner described this movement as proceeding from the claim that,

[93] 'Erfahrungen eines katholischen Theologen', 140.
[94] *Prayers for a Lifetime*, 3, *12* (text 1st pub. 1974). For interesting explorations of the issues raised see Ron Highfield, 'The Freedom to Say "No"?: Karl Rahner's Doctrine of Sin', *Theological Studies*, 56 (1995), 485–505; and John R. Sachs, 'Current Eschatology: Universal Salvation and the Problem of Hell', *Theological Studies*, 52 (1991), 227–54, esp. 246–54.
[95] Zahlauer, *Karl Rahner und sein 'produktives Vorbild'*, e.g. 251, regards the resulting imbalance as decisive for interpreting Ignatius's effect on Rahner.
[96] Contrast the opening of 'Reflections on the Experience of Grace', 86, *105*, or 1956*b*, 146, *127*, with the radical incarnationalism at, say, the end of 'The Eternal Significance of the Humanity of Jesus', 45, *59*: 'the religious act *in any form* and *always*, if it is to attain God in reality, has and must have this "incarnational" structure'.

besides academic ('scholastic') theology . . . there could and should also be
a further, second theology . . . of such a kind that this latter was distinguished from 'academic' theology not only by virtue of a stressed practical
and pedagogical orientation (the formation of the pastoral clergy), but
essentially.[97]

Karl Rahner came to reject this disjunction:

all theology must be theology of salvation: it would betray its own subject-
matter (*Objekt!*) were it to neglect the fact that its subject-matter, revealed
truth, is given 'for us human beings and for our salvation', and can therefore be regarded as true only when this standpoint is not overlooked.[98]

Conversely, the disclosure of God in ongoing experience is not wholly
independent of academic theology. If, for example, people claim to
experience God in prayer, what they say will inevitably imply positions in speculative epistemology and metaphysics. In short: if grace
is a reality in consciousness, then theology is no more and no less than
disciplined reflection on ongoing experience, on 'spirituality'. All theology worthy of the name is ultimately practical theology. Karl Rahner could not accept a dualistic account of truth, and therefore parted
company with the kerygmatic theology movement. Nevertheless, he
acknowledged the validity of their concerns, and his whole scholarly
career was an attempt to respond to them in his own way.

The central point is that theology is always anthropology.[99] A
statement about God's revelation is also a statement about the
fickle, changeable creatures who receive that revelation. In a speech
honouring Rahner's seventieth birthday in 1974, Metz spoke of how
Rahner's intellectual achievement was grounded in life-history,
how it amounted to a *lebensgeschichtliche Dogmatik.* Such a theology,

---

[97] 'Kerygmatische Theologie', 126. This article appears to summarize 'Über die
Verkündigungstheologie'. For general historical information on the kerygmatic theology
movement, see Karl H. Neufeld, 'Theologiegeschichtliches zur Innsbrucker "Verkündigungstheologie"', *Zeitschrift für katholische Theologie*, 119 (1993), 13–26.

[98] 'Über die Verkündigungstheologie', 340–1.

[99] The correct interpretation of this conviction has been well articulated by Hilberath,
Karl Rahner, 27: 'This does not mean that humanity becomes the measure of all things. What
it means is that all thought emerges from human experiences, and that even what far surpasses humanity, what is proper to God, must be demonstrated to be something significant
for human self-experience. Reality that means nothing for me does not exist; if it is supposed,
over and above any significance for me, to exist in and of itself, this can make no difference to
how I function. In other words: even if I describe God as the wholly Other, as the absolute
mystery, I still need to clarify for myself as a human being how I am related to this unfathomable mystery.'

brings the subject into theology's dogmatic awareness. This in no way implies the advocacy of a new form of theological subjectivism . . . To bring the subject into systematic theology means . . . to make the human person, with his or her religious history of life and experience, the objective theme of systematic theology. It means, thus, the reconciliation of systematic theology and life-history. It means, finally, the bringing together of doxography and biography, theological praise of God and mystical life-narrative.[100]

Theology's referent is the ongoing self-communication of God. It follows that the importance of dogmatic theology, the articulation of the universal structures of grace, though real, remains secondary: it abstracts from an unfinished, unpredictable lived reality. Theology names conditions which any possible future self-disclosure of God will satisfy, but does not constrict or exhaustively specify this disclosure. That disclosure remains to be discovered, in ever new ways.[101]

Thus it is that Rahner could speak of the Ignatian Exercises representing Christianity more fundamentally and radically than systematic theology ever can. Bonaventure's 'spiritual touch' took place at the *apex affectus*—a level of the self deeper than the separation between intellect and will. In his old age, introducing the published version of a doctorate on Ignatius that he had supervised, Rahner described the ultimate principles of Ignatian spirituality in terms that are at least structurally similar. What happens in the Exercises is 'a unity-in-accomplishment' which 'precedes the difference between theoretical dogmatic theology as such and mere (secularized) psychology'.[102] When Rahner relativizes his systematic theology to spirituality, he is not rejecting the academic in favour of devotion, nor abandoning conceptual rigour, nor discrediting the cognitive status of theology. Rather, he is asserting that Christian theology—the study of God's self-communication *to human beings*—remains permanently referred to ongoing human experience. Subjective and objective, academic theology and kerygmatic (or pastoral) theology, grace and mysticism—such distinctions, methodologically justified though they may be, remain abstractions from a single lived reality, one to which Rahner found privileged access in the Ignatian Exercises.

---

[100] Metz, *Faith in History and Society*, 220.
[101] The German phrase, '*eine Erfahrung machen*'—making rather than simply having experience—suggestively evokes our co-operation in the process.
[102] 1976, p. xiv.

4

The Rahner Brothers and the Discovery of Jerónimo Nadal

So far, this study has centred on what the elderly Rahner said and wrote about Ignatius, notably the 1978 testament. As he looked back on his life's work, Rahner attributed to Ignatian influence a fusion between the theologies of grace and mysticism that had been foundational to his whole theological achievement. In this chapter, the focus moves to the beginning of Rahner's career, in particular to work he did in collaboration with his elder Jesuit brother, Hugo, on editions of early Jesuit texts.[1] There are important aspects of Karl Rahner's theological creativity that can be traced back to this material, touching in particular the themes of contemplation, holiness, and the God–world relationship.

Discoveries from the Sources

In 1922 Hugo Rahner produced a catalogue of primary sources regarding Ignatius and the early Jesuits. The text seems to have circulated informally, and the Karl-Rahner-Archiv currently holds two versions of it.[2] The earlier of these attributes the authorship of the catalogue to Hugo in 1922, and adds 'extended by Brother Karl Rahner 1925'. Another, shorter version purports to be 'compiled by Frs Karl and Hugo Rahner S.J.', and bears the date 'January 1 1937'. The Rahner brothers also produced, in 1935, a German version of an address on prayer by Jerónimo Nadal.[3] Their intention was to

---

[1] Karl Neufeld's joint biography of the Rahner brothers has not rendered obsolete his 1979 pioneer essay on their early work together: 'Unter Brüdern'.

[2] The published version of this text (1922/5) has been tidied linguistically by Neufeld. In a note left with the archive versions, Neufeld outlines the editorial problems the text presents, and makes clear that his choices were determined more by an interest in the subject-matter than by text-critical considerations.

[3] The Rahner brothers date the address to 1553 (1935, 400)—hence in Ignatius's lifetime. Their principal ground appears to be a footnote in MHSJ *MN*, iv. 670, which in fact refers to

introduce this figure—whom we have already briefly met—to a Jesuit readership extending beyond the circle of Ignatian specialists. In both these pieces, the Rahner brothers present Nadal as a figure of prime importance for the understanding of early Jesuit tradition.[4] In Nadal, the Rahner brothers found two formulae that they, and many Jesuits after them, took as epitomizing the distinctive charism of Ignatius: 'finding God in all things', and 'contemplative in action'. In their introduction to Nadal's address on prayer, they write:

Again and again, Nadal comes back to what is most fundamental and distinctive in the Jesuit calling: to find God in all things, to unite Martha and Mary, to be 'contemplative in action', as he says in another conference and as he learnt from his father Ignatius.[5]

We can easily trace 'finding God in all things' back to Ignatius himself. The culmination of the Spiritual Exercises is a prayer for 'interior knowledge' of the good received from God, 'so that I, in full recognition, can in everything love and serve his divine majesty'.[6] In the *Constitutions*, Ignatius writes of how the novices,

should often be exhorted to seek God our Lord in all things, distancing from themselves love for all creatures to the extent that this is possible, in order to place it in their creator, loving him in them all and them all in him, in conformity with his most holy and divine will.[7]

'Contemplative in action', by contrast, is not an Ignatian phrase at all. It comes from notes written by Nadal, probably in 1557. Nadal has been describing Ignatius's familiarity with the Divine Trinity: sometimes he would contemplate the unity, other times the single persons. 'Fr Ignatius received this method of prayer through a great and most exclusive privilege.'

another document. Nicolau, *Jerónimo Nadal*, 103, cf. 78, gives good grounds for dating the address to 1562.

[4] Jerónimo Nadal (1507–80) joined the Society of Jesus in 1545. Most authorities believe he played a key role in the consolidation of the early Society of Jesus, particularly through his travels to promulgate the *Constitutions*. The definitive study on him is still Nicolau, *Jerónimo Nadal*, updated in 'Nadal, Jerónimo'. For biographical details, see Manuel Ruiz Jurado, 'Cronología de la vida del P. Jerónimo Nadal S.I. (1507–1580)', *Archivum historicum Societatis Jesu*, 48 (1979), 248–76, and William V. Bangert, *Jerome Nadal, S.J., 1507–1580: Tracking the First Generation of Jesuits*, ed. and completed Thomas M. McCoog (Chicago: Loyola University Press, 1992). On Nadal's theology of prayer, see Joseph F. Conwell, *Contemplation in Action: A Study in Ignatian Prayer* (Spokane: Gonzaga University, 1957). On his understanding of religious life, see Anton Witwer, *Die Gnade der Berufung: Allgemeine und besondere Berufung bei Hieronymus Nadal am Beispiel der Gesellschaft Jesu* (Würzburg: Echter, 1995).

[5] 1935, 401.   [6] *Exx*, n. 233.1.   [7] *Const*, III. i. 26 [288].

Then there was also this: in all things, activities and conversations, he could feel and contemplate the presence of God and a love for spiritual things—at the same time he was a contemplative in action (which he used to explain by saying that God was to be found in all things).[8]

The Rahner brothers follow Nadal in using these ideas to ground a claim in the theology of consecrated life: that the particular charism of Ignatius and the Society of Jesus lies in the ability to find God not just in prayer but also in action. Holiness depends not on flight from the world, but on engagement with the world. But underlying this thesis is a broader and more radical claim in fundamental theology: an understanding of God as one who can be found, and found to the highest degree possible, in human life and history.

For the Rahner brothers, Nadal's writings exhibit paradoxes, and thus point to a reality transcending conventional distinctions. The Rahner brothers point out how Nadal's exhortation on prayer fails to distinguish the ascetical and the mystical:

It shows a deep and devout familiarity with the spirit of prayer, a familiarity which knows how far grace leads those 'who serve him and love him with a humble and pure heart'. It finds no real need to draw a distinction between asceticism and mysticism, but rather lets ideas and hints pertaining to both mingle freely.[9]

At one point, Nadal presents a long list of material for meditation. Ordinary though this material is, says Nadal, 'from it will come out the grace of contemplation, or of illumination of mind and of union of our will with God in pure and sincere love'.[10] There are passages

---

[8] MHSJ *MN*, v. 162: *Hanc rationem orationis concepit Pater Ignatius magno privilegio selectissime; tum illud praeterea: in omnibus rebus, actionibus, colloquiis, ut Dei praesentiam rerumque spiritualium affectum sentiret atque contemplaretur, simul in actione contemplativus (quod ita solebat explicare: Deum esse in omnibus rebus inveniendum).* The linguistic difficulties with this passage are considerable, but they do not affect my argument. The Rahner brothers used an older edition of the text (MHSJ *MN*, iv. 651).

[9] 1935, 400. For the original of the quotation, see MHSJ *MN*, iv. 676. In general I cite Nadal directly from the original, referring to the Rahner brothers' German version only if the translation itself is of substantive theological interest. The only full published English translation of the text is too inaccessible to be worth citing. 'Asceticism' and 'mysticism' here have a precise technical sense, established in the eighteenth century, and popularized by the Italian Jesuit, Giovanni Battista Scaramelli (1687–1752). They refer to what were seen as different stages of the spiritual life: 'ascetical' before and 'mystical' after the onset of passive mystical experience.

[10] MHSJ *MN*, iv. 676. Since Nadal's list appears also in another instruction (MHSJ *MN*, iv. 576–8), the editors omitted it here.

in the text which could be read as proscribing mystical prayer,[11] and
the text will only be interpreted adequately when we have a clearer
idea of the deep conflicts about mysticism and authority in
sixteenth-century Spanish religion. But, for the Rahner brothers in
the early twentieth century, the text's main significance must have
lain in its subversion of the manualist spiritual theology in which
they were being educated. Nadal can use the language of abandonment, and speak of God's own action, in contexts which clearly do not
exclude normal human activity. Referring to the Exercises, he says:

For them and for all prayer, the main thing that matters in our Lord is a
great generosity and handing over to God of all one's abilities and activities, and of whatever it is to be human; and, without ceasing to play one's
own part under God's grace in the use of every virtue and path of perfection, to hope always, to desire intensely, and to ask God to do whatever is
for his greater glory and praise in them and in everyone.[12]

The mystical is not a branch of human activity, but a qualification
of the whole; conversely, 'ascetical' activities on our part—virtue
and methods of prayer—are in union with the divine action.[13]
    Nadal's vision also subverts what were, in the early twentieth cen-
tury, conventional accounts of action and contemplation. For
Nadal, these two realities intermingle. In their catalogue, the Rahner brothers describe the Nadal text which they were later to translate, and refer to what they call Nadal's favourite theme: 'Mary and
Martha, the active and the contemplative life, which come together
in a higher life where deed and contemplation have become one.'[14]
Towards the beginning of the address, Nadal stresses the apostolic
purpose of Jesuit prayer:

And this is how prayer is to be regulated. It should fill out and guide and
give spiritual relish to activities through its after-effects and its strength in

    [11] For example MHSJ *MN*, iv. 673: 'The feeling for prayer, and an attachment to it, that
incline a person to recollection and solitude beyond what is necessary—the prayer proper to the
Society does not seem to be this, but rather that which inclines a person to the exercise of its
vocation and ministry, and particularly to perfect obedience in accordance with our institute.'
    [12] MHSJ *MN*, iv. 672–3.
    [13] Contrast a fuller discussion of Nadal's teaching on prayer within a neo-scholastic
framework in Nicolau, *Jerónimo Nadal*, 254–64, 318–41. 'Nadal's teachings contain a
language which does not have the technical exactness with which the questions are put today,
nor the approach which is taken today. But, even given the vagueness of the expression, we
have been able to observe the mystical leanings which are there in abundance in his
teachings' (p. 263).
    [14] 1922/5, 432. The typescript is here corrupt, and Neufeld had to reconstruct.

the Lord. And activities should fill out, strengthen and give exhilaration to prayer. Thus, with Mary and Martha united in this way and helping each other, it will not be just one part of the Christian life, the contemplative, that is being embraced—better though it is—but rather that Mary, detached from the worry and fret over many things, helps Martha and is united with her in our Lord.[15]

Already, Nadal is qualifying the tradition whereby contemplation was superior to action. Later, he is more explicit:

One should bear in mind that the active and the contemplative lives have to run together. But the *period of* testing—which is so exacting—brings it about that the active life *arrives* at a certain perfection *and then* predominates over the contemplative. It regulates it and governs it with peace in the Lord and his enlightenment; and thus one arrives at the higher active life, which surpasses the active and the contemplative, and is capable of instilling these latter into everyone, in accordance with the greater service of God. In short: the action of love united with God is an action which is perfect.[16]

Nadal seems here to be drawing on a Thomistic, Dominican theology of consecrated life. Within a tradition that prized contemplation highest of all, Aquinas distinguishes between orders involved in 'outward occupation, for example almsgiving, receiving guests, and the like', and those who teach and preach 'from the fullness of contemplation'. This latter vocation, which is active but which draws on contemplation, represents 'the highest place in religious orders':

For even as it is better to enlighten than merely to shine, so is it better to give to others what one has contemplated than merely to contemplate.

Aquinas then incorporates the traditional preference for contemplation by placing a purely contemplative vocation in the second place, and a purely active vocation merely third. Nadal seems straightforwardly to be taking over the idea of the higher active life, and using it to articulate Jesuit identity.[17]

---

[15] MHSJ *MN*, iv. 674.

[16] MHSJ *MN*, iv. 679: '*y brevemente: la acción de la caridad unida con Dios es de perfecta acción*'. The words italicized in the translated quotation indicate Nadal's manuscript corrections: he is bringing out that it takes time to attain this state. The odd phrase *de perfecta acción* (as opposed to simply *perfecta acción*) I take as stressing that action and perfection are not incompatible, against a model of perfection in terms of static contemplation. In this respect, the Rahner brothers' translation (1935, 409) is more straightforward, but reduces the sentence to a conventional piety: '*Das Wirken der Liebe, die ganz eins ist mit Gott: das ist das vollendete Tun!*'

[17] Thomas Aquinas, *Summa theologiae*, II–II. 188. 6.

The Rahner brothers came to these texts from a tradition whereby religious life, beginning with desert monasticism, was thought to consist in a withdrawal from the world.[18] Admittedly the tradition had developed: Benedict, the mendicants, and finally the apostolic orders represented successive enrichments, and one could plausibly interpret these as the gradual incorporation of pastoral ministry, with the foundation of the Jesuits marking a climax. But 'flight from the world' remained the abiding common feature, the 'essential element', to use modern Vatican terminology. The prevailing conceptual model suggested that ministry was ultimately a distraction from the spiritual life—often excusable, sometimes necessary, occasionally laudable, but a distraction none the less.[19] By contrast, as the Rahner brothers and their contemporaries gradually appropriated the newly edited Jesuit sources, they found a form of mysticism that involved commitment to, and affirmation of, the world. Christian perfection and union with God were to be found in a cooperation between ourselves and God rather than in mystical passivity—in involvement in the world, rather than in the supposed isolation of a monastery or in rarefied states of prayer. At the time, the idea was a challenging one.

It would seem Nadal's theology of Jesuit life had fallen into oblivion shortly after his death, and that it only became accessible to Jesuits at large when the fourth volume of the *Monumenta Nadal* was published in 1905.[20] By the middle of the century, 'contemplative in action' had become a Jesuit slogan; official documents were describing the Jesuit as 'a man called by his vocation to be a contemplative in action', and Jesuit prayer as in line with a special grace given to Ignatius, whereby 'he found God in every thing, every word, and every deed'.[21] It seems likely that the Rahner brothers

[18] See O'Malley, 'Priesthood, Ministry, and Religious Life: Some Historical and Historiographical Considerations' (1988), in *Tradition and Transition*, 127–71, esp. 132.

[19] See Coreth, 'Contemplation in Action', esp. 199: the traditional understanding of action and contemplation sees action, 'more or less explicitly as a lapse from the essential—even if this lapse appears relatively justified by the practical necessities of life, the exigencies of relationships in the Church and civil society, pastoral need, or other such considerations. But these needs are regrettable: the ideal is a life as far as possible purely contemplative.'

[20] Such, at least, is the impression given by standard bibliographies and by the work of Nicolau.

[21] John W. Padberg (ed.), *Documents of the 31st and 32nd General Congregations of the Society of Jesus* (St Louis: Institute of Jesuit Sources, 1977), pp. 138, 139, 436, 460, 469, 471.

were, at least indirectly, responsible for this development in Jesuit self-understanding.[22]

At least on two counts, however, the development can be questioned. Firstly, what became the standard Jesuit reading of Nadal's phrase may have no basis in Nadal's own thinking. Only once does the expression 'contemplative in action' appear in Nadal's published writings, and Nadal never systematically developed it.[23] Nicolau's interpretation of this phrase—which is by no means his alone—sees it as expressing a significant distinction: 'it is not here a case of the simple ideal of *contemplata aliis tradere* (of a contemplation preceding action); the ideal is a contemplation accompanying action, of becoming *in actione contemplativus*'.[24] Nicolau takes Nadal to be contrasting Jesuit and Dominican spiritualities. So Alfred Delp:

> Thomas Aquinas develops the doctrine of the *vita mixta*. To contemplate and to hand on what one has contemplated is the Dominican order's motto. Ignatius demands of us . . . what we call the higher active life: contemplation in action. 'They should seek God in all things' articulates this outlook.[25]

But, as we have seen, Aquinas himself equiparates *contemplata aliis tradere* and the *vita activa superior*; moreover, *vita activa superior* is a concept which Nadal uses frequently and systematically.[26] The strong contrast between *contemplata aliis tradere* and *in actione contemplativus* found in Nadal's twentieth-century Jesuit interpreters, therefore, is probably foreign to his thought. This interpretation moves beyond Thomas in suggesting that one finds God actually in activity, including the so-called corporal works of mercy: Christ is

---

[22] A reasonably thorough search has yielded only one discussion of 'contemplative in action' prior to that in Hugo's 1922 catalogue (1922/5, 429): Henri Watrigant, 'Des méthodes d'oraison dans notre vie apostolique selon la doctrine des Exercices', *Collection de la bibliothèque des Exercices de St Ignace*, 45–7 (1913), 115 ff., esp. 145–7. It is only, however, in the 1930s that the idea begins to recur frequently, initially in the writings of German Jesuits—a development that seems attributable to Hugo Rahner. Miguel Nicolau, who was responsible both for the definitive theological study of Nadal and for editing many of his texts, wrote a thesis on Nadal at Innsbruck under Hugo's direction in 1937: 'El pensamiento ascético del P. Jerónimo Nadal, S.I.: fuentes e influjos'.

[23] Coreth, 'Contemplative in Action', 184: 'The context of the one place where Nadal uses this phrase shows clearly that it was not his intention thereby to give a final, well-honed formula in the form of an essential definition. Rather, in the course of a spiritual instruction, he is coining a phrase for the occasion: a phrase intended to make the reality it denotes more accessible by using familiar concepts taken from the tradition.'

[24] Nicolau, 'Nadal, Jerónimo', 11; cf. *Jerónimo Nadal*, 466–7.

[25] Quoted in Neufeld, *Geschichte und Mensch*, 267. Cf. Nicolau, 'Nadal, Jerónimo', 12.

[26] e.g. MHSJ *MN*, v. 124, 144, 168, 362–3.

encountered through the least of his sisters and brothers. However edifying and valid this thought may be, it is probably absent from Nadal's text.[27]

The second qualification to be made is that 'contemplative in action' and 'finding God in all things' cannot denote specifically Ignatian, still less specifically Jesuit, characteristics. What these expressions name is an attitude proper to Christianity as such. Karl Rahner himself saw this: in his first set of retreat conferences, he named 'finding God in all things' as 'the fundamental truth in which Christianity consists'.[28] But much Jesuit and Jesuit-inspired material misses the point.

Christian theology perennially struggles to maintain a doctrine of God consistent with the realities of grace and incarnation. In the nineteenth and twentieth centuries, it has also struggled to come to terms with historical consciousness and technical rationality. In this context, Nadal's description of Ignatius as 'contemplative in action', even if misinterpreted, seems to have caught the collective Jesuit imagination. The Rahner brothers are two in a school of twentieth-century Jesuit thinkers influenced by the retrieval of Ignatian sources. In the German-speaking world, other such figures include Alfred Delp (1907–45), Erich Przywara (1889–1972), Johannes Baptist Lotz (1903–92), Emerich Coreth (1919–), and Hans Urs von Balthasar (1905–88). These had important counterparts in France and Spain.[29]

[27] Parmananda R. Divarkar, *The Path of Interior Knowledge: Reflections on the Spiritual Exercises of St Ignatius of Loyola* (Anand: Gujarat Sahitya Prakash, 1983), 145–53, offers a suggestive discussion of 'contemplative in action', linking Nadal's phrase to the anonymous Franciscan treatise, *Stimulus divini amoris*, II. vi. Here the idea is presented along lines much closer to the standard Jesuit interpretation: 'when he sees his neighbour sick in bed he thinks that he sees his Christ'. The Thomist background to 'higher active life' may make the exegetical suggestion unlikely, but it is worth noting a medieval Franciscan antecedent to what twentieth-century Jesuits presented as new. The text is available, under the title *The Goad of Divine Love*, in a seventeenth-century English translation, ed. W. A. Philipson, with the authorship attributed to Bonaventure (London: Washbourne, 1907); and also in a translation by Walter Hilton, ed. Clare Kirchberger, as *The Goad of Love* (London: Faber, 1952).
[28] 1954/5, 276, 276. Cf. Coreth, 'Contemplative in Action', 184, 203.
[29] Alfred Delp (1907–45) was a philosopher and sociologist hanged by the Nazis for involvement in resistance work, and was clearly aware of the Rahner brothers' publications on Nadal. See references in Karl H. Neufeld, *Geschichte und Mensch*. Erich Przywara produced a theology of the Exercises: *Deus Semper Maior: Theologie der Exerzitien*, 3 vols. (Freiburg: Herder, 1964). Karl Rahner's contemporary as a graduate student in philosophy, Johannes Baptist Lotz, later a noted spiritual writer also, published 'Die ignatianische Betrachtungsmethode in Lichte einer gesunden Wertlehre', *Zeitschrift für Aszese und Mystik*, 10 (1935), 1–16, 112–23.

The rediscovery of *in actione contemplativus* was the vehicle for a Roman Catholic version of what Bonhoeffer prophetically saw from his Berlin prison cell:

God's 'beyond' is not what is beyond our cognitive faculties! The transcendence of epistemological theory has nothing to do with the transcendence of God. God is beyond in the midst of our life. The church stands, not at the boundaries where human powers give out, but in the middle of the village.[30]

For Bonhoeffer at this stage, a theology based on 'the transcendence of epistemological theory' entails a crude 'God of the gaps'. Rightly, he will have none of it. Ignatian spirituality, as mediated through Nadal's formulae, may have stimulated a similar realization in Rahner: openness to the transcendent God does not preclude human activity, but indeed demands it. Bonhoeffer draws on an anti-speculative tradition in Reformation theology, adopting an idiom of prophetic challenge. Karl Rahner's Roman Catholic instincts, by contrast, required him still to pay attention to the God of the philosophers, and thus to renew and develop the fundamental theology he had inherited.

One further passage from Nadal's 1562 instruction needs to be cited. Nadal distinguishes two approaches to prayer. The first consists in,

simple and humble meditation on creatures, whether natural or supernatural, such as the Incarnation of Christ, his humanity, the sacraments, all the infused graces: and in these one should gently consider the divine power, and thus the truth of it in God (*la virtud divina, y así la verdad della en Dios*).

On Hans Urs von Balthasar, a Jesuit till 1950, see his *Texte zum ignatianischen Exerzitienbuch*, ed. Jacques Servais (Einsiedeln: Johannes Verlag, 1993), and Jacques Servais, *Théologie des Exercices spirituels: H. U. von Balthasar interprète saint Ignace* (Brussels: Culture et vérité, 1996). Two major French contributions should also be mentioned: that of Gaston Fessard, most accessible to English-speaking readers through Edouard Pousset, *Life in Faith and Freedom: An Essay Presenting Gaston Fessard's Analysis of the Dialectic of the Spiritual Exercises of St. Ignatius*, trans. Eugene L. Donahue (St Louis: Institute of Jesuit Sources, 1980); and the early volumes of the spirituality review *Christus*, founded in 1954. Among Spaniards, besides Nicolau's work, one should note the ongoing editing of the MHSJ by such figures as Ignacio Iparraguirre and Cándido de Dalmases. Fischer, *Der Mensch als Geheimnis*, 19–80, gives further information on the German-speaking wing of this movement, and represents a pioneer attempt to place Karl Rahner in this context. Michael Schneider, *'Unterscheidung der Geister'*, offers a comparative study of Przywara, Rahner, and Fessard.

[30] Dietrich Bonhoeffer, *Letters and Papers from Prison*, ed. Eberhard Bethge, trans. Reginald Fuller et al. (London: SCM, 1971), 282.

The Rahner brothers translate Nadal's account of the second approach rather creatively, so I present the text in two versions:

Nadal's Original

The other is, with a prevenient grace combined with some higher enlightenment, to come to consider and contemplate God in everything lower; or in that light gently to seek greater force of the divine power in greater and clearer truths. This latter is higher, when God gives a very exalted grace and light, in which the highest truths are contemplated in a unity, which those who experience them feel; and with this enlightenment they look at and contemplate all the rest in our Lord, etc.[31]

The Rahner Brothers' Translation

The second kind is such that grace now comes to us with a higher enlightenment. Then we can feel and regard the eternal God's own self in all other things. Or in this light we seek to understand in spiritual consolation how the power of God works itself out powerfully in higher, purer truths. The second way is the higher. For then God gives a much more refined light of grace, in which one can see the highest truths as if in one single view. Those who have experienced this in itself, and those who through this enlightenment of the Spirit look at and behold everything which is *outside* God *in* our Lord—those people know what this means.[32]

The passage may seem eccentric and isolated, but it is significant for this study on at least two grounds. Firstly, Hugo Rahner—perhaps idiosyncratically—connected it with what, on any account,

---

[31] MHSJ *MN*, iv. 678–9: *Otro modo es con prevención de la gracia con alguna ilustración superior, venir a considerar y contemplar a Dios en todo lo inferior, o en aquella luz buscar con suavidad mayor fuerza de la virtud divina en mayores y más claras verdades. Otro es más alto, cuando Dios da una gracia y luz muy subida, en donde se contemplan las sumas verdades en una unión, cual sienten los que las experimentan, y con aquella illustración miran y contemplan todo el resto en el Señor, etc.*

[32] 1935, 408: *Die zweite Art ist so, daß uns da die Gnade mit einer höheren Erleuchtung zuvorkommt. Dann können wir erspüren und betrachten den ewigen Gott selbst in all den anderen Dingen. Oder wir suchen in diesem Licht in geistlichem Trost zu verstehen, wie sich die Gotteskraft in höheren, reineren Wahrheiten machtvoll auswirkt. Der zweite Weg ist der höhere. Da gibt Gott ja ein viel feineres Gnadenlicht, in ihm betrachtet man die höchsten Wahrheiten wie in einer einzigen Schau. Diejenigen wissen, was das heißt, die es an sich erfahren haben und die in dieser Geisteserleuchtung alles anschauen und betrachten, was außer Gott ist in unserem Herrn.*

are key elements in Ignatian mysticism: Ignatius's experiences at Manresa, his Trinitarian prayer, the finding of God in all things. In his important essay on Ignatius's vision at La Storta, Hugo quotes the Nadal passage in support of a general assertion: 'it was the grace of Ignatius's life to behold the organic coherence of all the truths of faith, to see all together (*zusammenzuschauen*) everything that is created—all that is outside God—from God's side'.[33] What is significant here, however, is not the justification for the connections Hugo made, but rather the simple fact that he made them, and the fact that they point forward to Karl's speculative innovations. Nadal's description of Ignatius as 'contemplative in action', together with the idea of finding God in all things, comes after a description of Ignatius's familiarity with the Trinity. Hugo Rahner interprets these ideas as materially equivalent. As exegesis, this claim goes beyond the evidence: Nadal simply connects the two ideas with *tum illud praeterea*—'then this as well'.[34] It is Karl Rahner's theology that enables us to see mutual entailments between human experience of God, divine self-communication, and the doctrine of the Trinity. If God's own self can be found by human beings in creation, then the structures of human mental life must reflect the ontology of God.[35] There are also other motifs in Hugo's La Storta essay foreshadowing Karl's speculative creativity: all the mysteries of faith reduce to one mystery, that of a self-communicating, Trinitarian God; each person of the Trinity has a distinctive relationship to the creation; the humanity of Jesus remains permanently our mediation to the Father.[36]

Secondly, there may be connections between the Nadal passage and Karl's claim that grace entails a supernatural formal object of knowledge. Hugo claims to find in Ignatius and Nadal a claim that we can come to know 'all things' as God knows them. Hugo did not develop the epistemology implicit in such a claim at all, while Nadal

[33] Hugo Rahner, *The Vision*, 79–80. This essay was first published as a four-part article in *Zeitschrift für Aszese und Mystik*, 10 (1935).
[34] MHSJ *MN*, v. 162. Hugo Rahner renders this phrase blandly with *ebenso*—likewise (*Ignatius von Loyola als Mensch und Theologe*, 81—cf. *The Vision*, 72: 'It was the same with that grace . . .').
[35] See, for example, 'Remarks on the Dogmatic Treatise "De Trinitate"', esp. 4.96–9, 4.125–9.
[36] Hugo Rahner, *The Vision*, 79–80, 83–4. Cf. Karl Rahner's essays, 'The Concept of Mystery in Catholic Theology'; 'The Eternal Significance of the Humanity of Jesus'; and the final section of 'Some Implications'.

himself offers a vague and crude contrast between two kinds of knowledge: one mediated through creatures (including Christ), the other somehow higher. Karl Rahner's account of the supernatural formal object, however, can be read as a gloss on the Nadal text. God's knowledge of creation is radically different in kind from ours:

> God, as pure *Sein*, is present to himself from the outset, and apprehends his own essence through the fact that pure *Sein* is completely self-reflective. Thus God knows himself as also the almighty, creative ground of finite beings, and in that way knows the beings themselves.[37]

On Karl Rahner's theology of grace, however, our normal mode of knowledge is transformed:

> grace entails an active, effective tendency in the mental faculties towards the supernatural goal; the psychological structure of the acts which spring from this divinizing life-principle is necessarily different from that of natural acts . . . If the understanding and the will are raised to the supernatural, this means that they are ordered to God in a new and distinctive way: in other words, they have a supernatural formal object.[38]

This new formal object is 'that which exists in simplicity, or, if you like, the triune God'.

A natural intentional act has as its *a priori* formal object 'the existent in general' (*ens ut sic*). By contrast, the person under grace somehow shares in God's own mode of knowledge:

> An understanding raised to the supernatural—given that this implies a participation in the divine understanding, the understanding natural to God alone—perceives everything no longer through a structure determined by existence in general, existence in the sense that applies to all existents, but through a structure determined by the simple existent, unbounded existence itself, concretely the triune God. For if God knows and desires everything, not in so far as he is carried towards existence in general but rather towards simple existence, i.e. towards himself (and only for God is this connatural), the one who participates in this divine understanding as such must have the same formal object. For human intellectual nature is ontologically changed by being raised to the

---

[37] *Hearer of the Word*, 99*, *151* (*KRSW*, iv. 182): '*In dieser Weise erkennt z.B. Gott die von ihm verschiedenen Dinge. Er ist als reines Sein von vornherein bei sich selbst und erfaßt in der Insichreflektiertheit des reinen Seins sein eigenes Wesen und erkennt sich darum auch als den allmächtigen schöpferischen Grund endlicher Seiender und damit diese selbst.*' The commendable concern in the published translation to avoid gender-specific language leads to the loss of important nuances here.

[38] Alfaro, 'Formalobjekt, Übernatürliches', 207.

supernatural, in such a way that it becomes a participation in the divine understanding as such.[39]

There are obvious parallels here with Hugo's comment on the 'contemplative in action' passage, shaped as this is by Hugo's identification of 'finding God in all things' with Ignatius's Trinitarian prayer:

> we recognize already from this passage the special nature of Ignatius's Trinitarian mysticism: his union with the Trinitarian 'Creator and Lord' is not just a resting abandonment to the mysteries of mystical vision. Rather, it is a 'finding of God in *all things*', or, to put it even better, a viewing of all things from the standpoint of the Trinitarian God.[40]

As we are about to explore further, there are major differences between what Hugo and Karl made of Ignatius. Nevertheless, both see him as teaching how human consciousness is drawn into the life of the Trinity, with transformative effects for how we regard the whole of creation.

Hugo Rahner and Ignatius the Mystic

Anyone who knew my brother was aware of how he was a very different man from me. He was more cheerful, wittier, and perhaps more interested in history. But we shared from the beginning a devotion to our common founder, Ignatius of Loyola. Hugo did a lot for Ignatian research: he was a real historian of our founder. He wrote excellent books about him, while I perhaps tried more to see some things that are directly there for the taking in Ignatius in terms of existentialist philosophy.[41]

In this interview statement from the last months of his life, Karl Rahner is thinking primarily of his work on Ignatian choice and

---

[39] *De gratia Christi*, 306: '*Si quaeritur, quale sit hoc obiectum formale supernaturale aprioristicum, dicimus id esse ens simpliciter, seu, si placet, Deus trinus. Actus naturalis intellectualis habet tanquam obiectum formale aprioristicum immutabile ens ut sic, sive ut verum ut sic (pro intellectu) sive ut bonum ut sic (pro voluntate). Intellectualitas supernaturaliter elevata, quippe cum sit participatio intellectualitatis divinae, prout Deo exclusive naturaliter propria est, percipit omnia non iam sub ratione entis ut sic, entis communissimi, sed sub ratione entis simpliciter, ipsius esse illimitati, quod est in concreto Deus trinus. Si enim Deus omnia cognoscit et appetit, non prout fertur in ens ut sic, sed in ens simpliciter, i.e. in se ipsum (quod ei soli naturaliter convenit), is qui hanc divinam intellectualitatem ut talem participat, idem obiectum formale habere debet. Ipsa enim elevatio supernaturalis ontologice naturam intellectualem humanam sic afficit, ut sit participatio intellectualitatis divinae qua talis.*'

[40] Hugo Rahner, *The Vision*, 73. In the 1935 edition, *ruhendes* (resting) is stressed.

[41] *Glaube in winterlicher Zeit*, 28–9 (not translated in *Faith in a Wintry Season*).

the theology of grace. But it also describes well the relationship between the two brothers' approaches to 'finding God in all things'. Hugo was a creative historian whose underlying theological assumptions were conventional; Karl took up some of Hugo's findings to refashion speculative theology. A comparison of how the two brothers handled Ignatius's mysticism can help us appreciate Karl's originality.

The abiding value of Hugo's work on Ignatian spirituality lies in its highly original and intuitive retrievals. For all his innocence of critical hermeneutics,[42] it is Hugo Rahner above all who established that Ignatius was not simply a soldier who had donned a soutane. His collation of Ignatius's letters to women in 1956 revealed aspects of Ignatius's character which were then hardly known, and the subsequent universal acceptance of Hugo's findings has obscured their originality.[43] Again, Hugo's 1935 presentation of Ignatius's mysticism is groundbreaking: it implies a coalescence of mysticism, ethics, and Christology that was then new. Hugo's explicit analysis of this mysticism, however, implies just the kind of religious epistemology that Karl, in *Spirit in the World*, exhaustively discredited.

As we saw in the last chapter, *Spirit in the World* rejects the claim that we know of metaphysical reality through 'a metaphysical intuition with a distinctive kind of grounding'.[44] Yet it seems that precisely such a conception underlies the final part of Hugo's study of Ignatius's La Storta vision, devoted to its mental structure, or *Psychologie*. In 1537, Ignatius and his companions moved to Rome. On the outskirts, at La Storta, Ignatius received what he took to be an assurance of God the Father's favour, together with a sense that the Father was 'placing' him with the cross-bearing Christ.[45] Hugo Rahner's analysis of this tradition presupposes that spiritual growth progresses from the material, through the imaginative, to the 'intellectual':

The mystical vision is an event that takes place in the purely intellectual part of the soul and in a wholly different dimension of knowing.[46]

[42] This is pitilessly exposed in Boyle, 'Angels Black and White', esp. 244, 253, 257.
[43] Hugo Rahner, *Saint Ignatius Loyola: Letters to Women.*
[44] *Spirit in the World*, 28, *13* (*KRSW*, ii. 33): '*eigengründige metaphysische Intuition*'.
[45] On the details, see Hugo Rahner, *The Vision*, 7–68, updated in Robert Rouquette, 'Essai critique sur les sources relatant la vision de saint Ignace à la Storta', *Revue d'ascétique et de mystique*, 33 (1957), 34–61, 150–70; more briefly, see Ignatius, *Personal Writings*, 376 n. 153.
[46] Hugo Rahner, *The Vision*, 124.

La Storta appears as a moment of decisive transition, the moment where Ignatius begins to leave imaginative vision behind and to embark on genuine mysticism.[47] The account depends on fundamentalist uses of authorities such as Teresa of Avila (in questionable German translation), and at a number of places Hugo Rahner invests Ignatian source material with significance it cannot bear.[48] Moreover, the facts of Ignatius's biography quite simply discredit such an account of spiritual growth. Ignatius's earlier key experience, by the River Cardoner near Manresa in 1522, cannot but, on Hugo Rahner's conventional terminology, count as 'intellectual'—'not that he saw some vision, but understanding and knowing many things'[49]—while the La Storta vision at least sounds primarily 'imaginative'.

Hugo handles the difficulty by drawing on the early Jesuit author Diego Alvarez de Paz.[50] For Alvarez, La Storta is a moment of intellectual vision: Ignatius was 'in ecstasy, totally deprived of the use of his senses, and his soul was resting in the most exalted contemplation':

> But in this state the visions are in the purely intellectual power of knowledge (*in der rein geistigen Erkenntniskraft*)—or at least they begin there and only from there do they communicate themselves to the lower powers of the soul.[51]

The last point enables Hugo to make a distinction in his account of La Storta. The deepest reality of the incident is purely 'intellectual': 'the immediate and real "being placed with"', and what the Father

---

[47] Ibid., e.g. 107, 114–16.

[48] For example, Hugo Rahner claims that Nadal's description of Ignatius as occupied *in pure intellectualibus* dates from the last years of his life (*The Vision*, 104). Nicolau's subsequent edition dates the text to 1545, nearly eleven years before Ignatius's death. Again, Hugo Rahner claims of Ignatius that 'the freedom from any accompanying bodily appearances was for him virtually a sign of progress' (*The Vision*, 106), adducing three Ignatian texts as sources (MHSJ *FN*, ii. 345; i. 638–9; *Aut*, n. 99). The first two of these are about Ignatius's ability to detach himself from such visions, not about their absence, while *Aut*, n. 99, offers no support for the claim whatever. Interestingly, all the texts cited in this note are taken up in Karl's Ignatian writings, e.g. 1937, 291, *346*; 1978*d*, 18–19.

[49] *Aut*, n. 30.2–3. Hugo Rahner, *The Vision*, 111, acknowledges the anomaly in passing, seeing it as an example of how Ignatius's life 'defies neat classification'!

[50] See the article on him by E. Hernández in *Dictionnaire de Spiritualité*, i. 407–9. Interestingly, this influential figure wrote from Peru.

[51] Hugo Rahner, *The Vision*, 108, over-creatively translating Alvarez de Paz, *De inquisitione pacis*, v. iii. 12 (n. 178): '*Erat enim tunc sanctus Pater in raptum abstractus a sensibus et altissima contemplatione defixus; in qua visiones solent in intellectu fieri vel saltem ab illo inchoare et se ad vires inferiores dimittere.*'

'imprints' upon Ignatius's heart. The images of the cross are '"seen" later', and depend on a subsequent communication to the soul's lower powers.[52]

What is already a contrived account collapses into incoherence when Hugo draws on the idea of the spiritual senses to interpret Ignatius's mature state. On the one hand, Ignatius is meant to have attained a non-sensory state of love, in which,

the laws of our sense-dependent knowledge of the 'before and after', of 'mere' knowledge, are no longer valid.[53]

On the other hand, however, sensory language can still be used in a transferred, figurative sense:

The transformation of heart in the purely intellectual vision of supernatural reality presents itself to the mystic's most inward consciousness (if they must speak of this with our sense-bound words) as a parallel to immediate sensory knowledge. Hence he or she has a certain preference for speaking of the 'five senses of the soul'—for so they feel they can best 'translate' their mystical experience.[54]

Talk of two kinds of human senses raises the difficult question of the continuities and discontinuities between them, the issue of nature and grace. Hugo Rahner fails to see that there is a problem here, and implies a naive extrinsicism. But there is also a more fundamental philosophical difficulty. The passage just quoted tells us that the language of the spiritual senses gives figurative expression to non-sensory reality. Hugo Rahner uses this imagery elegantly and poetically, and his writing may come as a relief after his brother's austere tortuousness. But Hugo's pious fluency masks conceptual muddle.[55] For Hugo Rahner still wants also to distinguish spiritual sight and spiritual hearing, not only from the normal varieties, but also from each other: God speaks to Hugo Rahner's Ignatius with 'ineffable (*unaussprechlichen*) words'![56] If, however, the referent of this

[52] Hugo Rahner, *The Vision*, 110, drawing on Laínez's recollection of how Ignatius described the vision (MHSJ *FN*, ii. 133).

[53] Ibid., 124*.   [54] Ibid., 125–6.

[55] Famously, Hugo used to say that he would spend his retirement translating Karl's work into German. In his old age, Karl formulated a retort: 'my dear Hugo, you'd never have managed it—for you were a good and interesting Church historian, but with sophisticated modern theology, I think you had rather less idea' (*Glaube in winterlicher Zeit*, 13, not translated in *Faith in a Wintry Season*).

[56] Hugo Rahner, *The Vision*, 128.

language is non-sensory, it is impossible to see on what basis we can distinguish individual instances of it in the way that Hugo Rahner's use of the metaphor still requires.[57] More fundamentally, given that to be human is to be bodily, the idea of a purely intellectual, or mental, human experience involves a contradiction.

Towards the end of his 1956 essay on discernment, Karl Rahner draws on Hugo's account of Ignatius's mysticism, and indeed refers to Ignatius's 'purely intellectual (*intellektuelle*) mysticism'. But 'intellectual knowledge' here is in some strong sense consistent with knowledge of particular sensory objects, specific options that the discerner may or may not take. Only rarely did Karl Rahner discuss what his brother had written on Ignatius, and never in detail. In 1981 he referred to Hugo's 'loving, profoundly sympathetic understanding of Ignatius', and noted the 'decisive stimuli' he had given to the theology of the Exercises.[58] But the systematic assumptions underlying Hugo's presentation needed drastic reform, a task addressed in Karl's theological metaphysics.[59]

Towards a Spirituality in the World

Already in *Hearer of the Word* it is clear that Karl Rahner does not accept what was then the conventional understanding of mysticism. Towards the end of chapter 13, he entertains the suggestion of a miraculous form of revelation, which somehow tore us 'permanently, in miraculous fashion, out of our natural thinking and acting'—a suggestion paralleled in the claim that mystical knowledge is 'purely intellectual'. This suggestion would entail two unacceptable consequences. It would amount to God creating another creature altogether, because, on this account of the matter, grace and revelation would no longer be accessible to human beings as such.

---

[57] For fuller discussion of the issues, see my 'The Ignatian Prayer of the Senses', where I suggest that 'spiritual' in 'spiritual senses' needs to be opposed, not to 'material' but to 'unconverted' (Pauline *sarkikos*).

[58] Foreword to Hugo Rahner, *Worte, die Licht sind*, 15. See also 'Ein brüderlicher Geburtstagsbrief', esp. 72.

[59] A recent, pioneer study of Hugo Rahner presents Hugo and Karl as having 'two conflicting types of theology' leading to 'contradictory images of Ignatian mysticism', and reports the matter far more favourably to Hugo: Johannes Holdt, *Hugo Rahner: Sein geschichts- und symboltheologisches Denken* (Paderborn: Schöningh, 1997), quotation from 143.

Moreover, it would compromise the gratuity of revelation. For revelation has to be a reality precisely *not* required for the fulfilment of
the creature's natural essence, whereas this new creature, *ex hypothesi*, would have an essence correlative to the revelation. If
revelation is to appear as radically other, as gratuitous, the standards enabling this otherness to appear as other must remain. Grace
may transform nature, but it is still the same nature; the drama of
revelation depends on this tension being maintained. The gratuity
consists, not simply in the divine reality of the revealed, but in
the fact that this divinity can 'transpose itself' (*sich umsetzen*) into
the normal structures of human knowledge.[60] Thus, if ordinary
knowledge is sense-dependent, then God's revelation must be
sense-dependent too.

A more theological argument appears earlier, in chapter 6. Rahner here raises the suggestion that our knowledge of God through
the *Vorgriff* might occur 'without the intermediary of a finite object'.
He notes the influence of such a conception on pagan mysticism,
and through Plotinus on Gregory of Nyssa, on Denys, and on some
readings of John of the Cross. On such a view, verbal revelation
from God could be superseded by a knowledge within unaided
human power that was nevertheless somehow deeper. Rahner's
objections to such a position concern not only the conceptual inco-
herences it presupposes, but also its 'destructive consequences for
the possibility of a free revelation of God'.[61] Such a concept of
mysticism relativizes gospel revelation unacceptably. Nevertheless,
Rahner was well aware that he was advocating a minority position.
Writing in 1959 on *Dreifaltigkeitsmystik* (Trinitarian mysticism) in the
Lexikon für Theologie und Kirche, Rahner noted,

that from Evagrius Ponticus, through Ps-Denys the Areopagite and into
the post-Renaissance period, the predominant foundational model for
the theory of mysticism was that of union with the absolute, simple (ἕν),
'modeless' God in the still desert of the 'divinity'.[62]

Rahner's most sustained treatment of the issue comes in his
1944 essay, 'Reflections on the Problem of the Gradual Ascent to
Christian Perfection'. The opening section of the essay exposes the

[60] *Hearer of the Word*, 135, *198–9* (*KRSW*, iv. 240). Cf. the intricate argumentation in 'On
the Relationship between Nature and Grace'.
[61] *Hearer of the Word*, 60–1, *96–8* (*KRSW*, iv. 116–18).
[62] 'Dreifaltigkeitsmystik', 563.

inadequacy, as Rahner sees it, of traditional accounts: either they reduce to simple, unelaborated statements that growth is possible, or else they are conceived in terms of a quasi-gnostic ideal.[63] Rahner then makes various suggestions towards alternatives. One might invoke what we now call life-cycle theory; Rahner's renewal of the concept of concupiscence suggests that the psychological intensity of our faith-commitment can deepen over time. We might also develop theologically the concept of approximation to Christ. More generally, the older formulations about mysticism might be rescuable if purged of ideas owing more to Neoplatonism than to Christianity.[64] Typically, however, he does not develop any of these suggestions fully.

Rahner's 1937 essay, 'The Ignatian Mysticism of Joy in the World', also exhibits the tension between Rahner's positions in fundamental theology and the rhetoric of mysticism that he inherited. The piece was an occasional one, written to match a title which was not of his own choosing, and with which he seemed uneasy.[65] It begins with a laboured discussion of how the two key terms in the title— 'mysticism' and *Weltfreudigkeit*—can be compatible. This preamble contains, in succession, three approaches to the issue that are not obviously consistent with each other. Firstly, Rahner insists that we must allow the Ignatian tradition to shape our theology, not the other way round.[66] Then, secondly, he takes a more defensive position: he names a list of technical theological problems raised by the concept of mysticism—a different list in the two editions—before simply invoking a vague sense of the word, and affirming that at least in this sense, without further precision, Ignatius was a mystic. Rahner supports this claim by quoting a number of features, notably the Laínez–Nadal passage about Ignatius's being taken up with *pure intellectualibus*. Most come from Hugo's La Storta essay.[67]

---

[63] 'Reflections on the Problem', 6, *4–15*: 'either the steps of the spiritual life are oriented towards and aimed at a mystical ideal of knowledge, or this doctrine never really gets beyond certain very formal divisions'.

[64] 'Reflections on the Problem', 15–16, 21–3; *25–6, 32–4*.

[65] In Rahner's appointments notebook, the untranslatable *Weltfreudigkeit* appears as *Weltbejahung*—'world-affirmation'.

[66] 1937, 278, *330*.

[67] 1937, 278–80, *330–3*. In the original publication (p. 123), Rahner describes mysticism as 'the experience of the immediate dealing (*die . . . Erfahrung des unmittelbaren Handelns*), based on the grace of Christ, between the personal God and humanity'. This is more than knowledge of God; nor is it union with God in the sense that these words are likely to be understood,

'But', Rahner continues, 'all this is not actually what we should be talking about', and proceeds to offer yet a third approach: we can prescind from questions of how mystical and ordinary piety differ, because our only concern is to clarify Ignatius's *Weltfreudigkeit*. We can therefore leave the specifically mystical aside, and focus instead on the much broader notion of 'piety' (*Frömmigkeit*).[68] In the main body of the piece, as we shall see, Rahner implicitly abandons conventional concepts of mysticism, and at least begins to replace them with an approach more organically connected to gospel revelation. If the prolegomena appear defensive and uncertain, this is because the approach Rahner develops is theologically subversive—perhaps more so than he realized at the time.

Following God's Action

The central argument of Rahner's 1937 essay on Ignatian *Weltfreudigkeit* depends on two moves. Firstly, Rahner takes as central to the concept of mysticism, or 'piety', a monastic commitment to the Cross. Even if they live in a city rather than the desert, Ignatius's disciples try, through a life of discipline and asceticism, 'to allow that dying with Christ, which was in essence and in principle brought about in Baptism, to become a reality throughout a whole life and in its complete significance'.[69]

Secondly, Rahner construes *fuga saeculi* theologically rather than spatially: flight from a life lived by the standards of 'pure nature' rather than flight from the world of space and time. Holiness consists, not in an escape from the constraints of creatureliness, but rather in the creature's following God's initiative of free, gracious

given the then widespread distinction between prophetic and mystical piety. On this distinction, see Friedrich Heiler, *Prayer: A Study in the History and Psychology of Religion*, trans. from 5th edn. Samuel McComb (London: Oxford University Press, 1932 [orig. 1st pub. 1918]), 135–6: 'Mysticism is that form of intercourse with God in which the world and self are absolutely denied, in which human personality is dissolved, disappears, and is absorbed in the infinite One of the Godhead.'

[68] 1937, 280–1, *333*. Rahner makes the qualification that the piety of a mystic will, as such, have a special depth and power. Explaining the complex decision to translate Viller's title, *La Spiritualité des premiers siècles chrétiens*, in terms of *Aszese und Mystik*, Rahner stated that *spiritualité* does not include everything covered by the German *Frömmigkeit* (*Aszese und Mystik in der Väterzeit*, pp. xix–xx [*KRSW*, iii. 126], Neufeld, 'Unter Brüdern', 23).

[69] 1937, 281–2, *334*.

self-communication. According to Christian conviction, God has 'broken in upon human existence and has burst open the world— what theology calls "nature"'. Because of the demands this initiative makes on us, any Christian holiness can be thought of as a flight from the world. But it is not that we cease to be worldly in the physical sense: rather, 'God steps directly before humanity with a demand and a call which fling human beings out of the track laid down previously for them by nature, the track that they would have run within the world's horizon'.[70]

Consequently asceticism is relativized: 'this new centre of our existence is bestowed on us exclusively by the free grace of God, and therefore not by the sacrificing flight from the world itself'.[71] What matters is an openness to the divine freedom. If asceticism is undertaken 'as being *the* means which of itself and with nothing further compels the awareness of the Absolute' it misses the point, just as much as a purely philosophical belief in God does.[72] Conversely—and here Rahner grounds an Ignatian openness to the world—God's freedom may lead us, paradoxically, into 'a normal, commonsense lifestyle':[73]

Once someone has placed themselves under the Cross and has died with Christ, once they have entered the darkness of faith and the ecstasy of love for the distant God, then (to use the specialist language of theology) every act which is good in itself—and thus even an act which is meaningful simply within the world order—can be supernaturally elevated by grace in such a way that its goal and its meaning extend beyond this inner-worldly significance, beyond the order of natural law, into the life of God's own self.[74]

Ignatian piety thus exhibits a mixture of detachment and commitment. On the one hand it is marked by 'indifference':

the distinctiveness of Ignatian piety lies not so much in a material element, in the cultivation of a particular thought or a particular practice. It is not one of the particular ways to God, but something formal: an ultimate attitude regarding all thoughts, practices and ways, an ultimate reserve and coolness regarding all particular ways, because all possession of God must allow God to be greater than any possession.[75]

---

[70] 1937, 285, *339*.   [71] 1937, 288, *342*.   [72] 1937, 289, *343*.
[73] 1937, 291, *346*.   [74] 1937, 289, *343–4*.
[75] 1937, 290–1, *345*. In the journal version, in *Schriften*, and in the published translation, this word is consistently written in misspelt Spanish as *indiferençia*. The noun form is not found in the *Exercises*, though Ignatius does use it once elsewhere (*Dir*, n. 1.17).

Equally, there is nothing which cannot, in principle, be a way to God. God can be found in all things. For Ignatius, as Rahner reads him, God is really 'beyond all that is world (*jenseits aller Welt*) and not merely the dialectical antithesis to all that is world'. Therefore God can also be found '*in the world*, when his sovereign will commands us to take the way into the world'.[76]

This last formulation, however, also points up some of the unfinished business in this essay. It implies that finding God in the world is one possible way, among others, of finding God. The Ignatian 'contemplative in action', Rahner tells us, finds God in the world 'should that please God'.[77] The implication seems to be that God could will something else. In fact, however, Rahner is not developing an interpretation of the specifically Ignatian or Jesuit vocation at all, but rather of Christianity as such. As Rahner has mentioned earlier in the essay, the version of 'flight from the world' he advocates is in reality 'not merely reasonable but also necessary', and Christian faith represents its beginning.[78] Moreover, human beings are *essentially* worldly: what Rahner says, despite his disclaimers at the beginning, subverts conventional accounts of mysticism at their root.

The occasional nature of the piece, and the fact that this business is unfinished, obscure the argument's metaphysical basis. For Rahner, it is not, despite what some of his formulations might suggest, that God 'accepts' worldly action 'as if' it were true, 'otherworldly', mysticism. On the contrary, there is a true ontological union between creator and creature, realized through the creature's action in space and time, in the categorical. Moreover, there is no other way in which human beings, spirits in the world, can attain such union.

Rahner at one point describes his reformed version of *fuga saeculi* as an 'existential action-following'—*existentieller Nachvollzug*—of God's 'always already enacted' reorientation of our being.[79] *Nachvollzug* and *Mitvollzug* are Rahnerian jargon, not ordinary German words, and accordingly I translate them, where possible, by two non-standard

---

[76] 1937, 291–2, *346*.   [77] 1937, 292, *347*.

[78] 1937, 340, *286*. Rahner acknowledges at the end that he has not worked out how Ignatian religious life and an Ignatian interpretation of lay discipleship (or Christian life at large) relate to each other (p. 292, *347*).

[79] 1937, 288, *342*.

English idioms–'action-following', 'action-accompanying.'[80] The expressions appear repeatedly in Rahner's Ignatian writings. In the 1978 testament, for example, the account of Ignatian vocational choice emerges from an evocation of God 'becoming flesh' in the creature. We are then told that this creature makes a *Mitvollzug* of— an action-accompanying—the divine descent.[81]

To understand these expressions, we need to refer to Rahner's most extended use of them: in *Hearer of the Word*.[82] As we saw in the previous chapter, this text develops a philosophy of mind related to Bonaventure's 'immediate experience of God' in spiritual touch. Though we cannot directly see the absolute, we are permanently in a questioning, dark contact with it. In chapters 7 and 8 of the book, Rahner brings out the implications for our understanding of human action.

The argument starts from the phenomenon of human questioning about the meaning of reality, from the fact that all human knowing and willing presupposes some stance or other with regard to the absolute. This reveals—in an idiom with obvious Heideggerian echoes—a curious interplay of necessity and contingency:

> Insofar as they must *inquire*, human persons affirm their own thrown finitude; insofar as they *must* inquire, they affirm this thrownness of theirs necessarily. And as they affirm it necessarily, they affirm their existence, in and despite its thrownness, as unconditioned, as absolute. In other words, because the affirmation of the *contingent* fact is inescapably *necessary*, there is an absoluteness disclosed in the contingency itself: the inescapability with which the contingent fact, of itself, demands its affirmation.[83]

Rahner is here reworking the cosmological argument for the existence of God, but in an idiom shaped both by his reading of Heidegger and by his transcendental approach to the scholastic tradition. Rahner resolves the paradox he has set up by introducing the concept of will. If something contingent exists, in a way that cannot be denied, then a will must have established it. Further, creatures themselves cannot furnish their own reason for existing; and reality must, in principle, be intelligible. Only one explanation,

---

[80] The translational issue is discussed by Andrew Tallon in his introduction to *Hearer of the Word*, pp. xii–xiii.

[81] 1978*b*, 18*, *382*. See also, for example, 1954/5, 272*, *272*; 1961, 270, *294*; 1975*b*, 10.

[82] In the *Schriften* edition of the 1937 essay (1937, 283–4, *337*) a footnote connects the two texts, which were written in the same year.

[83] *Hearer of the Word*, 67–8, *107* (*KRSW*, iv. 128–30).

therefore, remains possible: the volitional self-affirmation we cannot but make is grounded in God's creative affirmation of us. Or, to use Rahner's own terms, our part is always 'an action-following a *free* and absolute establishing of the not-necessary'.[84]

Mitvollzug and *Nachvollzug* thus denote the creaturely dependence of our action on God's. For us, God's action remains mystery, unfathomable. Although we must affirm *that* our human reality is grounded on God's free act, the *how* remains completely opaque and mysterious to us:

we see the act of establishing only in that which has been established. Hence for us, for whom the free act of establishing as such does not show itself, this act remains as opaque as that which has been established.

To affirm the intelligibility of reality is not to claim that we must understand all that occurs:

we are not trying to reconcile the contingency of the finite being with *our* finite knowledge of reality, but with the intrinsic luminosity of reality in itself.[85]

The concept of 'transparency' (*Gelichtetheit*) or intelligibility put forward here must allow free divine decision as a category of explanation. The absolute's free action is intelligible to us, not through our comprehension, through our 'seizing' or 'grasping' it and subsuming it under laws of cause and effect, but rather through our 'under-standing' it in loving, actively participative, responsiveness. Of the Absolute's free act, including its creative acts, Rahner writes,

It can only become luminous and intelligible for another when this other acts-accompanying in the action as a free one (*wenn er sie als freie Tat selbst mitvollzieht*), when the other as such loves the action. The free action is thus intelligible, in itself. And if it seems obscure and incomprehensible, this is so only for a knowledge which tries to understand the action while standing outside the action itself. Yet this does not detract from its intelligibility; but is merely the command addressed to knowledge to swing itself, as it were, into the free act (*sich selbst in die freie Tat gleichsam hineinzuschwingen*) in order to understand it and what it establishes. But this happens when the understanding does not seek to apprehend the free action of the other as something previously established, but to act-accompanying the very

---

[84] Ibid., 69, *108* (*KRSW*, iv. 130): '*Diese notwendige willentliche Bejahung kann nur aufgefaßt werden als der Nachvollzug einer freien Absolutsetzung des Nichtnotwendigen.*'

[85] Ibid., 79, *122* (*KRSW*, iv. 146). Donceel translates *Setzung* and its cognates in terms of 'creation'.

establishing, to allow it to emerge also from itself, as it were in action-following (*die Setzung selbst mitvollzieht, sie gleichsam im Nachvollzug auch aus sich selbst entspringen läßt*). In this very emergence, the free is present—and understood—in itself.[86]

Le cœur a ses raisons que la raison ne connaît pas.[87] God's knowledge of creation is encompassed in the divine self-knowledge. As creatures, we can be in loving contact with this. Here, perhaps, Rahner is echoing Nadal's talk of seeing creation as God sees it. But this contact is dark and obscure: it involves unknowing and surrender, not the clarity of Hugo Rahner's spiritual senses. We act-accompanying and act-following something we do not originate or understand.

Rahner then goes on, following a properly restrictive definition of terms, to talk of love as the necessary condition of knowledge. However, this language can easily mislead, and should probably be replaced. It is perfectly possible for the *Mitvollzug* and *Nachvollzug* to take the form of resistance, of suicide, self-hatred, and hatred for God.[88] Rahner's point is that whatever we do and whatever we know are always in some way responsive to a divine initiative which we do not comprehend. All our mental activity is encompassed in a lived emotional stance, some degree of trust or lack of it, some degree of acceptance or rejection of what God has set in motion. Even the rejection of God is grounded in this dark contact between God and the self.

Conversely, our only access to God is through the categorical. In 1975, Rahner was asked to collaborate in producing a theological dossier designed to help his fellow Jesuits come to terms with the 1974–5 General Congregation (chapter), which had made powerful statements identifying the contemporary service of faith with the promotion of justice. Rahner's main contribution was simply to repeat his 1965 essay, 'Reflections on the Unity of the Love of Neighbour and the Love of God'. Drawing on familiar Rahnerian arguments, this essay insists that for us who are worldly beings, access to God always depends on our worldly interactions.[89] In a draft for a postscript, not

[86] Ibid. 80, *124* (*KRSW*, iv. 148).   [87] Pascal, *Pensées*, iv. 27.
[88] *Hearer of the Word*, 85, *130–1* (*KRSW*, iv. 156).
[89] 'Reflections on the Unity', esp. 244–6, *292–5*. Arguably, Rahner's decision to recycle this essay avoids the Congregation's real challenge, which was also that of liberation theology. No one disputed that faith had to be realized through love; the controversial question was how far such love could or should be informed by social (Marxist?) analysis of ideological, and indeed ecclesiastical, structures.

published with the dossier, he invoked the idea of an irreducible 'duality' in the God–world relationship. The dualities of love of neighbour and love of God, of faith and justice, ultimately reflect,

> the mystery whereby an infinite God co-exists with the finite world—a God who in freedom has willed to exist only as one who establishes the world . . . in the sense that the world is constantly being established by God, so that the duality is itself enclasped in God's unity.[90]

Rahner is radically rejecting a model of holiness which involves transgressing the distinction between creator and creature. The duality is irreducible, and remains under grace. Grace is not the fusion between creator and creature, but the creator's self-communication to a distinct reality.[91]

Following God's Descent

In the 1937 essay, then, Rahner's interpretation of Ignatian *Weltfreudigkeit* depends primarily on a formal metaphysical principle: our existence in space and time is constitutive of who we are as creatures, and conceptions of mysticism which fail to respect that principle are incoherent. The essay's rhetoric, however, stresses more the fact that God is a free, self-giving God. Revelation thus specifies, decisively, the formal truth accessible through metaphysics. We act-following 'God's creative and redemptive descent of God to God's world', and it is on that basis that 'we find God, not just in the divine modeless unfathomability, but in everything'.[92] In Rahner's Ignatian writings, two theological groundings for 'finding God in all things' co-exist. On the one hand, there is a metaphysical argument: only through 'things' can human beings find the metaphysical. On the other, there is the conviction of Christian revelation that God's own self has been identified with the creation. It is time to look at how Rahner puts this latter argument.

[90] 'Konsequenzen und Ergebnisse', 2.
[91] Compare how this principle recurs in Rahner's mature Christology, e.g. *Foundations of Christian Faith*, 202, 202; 292, 285–6 (*KRSW*, xxvi. 195–6, 277–8). Jesus may be, truly, God's own self, but he also exists 'with a created, active, and lived centre of activity vis-à-vis God, and in an absolute difference from God'. To conceive the union of divine and human other than in this radically relational fashion is to fall into docetism.
[92] 1975*b*, 10: '*vollzieht er den schöpferischen und erlösenden Abstieg der Liebe Gottes zu seiner Welt mit, um Gott nicht nur in seiner weiselosen Unbegreiflichkeit allein, sondern in allem zu finden*'.

An important text in this connection is the last of Rahner's 1961 retreat conferences, entitled, simply, 'Love'. In it, he is expounding the Ignatian Contemplation to Gain Love:[93]

Why can we find God in everything? Because *God*—precisely as the eternal glory and vitality that can never be confused with the world—this God as such has made a gift of self to the world. This 'seeking and finding God in all things' is not a philosophical truth, nor a spiritualisation of the mind's simply experiencing its transcendentality through the necessary mediation of the finite and objective (*Gegenständliche*).[94]

In the Word, God has made an absolute and irrevocable commitment of self to the world: God has 'lost himself—in his own reality—as love in his creation, and never turns back from that'.[95] Later in the conference, Rahner invokes the commitment of an Ignatian disciple to specific service, explaining it in terms of God's gracious initiative:

we find God, because God in person, in absolute immediacy, has sought and found us through his Holy Spirit. It is only as a result of this that God gives us this radical relationship to earthly reality in itself. This relationship can rely on the fact that it is dispensed to us by God as the specification of God's holy will. Thus it is that the Ignatian person can be *in actione contemplativus*.[96]

In one striking passage, Rahner reinterprets the traditional formula, *reditio creaturarum in Deum*—the return of creatures to God. If the beatific vision is still to be a human experience, then probably—Rahner is not one to abandon caution—it occurs in and through the incarnation of the Logos; it is hard to see how otherwise we, finite creatures, could be capable of the infinite without simply being consumed. The *eschaton* may be a mystery, but it cannot involve contradiction; its 'unfathomability' must be something we can experience (both *erleben* and *erfahren*):

How can anything like this occur at all? In the last analysis, a minimal condition for this to be possible is that God as such, without ceasing to be God, can make a gift of self to the world. This means, again as a minimal condition, that the Incarnation of the eternal Word amounts to God becoming worldly, God stepping out of Godself as love, the fundamental truth of God's own self, what God's own self actually does, what God's own self can do.[97]

[93] *Exx*, nn. 230–7.   [94] 1961, 273, 296–7.
[95] 1961, 271, 294.   [96] 1961, 276–7, 300.
[97] 1961, 271, 294–5. '*Freilich als des unendlichen Geheimnisses des unbegreiflichen Gottes, aber eben als die Unbegreiflichkeit, als diese Unmittelbarkeit erfahren und erlebt—wieso ist so etwas überhaupt möglich?*'

We may still use the traditional metaphors of ascent, but their real referent must be our 'action-following God's descent into the world'.

Rahner's two retreat conferences on the Ignatian Contemplation to Attain Love both make brief, cryptic allusion to the human person as *imago Trinitatis*. In themselves, these references should probably be taken as throwaway lines: the connections with the Augustinian tradition are not developed, and the allusions may simply have been prompted by Ignatius's reference to memory, understanding and will.[98] Equally, however, the conception of God underlying these conferences is plainly Trinitarian. If creatures can find God in all things, then the structures of human knowing and willing must be reflected in the ontology of the Godhead.

From this vision flows a radical Christian humanism. If a person acts-following God's 'inclination and descent into the finite', they,

can no longer be the person whose innermost torment and desire at once it is to lay bare the relativity and meaninglessness of everything and anything; they can no longer be the person who either idolises or (ultimately) makes a nothing of a distinct finite reality. . . . The love of God, which seems to let the world sink away, is a love for the world. It loves the world with God. Thus in fact it is what enables the world to rise, eternally.[99]

Our responsive love takes the form of service, following Christ's action in the world. It is not, however, that we have to prove our inner attitude through deeds. Rather, our love takes up the move-ment of God's love, moving outwards into the world. Our love sim-ply is 'a service with God in descent to what lies outside, to what is lost, to what is sinful in this world'.[100]

Thus Rahner interprets 'finding God in all things' and 'contem-plative in action' both by invoking formal philosophical arguments about how our knowledge of God depends on the material, and by appealing to New Testament revelation. As his general views on nature and grace might lead us to expect, the two approaches cannot be cleanly separated in his work. There may, however, be a

---

Letzlich kann es mindestens nur darum möglich sein, weil Gott selbst, ohne aufzuhören, Gott zu sein, sich der Welt geben kann, d.h. aber mindestens, weil die Inkarnation des ewigen Logos die Verweltlichung, das Aus-sich-Heraustreten Gottes als Agape, die Grundwahrheit und Wirklichkeit und Möglichkeit Gottes selber ist.'

[98] 1961, 275, *298–9*; 1954/5, 272, *272*; see *Exx*, n. 234.4. The later reference is more fully articulated. For Rahner's complex, innovative position on the so-called psychological ana-logy, see *The Trinity*, 115–20, *393–6*.

[99] 1978*b*, 18, *382*.   [100] 1961, 272–3, *296*.

tension between them, particularly as regards their handling of canonical revelation itself. The metaphysical approach, on its own, leads us to relativize any particular reality: God is always greater. The more theological approach ascribes unconditional value to one set of particulars, namely Jesus Christ and the canonical symbols associated with him.

A text which illustrates the tension is an address given by Rahner to Jesuit students improvising their theological studies in Vienna during the war.[101] Rahner is reflecting on what he sees as the characteristic eclecticism of Jesuit scholarship, its *grundsätzliche Systemlosigkeit*, its refusal to commit itself to any one particular approach. Rahner relates this trait to the characteristic Jesuit spirit, the *Geist* of the order. Though the danger of this spirit is one of heartlessness— 'Is our spirit so to speak the spirit of an SS in the Church?'—it emerges from a reverent wish to avoid idolatry, from a sense of how God is always greater:

It is because the Jesuit knows that his whole life and his every moment has been taken into service by the Divine Majesty of his only Lord, who is always greater than anything that could be thought or accomplished in the finite order, that he keeps this distance, this coolness towards everything.[102]

And yet a few lines later Rahner speaks of an unreserved commitment to the Church and the Eucharist:

Because it has irrevocably pleased this Lord of his to make an earthly body and a Church of human finitude the locus of his grace, the Jesuit thus loves and serves this body as a priest and this Church as an apostle in silent, unconditional loyalty. And this too, when the form of a servant which it takes, and its wretchedness, touch him a thousand times more bitterly than they do all those who want to find God elsewhere—people who complain on account of so many such things, of such humanness, repelled by the knowledge that God is only to be found on the Cross driven right through this world.[103]

There is a tension in Rahner's Ignatian writings between a readiness to find God in all things and what, for Christian tradition, is the

[101] For the background, see Neufeld, *Die Brüder Rahner*, 159–62; ' "Aufhebung" und Weiterleben der theologischen Fakultät Innsbruck', *Zeitschrift für katholische Theologie*, 119 (1997), 27–50.
[102] 'Ansprache zur Bedeutung des Studiums in der Gesellschaft Jesu', 3*a*.
[103] Ibid., 4.

unconditional presence of God in one particular set of places, namely Christian revelation. The two motifs seem to jostle uneasily in a difficult, dense passage in the 1978 testament. God is transcendent, but must also, somehow, remain in the believer's sight:

The nameless, unfathomable, unmanipulable, incalculable God may not, in this process, vanish from the sight of the one praying and acting. God may not become the sun which makes everything visible and itself remains unseen. God must remain in immediacy and must hold everything else fast in its finitude and relativity with—as I would almost like to say—merciless clarity.[104]

The testament, however, fails to resolve the conflict. Von Balthasar once put the underlying point pithily. Ignatian indifference is all very well, but 'who could, on beholding Christ's suffering, remain indifferent towards him?'[105]

A Rahnerian answer might invoke the concept of Christ, not as the one who alone is divine and human, but the one who uniquely guarantees God's self-communication to the whole creation. Thus in 1955, speaking to seminarians in Innsbruck about Ignatian spirituality and the Sacred Heart, Rahner sees the Incarnation as grounding the possibility of our love for what is fragile and fickle:

the ultimate guarantee that such a love is possible occurs when unconditioned, infinite love has accepted something finite in absolute, unsurpassable love, and absolutely identified itself with it. And that of course happened in that God accepted the finitude of Christ's humanity as God's own reality. In that act of love which was the hypostatic union, God accepted the finite centre of a human reality in a way that was so real, so absolute and so unconditional that this reality is God's own for all eternity. This finite reality really participates—in a way that cannot be surpassed— in the absoluteness of God, without its ceasing to be finite in itself; it belongs to God in such a way that one would be relativizing the very reality of God if one's manner of life were such as lovelessly to relativize this reality that God has accepted.[106]

But the promise guaranteed us in Christ is intrinsically linked to the fulfilment, where the divine self-gift is 'all in all'. Christ's uniqueness consists in his being the guarantee of the divine self-communication as it continues over the whole creation. Only in those terms is it

[104]   1978*b*, 18, *382*.
[105]   Hans Urs von Balthasar, *Homo Creatus Est* (Einsiedeln: Johannes, 1986), 272.
[106]   1955, 195–6, *523–4*.

rightly understood. Christ, as one 'thing', or as originator of one set of 'things', guarantees the possibility of finding God 'in all things'.

Further development of this issue must wait until this study moves into a more critical, constructive phase. In this chapter, one further point remains to be noted. Rahner's interpretation of 'finding God in all things' has strong ethical implications. Nadal's 1562 prayer text had already anticipated the point, especially as the Rahner brothers translated it:

One also takes very well from the Exercises, with the Lord's grace, a further very distinctive grace—an understanding and a very delicate feeling for one's own, quite particular vocation, and with this a quite distinctive tranquillity and unity with God, in spiritual obedience and in unremitting journeying along the way which one should take on one's pilgrimage to God.[107]

Karl Rahner's 1937 essay on Ignatian mysticism and world-affirmation stressed that the free working of God's grace must affect the ways in which Christians take decisions. The 1961 conference on love in Ignatius speaks of how God's presence, in the Holy Spirit, to an individual reveals,

a will of God which the individual cannot fully and unambiguously deduce from the objective norms of morality, not even from supernaturally revealed Christian morality.[108]

Through the Exercises, we become able to let God's sovereign will hold sway over us, and thus 'to fall divinely in love, as it were, with the particular things of the world'.[109] For Karl Rahner, Ignatius has a significance, not only for systematic theology (both fundamental and dogmatic), but also for practical theology. This theme we must now explore.

[107] 1935, 403, cf. MHSJ *MN*, iv. 673. Though the Rahners' translation in general stresses the particularity of the call more than the original does, their 'unremitting journeying along the way' is a strange rendering of *particular ejecución del camino*.
[108] 1961, 266, *289*.   [109] 1961, 277, *301*.

5

Transcendence Becoming Thematic

In the early 1940s, Karl Rahner was working with Jesuit seminarians in Vienna. The conditions were difficult, almost clandestine. One November, he preached during Mass for one of the communities, in a Jesuit house located in Am Hof, a Vienna square.[1] It was the feast of St Stanislaus Kotzka. Stanislaus had been a young Polish noble, and an early student at the Jesuit college in Vienna. In 1567, he had expressed his desire to become a Jesuit. Legend has it that the local Jesuits were cautious, and feared his family's reaction. Nothing daunted, he left Vienna and walked to Bavaria, dressed as a beggar. From there he went on to Rome, where he had finally entered the novitiate, only to die within a year.[2] Rahner began by evoking the 'unambiguous decision' Stanislaus made, the responsibility he took for himself:

Stanislaus had to make up his mind alone regarding his way. The decision he took had no-one else to support it—there was no-one else to ask, no-one else onto whom he might have unloaded his responsibility. The people around him were against it. Quite unequivocally against it. The Jesuits, then as now, were very cautious and reserved, and didn't want anything to do with the matter. And of course prudence is a virtue. But not the only one we have to consider . . . (Stanislaus) made his decision against the people around him, against so-called common sense, and despite the caution of the Jesuits regarding the risk he was taking. And he was right.

Stanislaus, Rahner continues, has much to teach the Jesuits of 1942. It will not do simply to be obedient and keep the rules: 'If we no longer feel that, in the end, it is we ourselves who alone are responsible for our lives, and that this responsibility is a serious, indeed *the*

---

[1] 'Homily for St Stanislaus'. No title is given in the manuscript, and the dating is conjectural. In Rahner's appointments diary there is an entry for 18 November 1942: 'Mass with sermon for scholastics—Stanislauskapelle, Vienna'. Stanislaus, however, is normally celebrated on 13 November.

[2] See entry on Stanislaus in Ludwig Koch, *Jesuiten-Lexikon: Die Gesellschaft Jesu einst und jetzt* (Paderborn: Bonifaz, 1934), 1687–8.

serious concern of our lives before God, then we are no true companions of this saint.' The future was ominous. Jesuits had been dis-
charged from the armed forces the year previously, and the threat of
serious persecution from the Nazi regime seemed real.[3] Rahner
reminds them that Stanislaus knew something of how God's wisdom lies hidden in the folly of the Cross. The feast, the place, the
Eucharist—all these should encourage them to pray 'that when the
sacrifice to which we have pledged ourselves touches us in our
hearts, as it must, differently from how we expected it, we can say
yes—as a matter of course, without fuss, and yet in faith and with
gladness'. Stanislaus committed himself to Jesuit community,
despite his negative experience in Vienna. From him, the Jesuits of
1942 can draw courage to stay together in a difficult situation, and
to find the new forms of community which the situation demands.
'Let us look for these ourselves, and not wait for decrees from on
high.'

In this early text, from a setting of insecurity and breakdown that
would be formative for his later career,[4] Rahner names a theme that
would become central to his reading of Ignatius: our experience of
God reveals imperatives to us—imperatives which no other source
can yield. Later, in the mid-1950s, Rahner gave a retreat at the Germanicum, the German-language seminary in Rome. Rahner's
stress on the importance of personal decision clearly struck the seminary's chronicler:

Each of us was clear in his mind that this retreat would be different from
any previous one. It was not Fr Rahner's intention to give Exercises: the
idea was that we should make them—*exercitia spiritualia*, ways of growing
into Christianity (*Einübungen ins Christentum*). There were no shocking or
amusing experiences about life at the ministerial coal-face to interrupt the
intense, compressed, and yet precisely judged philosophical and theological expositions. And in our meditation, we were meant not to go over
the talk again, but rather to begin where he had left off, and to take a
balanced look at reality. In this we were not supposed to run away from
ourselves towards an unsubstantiated ideal, but to make a decision—not

---

[3] For careful interpretation of this emotive, but obscure, situation, see Roman Bleistein,
Augustin Rösch—Leben in Widerstand: Biographie und Dokumente (Frankfurt: Knecht, 1998), 94–6;
Erwin Bücken, ' "Wehrunwürdigkeit" der Jesuiten im zweiten Weltkrieg? Widerlegung
einer hartnäckigen Fehldeutung', *SJ Nachrichten der Norddeutschen Provinz* (1997/4), 129–35.
[4] For suggestive reflections on how the experience of wartime Vienna shaped Rahner's
subsequent theology, see Neufeld, *Die Brüder Rahner*, 172.

to go beyond our strength, but to be modest and realistic. They were good, but also difficult days.[5]

Another witness, who heard both published sets of Rahner's retreat conferences, has similar memories: 'He hammered it into us that *we ourselves* had to work out what it was to be a Jesuit in the twentieth century. We couldn't just carry on, withdrawn into our shells, thinking and regurgitating what had been said and thought before.'[6]

For Rahner, the Exercises were a process of individual decision under God, and he stressed the point in ways which were, for his time, original. Since the 1960s, it has become conventional to interpret Ignatius in these terms, a development fostered also by the rediscovery that Ignatius gave retreats individually.[7] The effect has been that many, especially in the English-speaking world, have abandoned the practice of giving the Exercises through talks addressed to a group. As we have already noted, Rahner came to see his own writings on the *Exercises*—implicitly including his two books of retreat conferences—as theological treatises, rather than Exercises in the proper sense.[8]

Ignatius describes 'spiritual exercises' as any activity designed to free a person from inordinate attachments, enabling one to 'seek and find the divine will in the disposition of one's life for the salvation of the soul'.[9] They are a way of finding out what we should do; they represent an epistemology of practical reason. In the *Exercises* Ignatius sets out three kinds of process for taking a life-decision:

---

[5] *Korrespondenzblatt für die Alumnen des Collegium Germanicum-Hungaricum*, 62 (1955), 126–7, cited in Neufeld, *Die Brüder Rahner*, 219.

[6] Reinhold Iblacker, 'Geistliche Wegweisung—Exerzitien', in Imhof and Biallowons (edd.), *Karl Rahner: Bilder eines Lebens*, 127.

[7] Decisive here was the first volume of Ignacio Iparraguirre's history of the Exercises: *Práctica de los Ejercicios de San Ignacio de Loyola en vida de su autor (1522–1556)* (Rome: Jesuit Historical Institute, 1946). For a provocative historical and geographical survey of twentieth-century practice, see Joseph A. Tetlow, 'The Remarkable Shifts of the Third Transition', *The Way Supplement*, 95 (Summer 1999), 18–30.

[8] 1978c, 175, 32. In 1982, Rahner was invited to give a retreat to seminarians at Tübingen. The correspondence is moving. Having consulted a younger Jesuit, Rahner was hesitant about accepting. 'It has become clear to me how old-fashioned I have become in these things, without being able to change this at my age' (KRA, I. D. 126). Nevertheless, the invitation was pressed, and he noted some time later, that his retreat, given 'the way people did it thirty and forty years ago', had nevertheless gone 'quite well' ('Das Noviziat heute', 10).

[9] *Exx*, n. 1.4.

THREE TIMES FOR MAKING—IN ANY ONE OF THEM—A SOUND AND GOOD ELECTION

The first time is when God our Lord so moves and attracts the will that, without doubting or being able to doubt, such a devout soul follows what is shown; just as St Paul and St Matthew did in following Christ our Lord. *The second*, when enough clarity and knowledge is acquired through the experience of consolations and desolations, and by the experience of discrimination of various spirits. *The third time* is quiet, considering first what the human person is born for, that is, to praise God our Lord and save their soul; and, desiring this, one chooses as a means a life or state within the limits of the Church for the purpose of being helped in the service of one's Lord and the salvation of one's soul. I said 'quiet time'—when the soul is not agitated by various spirits and uses its natural powers freely and peacefully.[10]

On Rahner's interpretation—which, as we shall see, is questionable—the second of these is normative. Regarding the first, Rahner is not entirely consistent: sometimes he presents it as a miraculous exception; at other times, he sees it as an accelerated variant of the second.[11] The third, claims Rahner, is a deficient form of the process. For Rahner, the *Exercises* are informed by a sense that obligations under God need not consist simply in the application of general principles, whether of secular ethics or of divine revelation. As we have seen, Rahner contrasted 'the immediate experience of God' with the inferential knowledge of God that follows—on his Thomist presuppositions—from the experience of a created reality. This contrast carries through into the practical sphere. Christian practical reasoning involves more than a reverent readiness to do God's will as manifest through the sheer fact of creation. God is present, not merely as creator, but also as self-giver—a distinction which can imply a difference in our obligations. Moreover, God's gracious presence differs between individuals: hence the consequences of God's grace for our practice cannot simply be deduced.

Rahner thus took issue with what he took to be the received view

---

[10] *Exx*, nn. 175–7. *Discreción*—here rendered as 'discrimination'—is more conventionally translated as 'discernment'.

[11] The former interpretation fits most naturally into the position Rahner put forward in 1956a (see e.g., 159, *138–9*). However, even in that essay, there are hints also of the latter view (1956a, 105, *92*), and after receiving Peter Knauer's 1959 letter criticizing his reading of 'consolation without preceding cause', Rahner may have, more or less consciously, adopted it definitively (1969, 293, *247*; 1976, pp. xvi–xvii). For further discussion, see Chapter 7 and the Appendix.

about prayer and ethics, namely, that it was some kind of illuminist or modernist mistake to look for particular ethical imperatives or inspirations from God. For Rahner, it shows a misunderstanding of Ignatius,

> if one tries to start from the assumption that the only real point is whether something is good or bad, and that the further question of 'how' it arose is fundamentally unimportant—and that there is no need to rack one's brains over whether it came directly from God or not, on the ground that in the end everything good comes from God, whether directly or indirectly. Such views and interpretations, which can not infrequently be met with in the standard tradition and interpretations of the Exercises, are diametrically opposed to the conception of St Ignatius. For him the whole point is that one *only* knows whether an impulse is good when one has determined its source.[12]

In the Ignatian Exercises, therefore, Rahner saw a process of discovery essential to Christian discipleship. To summarize it in anticipation: the self can be led to focus on its 'transcendence', and the basic features of consciousness which are normally just the tacit accompaniments and enabling conditions of particular mental acts can become 'thematic'. The Exercises foster such moments. The effect can be to transform our reflective self-understanding, and the patterns of significance and value that shape our perceptions—a transformation with practical consequences.

Rahner saw this theology as challenging conventional approaches to at least three sets of issues: the nature of judgements about priestly and religious vocation; the role of natural law in ethics; and the dynamics of the decision to believe in Christianity in the first place. In the first part of this chapter, we will look at these issues in turn. Then we will move on to Rahner's account of how Ignatius's process worked. We find different approaches not explicitly connected: one is strongly Christological, while others are couched in more metaphysical idioms.

Lahitton, Hürth, and the Theology of Vocation

Like his claim that grace is an experienced reality, Rahner's theology of Ignatian choice arises partly in reaction against what he

---

[12] 1956a, 118, *113.*

himself had been taught at Valkenburg, this time by Franz Hürth
(1880–1963), professor of moral theology.[13] Hürth appears to have
taught a position attributed to Joseph Lahitton's *La vocation sacerdotale: traité théologique et pratique*, a book first published in 1909.[14]
Lahitton had attacked the view—which he took to be standard at
the time—that the theological nature of vocation rested in an 'attraction' (*attrait*): 'a supernatural, spontaneous, and steady inclination
towards ecclesiastical functions, i.e. liturgical prayer, the ceremonies
of worship, the care of souls'.[15] Such concentration on inner
dispositions, claimed Lahitton, was misplaced. It was the call from
ecclesial authority that constituted priestly vocation: 'The call of a
person to the priesthood by the legitimate ministers of the Church
does not presuppose the presence of a vocation in the person concerned, because this very call itself creates the vocation within
him.'[16] The bishop simply had to find suitable qualities within the
candidate—*vocabilité, idonéité*, or *vocatio in potentia*—and their free
assent. Moreover, though these might be necessary conditions for
vocation, they were not identical with it.[17] Lahitton's book provoked
serious controversy, for reasons which are now obscure,[18] and the
matter was referred to the Vatican. Pius X set up a commission of
cardinals to investigate the book, and, in July 1912, the Secretary of

---

[13] See Neufeld, *Die Brüder Rahner*, 97. The anecdotes given there, and in Vorgrimler, *Understanding Karl Rahner*, 136, indicate considerable conflict between Hürth and Rahner. See also
extensive obituaries on Hürth in *Mitteilungen der deutschen Provinzen der Gesellschaft Jesu*, 20
(1964), 445–52, and *Periodica de re morali canonica liturgica*, 52 (1963), 411–16.

[14] Citations from this work come from the first edition (Paris: Lethielleux, 1909). A second
edition (Paris: Beauchesne, 1913), which Rahner cites (1956*a*, 98–9, *86*), involved a total
reworking, and the book ultimately went into a seventh edition (1931). Some sense of the controversy's bizarre quality can be gained from the prefaces to the second and sixth editions.
For further information, see entries in the *Dictionnaire de théologie catholique*: L. Sempé, 'Vocation', xv. 3148–81, esp. 3168–71, and 'Lahitton, Joseph', Tables Générales, 2586–7; A. Bride,
'Lahitton, Joseph', in *Catholicisme: hier aujourd'hui demain* (Paris: Letouzey et Amé, 1948–),
v. 1626; Josef Brandenburger, 'Vocatio sacerdotalis: Eine Kontroverse', *Zeitschrift für kathol-
ische Theologie*, 38 (1914), 63–74; Hans Urs von Balthasar, *The Christian State of Life*, trans. Mary
Frances McCarthy (San Francisco: Ignatius, 1983), 442–8; Friedrich Wulf, 'Kriterien der
Eignung: Ein geschichtlicher Überblick', in Hermann Stenger (ed.), *Eignung für die Berufe der
Kirche: Klärung—Beratung—Begleitung* (Freiburg: Herder, 1988), 11–30.

[15] Sempé, 'Vocation' (as n. 14 above), 3170. Sempé links this approach to the Sulpicians,
who nevertheless did not press the dogmatic issue in the way Lahitton himself did.

[16] Lahitton, *La vocation sacerdotale*, 31–3.   [17] Ibid., 34–8.

[18] Brandenburger, 'Vocatio sacerdotalis', 65: 'Lahitton's narrow and curt presentation,
some weaknesses in his argumentation, and the alleged affinity between his opponents and
Modernism, Quietism, Illuminism, Protestantism, and fanaticism etc. aroused deep antagon-
ism and intense opposition.'

State wrote to Lahitton's bishop, conveying the commission's verdict. While not endorsing Lahitton totally, this verdict did support his major contentions.[19]

Rahner presents Lahitton as denying that a person could receive some kind of individual call from God, and claiming instead that everything in the spiritual life reduced to general principles. Thus Lahitton is an authority against whom Rahner, in the 1950s, reacts.[20] In 1959, setting out for a Jesuit audience the ethical implications of Ignatius's process, Rahner comments:

> It is just not true to say that everything can be deduced rationally, as it were. It is not true that the individual, in his or her distinctiveness, in his or her decision, is simply the particular case of general abstract principles. These are difficult and obscure questions—how much so, you can see from the fact that Fr Hürth in Valkenburg used to teach us as something self-evident—didn't he—that Lahitton's opinion about priests (i.e. the recognition of a priestly vocation) was right.[21]

In fairness, we should note that Lahitton's direct concern was narrower than Rahner, fifty years later, implies. In the first edition of his book, Lahitton had explicitly denied that his arguments applied to other vocations, such as that to consecrated life: 'This little treatise speaks only of the *priestly* vocation. One would be wrong in extending the principles here set forward to other vocations. With regard to religious profession, one is free to think that a divine call is

---

[19] *Acta Apostolicae Sedis*, 4 (1912), 485, quoted in Balthasar, *The Christian State of Life*, 443–4. Lahitton's arguments are more than a historical curiosity. Thomas O'Loughlin, in 'Eucharist or Communion Service?', *The Way*, 38 (1998), 365–74, invokes similar principles in reflecting on the contemporary perceived shortage of Roman Catholic priests: 'finding suitable men to celebrate the eucharist is not a matter of an individual's sense of his personal calling, but an objective decision of the Church to find those most suited to the task, call on them, and appoint them . . . If we have a group of Christians in a place, we must trust that the Spirit has provided one of them with what it needs to preside at the eucharist. It is the Church's task to find this individual and empower him' (p. 372).

[20] Beside the long footnote in 1956a (98–100, *86–7*), in which Rahner exercises his ingenuity to reconcile his own position with what he takes to be the official sanction of Lahitton's theory, and the 1959 passage cited above, see 'On the Question of a Formal Existential Ethics', 233, *244*. There are also two much later references: 'Das Noviziat heute', 20 (though the transcriber failed to understand Rahner's allusion), and 'Bin ich berufen?', 42–4.

[21] 1959, 42, *48–9*—though I quote here, with tacit corrections, from the original transcript of the tape recording (p. 26), in order to incorporate the biographical point about Hürth. See Hurth's unpublished codex, *Theologia moralis de sacramentis*, 1926/7, n. 633. Rahner's copy of this work has survived (KRA, IV. A. 6); below the relevant passage we find an enigmatic doodle.

necessary, or that one can be carried by one's own choice.'[22] More-over, Lahitton's claim was about canon law rather than the theo-logical interpretation of human experience. Neither Lahitton nor Pius X's cardinals were denying that some kind of call-experience was normal in candidates for the priesthood; their concern was simply to deny that such a reality should be thought of as constitu-tive of vocation, and as a constraint on the bishop's authority.[23]

Rahner's real concern was not with what Lahitton had actually said, but with the mythology he had generated. In Rahner's per-ception at least, the Lahitton controversy had led to a consensus that charismatic conviction was marginal, if not irrelevant, to ques-tions of vocational assessment:

> A French theologian, Lahitton, had defended the view that the only things required for sureness about God having willed a particular vocation for a particular person were, firstly, a genuine suitability for such a vocation, and, secondly, the person's free choice informed by motives appropriate to the vocation. If both these things were there, then there was no need to wait for a special inspiration from above, coming down for the purpose.[24]

Against this view, Rahner was concerned to insist that some kind of divine illumination was a normal feature of vocational choice. Such choice could not be reduced, either to an arbitrary choice between equally permissible alternatives, or to obedience to authority. Moreover, God's action in an individual's experience could, indeed should, affect the choice they made.

The Wisdom Behind 'Situation Ethics'

On Rahner's reading, however, Ignatius's process is of relevance to a far wider range of decisions than those connected with priestly or religious vocation. The epistemology of Christian practical reason

[22] Lahitton, *La vocation sacerdotale*, 1. In the second edition, however, Lahitton blurs the issue: 'This work, as the title indicates, has as its main concern the priestly vocation. No doubt it would not be difficult to find in it general principles applying just as well to other states of life, and, more particularly, to religious profession. Nevertheless, the plan here has been to speak directly of the priestly vocation.' Cf. Franz Hürth, 'Zur Frage nach dem Wesen des Berufes', *Scholastik*, 3 (1928), 94–102, here 100: 'the essential content of the Roman decision of . . . 1912 can and must be applied to the religious vocation, even if this content concerns itself directly only with the priestly vocation'.

[23] Hürth, 'Zur Frage', 101–2.   [24] 'Bin ich berufen?', 42.

implicit in the *Exercises* applies to moral theology generally. Rahner's advocacy of this claim feeds into discussions about what was then called 'situation ethics'.[25] For Rahner, a situation ethics was a moral theory denying the binding force of general norms. Duty was to be considered exclusively as an answer to,

> the call of the always unique situation, in which the human person must defend themselves at the bar either of the inalienable judgment which is their own personal decision, or at the bar of God, whose direct presence in the situation, in conscience, and in faith, cannot be thought of as mediated through a general law.[26]

The historical development of the term 'situation ethics' is far from clear.[27] Pius XII expressed himself on the matter in two addresses given in 1952; more formally, the Holy Office in 1956 issued an instruction forbidding the teaching or praising of the 'new morality' or 'ethics of situation'. The target is not precisely defined, but it is clear that the Holy Office was against any theory giving significant weight to a 'direct interior enlightenment' within the individual, and denying the decisive role of general principles of natural law.[28] The instruction implies that a naturalist ethics—one which,

---

[25] The primary materials most directly relevant here are 'The Appeal to Conscience'; 'On the Question of a Formal Existential Ethics'; 'Principles and Prescriptions' (better translated as 'Principles and Imperatives'); the introduction to *The Dynamic Element in the Church*, 7–12, *9–13*; 'Der Anspruch Gottes und der Einzelne'; 'Situation Ethics in an Ecumenical Perspective'. For a useful introductory summary and critique, see Donal J. Dorr, 'Karl Rahner's "Formal Existential Ethics"', *Irish Theological Quarterly*, 36 (1969), 211–29; for a more exhaustive Germanic account, see Ludwig Sanhüter, *Das Dynamische in der Moral: Zur Aktualität der Existentialethik Karl Rahners* (St Ottilien: EOS, 1990). Bernard Fraling, a doctoral student of Rahner's, shows the relevance of Rahner's theory to more recent issues in moral theology in 'Existentialethik—spirituelle Mitte der Moraltheologie', *Geist und Leben*, 70 (1997), 12–27.

[26] 'On the Question of a Formal Existential Ethics', 218, *228*. See also *Concise Theological Dictionary*, 478–9, *385–6*.

[27] Rahner professes ignorance at the beginning of 'On the Question of a Formal Existential Ethics'. Waldemar Molinski, 'Situation Ethics', *SM*, vi. 94–8, begins by attributing the term to Theodor Steinbüchel, citing in the bibliography a work dating from 1938. Note that the (German) Roman Catholic pejorative use of the term antedates considerably Joseph Fletcher, *Situation Ethics: Beyond the New Morality* (London: SCM Press, 1966), which popularized the idea in the English-speaking world. Often used as a smear-word, the term covers a diversity of positions. For a brief, lucid analysis, see James M. Childress, 'Situation Ethics', in Macquarrie and Childress (edd.), *A New Dictionary of Christian Ethics*, 586–8.

[28] *Acta Apostolicae Sedis*, 48 (1956), 144–5; see also 44 (1952), 270–1, 413–19. Coincidentally, it was Franz Hürth who was probably responsible for drafting this material. By this stage, he was a consultor to the Holy Office on moral matters, and six weeks after its being issued he published a long commentary on it in a Roman academic journal: 'De ethica situationis', *Periodica de re morali canonica liturgica*, 45 (1956), 137–204.

directly or indirectly, derives 'ought' from 'is'—must necessarily be an ethics of natural law, an ethics exclusively of general principles. The 'right objective order' is 'derived from the natural law', and to deny the latter is to deny the former.[29]

But what, Rahner asks, if there is a dimension of 'nature', of 'objective reality', unique to individuals or to particular groups? Then, a corresponding naturalist ethics has itself to be 'existential' or individual, not dependent exclusively on general laws and syllogistic reasoning: 'God is interested in history, not only in so far as it is the putting into practice of norms, but also in so far as it is an unrepeatable unity, and precisely thus of significance for salvation.'[30] A naturalistic ethics may involve more than natural law. The duties and obligations laid upon us by the way things are cannot always be established deductively. We also need an individual, intuitive procedure. An ethics of essences must be complemented by what Rahner called an 'existential ethics', addressed to the specific individual:

> There is a summons of God which cannot be reduced to any other terms, and which is individual. It cannot be regarded simply as the sum and the application of general material principles of ethics and Christian morality. And this irreducible, individual summons of God is not only a call to something within the bounds of what is possible and permissible as a general principle. It can be—admittedly not always, but, in certain circumstances, nevertheless quite absolutely—a summons to something significant for salvation, both personally and collectively, a call to an ought entailing a genuinely strict obligation.[31]

Ignatius is important for moral theology because he gives us, in the *Exercises*, a systematic process for discovering such obligations. Moreover, though Rahner's idiom is often individualist, such existential obligations can apply to groups as well; in 1974 Rahner wrote at some length on how the moral epistemology he found in Ignatius could be used collectively.[32]

[29] From the instruction: '*Auctores qui hoc systema sequuntur decisivam et ultimam agendi normam statuunt non esse ordinem obiectivum rectum, naturae lege determinatum et ex hac lege certo cognitum, sed intimum aliquod mentis uniuscuiusque individui iudicium ac lumen, quo ei in concreta situatione posito innotescit quid sibi agendum sit.*' For brief and helpful orientation on the philosophical issues, see John Langan, 'Metaethics', in Macquarrie and Childress (edd.), *A New Dictionary of Christian Ethics*, 382.
[30] 'On the Question of a Formal Existential Ethics', 228, 239.
[31] 'Der Anspruch Gottes und der Einzelne', 536.
[32] 'Principles and Prescriptions', 22, 21–2; 'Der Anspruch Gottes und der Einzelne', 534; 1974a. Another rich Ignatian source for communal discernment is the *Constitutions*: see my 'The Draughthorse's Bloodlines', and other articles in *The Way Supplement*, 85 (Spring 1996).

Rahner suggests two kinds of reasons why an existential ethics is necessary. One approach depends on metaphysics, technically and cryptically expressed: human beings are not simply instances of a general kind, as a Thomist or Suarezian ontology would suggest, but individuals uniquely sustained by God. Moreover, even if this claim could not be justified, it would still be the case that every human being has a unique history, and hence that the application of universal laws would involve individual judgements.[33]

A second approach is more empirical. Common sense tells us that the moral life involves more than a purely deductive approach. Any application of principle must be grounded in more informal, intuitive reasoning:

all reflection which seeks to offer grounds for a decision is itself conducted within a given horizon of understanding and under the influence of selective patterns of salience. Attempting such reflection is obviously legitimate and partial success is always possible. But nevertheless it depends on psychological, historical, cultural and social conditions that cannot themselves be critically appraised in the same kind of reflective way without our falling into infinite regress.[34]

Rahner also appeals to everyday experience. We often have to take crucially important decisions where no general rule will guide us. A career choice, for example, 'is of the greatest importance for individuals and their salvation', yet it would be unthinkable for the Church to impose any such choice on a person. Within social ethics, too, the Church rightly claims no direct competence in adjudicating complex situations. 'Yet the choice between . . . several alternatives cannot be dismissed as indifferent and unimportant, for on just this choice, which the Church declares beyond its own competence, everything may depend historically, the rise or fall of a nation or a civilization.'[35]

If morality were just the following of rules, it would follow that many decisions, felt by the individuals concerned to be of the highest existential significance, were in fact not ethical at all. In the 1978

[33] 'Principles and Prescriptions', 16–18, *17–18*; 1956a, 109–14, *96–100*. For an exegetical discussion of Ignatius's implicit understanding of individual cases and general laws, crystallized in his concept of *discreta caridad* (*Const*, VI. iii. 1 [582.4]), see Antonio M. de Aldama, *The Constitutions of the Society of Jesus Part VI: Jesuit Religious Life*, ed. and trans. Ignacio Echániz (Anand: Gujarat Sahitya Prakash, 1994), 81–6.
[34] 1972, 160, *202–3*.   [35] 'Principles and Prescriptions', 25–6, *24–5*.

testament, Rahner's Ignatius denounces this view as absurd: 'it would be crazy just to say that everything in reality—just because it is real and originates in God—must offer equal access to God for every human individual. For then no decision of our freedom, even unavoidable ones, would have any special significance.'[36] The idiom here brings out how Rahner's ethical claims are linked to his theology of grace, alluding as it does to Rahner's distinction between two modes of God's presence to creatures: a creating presence through instrumental causality, and a self-giving presence through formal causality. According to Rahner, Ignatius's prime concern is with divine promptings in consciousness grounded on the latter.

Moreover, an ethics based solely on general principles will lead to moral inertia, a reactionary existence tacitly supporting the *status quo*, avoiding change by invoking endless ifs and buts. But 'it is perfectly possible for something to be completely in conformity with the Church's principles, and with general considerations, or at any rate for it not to be demonstrably wrong on that basis, and yet for that same thing here and now nevertheless to be in fact wrong'. The example Rahner then takes is the lack of progress in the ecumenical movement: as long as one has to proceed from general principles, nothing will happen, because one can always say, ' "Of course we must obviously do something about reunion, but then we must also take this and that into account", and so on *ad infinitum* . . . both sides carry on talking, without anything serious and radical, anything which requires courage, in the end happening.'[37] Rahner invokes a similar argument when expressing his misgivings about how Catholic priests, including himself, behaved during the Third Reich:

Think back to the time of the Third Reich. I think there were relatively few priests whom you can really prove to have clearly transgressed moral principles in their dealings with the ideology prevailing at the time, with the persecuted Jews etc. But can you then say with equal clarity that we all always really did the right thing (and I don't except myself here)? That much is certainly not clear to me.[38]

Rahner did not work out fully the relationship between essential and existential ethics, nor that between the two different reasoning

---

[36] 1978*b*, 17*, *381.*   [37] 'Der Anspruch Gottes und der Einzelne', 534–5.
[38] Ibid., 531.

processes of deduction from principles and Ignatian discernment. It is unclear whether he sees his 'existential' ethics as a dimension of every decision we have to take (albeit one that is often only implicit), or whether there remain some decisions which principles alone can settle. Out of an understandable defensiveness with regard to Church authority, Rahner tends to write as if he holds the latter. But if the decision as to *which* principle(s) should apply in a situation is one that cannot itself be made through recourse to a principle, then it follows that there is an intuitive, spiritual aspect to *any* Christian moral decision.[39] Moreover, when Rahner wrote directly on the natural law, he implied a much more nuanced conception than the one he presupposes in the essays on existential ethics.[40]

Within Roman Catholic moral theology the underlying issue remains controversial, and survives as the debate between proportionalists and upholders of exceptionless moral norms.[41] Rahner in no way offers a solution; but he does insist that a purely syllogistic ethics is inadequate. He also at least gestures towards an alternative, even if it remains unclear whether he is seeking to refine natural-law ethics or to provide some kind of independent supplement to it. Finally, he points to the importance of Ignatius's *Exercises* for Christian moral epistemology.

Faith and Rationality

What the *Exercises* imply about Christian practical reasoning has, however, still broader relevance. Ignatius's process, Rahner believes, illustrates how we can responsibly commit ourselves to Christian revelation.

[39] 1956a, 111, 97; 'On the Question of a Formal Existential Ethics', 225, 235.

[40] See 'Naturrecht IV: Heutige Aufgaben hinsichtlich des Naturrechts'; and the first part of Rahner's article reviewing Josef Fuchs's influential book on Natural Law, 'Bemerkungen über das Naturgesetz und seine Erkennbarkeit'. A helpful discussion of these issues in Rahner's theology can be found in James F. Bresnahan, 'Rahner's Ethics: Critical Natural Law in Relation to Contemporary Ethical Methodology', *Journal of Religion*, 56 (1976), 36–60. Contemporary scholarship has developed considerably Rahner's attempts to link ethics and spirituality, and in doing so discovered a far more nuanced approach to principles and situations in Aristotle and Aquinas than was ever suspected in the conventional theology attacked by Rahner. See, for example, Hughes, 'Ignatian Discernment'; Jean Porter, 'Virtue Ethics and its Significance for Spirituality', *The Way Supplement*, 88 (Spring 1997), 26–45.

[41] For an overview of the conflict, see Bernard Hoose, *Proportionalism: The American Debate and its European Roots* (Washington: Georgetown University Press, 1987).

Before the 1960s, Rahner seems to have left this idea implicit in his Ignatian writings. Only rarely does it surface, and without being developed. In his first set of retreat conferences, for example, Rahner has a throwaway line about how Ignatian choice is central to the proper understanding of God. Commenting on Ignatius's Principle and Foundation, a bald statement about God and humanity placed near the beginning of the *Exercises*, Rahner says: 'the Christian understanding of God—the theme of this meditation—is essentially tied up with what one *does* (*ist wesentlich "praktisch"*). It calls upon us to decide for or against this God—and, moreover, one can only attain such an understanding in and through decision.'[42]

Later, Rahner became more explicit. Two texts are particularly important here: his 1972 essay on the Exercises and fundamental theology, and a passage from a 1968 address on how Jesuits should come to terms with changes in Roman Catholic ecclesiology. The immediate context of the talk was the publication of Paul VI's highly controversial encyclical, *Humanae vitae*. Rahner begins by rehearsing his standard positions on the individual within the Church, and on Ignatian vocational discernment. Then he becomes more radical:

> The reason for citing all this here is as follows. The fundamental decision which a human person makes for Jesus Christ, for discipleship of Jesus, and for the Church must fundamentally, if it is to be genuine and unconditional in the way that it should, occur through the method of existential logic that Ignatius teaches us. His teaching is in fact in no way restricted to those objects of choice initially envisaged in the *Exercises*, to what one imagines when those charged with spiritual formation give instructions for the spiritual life in the narrower sense of the word.[43]

Ignatian spirituality touches a classical problem of fundamental theology: the so-called *analysis fidei*. How does one bridge the gap between the absoluteness of Christian commitment, and what is at best only a conditional certainty regarding the rational arguments for it? How can we honestly acknowledge that the arguments for commitment fall short of deductive certainty without reducing commitment to some form of irrational arbitrariness? If fundamental theology is to reflect on the decision of faith itself, and not just on the rational presuppositions for such a decision, then, says Rahner,

---

[42] 1954/5, 15, *19*.   [43] 1968, 18.

it must be prepared to apply something like the Ignatian epistemology of existential decision to such historical realities as Jesus and the Church. 'For, in the case of these specifically Christian realities, we are dealing with concrete historical realities which cannot be fully traced back to transcendentally necessary principles, and to which nevertheless freedom is meant to entrust itself, unconditionally.'[44] According to Rahner, Jesuits have often not only misunderstood and misapplied Ignatius's logic even when giving the Exercises; they have also 'practically totally overlooked its significance for Christianity as a whole'. If faith is to be more than the mere repetition of inherited habit, it must occur,

in that experience of the Spirit in immediacy to God which Ignatius describes in the *Exercises*, in that experience in which the contingent, historical object of choice is taken up into a mysterious union with God, without the object's obscuring that infinitely free immediacy to the mystery beyond speech which is called God.[45]

The commitment of faith presupposes that something like this experience has taken place, at least unreflectively and diffusely, with regard to the historical realities of Jesus and the Church. Thus it is that Rahner's 1974 Christmas homily can invoke the experience of Ignatian choice as a source of insight into the Incarnation: conversely, in 1978, Rahner's Ignatius describes the experience of choice as that of 'God's "taking flesh" in his creature'.[46] Again, in the *Entschluß* article of the same year, Rahner could speculate that a theology of the Exercises might illuminate a problem simply ignored—as he saw it—in standard fundamental theology: the psychological structure of canonical revelation. The manuals were content to talk of confirmation by external miracles:

How it is with the revelation-bearer themselves—whether they too know something of the divine causality of their inner ideas (which they feel as revelation) only through the external miracles that accompany their psychological experiences, or whether the original revelation-bearer becomes aware of the divine causality of these inner ideas in a quite different way—this is in fact hardly thought about in today's average fundamental theology.

Yet Ignatius presupposes that God can touch the human person even without there being an external miracle, enabling us to

---

[44] 1968, 19.   [45] 1968, 19.   [46] 1974*c*; 1978*b*, 18, *381*.

recognize 'maxims present within as the genuine, true will of God'.[47] Finally, a short piece on the *Exercises* published in 1974 contains the following bold statement:

> Only by admitting, and not repressing, a concrete question regarding his or her concrete existence, only by accepting this in a free and responsible act—only so can what is really meant when people say 'God', 'sin', 'grace', 'forgiveness', 'Christ', 'Christian discipleship', and 'cross', come home to a person in a way that touches them.[48]

Clearly these late texts need clarification. But even to quote them fills out what Karl Rahner had written to mark Hugo Rahner's sixty-fifth birthday in 1965. Ignatius was not just a holy man: rather, 'with him, a new theology begins to be lived out, and the task of articulating this theology reflectively has not yet really been tackled. And the success of this enterprise will be a very substantial factor among those deciding the fate of future Catholic theology.'[49]

The Varieties of Transcendental Experience

So far, we have surveyed a range of issues which, for Rahner, this 'new theology', unreflectively lived out by Ignatius, could clarify. We need now to explore how this 'new theology' works. For Rahner, Ignatian decision occurs in a kind of synthesis or harmony between the imagined object of choice—a particular vocation, a course of action, membership of the Christian Church—and a particular privileged moment in experience. In 1956, Rahner describes the second model, or 'time', of Ignatian choice as,

> the time of experiment, of *experiencia* in the root sense, the time of experiential testing how an initial decision, taken provisionally, matches the fundamental directedness of the mind—a directedness which has become a focus of awareness, and which exists otherwise either as only a tacit

[47] 1978*d*, 11–12: a more pious translation of '*innerlich gegebenen Maximen*' could be defended. This piece is, as we have already seen, a uniquely valuable source for Rahner's understanding of Ignatius, but its disjointed, table-talk quality also makes it hazardous to build too much on it. In 1956*a*, Rahner gives conflicting indications of how he sees the relationship between the Ignatian choice and canonical revelation: towards the end (p. 159, *138–9*) he insists on the disjunction, but earlier (p. 129, *112–13*) he speculates on a structural similarity. The unclarity here is linked to that surrounding Rahner's understanding of the first Ignatian 'time'.
[48] 1974*b*, 102, *99*.   [49] 'Ein brüderlicher Geburtstagsbrief', 72.

condition enabling dealings with the individual realities of life and of the world around, or else merely as a reflected object of theoretical thought (in sentences which have become generally applicable).[50]

The self focuses on its 'transcendence'; transcendence becomes 'thematic'.

In Rahner's thought, the concept of 'transcendence' takes on different nuances and connotations, depending on the different ways in which he situated himself, at various points in his career, in the hinterland between philosophy and theology.[51] When Rahner is writing more philosophically, 'transcendence' refers to what must be present for human knowing and willing to exist *at all*, in any possible world, or in a world of *natura pura*. When he is writing more theologically, 'transcendence' refers to conditions present within the self in the actually existing, graced world. It is this latter sense that is operative when Rahner interprets Ignatian discernment as dependent on moments of 'transcendence becoming thematic'. An alternative jargon might speak of identity, of the subjective conditions which shape our every mental and physical act, and of moments when it is this identity itself, rather than any object outside the self, on which our awareness focuses. Such moments may transform the patterns of significance and value we find in the external world, and thus lead to particular choices. A biblical model comes in the parable of the prodigal son. In his pigsty, he 'came to himself' (Luke 15: 17), and took a decision accordingly.

Rahnerian transcendence—which we might therefore gloss as human identity under God's grace—is pluralist. Even if we assume that Christian theology must be ascribed a defining role in any account of it, it remains the case that each of us is called to a different quality of intimacy with God, and each of us moves within God's grace to our goal along a meandering path. 'The essential nature' (*Wesenheit*) of the basic Ignatian experience can 'adapt itself in different—and ever higher and existentially deeper—ways'.[52] Moreover, this process of growth is a complex one, and a full Christian theological account of it would integrate various aspects.

[50] 1956*a*, 161–2, *140–1*: '*wie sich ein hypothetisch einmal angenommener Einzelentschluß verträgt mit der thematisch gewordenen Grundrichtung des Geistes, die sonst entweder nur als unthematische Bedingung der Möglichkeit der Befaßtheit mit den Einzelwirklichkeiten des Lebens und der Umwelt oder als bloß in reflexer Vergegenständlichung (in den allgemein gewordenen Sätzen) des begrifflichen Denkens gegeben ist*'.

[51] See Nikolaus Knoepffler, *Der Begriff 'transzendental' bei Karl Rahner: Zur Frage seiner Kantischen Herkunft* (Innsbruck: Tyrolia, 1993), esp. pp. 177–8. [52] 1956*a*, 151, *131*.

Towards the end of his 1956 essay on Ignatian discernment, Rahner begins to speculate how anonymous Christians might be anonymous Ignatian discerners, invoking the principle that people often make good moral decisions without being reflectively aware of all the relevant factors.[53] The principle applies to his own accounts as well. In Rahner's Ignatian writings, there are accounts of the process building on three particular aspects: Christology, general metaphysics, and grace.[54] Though these must somehow cohere,[55] Rahner does not spell out the connections between them. Later chapters of this study will explore such connections; the task remaining for this chapter is to look in turn at these three approaches.

Following after Christ

In Rahner's first set of published retreat-conferences dating from 1954/5, he presents the Ignatian choice in Christological terms.[56] The key text in this connection is what appeared in the published version as the thirteenth chapter: *Nachfolge Christi*, 'Following after Christ'.[57]

Rahner begins by drawing an inference from the Christmas kerygma: 'the most central feature in the world's constitution is that of being the "surroundings", the "life-space" for the God who, in person, becomes world'. It follows that, ultimately, human beings exist only so as to make possible for God 'this adventure of love for what lies outside'. This enabling occurs through their lives and existence being 'shared with the Word made human':

---

[53] 1956a, 165, *143–4*.

[54] 1974b, 101, *97*, describes the key Ignatian moment as one of *metanoia*. Given Rahner's early interest in the theology of penance, the connection is suggestive; but Rahner did not explicitly develop it.

[55] In the foreword to the published version of 1954/5 (8–9, *12–13*), Rahner reminds us that its account of Ignatian choice must be complemented by 1956a.

[56] It may be significant that this talk, which is our only source for key elements in Rahner's understanding of Ignatius, was given with 'no written notes', and that its preservation is due only to the industry of transcribers among the audiences (1954/5, 7, *11*).

[57] The later 1961 conferences were given as an immediate preparation for ordination. Hence Rahner presumes that the major decision has already been irrevocably taken, and focuses more on issues connected with priestly life (1961, 64, *76–7*). For general background to the ideas expounded here, see Gerd Lohaus, 'Die Lebensereignisse Jesu in der Christologie Karl Rahners', *Theologie und Philosophie*, 65 (1990), 349–86.

For this purpose, God really does need humanity, because the finite human person, such as God became, is essentially oriented to his or her other, his or her human companions. Therefore, the whole human race is in this sense centred, from the beginning, on the Son of Man, in so far as he is the core of its meaning. From the beginning, the human race is the 'filling out (*pleroma*) of Christ'.[58]

Human being is realized in relationship, and therefore what we believe about Christ affects our understanding of the whole human race. The world belongs to God, not just because God created it, but also because the realities of creation constitute 'God's substantial specification (*substantielle Bestimmung*), God's own environment'.[59] Rahner here echoes Barth's Christological account of humanity and creation: 'because this One is also human, they too, every human being in their place and time, are changed, i.e. they are people other than who they would have been if this One had not been human too. It belongs to their human essence that Jesus too is human, and that in Him they have a human neighbour, companion, and brother.'[60]

Given, further, a naturalist approach to morality, it follows that Christ is a distinctive and indispensable source of practical wisdom.[61] The Christian life cannot consist merely in following principles that could be established independently of Jesus. It must involve 'an actively participative resonance with *his* life, and thereby with the life within the Godhead with which we are gifted'.[62]

Christ's call specifies our nature, however hard it is to articulate this point philosophically.[63] This vision is nevertheless pluralist. Some people can name Christ, others not; acceptance and rejection of the reality he represents lie on a spectrum. One can be an anonymous Christian or an ecclesiastical apostate.[64] But there is an

[58] 1954/5, 114, *117*.   [59] 'The Theology of the Symbol', 239, *237*.

[60] Karl Barth, *Church Dogmatics*, III/ii, trans. H. Knight et al. (Edinburgh: T. and T. Clark, 1960 [orig. 1st. pub. 1948]), 133.

[61] See Engelbert Guggenberger, *Karl Rahners Christologie und heutige Fundamentalmoral* (Innsbruck: Tyrolia, 1990) for a use of Rahner's theology to mediate problems regarding natural law and the distinctiveness of Christian ethics: also Brian F. Linnane, 'Rahnerian Christology as an Anthropological Foundation for a Theocentric Ethic', Ph.D. thesis (Yale University, 1994).

[62] 1954/5, 118, *121*: '*das mitvollziehende Einschwingen in gerade sein Leben und darin in das uns geschenkte innergöttliche Leben*'.

[63] 1954/5, Germanicum text, 67: '*der Plan, der Ruf Gottes ist die realste ontologische Bestimmung, so schwer das in unserer scholastischen Ontologie kategorial einfangbar ist*'.

[64] 1954/5, 115–16, *118–19*.

even more fundamental source of pluralism. Our relationship with Jesus is radically unique and individual. Our task is to let ourselves be loved into existence by God in a way that is inalienable and unrepeatable. For only so can Jesus be fully human:

> If human persons are to find their own existence, they need those who are human with them genuinely to be other, to be different, i.e. precisely not clones (*Doppelgänger*). Human beings find their own perfection only in the otherness of those who are human with them, an otherness acknowledged, affirmed and sheerly loved. This applies also to Christ, indeed especially so. We must say also of him: through the Word made human loving human beings as others and because they are others, he too attains the fullness of his nature.[65]

Again one might cite a parallel in Barth:

> the solidarity with which Jesus binds Himself to His co-human beings is a quite real one. There is not in Him some kind of deep, inner, secret recess in which He is alone in Himself or with God, existing in stoical calm or mystic rapture apart from His co-human beings, untouched by their state or fate. He has no such place of rest. He is immediately and directly affected by how his co-human beings exist. His relationship to His neighbour, His participation in His neighbour, occurs precisely in his innermost being, just as surely as this relationship is something primordial and proper to him.[66]

There is a distinction to be made between 'following after' Christ and 'imitating' Christ, between *Nachfolge* and *Nachahmung*.[67] What is at stake is precisely not the vision expressed by Hopkins in his poem on the resurrection and nature as a Heraclitean fire: 'I am all at once what Christ is, since he was what I am'. Hopkins came closer to the matter in a letter about the poem, commenting on the differences between his own writing and that of Heraclitus: 'the effect of studying masterpieces is to make me admire and do otherwise'.[68] Through our responses to him, individual and inalienable as they are, Christ can realize unique and unrepeatable potentials in his own existence.

---

[65] 1954/5, 118, *121–2*.   [66] Barth, *Church Dogmatics*, III/ii. 211.

[67] For a stimulating development of this distinction in an Ignatian context, drawing both on Bonhoeffer's seminal discussion and on René Girard's account of imitation and rivalry, see Raymund Schwager, 'Imiter et suivre', *Christus*, 34 (1987), 5–18.

[68] Claude Colleer Abbott (ed.), *The Letters of Gerard Manley Hopkins to Robert Bridges*, 2nd edn. (Oxford: Oxford University Press, 1955), 291.

The decisions which emerge from the Ignatian process are thus quite individual. Blind reproduction of Christ's life is sub-personal. Because our relationships with Jesus are unique, the form of our 'following after' must be a matter of discovery and improvisation. It cannot be deduced from material laws or from the dictates of authority. We must face the loneliness the process involves, and avoid the temptation to unload the task on to some outside authority: 'such discovery is always an individual, inalienable decision. Thus an essential aspect of the following of Christ is the taking of responsibility for what no-one, no ethics text book and no spiritual director, can tell us.'[69]

In the 1978 testament, the theme briefly recurs. We find God in Jesus, once and for all, 'in him, just as he is, quite concretely, so that love alone, not reason with its distinctions (*die scheidende Vernunft*), can say how the disciple who follows him should also imitate him'.[70] Nevertheless, it seems that not everyone who is saved by God, even as an explicit Christian, is called to follow 'the specific ways of Jesus's prosaic life' in the way Rahner's Ignatius felt himself to be. Moreover, there are many ways in which 'following after Jesus' occurs. One may be tempted to see the diversity among Christ's disciples as a 'unity in the Spirit', but, Rahner's Ignatius implies, this 'does not make all that much sense' when considering conflicts such as that between Francis of Assisi and Innocent III: 'there are concrete forms to this "following after" that are different, that remain terrifying different, that even seem to threaten and negate each other'.[71] However, Rahner is not advocating anarchy. The following of Christ will always be marked by certain basic structures within which any decision must be taken. And even the individual decision within those limits will still be a matter of obedience,

of hearing the individual imperative from God, God who has placed me into my situation so that I might carry forward Christ's life in a way befitting this situation: the submissive love which has no desire to plan independently and self-centredly even the most personal flourishing of what is its own, but rather still to receive even this from the hand of God: more precisely, fealty towards Christ, who faces me concretely, one person to another, and, in his freedom against which no appeal is possible, allocates me my place in his discipleship.[72]

[69] 1954/5, 119, *122*.   [70] 1978*b*, 20, *385*.   [71] 1978*b* 21, *386*.
[72] 1954/5, 120*, *123*.

On the basis of this theology, Rahner offers an original reading of the imaginative contemplations on Christ's life, death, and resurrection that take up the greater part of an Ignatian retreat. Central to these are the retreatant's own reflections: the retreatant must be 'always seeing to my drawing profit from it', and each contemplation ends with an imaginative conversation, or colloquy, shaped by the retreatant's reactions—'asking according to what I feel in me'.[73] Their point is not so much that the exercitant may learn what the New Law entails, but rather that 'from the life of Christ, I can read the imperative which applies individually to me, and arrive at a corresponding choice regarding my way of following him'.[74]

Rahner had already articulated the principle invoked here in 1936, towards the end of his successful doctorate, submitted to the theology faculty in Innsbruck: *E latere Christi*, a study of the tradition that the Church originates from the pierced side of the crucified Christ. Rahner is speculating on some systematic implications of this tradition and the use of Scripture on which it depends. If it is legitimate to read the gospels typologically, then the events of Christ's life 'work themselves into the life of the Christian with a salvific power, over and above the moral example they embody'. They are not just signals of Christ's time-transcending work, but rather an invitation, an 'address' (*Anrede*) to us who come later in history. As such, then, what we make of these invitations constitutes an aspect of their identity as created by God: what God did in Christ must be 'intrinsically and from the outset simultaneous with the "later" person'. Moreover, such an approach leads us to an enriched understanding of gospel meditation. Our responses to the narratives—however diverse, limited, or even inauthentic—constitute under God part of the very meaning (*Sinn*) of the salvific events:

meditation on the life of Jesus will never be able to avoid making 'applications' of the events in Jesus's life which are being contemplated. Now, if one can read the New Testament typologically, then this yields 'applications' which really from the outset belong to the meaning of the narrated events themselves, and thus count as God's thoughts—they are not just 'pious meditations'.

This is why, Rahner says, reference to Christ is important for Christian decision-making.[75]

[73] e.g. *Exx*, nn. 106–9, 121–6. See further my 'To Reflect and Draw Profit'.
[74] 1954/5, 127, *129–30*.   [75] '*E latere Christi*', 115.

Rahner also uses his account of 'following after Christ' to interpret the distinctive references to the Cross set by Ignatius close to
the choice process. Ignatius encourages a person preparing for decision to pray for 'the highest spiritual poverty', and even, if it can
happen without dishonour to God or without anyone sinning, for
'actual poverty', together with 'insults and injuries'.[76] Ignatius also
invites us to consider three styles of 'humility', or 'submissive love':
that which refuses to countenance mortal sin, that which refuses to
countenance venial sin, and that which, all other things being equal
under God, chooses poverty and insults with Christ.[77]

Traditionally, these texts led retreat-givers to deliver themselves
of *fervorini* that were questionable both theologically and psychologically, exhorting their listeners to desire suffering. Rahner takes a
different line. Cross-centred prayer should foster not a desire for
suffering, but a readiness to be open for however God may speak.
These exercises lead us beyond a simple readiness to suffer with
Christ into a surrender 'to the love of God which is always greater
still'. This is not to deny the importance of the Cross, but to set it in
a richer context: 'it remains all the more valid in a still greater,
broader, and totally unsearchable dimension of God's absolutely
free love, of the quite underivable disposing of God's holy will: the
will that touches me and only me'.[78] What is at stake is a love which
no longer cares for 'objective considerations' (*sachliche Gründe*) of
God's greater glory: instead, it is handed over to the 'underivable
disposing' of God's love.[79] Ignatian meditation on the Cross dis-
closes to us 'the ultimate law of our life, one that cannot be criticized
from any higher standard'. But obedience to that law takes us into a
sphere where general theory no longer applies.

Before Rahner, interpretations of Ignatian prayer depended on a
concept of the mystical very different from that which Rahner
developed. There were thus fruitless debates about whether Ignatian spirituality could attain this version of mysticism, or whether it
remained a form of prayer for beginners and the spiritually second-
rate.[80] Rahner's reworking of 'the mystical' enables him to evade
this dilemma, and to find new meaning in gospel contemplation.

[76] *Exx*, n. 141. 1–3.   [77] *Exx*, nn. 164–8.   [78] 1954/5, 189, *189–90*.
[79] 1954/5, 199–200, *200–1*. See also 1961, 194–207, *213–27*.
[80] De Guibert, *The Jesuits*, struggles throughout with this problem. More contemporary,
but also far briefer reflections can be found in Joseph Veale, 'Ignatian Prayer or Jesuit Spirituality', in Philip Sheldrake (ed.), *The Way of Ignatius Loyola* (London: SPCK, 1991), 248–60;

More questionable, however, is how Rahner interprets Ignatius's use of the Cross. Certainly Rahner's concern for indifference is a theme of the whole Ignatian process, but Ignatius's specific concern in such passages as the Three Manners of Humility seems to be something other than encouraging detachment. Ignatius himself seems to have had a strong devotion to the crucified Christ, which he came to moderate for the sake of his ministry. Following a helpful review of earlier discussion, Cantin plausibly finds this attitude reflected in Ignatius's expectation of a retreatant inclined to choose 'poverty with Christ poor rather than riches', and for whom it is a psychologically secondary proviso that this poverty should be in accord with God's 'praise and glory', with the furtherance of God's reign.[81] But not all exercitants were like Ignatius, and there are conceptual and psychological problems with the desire for insults.[82] Thus, with some support from Ignatius himself, commentators have repeatedly tamed Ignatius's powerful rhetoric of the Cross, seeing it as merely an application of a prudential maxim placed near the beginning of the *Exercises*: the so-called *agere contra*. To enable 'the Creator and Lord to work more surely, it is very appropriate, should it happen that the soul is attached or inclined to a thing inordinately, that it should move itself, putting forth all its strength, to come to the contrary of that to which it is wrongly affected'.[83] A third interpretation begins by noting that the conditions placed on the desire Ignatius is trying to encourage are so stringent that the desire can never be realized. It is as though Ignatius is abstracting from the sinfulness involved in Christ's death,

Paul Begheyn, 'The Controversies on Prayer after the Death of Ignatius and their Effect on the Concept of Jesuit Mission', *CIS*, 24/1 (1993), 78–93; and my 'Foreword' to *The Way Supplement*, 82 (Spring 1995), 3–6—the theme was 'Ignatian Prayer'.

[81] Roger Cantin, 'La troisième degré d'humilité et la gloire de Dieu selon saint Ignace de Loyola', *Sciences ecclésiastiques*, 8 (1956), 237–66. See *Exx*, n. 167, cf. n. 147.2–3.

[82] Very few pieces on Ignatian prayer, even now, face the hard questions raised by critical exegesis and hermeneutics. The psychological and ethical problems connected with a 'desire to suffer' are also generally passed over in silence. One stimulating exception—though it states rather than solves the issues—is John Ashton, 'The Imitation of Christ', *The Way Supplement*, 16 (Summer 1972), 28–45.

[83] *Exx*, n. 16.1–2; cf. *Dir*, n. 1.17 (by Ignatius himself), n. 20.78 (by Polanco his secretary). See also Brian E. Daley, ' "To Be More Like Christ": The Background and Implications of "Three Kinds of Humility"', *Studies in the Spirituality of Jesuits*, 27/1 (January 1995), 1–39; Stefan Kiechle, ' "Schmerz mit dem schmerzerfüllten Christus": Zur Kreuzesnachfolgeschaft in der ignatianischen Spiritualität', *Geist und Leben*, 69 (1996), 243–59; and *Kreuzesnachfolge: Eine theologisch-anthropologische Studie zur ignatianischen Spiritualität* (Würzburg: Echter, 1996).

and inviting us only to desire his kind of disposition that enabled good to come from evil. An openness to that possibility, indeed a positive desire to take on such a disposition, might subtly free a person, and enable them to consider possibilities that might otherwise seem just too threatening.

Rahner's account specifically of the Cross in Ignatius differs from all three of these interpretations, and has little support in Ignatius's text. Otherwise, however, Rahner's retreat conferences yield a rich and suggestive Christological account of Ignatian discernment. The transcendence that becomes thematic, the identity that comes into focus, is specified by Christ's membership of the human race, and by the irrevocable divine solidarity with us that the Incarnation guarantees. What remains a puzzle is why, in other contexts, Rahner remained almost silent on Christ's role in Ignatian discernment. His 1974 Christmas homily is, admittedly, a dense reflection on the links between Ignatian choice and Chalcedonian doctrine, and in 1975 he could write of how indifference always occurs 'in action-with the poor life of Jesus, dying into God's unfathomability'[84]—ideas which a later chapter will explore. But nothing else in Rahner's Ignatian writings parallels the bold statements about Christ in his 1954/5 retreat conferences.

The 'Ever Greater' God

Not surprisingly, Rahner's published expositions of 'transcendence becoming thematic' are mostly couched in a more abstract and philosophical idiom than the Christological account given in 1954/5. A good place to start is a talk Rahner gave in 1959 to a Jesuit audience about the Jesuit motto, 'for the greater glory of God'—*ad maiorem Dei gloriam.*[85] After lengthy preambles, he states the basic thesis. What this motto expresses is not in fact a distinctively Jesuit attitude, but rather an aspect of Christian identity and commitment in general. It is associated with Ignatius and the Jesuits only because Ignatius marks the emergence of this aspect of Christianity into

---

[84] 1975*b*, 10: '*im Mitvollzug des armen und in Gottes Unbegreiflichkeit hinein sterbenden Lebens Jesu*'.

[85] The phrase or its equivalent recurs constantly in Ignatius's writings, and expresses his principal conscious motive. Its use as a motto and in iconography cannot, however, be traced back to any formal act on Ignatius's part—nor do we have an Ignatian text explicitly reflecting on its significance.

reflective awareness—an emergence conditioned by the dawn of modernity. The motto expresses the subject's inner detachment from its present state, a permanent openness to something greater, something more. Though human subjectivity is realized through relationship to the other, no particular other can exhaustively define human identity. What happens at the key Ignatian moment is that this 'transcendence' becomes the focus of awareness:

the subject's own subjectivity itself comes into the subject's focus, instead of being merely a means through which the subject realizes itself. This is something typical of the post-Renaissance period. The Christian knows that what he or she now does, what is here and now imposed on them, falls essentially short of the totality of possible ways in which they could live out their Christian life. Thus they can always set this particular individual decision within the boundless range of other Christian possibilities, and so know themselves as the subject, not only of what actually is, but also of what might still be possible beyond that, and come to appropriate themselves also as such. And it is only from such a standpoint that one is in fact able to ask what in the here and now is and is not *ad majorem Dei gloriam*.[86]

Rahner claims, perhaps questionably, that such a psychological capacity is found only in recent centuries, and, more plausibly, only in certain people at certain times. He contrasts the attitudes of Francis of Assisi and Ignatius to the gift of tears. When the doctor warned Francis that he would lose his sight if the tears continued, Francis carried on regardless. For his part, Ignatius, when faced with similar medical advice, sought to restrain the tears.[87] Rahner sees in Ignatius a distinctive kind of detachment:

Had God taken away this gift of tears from him, St Francis would obviously have allowed himself to be disposed, and would have been quite content with this. But at the moment when God, so to speak, is there for him in this way, he has absolutely no hesitation but follows through (*vollzieht*), as it were unreflectively, on this gift of God's grace and this providence of God's. One could, in a certain sense, say that this was naive. With Ignatius it is different. Here the subject is self-aware in a far more radical and intensive way. They distance themselves in a quite extraordinary way from all these things once again, and to a certain extent withdraw from the par-

---

[86] 1959, 38, *45*.

[87] For primary sources see Bonaventure, *Opera Omnia*, viii. 518, and MHSJ *FN*, i. 638–9. Hugo Rahner alludes to the Ignatian incident in *The Vision*, 106, and Karl makes this contrast on a number of other occasions in his Ignatian writings, e.g. 1937, 291, *346*; 1954/5, 274, *274*; 1955, 183, *522*.

ticular concrete way in which they are living out their own existence. They set this latter in front of themselves, and ask, 'Is this really and unambiguously the right thing? Clearly, it is a good thing—but is it for the greater glory of God?' The particular way in which they live out their existence—even in so far as it is something willed by God, perhaps even commanded by God, certainly something under God's providence and permitted by God—is expressly set against a higher norm. Thereby of course the subject is detached from it.[88]

It is in such a moment of detachment that the Ignatian choice can be made. One draws oneself back to 'an absolute point . . . so as from *there* to test reflectively what one should do'. Rahner contrasts this with a more 'rational' approach, to which people aim to reduce Ignatius's process. But this latter interpretation is wrong-headed, he says. Ignatius's Exercises represent the first, and still almost the only, expression of a 'logic of choice . . . which we apply in our practice, as far as we can manage, because we *have* to apply it, but we have not yet really got a grip on its theological and metaphysical foundations and presuppositions'.[89]

Human knowing and willing involve a permanent openness to something greater than the categorical. There is a detachment and reserve regarding external objects rooted in the fact that it is always *I* who am apprehending them. The big 1956 essay had focused more explicitly on how this 'transcendence' is always 'supernatural', shot through with grace.[90] Nevertheless, some of its formulations are clearly rooted in Rahner's metaphysics of mind. The key moment is one,

of transcendence as such becoming a focus of awareness . . . supernatural transcendence, and *in* this transcendence God (in so far as God is what sustains this *Vorgriff*): the transcendence which is the necessary condition of all knowledge, and the presupposition of any argument, the sustaining ground of all these mental acts, always and everywhere—this transcendence becoming a focus of awareness.[91]

[88] 1959, 40, *47*. [89] 1959, 41, *48*.

[90] In the published version of the 1959 talk, Rahner is comparatively restrained on the role of supernatural grace. One explanation for this may lie in the topic he chose (or was given); another in the influence of Knauer's letter. Moreover, the 1959 text is a transcription of a tape-recording; and as Rahner did begin to touch on issues regarding grace, the tape had to be turned over (KRA, I. A. 328). Hence the published text at this point (1959, 43, *49–50*) is more than normally obscure and cryptic.

[91] 1956a, 148–9, *129*: '*Es handelt sich um ein Thematischwerden . . . der Transzendenz als solcher und übernatürlicher und darin Gottes (als des Woraufhin dieses Vorgriffes).*'

The core of the self-conscious person (*der Kern der geistigen Person*) comes into play, and becomes something 'expressly, explicitly experienced'.[92] The principle of choice (*Wahlprinzip*) is that 'God—or, more precisely, that concrete, unique orientation towards God which constitutes the innermost nature of the human person—this orientation becomes present and actual'.[93]

As we have already seen, Rahner also links the subject's transcendence with the Ignatian concept of 'indifference'. In 1961, Rahner could tell the Innsbruck Jesuit ordinands that indifference is a 'fundamental structure of mental existence (*Grundstruktur des geistigen Daseins*)':

> Wherever we know the finite as finite, the good as a provisional good, the individual as something which need not be, wherever we tell the tiny truth of an affirmative statement in the power which comes from the affirmation of absolute truth, whenever we are free, then we are in fact saying: 'there is present in the depths of our being as its ground an indifference with regard to what is finite and individual—an indifference which, if we do not become indifferent, we are denying, and are thus acting destructively against the grain of our existence'.[94]

Our ethical task—which we will accomplish only in the teeth of a mysterious, painful resistance arising from sinfulness—involves coming to terms with this reality, and freely appropriating it.[95] The 'consolation'—to use an Ignatian word—which issues in decision can be defined as the *Erfahrung* of indifference and of freedom, the experiential realization of human identity: 'for Ignatius, indifference and freedom occur in the full sense only when people come to a choice out of . . . infinite freedom—the freedom that he calls "consolation" when it is experienced'.[96]

One final point should be noted under this heading. Though for Rahner the human mind transcends the particular and categorical, this transcendence remains inseparable from its relationship to the other. This interplay of transcendence and dependence is radicalized in death: to focus on human transcendence is also to focus on mortality.[97] Ignatius himself, while outlining the third of his models of choice, invites us to imagine our deathbed, and ponder how then we will regard the choice now facing us.[98] Thus in the 1978 *Entschluß*

---

[92] 1956*a*, 154, *134*. [93] 1956*a*, 160–1, *140*. [94] 1961, 31, *42*.
[95] 1961, 31–4, *42–5*. [96] 1974*c*, 5, *331*.
[97] I follow here Mannermaa, '*Lumen Fidei*', 102–13. [98] *Exx*, n. 186.

article, Rahner could gloss Ignatian indifference in terms of a gradual letting-go:

The distancing, the existential casting-off of the individual reality of my existence—this is not something that I can just summon up and then it's done. Rather, it is a difficult, slowly executed, mystical development. Where at least this begins in this slow way, where there is death, where there is renunciation, where the straightforwardness of the world slowly crumbles in a night of the senses and the spirit—there will a person slowly (now once again we can talk philosophically) feel and experience the transcendence of humanity towards God as it really is, and not merely as the unavoidable condition under which our categorical dealing with the world is possible.[99]

In the 1978 testament, the brief references to Jesus's own life centre on the godforsakenness of his death, 'the ultimate in modeless mysticism'. But the point's most poignant documentation can be found in the typescript of the 1961 retreat conferences. Presumably because some of the typescript was lost, the first conference was not published. The fragment we have breaks off in mid-sentence: 'The most important Exercises in life are mostly not made during the Exercises as such. Rather they happen where God brings us up against life's final, bitter, serious moment.'[100] The audience for this talk was a group of young Jesuits preparing immediately for priestly ordination. Among them was Ignacio Ellacuría, who was, in November 1989, to be murdered at the University of Central America in El Salvador, along with five other Jesuits and two women friends of his community.[101]

Grace, Consolation, and the Absence of Object

It is now time to turn explicitly to the 1956 essay on Ignatian discernment: Rahner's most substantial piece on the *Exercises*, and the

---

[99] 1978*d*, 20–1.   [100] KRA, I. A. 173*a*, 4.

[101] On the links between Rahner and Ellacuría, see Martin Maier, 'La influencia de Karl Rahner en la teología de Ignacio Ellacuría', *Revista latinoamericana de teología*, 39 (Autumn 1996), 232–55; 44 (Summer 1998), 163–87, and also the summary of an obituary of Ellacuría, reproduced in *America*, 162 (Jan.–Jun. 1990), 254. During his years of training, Ellacuría sought to attach himself to 'great men, who in his opinion were few. The "greats" were not those of towering intellect, but those who understood and taught in an integrated, convinced, concrete and innovative way, not tied down by rules. He always cited Karl Rahner, about whom he used to say that Innsbruck wouldn't have been worth the trouble except for him.'

chief focus of all earlier discussions regarding Rahner's use of Ignatius.

Set against Rahner's work as a whole, this piece seems unusual, even maverick. If one is to do it justice, something more than straight exposition is required. This essay contains passages which seem, at least initially, to contradict basic principles of Rahner's theology. Elsewhere Rahner presents the awareness of God latent in human consciousness—through the *Vorgriff*—as something that occurs only in and through our awareness of a finite reality. Here, in the 1956 discernment essay, God is not only 'what sustains this preliminary idea *(das Woraufhin dieses Vorgriffes)*' latent in all consciousness. In the key experience on which discernment depends, God is present in another way: 'God's own self is present and nothing else at all can be.'[102] Again, in *Foundations of Christian Faith* Rahner denies that God can function, or intervene, within the chain of secondary causes—such a view compromises God's transcendence. Here, in the 1956 discernment essay, Rahner implies the opposite. In the key Ignatian experience, such divine intervention is just what happens—it is, in Rahner's patronizing phrase, 'average school-theology' which denies the possibility of such intervention, in a way that could never, Rahner says, satisfy Ignatius.[103] The essay also includes some questionable exegesis of Ignatian texts. Finally—though this difficulty is hardly peculiar to the 1956 essay—there are problems arising from Rahner's attitude to language. Many words are used about a reality alleged to lie beyond words.[104]

Given the need to resolve such tensions and contradictions, much in the 1956 essay must be deferred to the more critical and constructive phase of this study. Moreover, some of the essay's major themes—notably the insistence that there can be divine imperatives not reducible to general principles—have already been documented, and need not be repeated here. The one strictly expository point outstanding concerns the specifically supernatural, gracious

[102] 1956a, 148, *129*. The discrepancy has already been noted by Maier, 'La Théologie des Exercices de Karl Rahner', 552–3, and by Ashley, *Interruptions*, 182–3. Both these authors take Rahner's 1956 rhetoric at face value, and understand this key experience as involving some kind of transposition of normal consciousness into an extraordinary state; my interpretation departs from the continuities between Rahner's Ignatian writings and his general metaphysics of mind.

[103] *Foundations of Christian Faith*, 86, *93–4*; 1956a, 119, *104*; 122, *106*.

[104] Readers of O'Hara's otherwise generally reliable English translation are not helped by his tendency to render *Gegenstand* (object over-against) and its cognates in terms of 'concept'.

dimension of the key Ignatian experience. The 1959 talk approached Ignatian discernment through Rahner's metaphysics; the 1954/5 retreat talks took Christology as a basis for interpreting the process. Here in 1956, Rahner's distinctive theology of grace plays a significant role, and it is this which we need to document here.

For Rahner, the key Ignatian experience is one where our basic idea of God 'becomes present and actual in its distinctive functioning, and not just in the concepts of an objectifying reflection'.[105] The question then arises: if the experience is one not focused on a particular object but on the subject's own 'transcendence', how can we make this distinction between the experience itself and the words we use about it? There is obviously some kind of distinction between the reality of a table and the idea of a table. But surely such a distinction cannot apply when 'the object over-against consciousness' recedes and the subject's 'transcendence' becomes the focus.[106] Insight into our transcendence or identity might vary from the intensely emotional to the coolly deductive, but all positions on the spectrum must surely involve *reflection* on subjectivity.

The passage raises a general problem with Rahnerian theology to which we will need to return. Here we need simply to note how Rahner himself acknowledges and handles the difficulty: namely, by invoking the idea of the supernatural.[107] It might sound, he says in a footnote, as though the difference between the Ignatian key experience and normal everyday experience is simply one of degree: what is normally tacit becomes explicit. But this need not be so. The difference can be more essential (*wesentlicher*). The more our self-awareness grows, 'the more the supernatural elevation of this transcendence makes itself felt'. Thus we become aware of our transcendence as something *more* than what we need in order to be aware of created objects and, through them, of God as their creator. Another significance in the *Vorgriff* becomes apparent. No longer does it appear merely as a means of knowing particular objects 'conceptually' and God inferentially as the creator of these objects. It also has 'an immediacy and its own status before God' (*Unmittel-barkeit und Fürsichständigkeit . . . auf Gott*). Thus, when human transcendence and that which sustains it become a focus of awareness,

[105] 1956a, 161, *140*.   [106] 1956a, 145, *126*.
[107] 1956a, 145–6 n. 34, *126–7 n. 48*. Rahner restated these ideas in 1978d, 21–2.

we are focusing not just on human consciousness as such, but on something 'qualitatively other'.[108] The only reason Rahner is reticent on this point in the text, he tells us, is because he does want to rule out the possibility of some 'purely natural' analogue to the whole process. He also mentions the need to keep theoretical space open for 'non-Christian spirituality and mysticism'. We might further add that Catholic theologians in the 1950s, in the wake of Pius XII's *Humani generis*, had a professional need to be cautious when discussing the gratuity of grace.

In earlier chapters we have seen how Rahner's theology of grace centres on a dark, loving contact between God and the self, and how Rahner habitually distinguishes his account from two other modes through which the self might be thought to know God: the clarity of the beatific vision, and an indirect consciousness of God as creator. An analogous pattern appears in Rahner's predominant interpretation of Ignatius's three times of choice. The second of Ignatius's times is taken as normative, the first as exceptional, the third as deficient. Correspondingly, the experience of God on which, for Rahner, Ignatian discernment centres can be distinguished both from privileged and from inferential awareness. The key Ignatian experience should be accessible to any Christian able to make the Exercises. It is not a foretaste of the beatific vision or a revelation in the strict sense, nor is it a miracle. Any suggestion of ontologism—the view that human knowledge depends on an immediate apprehension of the divine being itself—must be excluded. Still less must we see Ignatius as licensing irrationalism or an undisciplined illuminism.[109] Equally, however, God's grace makes a difference to what we could discover by purely deductive means. Ignatian discernment is more than an intuitive, affective method of discovering the truths of essential ethics.[110] In Ignatian discernment, we are distinguishing divine impulses 'not only from bad impulses, but also from ethically good tendencies arising within the person or from other people'.[111]

Rahner links the key Ignatian experience to a phrase in Ignatius's Second Week Rules for Discernment: 'consolation without preceding cause . . . that is, without any previous perception or understanding of any object such that through it consolation of this sort

[108] *'mit diesem Thematischwerden der Transzendenz und ihres Woraufhin ein qualitativ anderes als die bloß begleitende, unthematische Transzendenz gegeben ist.'*
[109] 1956a, 93, *81*; 106, *93*; 127, *111*; 148, *129*; 94 n. 9, *83 n. 23*; 101, *89*.
[110] 1956a, 106–7, *93–4*.   [111] 1956a, 117, *103*.

would come by the mediation of the person's own acts of understanding and will'.[112] There are other consolations which occur
'with cause', through a good or evil angel, or indeed through a
human agency; this one, however, is 'for God our Lord alone to do'.
Rahner sees Ignatius as pointing here to a metaphysical distinction.
It will not do to reduce 'consolation without preceding cause' to
'sudden consolation', or 'consolation out of proportion to its cause'.
Nor is the word 'preceding' significant—elsewhere in the Rules
Ignatius drops it. One should gloss the phrase, rather, as 'consolation without object'.[113] The difference between a 'purely divine
consolation' and one 'called forth by created causes' cannot be a
matter of the paranormal, the unconscious, or mere suddenness, for
these too are created realities. Rather it must consist 'in the essential
difference between the inner structures of the experiences themselves'.[114]

Rahner describes Ignatius's rule as 'a masterpiece of brevity but
not of clarity'.[115] Rahner's interpretation of the text may be less
brief, but it is hardly clearer. Central to it is the distinction between
God as author of nature and of grace, between God's instrumental
causality in creation and his formal causality in the divine self-gift.
This latter is 'direct' and 'unmediated' in the sense that God in
grace is constitutive of the self's identity: in *that* sense no creature
mediates the divine presence. There is a non-inferential contact
between the self and God. The status of the experience's efficient
cause—natural or supernatural, miraculous or more regular—is
irrelevant to the 'intrinsic evidence' it gives. One can have the security proper to this experience 'even if one does not know through
which kind of physical efficient causality it was brought about'.[116]

But this is not to exclude *any* form of categorical mediation whatever. We saw in Chapter 3 that God's quasi-formal causality gracing
our subjectivity must correlate with a quasi-material causality in the
external world. All reality—even God's own being—is symbolic.
This outer material is not an extrinsic sign (*Vertretungssymbol*) of
God's creative power, but an intrinsic symbol (*Realsymbol*) of God's
self-gift.[117] When the key Ignatian experience occurs, when we
become aware of who we are under God, this cannot be accounted

[112] *Exx*, n. 330.2. Translation from Toner, *A Commentary*, 28.
[113] 1956*a*, 131–42, *114–23*—cf. *Exx*, nn. 330, 336.   [114] 1956*a*, 137, *119*.
[115] 1956*a*, 131, *115*.   [116] 1956*a*, 147, *128*.
[117] 'The Theology of the Symbol', esp. 224–5, *278–9*.

for simply in terms of what happens externally. The change occurs within the self. But external matter is inevitably present. Thus, commenting on Rahner's account of 'consolation without preceding cause', Schwerdtfeger writes:

> If one reads these sentences against the background of Rahner's theory of the symbol, one is led to conjecture that Rahner's intention is that of rejecting a view whereby God is present in 'consolation without cause' only through a 'substitute', a 'secondary sign', a *Vertretungssymbol*. This does not, however, mean that Rahner is disputing a transparency to God mediated through a 'constitutive sign', a *Realsymbol*.[118]

Nevertheless, the word 'conjecture' indicates that this interpretation goes beyond Rahner's own formulations. As we shall see, there are phrases here and there in the 1956 essay which support such a reading. But in general, Rahner stresses the immediacy of God's presence in the key Ignatian experience, in terms which seem to suggest that the categorical has been left behind. Rahner describes 'consolation without preceding cause' as 'the pure, objectless brightness of one's whole existence being taken up—a taking up that is consoled and surpasses anything that can be pointed to—into the love of God'; 'consolation with cause', by contrast, is the experience of 'being consoled in connection with a definite object of a categorical kind'.[119]

Such formulations can suggest that Rahner saw the experience grounding Ignatian discernment as some kind of exception to his general accounts of metaphysics and grace. Moreover, Rahner sometimes attributes a certainty to the Ignatian experience of a kind which he repeatedly says does not obtain with the supernatural grace present in everyday Christian life. In *De gratia Christi*, Rahner explicitly states that the experience of God implicit in the idea of the supernatural formal object cannot serve as a premise for logical deduction. One cannot clearly distinguish nature from grace. In particular, to invoke such experience does not help us solve the problem of the *analysis fidei*, the question as to how faith can be rational.[120] Yet this is precisely what Rahner, in his 1972 essay on the *Exercises* and fundamental theology, claims that the Ignatian experience can do. Again, in the 1956 essay, Rahner explicitly raises the possibility that we can interpret Ignatian discernment by recourse to

---

[118] Schwerdtfeger, *Gnade und Welt*, 318.   [119] 1956a, 137, *119*.
[120] *De gratia Christi*, 307–8.

the supernatural formal object, only to reject the idea. Ignatian discernment requires certainty of a stronger kind.[121] In 1972, by contrast, Rahner explores significant parallels between the supernatural formal object and the key Ignatian experience.[122]

It is undeniable that Rahner in 1956, against the grain of his own best theology, flirted with the idea that Ignatian discernment depends on some kind of extraordinary experience. But the 1956 essay makes sense, and coheres with Rahner's other writings, only if we interpret Rahner's account of the key experience more modestly, as he himself, at least implicitly, came to do. The key Ignatian experience is one in which the dark contact with God present in all experience emerges into reflective awareness—a contact which cannot be cleanly distinguished from 'purely natural' transcendence. Christology, metaphysics, and the theology of grace led Rahner to formulate the same ideas in three different ways.

This interpretation obviously needs to be defended, and we will return to the issues in the more constructive phase of this study. We need to establish the connections between Rahner's different approaches, and to consider explicitly the senses in which our experience does and does not deliver knowledge and certainty about God. These tasks will require us to move beyond straightforward exegesis of Rahner's writings. Nevertheless, despite all the complications and despite the complexities of Rahner's jargon, the reality is simple and commonplace. Rahner's account of his own decision to become a Jesuit, given in an interview with schoolgirls in 1983, can serve as an illustration:

I must honestly admit that I do not recall a lightninglike illumination, or a sudden, almost mystical, experience of vocation. No, in my case it did not happen so dramatically. Of course there are people who feel called in an entirely different way . . . sudden experiences, which come as it were like bolts of lightning, are entirely possible. Whoever has had such experiences is to be congratulated on them. However, there is another way of being called, in quiet reflection, and in a prolonged process of testing and of finding one's way into a definite life-decision.[123]

Or let us return once again to a biblical image. The prodigal son comes to himself in a pigsty, and the pigsty triggers what happens. But the primary object of the young man's thought is not the actual

[121] 1956*a*, 123–6, *108–10.*   [122] 1972, 165*, *209.*
[123] *Faith in a Wintry Season,* 95, *117.*

pigsty—which is presumably the same as it always was—but his own situation. He comes to *himself*; the nature of his own identity becomes the focus of his awareness; he begins to recognize—even if only by remembering that the food is better at home—that he is made for something different. It is to such an experience that Rahner's theory is pointing. Particular situations trigger moments of self-awareness in us—moments when we recognize our identity as temples of grace.

6

Immediacy, Mediation, and Grounding

Ignatius Loyola's *Spiritual Exercises* inspired Karl Rahner to make creative innovations in dogmatic, fundamental, and practical theology. The preceding chapters have sought to present these innovations in Rahner's own terms. But such an approach, as we have begun to see, has limitations. It will not yield a satisfactory Rahnerian theology of the Ignatian Exercises, nor will it lead to a cohesive, unitary explanation of how Rahner's overall achievement can fairly be described as Ignatian. For those tasks an additional method is needed: a constructive attempt to make explicit the latent connections between different Rahnerian statements. This present chapter is critical in its thrust: it highlights the needs which such a method might satisfy. Later chapters will address the task itself.

The Transcendental and the Categorical

A central problem, both with Rahner's thought generally and with his Ignatian writings in particular, is that of how the transcendental and the categorical are related. Even in grace, Rahner's God transcends the particular, and may not be straightforwardly identified with any particular object. Nevertheless, Rahner also remains a Christian theologian, and therefore commits himself in some sense unnegotiably to the particular, historical Jesus Christ, and to the tradition stemming from him.

We can illustrate the issue by highlighting two contrasting passages. In the 1972 essay on the Ignatian choice and fundamental theology, Rahner speaks of the key Ignatian experience, bringing out how a particular object is involved. Then, however, the idiom changes: in the experience, 'God in person is present, "without mediation" and "without cause", and is not obscured by the object of the choice (*nicht durch den Gegenstand der Wahl verstellt*)'.[1] Now the

---

[1] 1972, 163, *206*.

tone suggests that the particular object is a source of alienation from the one thing necessary. Its role is limited to not getting in the way. In passages such as these, Rahner seems to be regressing to an uncritical sub-Platonism, inconsistent with Christian commitment. At the most central moment of Ignatian discernment, history seems left behind.

Contrast what we find in the first published set of Rahner's retreat conferences. Ignatius invites retreatants near a point of choice to imagine themselves as having acquired a considerable sum of money. The process has been legal, and has not involved overt sin. At the same time, it has been marked by an inevitable mixture of motives.[2] Three possible responses are considered. When expounding these, Rahner follows Ignatius's lead,[3] and takes a clerical position as an analogue to the money (he was, after all, speaking to students at a prestigious seminary for German-speaking dioceses):

> It is entirely possible that a cleric can also administer his office with perfect honesty from very natural motives; from an objective ethical standpoint, such a relationship between person and office is entirely justifiable. Humanly speaking it makes sense. But each of the clerics in our three groups of people must nevertheless say to himself: 'I have not acquired my office with that love of God which is pure, total, and unreserved. It is intrinsically possible for me to integrate it into this love. But I did not strive for it or accept it as a part of my life in the sense that this latter is purely a project of God's.' To this extent, but only to this extent, each of them feels his office as, so to speak, a foreign body unintegrated into his own existence as a Christian.[4]

For our purposes, the key phrase here is 'but only to this extent': the ideal is not to escape from the historical situation altogether, but rather to find some way of integrating ambiguous, even venal, circumstance into a Christian lifestyle. The benefice may be a foreign body; equally, it may not be. Authenticity consists in the attempt, not to leave the body behind, but rather to find appropriate ways of integrating one's bodily and social existence.

At least in his writings on Ignatian choice, Rahner himself did not resolve the tension between the different accounts of transcendence and history implicit in these two formulations. Thus his accounts of

---

[2] *Exx*, nn. 149–56.   [3] *Exx*, nn. 16.3, 16.5, 169.5, 171.2, 178.3, 181.1.
[4] 1954/5, 190, *190–1*.

Ignatian discernment remain unsatisfactory. In the 1956 essay, for example, Rahner described the second time of Ignatian choice— for him the fundamental one—as involving a frequent bringing together (*Konfrontierung*) of the object in question with the 'fundamental consolation' (*Urtröstung*). Over time, such comparison enables us to find out,

> whether these two phenomena are inwardly in harmony, and fit with each other (*innerlich zusammenklingen, sich gegenseitig finden*); whether the desire for the contestable object of choice leaves untouched that pure openness to God which occurs in the supernatural experience of transcendence, indeed even supports and increases it, or whether it weakens and obscures it.[5]

Despite the extravagant terms in which Rahner describes the fundamental consolation, the process is sober and tentative. Ignatius, he says, may acknowledge the possibility of God revealing imperatives directly, but does not reckon with it as a general possibility. The comparison turns not on objects but on dispositions:

> we are not dealing here just with a synthesis between the object of choice and the 'object' of the fundamental divine experience, because this as such raises no problem (the general ethical permissibility of the object of choice is already established). Rather, it is a matter of whether we can synthesize the *subjective* accomplishment (*Vollzug*) of the divine experience (as a basic religious attitude that should be preserved) on the one hand, with, on the other, the direction of the choice. But in both of these the subjective aspect is not there at the beginning sufficiently expressly and explicitly for it necessarily to be clear already at the first try whether this synthesis is possible.[6]

The problems arise with Rahner's account of how this synthesis is attained. Rahner uses a phrase based on Ignatius to name criteria: 'peace, joy, tranquillity'.[7] For Ignatius, however, such states are signs of God's leading only for those whose lives are already moving positively. Hence the most that such psychological well-being could indicate is a conditional certainty about God's will.[8] Rahner is clearly aware of the point, but believes it is irrelevant to the claim he wants to make. Without giving an Ignatian source, he suggests that

---

[5] 1956a, 158, *138*.   [6] 1956a, 159–60, *139*.

[7] 1956a, 150, *130*. Rahner is here paraphrasing rather than quoting Ignatius. What follows draws on this passage and its associated footnote.

[8] *Exx*, nn. 314–15, 335: see Toner, *A Commentary*, 49–54.

in the fundamental consolation the 'peace, joy, tranquillity' lie 'at a deeper place'—deeper, presumably, than mere empirical scrutiny. Somehow, God's presence is indubitable. Rahner's rhetoric at this point seems to lose contact with reality. Because self-awareness involves not just knowledge, but also freedom and love, the consolation in the central experience is not merely a sign of 'transcendence becoming thematic' but identical with it. The consolation in question is 'freedom itself, itself the affirming self-appropriation of the mind raised to the supernatural, in its pure essence as such a mind'.

Rahner nevertheless sees a need for some moderation, in particular a need to distance such an account from any claim that we can be certain about our state of grace. He therefore insists that the knowledge is of God's offer of grace, not of our acceptance of that offer. Moreover, the evidence given by such consolation is 'humanly finite and ultimately incommunicable', not susceptible of translation into a 'reflex, clear statement of a conceptual kind'. The 'experience' (*Erfahrung*) cannot be transposed into a 'knowledge' (*Erkenntnis*) that a person can express. But then such a concession seems to undermine any claim that the key Ignatian experience can serve as the basis for discerning specific options. If we cannot know and recognize when we have such an experience, how can it possibly function as a reference-point in the process?

It is a task for later chapters to explore further the questions which this passage raises and the possible answers to them. At present, the concern is simply to name the issues, and to bring out how Rahner's account of Ignatian discernment relates to his positions regarding fundamental issues of religious epistemology. There are questions about whether the idea of a pure 'experience', emancipated from all 'concepts', is an intelligible one. Moreover, even if it is, can such 'non-conceptual' experience be foundational to Christianity, given a Christian commitment to a historical revelation mediated by the word in community? Let us look more closely at these two issues in turn.

Experience without Mediation

In the 1978 testament, Rahner's Ignatius repeatedly echoes the statements about experiential certainty in the 1956 essay.

I experienced God . . . God, who, when he thus comes near in grace out of his own self, absolutely cannot be confused with anything else.[9]

The tone sometimes becomes teasing: 'have you never actually been startled by the fact that, in my *Autobiography*, I said that my mysticism had given me such a certainty in my faith that it would remain unshaken even were there no Holy Scripture?'[10] Rahner's Ignatius reminds his modern disciple that not all the first Jesuits were adepts at 'the immediate experience of God', and goes on to ask:

Is it *so* obvious that something like this exists, legitimately exists? Was it obvious for the churched culture of my time? Is it obvious for the atheism of yours? Obvious enough for it not to have been rejected in the old days as an anti-Church subjectivism and in your modernity as illusion and ideology?[11]

Rahner appears, therefore, to be claiming that a particular kind of experience can be somehow foundational in theological epistemology. It is in these terms that most, if not all, commentators on Rahner's Ignatian writings have interpreted him. For example, Harvey Egan, in a doctorate written under Rahner's own supervision and building on what he takes to be Rahner's position, describes 'consolation without preceding cause' in terms such as these:

This central, core, touchstone experience cannot deceive and cannot in itself be measured; it is itself the measure and the standard of all other experiences, hence, the one movement among various movements of 'spirits' which carries within itself its own indubitable evidence . . . and can serve as the Ignatian first principle in supernatural logic, because . . . (it) . . . is the becoming-thematic of supernaturally elevated transcendence, pure openness to God, and nothing else. It is essentially a consolation

---

[9] 1978*b*, 11*, *374*.

[10] 1978*b*, 12, *374*; see also 1974*a*, *179*, 140. The reference is to *Aut*, n. 29, and exaggerates slightly. In the context of the Manresa events, Ignatius, writing in the third person, is naming other experiences which he had subsequently, and comments: 'These things which he saw gave him confirmation and strength back then (*le confirmaron entonces*), and they always gave him such great confirmation and strength in his faith that he has often thought to himself: were there no Scripture to teach us these matters of faith, he would be prepared to die for them solely on the basis of what he has seen.' The MHSJ editors (MHSJ *FN*, i. 404) refer us back from the 1553–5 *Autobiography* to the long letter written by Diego Laínez, one of Ignatius's first companions, in 1547, which is the earliest major biographical text extant about Ignatius. Laínez records Ignatius as saying that 'if, *per impossibile*, the Scriptures and the other documents of the faith were lost, the knowledge and the impression of the things which our Lord had imparted to him at Manresa would suffice for him for all purposes relating to salvation' (MHSJ *FN*, i. 84).

[11] 1978*b*, 13, *376*.

'without conceptual object in the actual, concretely personal, radical love of God'.[12]

For Avery Dulles, 'careful study of the Ignatian texts' leads Rahner to postulate 'a privileged type of consolation which is incontrovertibly divine in origin', and which 'can then be applied as a criterion and prototype of all other movements of grace'.[13]

Rahner seems, then, to be suggesting that there is one identifiable kind of experience that can be guaranteed as an experience of God. Such a claim seems problematic for at least two kinds of reason. Firstly, the claim that the experience somehow transcends language—'God himself. God himself I experienced, not human words about him'[14]—raises questions about how we can distinguish and reidentify different instances of the same experience. It is not that we have experience and then clothe it, so to speak, in words: language is a necessary condition of our being able, at least in one sense of the word 'experience', to have an experience at all. Certainly linguistic competence must be vital for any process of discernment between experiences, because only through language can we distinguish our experiences one from another. The distinction between the experience of God's own reality and 'human words about God' is thus too crude.[15]

Epistemologically, our use of language is a constituent of what Rahner called our transcendence, or, in scholastic idiom, the formal object of knowledge. Linguistic competence is itself an *a priori* condition of experience—language's role is not confined to the categorical. The events we call our experiences are a synthesis between the objects to be experienced and the presuppositions we bring to them. Whether or not Ignatius actually said that his experience of the truths of the faith was so strong that he would have been prepared to die for them even without the witness of Scripture, the

---

[12] Egan, *The Spiritual Exercises and the Ignatian Mystical Horizon*, 15. Quotation from published version of 1956a, 134 n. 28*, *116 n. 42*: '*der gegenstandslose Trost in der existentiell radikalen Liebe zu Gott*'.

[13] Dulles, 'Finding God's Will', 145.   [14] 1978*b*, 12, *375*.

[15] These paragraphs are influenced by Wittgenstein's argument against the possibility of a private language, in particular as interpreted by Anthony Kenny, *Wittgenstein* (London: Penguin, 1973), 178–202. Kenny moved the debate about Wittgenstein decisively beyond tedious discussions about memory-scepticism: 'Wittgenstein is not arguing, "When next I call something 'S' how will I know it really is S?" He is arguing, "When next I call something 'S' how will I know what I mean by 'S'?" Even to think *falsely* that something is S I must know the meaning of "S"; and this is what Wittgenstein argues is impossible in the private language' (p. 192).

contrast the statement implies is overdrawn. For to have had such experiences at all, he must have been socialized into the Church—the Church of which Scripture is the foundational document. Pierre Rousselot, a figure who influenced Rahner, commented on this Ignatian tradition in a seminal article that Rahner must have known: 'for the saints, the proof taken from the "voice come from heaven" never renders empty "the prophetic message more fully confirmed"'.[16] As Nicholas Lash puts the matter during a discussion of Rahner: 'the accounts that we give, the interpretations that we offer, *make a difference* to the experience itself, constitute an internally constitutive feature of that experience'.[17]

An associated question is that of the sense in which spirituality, or experience, can serve as a warrant for theological claims. Since the mid-1970s, the claim that 'spirituality' lies at the centre of Rahner's theology has become a truism among his admirers:

Rahner's theology has grown out of prayer, is accompanied by prayer, and leads into prayer.[18]

Fischer makes the point by taking up Balthasar's 1939 review of *Spirit in the World*. Balthasar had perceptively noted the connections between this philosophical work and the collection of prayers, dating from 1937, entitled *Encounters with Silence*.[19] A typical statement of Fischer's position comes when he takes up Balthasar's comment:

Balthasar says of these 'literary and stylized prayers' that they 'repeat the basic insights of the theoretical works at the level of religious experience'. In fact, to avoid misunderstanding, the point should rather be put the other way round. Rahner's philosophical works (as *also* his theological works) repeat his religious experience at the level of abstract theory. They articulate the formal foundation (*formale Grundlegung*) of this experience; as such they are an echo of it, and are intended as such.[20]

---

[16] Rousselot, *The Eyes of Faith*, 79, quoting 2 Pet. 1: 18–19. For Rousselot's influence on Rahner, see the preface to *Spirit in the World*, p. xlvii, 9 (*KRSW*, ii. 6—see also the reference in the first edition preface, p. 5).

[17] Lash, *Easter in Ordinary*, 248.

[18] Herbert Vorgrimler, in his introduction to the collection of Rahnerian texts, *Sehnsucht nach dem geheimnisvollen Gott*, 15.

[19] In fact Rahner had compiled *Worte ins Schweigen* in order to cover the costs of publishing *Geist in Welt*—see *Faith in a Wintry Season*, 44, 53.

[20] Fischer, *Der Mensch als Geheimnis*, 62, quoting from Hans Urs von Balthasar, review of J. B. Lotz, *Sein und Wert*, and K. Rahner, *Geist in Welt*, *Zeitschrift für katholische Theologie*, 63 (1939), 371–9, at 378. For fuller English statements of this kind of position, see Wong, *Logos-Symbol*, 46–62, and Egan, '"The Devout Christian of Tomorrow will be a Mystic"'. For

Earlier in his study, Fischer had noted Rahner's stress on 'a basic human experience of being referred to God' (*Grunderlebnis einer Verwiesenheit auf Gott*), a stress for which the Ignatian Exercises were a decisive source.[21]

Clearly such claims raise questions. Fischer's book received a critical review from Peter Eicher, author of a major work on Rahner's philosophy. A brief controversy ensued. Terminating the exchange, Eicher wrote of,

> a danger not to be underestimated for contemporary theology, a danger arising from a concept of experience (*Erfahrungsbegriff*) that has not been fully clarified, not even in Rahner: on the one hand, the abandonment of coherent theological thought in favour of telling stories about experience; on the other, the increasing confusion in the use of such central terms as 'meditation', 'mysticism', 'experience of transcendence', 'transcendental experience', 'spiritual activity'.[22]

Eicher here puts his finger on a central issue. The claim that Rahner's theology proceeds from his experience of God is in danger of collapsing into the claim that his theological achievement depends on some form of private revelation.[23] Whatever their biographical origin, Rahner's theological insights must stand or fall on a basis generally acceptable at least to Christians at large, if not indeed to human reason as such. The fact that an insight emerges from 'prayer' cannot render it immune from speculative criticism.

The literature on how spirituality shapes Rahner's theology, then, raises both general and specific questions. The general issues

---

critical discussions of *Encounters with Silence*, see Karl H. Neufeld, 'Worte ins Schweigen: Zum erfahrenen Gottesverständnis Karl Rahners', *Zeitschrift für katholische Theologie*, 112 (1990), 427–36; Roman Siebenrock, 'Gezeichnet vom Geheimnis der Gnade: *Worte ins Schweigen* als ursprüngliche Gottesrede Karl Rahners', in Christian Kanzian (ed.), *Gott finden in allen Dingen: Theologie und Spiritualität* (Vienna: Thaur, 1998), 199-217.

[21] Fischer, *Der Mensch als Geheimnis*, 23.

[22] Eicher, 'Erfahren und Denken'. Previous contributions to the exchange, again in the *Theologische Quartalschrift*, were Eicher, 'Wovon spricht die transzendentale Theologie? Zur gegenwärtigen Auseinandersetzung um das Denken von Karl Rahner', vol. 156 (1976), 284–95; and Fischer, 'Wovon erzählt die transzendentale Theologie? Eine Entgegnung an Peter Eicher', vol. 157 (1977), 140–2.

[23] See e.g. Paul Imhof's introduction to *Karl Rahner: Bilder eines Lebens*, 6: 'The lived centre (*existentielle Wurzel*) out of which he thought was fundamentally his experiences of the Exercises, about which he spoke rarely, and then only in trusted circles.' Cf. the retort in Miggelbrink, *Ekstatische Gottesliebe*, 248 n. 12: 'The thought of a man whose life's work was taken up with conveying the rich wine of faith to everybody ill deserves that imitators should pretend to possess for themselves a secret revelation regarding the core of the whole received from the Master "among trusted circles"'.

concern the relationship between our religious or spiritual experience and the knowledge we acquire through language and community; these will be dealt with briefly in the concluding chapter. The more specific questions are about what grounds Ignatian discernment: both how Rahner thought it worked and how it actually works. The next chapter will argue that the reality grounding Ignatian discernment cannot be *one particular experience*, but rather a *factor conditioning all human experience* in a graced world. But there are further critical and methodological issues to be named before we can begin that constructive task.

The Role of Tradition

A second major unclarity in Rahner's Ignatian writings lies in the relationship between 'the immediate experience of God' and Rahner's institutional commitments as a Roman Catholic Christian. In the 1978 testament, Rahner's Ignatius tells us repeatedly that he experienced God 'im-mediately' (*unmittelbar*), but he also refers to a variety of mediations of God's presence. Though he does not mention Jesus in the first part of his message, this is only because 'the words spoken among you have to follow each other, and none of them says everything at once'. In fact, Jesus was 'already present within' everything previously said.[24] When Ignatius went as a pilgrim to the Holy Land in quest of the historical Jesus, the experience 'could be truly the journey into the pathlessness of God'.[25] The Roman Church, too, in all its ugliness and harshness, was 'transparent to God, and the specific locus of this inexpressible relationship of mine to the eternal mystery'.[26] Moreover, human words can also mediate the experience of God. At the very beginning of his message, Rahner's Ignatius solemnly declares:

As you know, I wanted 'to help souls' (as I said back then), that is, to say something to people about God and God's grace and about Jesus Christ, the crucified and risen one—something meant to redeem their freedom into that of God (*das ihre Freiheit in die Gottes hineinerlösen sollte*).[27]

However, Rahner himself normally refrained, at least in Ignatian

---

[24] 1978*b*, 19–20, *384*.   [25] 1978*b*, 20, *385*.   [26] 1978*b*, 27, *393*.
[27] 1978*b*, 11, *373*. 'To help souls' is a standard Ignatian phrase in such texts as the *Constitutions*.

contexts, from exploring how the paradoxes here could be resolved. A statement from a 1978 interview about the Exercises is typical:

> Why and how something like this (i.e. an immediate experience of God) is tied up with an immediate encounter with Jesus, why these two things are mutually dependent . . . is something which I cannot explain in more detail here.[28]

Rahner often presents Ignatius in terms of sweeping, unverifiable *Geistesgeschichte*—'history of the human spirit', 'cultural history', or 'history of ideas'. Ignatius is an individualist saint. He marks the end of medievalism and the dawn of the modern era, a figure parallel to Luther and Descartes.[29] The fullest articulations of such claims come in the 1959 talk on the Jesuit motto, and in the 1974 essay on collective applications of Ignatian discernment. For Rahner, medieval humanity 'thought and lived in terms of God and the world, from the general, and from the regular order that could be formulated in norms derived accordingly'.[30] By contrast, Ignatius marks a profound shift from medievalism, in tandem with all kinds of other social and cultural factors, ranging possibly from Thomas Aquinas—if one interprets the historical Aquinas as a transcendental Thomist—to the Enlightenment and the rise of modern science.[31] Despite all the diversities between these phenomena, Rahner discerns one underlying trend. In this 'modern' period, there is a 'turn to the subject'. The individual is no longer merely one instantiation of a general term, but an autonomous centre of freedom, in some sense over and above the non-human world:

> The initial datum is the individual subject. This remains the case, even if the subject, in his or her own freedom, has absorbed and accepted the realities handed on by a *philosophia perennis* and by the Christian faith—in other words, when this subject is and remains a member of the Church, and knows themselves to be not only profane and of the world, but religious and related to God. *The subject itself*, in its transcendental *a priori* constitution, is now the primary datum, the starting point, providing for itself the first and foundational certainty.[32]

Religiously, this entails 'a turn towards subjective anxiety about salvation, a subjectively perceived commissioning for the Church,

---

[28] 1978*c*, 175, *33*.   [29] 1978*b*, 13–14, *376*.   [30] 1974*a*, 139, *177*.
[31] 1959, 32–4, *39–41*; 1974*a*, 138–9, *177*.   [32] 1974*a*, 139, *178*.

towards reflection, towards the ever unique . . . It is the turn towards self-responsibility.'[33]

In Rahner's view, the cultural shift into modernity relativizes the institutional Church. In the Middle Ages, human beings understood themselves within an objective order: if they reflected on themselves, their mind and freedom, they did so 'on the basis of those objective realities into which they were incorporated as parts from the outset'.[34] At the Renaissance, the individual becomes crucial; the Church becomes merely a context within which the individual religious drama is played out. The structure of the standard Ignatian phrase, 'thinking with the Church',[35] is revealing: one 'thinks' for oneself first, and then adjusts to Church teaching. And Ignatius does this latter,

in a true sense 'despite'. This is because for Ignatius, the fundamental cultural-historical starting point, imposed on him unavoidably, is not the Church, but the modern subject. This modern subject is, for Ignatius, an ecclesial person 'despite': they are not subjective in a Calvinist or Lutheran sense, even though they have experienced exactly the same thing as Luther in his subjective question about salvation, and asked just as radically—in a way which previous centuries could not at all—whether there was a gracious God or not.[36]

Although ecclesial Christianity is somehow normative, it remains radically secondary to the immediate touch of God. Ignatius's apostolate 'stands at the beginning of the period when the confessional split caused the Church, which had been the taken-for-granted space for everyone and everything, to become a Church of the Diaspora and of the lonely individual'.[37]

In context, Rahner makes such claims to help his audiences and readers cope with the religious challenges implied by contemporary cultural transitions. Sometimes, Ignatius appears as a prophet of secularization, whom even after Vatican II the Roman Catholic Church has not yet fully understood.[38] Though he was a saint of the

---

[33] 1959, 33, *40*.   [34] 1974*a*, 139, *177*.
[35] *sentire cum ecclesia*—based on the official 1548 Latin version (Vulgate) of *Exx*, n. 352.
[36] 1959, 33–4*, *40–1*—the non-standard language reproduces that in the original. This passage also hints, however, at a contrast between Ignatius and the Reformers. Ignatius overcame the time-conditioned elements in the early modern turn to the subject, and 'carried them over to a certain extent into the realm of the permanent' (*überholt hatte in das Bleibende hinein*). The point is less than clear, and Rahner seems never to have returned to it.
[37] 1956*b*, 338.   [38] 1959, 33, *39*; 1974*a*, 142, *181*.

Counter-Reformation, of the baroque and of Catholic restoration, he also has a significance for the period that is just beginning as a saint of the individual before God.[39]

However, though the 1974 address responds to what was then a new interest in group discernment,[40] its basic thrust remains individualist. Admittedly, it acknowledges the advent of a post-modern era, distinguished by a new sensitivity to the interpersonal. Moreover, Rahner had always stressed surrender to mystery, and insisted that God, rather than the human ego, was the centre of the world's intelligibility—he had never completely subscribed to Enlightenment, technical models of rationality.[41] Now, in 1974, Rahner observes how people are searching for 'higher forms of human socialization in which the dignity and freedom of the individual will be reconciled both with his or her social nature and with the particular exigencies of survival imposed on them by the material and social situation of today and tomorrow'.[42] Rahner seems unimpressed, however, by wholesale critiques of modernity; 'Cartesian' is never for him a smear-word. The individual retreat is certainly not outmoded: even in this post-modern period, there are 'crucial decisions of an existential and religious kind, whose burden the individual as such must deal with'.[43] Rahner's version of discernment in common results from a free decision by a number of people to share their individual experiences and to use these as the basis of

---

[39] 1956*b*, 338–9.

[40] The idea was given official encouragement in the 32nd Jesuit General Congregation, meeting approximately a year after Rahner delivered this talk. Neufeld's footnote 19 (1974*a*, 145, *185*) indicates a debt to scholarly work in the early 1970s on the so-called Deliberation of the First Fathers. In 1539, Paul III took the early Jesuits up on their offer of themselves for mission all over the known world. The companions came together and prayed in a regular fashion, attempting to discern whether they should maintain some kind of union in their dispersal, and whether they should vow obedience to a superior from among themselves.

[41] Rolf Bauerdick, 'Tranzendentale Subjektivität oder Tranzendentalität des Subjekts: Die mystische Theologie Karl Rahners am Ende der Moderne', *Freiburger Zeitschrift für Philosophie und Theologie*, 32 (1986), 291–310, argues that Rahner's orientation to mystery renders his project closer to that of a critical thinker such as Adorno than to Kant's: 'Rahner's concept of the "absolute mystery" avoids the security-thinking characteristic of the ideologies of conviction and of the standpoint appropriated by the self-assured modern subject' (p. 308). 'It is no coincidence that "transcendental" in Kant betokens "never a relationship between our knowledge and things, but only *a capacity of knowledge*", whereas in Rahner the object of transcendental enquiry refers precisely to "the mutual *relationship* of connection and conditioning between knowing subject and known object, each as such"' (p. 303, quoting Kant's *Prolegomena to Any Future Metaphysics*, and 'Reflections on Methodology in Theology', 87, *98*, emphases Bauerdick).

[42] 1974*a*, 146, *186*.   [43] 1974*a*, 155, *196*.

a common decision. For all its originality, Rahner's text has not been informed by more radical versions of post-modernism, by more thoroughly relational accounts of the human person, and by accounts of experience making strong reference to a shared language and culture.[44]

Rahner's account of our experience of grace often seems radically to relativize the Church and the communal. The institutional in Christianity is secondary to, and at the service of, believers' immediate experience of God. One can understand why his critics see an inconsistency:

Rahner's most characteristic theological profundities are embedded in an extremely mentalist-individualist epistemology of unmistakably Cartesian provenance. Central to his whole theology . . . is the possibility for the individual to occupy a standpoint beyond . . . immersion in the bodily, the historical and the institutional. Rahner's consistently individualist presentation of the self emphasizes cognition, self-reflexiveness and an unrestricted capacity to know. It rapidly leaves time and place behind. It is not surprising if this mentalist-individualist conception of the self seems difficult to reconcile with the insistence on hierarchy and tradition that marks Rahner's Roman Catholic ecclesiology.[45]

In the 1978 testament, Rahner's Ignatius acknowledges unresolved conflicts in his attitude to Church authority. He presents the issue in terms of knowledge of God coming from two sources. Perhaps echoing Teresa of Avila, he imagines the human heart as soil for crops, and in need of irrigation. On the one hand, there is a Johannine well of living water in the heart of each believer; on the other, the Church provides a watering system coming, as it were, from outside. The image suggests two autonomous systems that might deliver conflicting results: the individual conscience, and authority. One way in which Rahner's Ignatius copes with this is to invoke the limitations of any metaphor: 'the image distorts the reality; there is no ultimate opposition between this source of one's own and the "watering system" coming from without'.[46] He also invokes the unity of divine providence: in the last analysis, obligations to conscience and to Church authority cannot conflict, even though

---

[44] For an interpretation of communal discernment in terms of a more relational understanding of the human, see Meures, 'The Ministry of Facilitation'.

[45] Fergus Kerr, *Theology after Wittgenstein* (Oxford: Blackwell, 1986), 14.

[46] 1978*b*, 15*, *379*.

there are no exact rules for negotiating the tensions now.[47] At one point he even resorts to a kind of gallows humour to mask the difficulty. He was lucky to have managed both to follow his vocation to radical, marginalized discipleship, and to have stayed on good terms with the hierarchy:

And you must try to bring about the miracle of this double identity (*Identifikation*) over and over again (*immer neu*). The sum will never quite work out. But try for it, over and over again. One of the two on its own is not enough. Only the two together are sufficiently crucifying (*Erst beides zusammen kreuzigt genug*).[48]

There is a general question, therefore, as to how Rahner's statements about subjective revelation relate to his ecclesial commitments and his belief in historical tradition. In the context of the Ignatian writings, the question could be focused in one of two ways. Sometimes, as we have seen, Rahner seems to present the key Ignatian experience as some kind of exception to the general principle that transcendental experience is always mediated. On that account, the question is one of clarifying and justifying the claim about exceptional status—a task which, as the next chapter will argue, is impossible.

An alternative account, however, aligning Rahner's interpretation more closely with his general theology of grace, can be imagined. We have already seen in Chapter 3 how 'the immediate experience of God' is compatible with the presence of an external object, and indeed requires its stimulus. It is to this principle that Rahner's Ignatius alludes when he says:

Every call (another image) in God's name from outside is only meant to make clear the self-pledge of God's own self within; and this latter also requires that call in some earthly form or other—even if this form can be much more diverse and unassuming than your theologians used to allow in earlier times, and even if, too, such a call from outside, a call of

[47] 1978*b*, 27, *394*. Such an approach has strong antecedents in Ignatius. See Schwager, *Das dramatische Kirchenverständis*, 127–52, summarized in my 'Ignatius and Church Authority'. Important subsequent contributions on Ignatius's ecclesiology are: Michael J. Buckley, 'Ecclesial Mysticism in the *Spiritual Exercises* of Ignatius', *Theological Studies*, 56 (1995), 441–63; Jesús Corella, *Sentir la iglesia: Comentario a las reglas ignacianas para el sentido verdadero de Iglesia* (Bilbao: Mensajero, 1995); and a decree of the 34th Jesuit General Congregation in 1995, reproduced with commentary in Gerald M. Fagin, 'Fidelity in the Church—Then and Now', *Studies in the Spirituality of Jesuits*, 31/3 (May 1999).

[48] 1978*b*, 23, *389*.

responsibility, love and fidelity, of a selfless commitment to freedom and justice in society, can sound much more worldly than your theologians might like to hear.[49]

On this account, there is no question that the transcendental is categorically mediated. The issue is rather one of articulating how, in different ways, Christian tradition and particular discerned options can have a *special* mediating role, granted that *all things*, at least in principle, are mediations of grace. This task will occupy Chapters 8, 9, and 10.

The Hermeneutics of Rahnerian Assertions

One final issue needs to be considered in this transitional chapter, namely the kind of interpretation of Rahner's achievement offered by this study. Rahner was well aware that his account of Ignatius left loose ends. He ended the Ignatian section of his valedictory lecture at Freiburg with a frank admission:

Of course I know that perhaps a great deal of what is said in my theology in no way fits together clearly and unambiguously, for a human being is in no way in a position to carry through an exhaustive and comprehensive reflection on how the particular things they say hang together, given that the sources of their knowledge are from the outset pluralist. A theologian can therefore only ask supporters and opponents of their theology to come at this theology with an indulgent benevolence, to see its approaches, basic tendencies, ways of putting questions, as more important than its 'results'—results which, in the end, cannot after all be definitively valid.[50]

In his last years, Karl Rahner would often speak of the permanent tension in his theology arising from its two different starting-points: the historical and the transcendental. He did not know how they fitted together. He could only retreat into piety: maybe God would show him the answer in heaven.[51]

The next four chapters of this study address this tension as it appears in Rahner's Ignatian writings. They neither repeat Rahner's Ignatian theology—that task is done—nor refute it; nor, equally, are they content simply to claim that no further synthesis is possible.

---

[49] 1978*b*, 16, *379*.
[50] 'Erfahrungen eines katholischen Theologen', 144.
[51] Information from an interview with Paul Imhof in Munich on 25 Feb. 1989.

During a major interview Rahner gave for his seventieth birth-day, the interviewer began to mention a criticism often made of Rahner: that his theology did not take the interpersonal sufficiently seriously. Rahner interrupted the question, and made two points. Firstly, he did not want to be held to every word in his early philosophical works, which were juvenilia, and in some ways distorted:

Secondly, here we are dealing with matters that, correctly understood, are abstract and formal, in such a way that they remain open for interpret-ation in the light of material content, for example through what people call the historical and the interpersonal.

Abstract principles, such as the principle of non-contradiction, apply in one sense universally. On the other hand, 'the principle only comes properly and fully into its own when it is brought into contact with a fuller and more concrete understanding of the human person or a fuller and more concrete theology'. Rahner then issues a challenge, which can serve as a charter for the chapters that follow: 'Given this, I would say to you, "go ahead and make all these charges against me. I accept them, if they are understood in the sense I have stated. But you must do more: do the job yourselves, better!"'[52]

The remainder of this study takes up the challenge which Rahner names here. Rahner certainly did see his Christological and transcendental accounts of Ignatian choice as complementary;[53] and the 1956 essay, with its austerely formal account, was origin-ally one essay in a collection of pieces, many of which handled explicitly historical topics. How can the connections be more fully articulated?

We need, however, to specify the issues more precisely. Rahner's table talk about 'the historical and the interpersonal' covers a num-ber of different issues, which commentators, even when concentrat-ing on the Ignatian writings, have begun to explore. Besides Fischer and Schwerdtfeger, we can cite the example of Wolfgang Kues. Kues has interestingly drawn on Jungian resources to describe more closely than Rahner can the process by which a particular option

[52] *Faith in a Wintry Season*, 22 ('Gnade als Mitte', 83–4).
[53] 1954/5, 8–9, *12–13*: a reader of the Christological account in the Germanicum confer-ences is directed to the account of the 'formal structure of the logic of existential knowledge and decision' given in 1956*a*.

appears as the will of God for an individual.[54] In so doing, Kues is drawing on an empirical science, psychology, to clarify how Rahner's transcendental theology can be *applied* in particular situations. Our concern here, however, is different: one more properly theological, and more crucial in determining the validity of Rahner's project. For, within Christian theology, we do not invoke 'the historical and the interpersonal' simply in order to determine how to apply theological principles in particular cases. On the contrary, certain historical and interpersonal realities, connected with Jesus Christ and the tradition stemming from him, are properly theological. Hence they must somehow be incorporated into the general principles *as such*. If Ignatian discernment depends on 'transcendence becoming thematic', this transcendence must somehow be decisively specified by Christology and ecclesiology. One important task outstanding is to clarify how this, on a Rahnerian account, can be so. Questions of application may properly remain a matter of empirical science and discovery, but questions of theological principle are vital to our purpose.

We also need to consider the ground rules under which developments of Rahner's published positions can nevertheless be called 'Rahnerian'. Rahner was challenging us, in the 1974 interview, to enter not so much into what he had said as into the problems which had preoccupied him. In doing so, he was echoing one of his long-standing convictions about interpretation, one that he may have learnt from Heidegger:[55]

---

[54] Kues, *Werde, der du sein sollst!* The following paragraph illustrates Kues's goals in drawing on Jung: 'Rahner investigates the existential-ontological presuppositions made by Ignatius. The existential-*ontological* presuppositions are the transcendental reference to reality as a whole and the reference to God as two moments of one and the same experience. But just what, over against this ontological structure found in humanity, is the *existential*-ontological presupposition? What is the content of the existential extra in this experience of the Exercises, the extra that makes, for this specific subject, the (divine [P.E.]) self-communication into a knowledge of the will of God for them, whoever they are, a knowledge that is not just formal but has a specific content? . . . In consolation during the Exercises, does the subject experience an existential-ontological structure, or themselves as something historical? Rahner does say that we are talking about a concrete historical subject. But he gives no satisfactory answer to the question of how this specificity is to be understood in connection with knowledge of the will of God' (p. 45).

[55] *I Remember*, 45, 47: 'Obviously . . . you can distinguish how Heidegger was a kind of mystagogue into philosophy for his pupils from what he actually put forward as a matter of systematic philosophy. I would say that it was the first of these functions that made Heidegger important for me. He taught how to read texts in a new way, to analyze, to see lines of

the true philosophical content of an earlier philosophy makes itself accessible only through a personal philosophizing-with. Such a method may involve greater dangers of interpreting the early philosophy perversely, but it is also my belief that we just have to live with and allow for this danger, because otherwise the actual *philosophical* content of an old philosophy is quite inaccessible.[56]

Nevertheless, the danger Rahner notes is also present when we apply such a method to his own texts. One can get so caught up with the problems underlying Rahner's formulations that 'the boundary between the presentation of Rahner's theology and one's own doing of theology dissolves'.[57] This study will make connections, with at best only limited direct support from Rahner's texts; sometimes, indeed, it will contradict them. Nevertheless, the result can still be presented as Rahnerian. As a 'constructive interpretation' its concern is to develop and safeguard Rahner's basic project, not to refute it.

The following chapters seek to reconcile, more fully than Rahner himself may have done, concerns that were always central to Rahner's theology. They respect Rahner's insistence on a philosophically responsible doctrine of God, an insistence grounded in convictions about the links between reality and awareness, and about the organic links between our knowledge of the metaphysical and the material. Theologically, this study continues Rahner's commitment to mainstream credal Christianity, and his belief in the presence of grace in all experience; it also follows Rahner in seeing 'spirituality' as something animating and renewing theology rather than as any kind of replacement or supplement. Whereas, however, Rahner's own formulations focused simply on the material, bodily,

connection between a philosopher's individual texts and statements that didn't occur to your conventional educated reader, and so on.' For links between Heidegger's *Wiederholung* ('retrieval') and Rahner, see Muck, 'Heidegger und Karl Rahner', 260.

[56] 'Begleittext zu *Geist in Welt*', 435. For a similar statement regarding theology, see 'The Prospects for a Dogmatic Theology', 8, *17*.

[57] Sandler, *Bekehrung des Denkens*, 41. Sandler shrewdly points up how an over-defensive attitude to what Rahner actually wrote 'weakens the persuasiveness of the justifiable concern', and does as much as unsympathetic criticism to bring Rahner's theology into disrepute. Instead he argues for a *Weiterinterpretation oder Rekonstruktion der Rahnerschen Theologie*. Cf. Schwerdtfeger, *Gnade und Welt*, 61–6, focusing more on textual issues; Reno, *The Ordinary Transformed*, 57–8, which echoes Rahner's own Heideggerian statements about hermeneutics; and McIntosh, *Mystical Theology*, 98–101, in the course of an exceptionally helpful discussion of the differences betwen Rahner and von Balthasar.

and sensory aspects of the human, the following chapters will argue also that language, culture, and tradition are integral to any full account of human experience, of human identity, of what Rahner called human transcendence. Rahner's failure to develop this point has, as we shall see, led some critics to miss how down-to-earth his theology is. If we are to interpret Rahner's Ignatian writings fruitfully, we must find creative ways of dealing with this lack.

7

First Principles

Ignatian discernment seeks to discover God's will. It thus represents an epistemology, a system of knowledge. For Rahner, this system is a foundationalist one: it depends on a 'first principle' which cannot be questioned without the system as a whole becoming discredited.[1] Thus, the properly systematic interpretation in the 1956 essay begins with this question:

> Is there for Ignatius something foundationally evident that is logically prior to the individual rules and techniques for the discernment of spirits (*eine den einzelnen Regeln . . . vorgeordnete Grundevidenz*), which performs in this branch of knowledge a function corresponding to the first principles of logic and ontology in other realms, and which, distinct from the Rules, fundamentally make these possible—in such a way that the Rules are the application and regulated putting into practice of this foundationally evident principle, represent something like a supernatural logic, and themselves refer back to their distinctive 'first principle'?[2]

Rahner answers this question affirmatively, with the claim that at certain moments our 'supernaturally elevated transcendence' becomes 'thematic'. This experience is 'without object', and 'non-conceptual'; it is also self-authenticating.

This question and answer reflect a tension throughout Rahner's Ignatian writings regarding the nature of this first principle. Sometimes Rahner seems to be writing about one identifiable, particular class of experience; at other points, such as this tortuously worded question, he appears to refer, not to one experience as such, but rather to a regulative principle that applies, in a graced world, to all possible experience.

---

[1] This sense of 'foundationalism' obviously differs from that in which 'post-modern' thought so zealously repudiates the term: the attempt to ground rationality in some indisputable, 'neutral' fixed-point. On Rahner's opposition, throughout his career, to such a strategy in theology, see further Chapter 10 below. But there are other, less objectionable versions of the claim that Christianity has some kind of axiomatic basis. For an exploration of the general issue in a Rahnerian context, see Reno, *The Ordinary Transformed*, esp. 212–19.

[2] 1956*a*, 130, *113*.

A similar tension can be found in the 1978 testament. When Rahner's Ignatius tells us how he wanted to mediate his experience of God to others, the experience itself seems located at quite definite points in his life-history. He says he met God 'first in an incipient way during my illness at Loyola, and then decisively during my time as a hermit at Manresa'.[3]

A few pages later, however, Rahner's Ignatius seems to elide towards a different kind of claim. He mentions once again 'the immediate encounter with God', but then adds a significant parenthesis: '(or should one say: towards the experiential realisation that the human person is always one who has already met God—and continues to meet God?)'.[4] *Immer schon*—'always already'. The parenthesis sounds like a clarification, but a shift has been made. Now Ignatius's key experience is not an event in isolation, but an 'experiential realization'—at this point the best translation of *Erfahrung*—of what is 'always already' the case, leading Ignatius to see the whole of reality as within the immediacy of God. It is not that the particular events are sacred and the rest of reality profane; rather, the particular events are symbolic, parts of reality revealing the meaning of the whole.

When Rahner talks about the experiential knowledge of God given in the Exercises, it is thus unclear whether such knowledge is meant to count as an exception to Rahner's general theology of metaphysics and grace, or as a further illustration of that theology. The point is an important one, given that the two possible interpretations imply quite different theologies of human experience, grounded through correspondingly different strategies. In favour of the former interpretation, there are passages where Rahner quite explicitly says that the Ignatian key experience offers a certainty about God's leading, a certainty contrasting with our indirect, fuzzy awareness of the supernatural existential.[5] In favour of the latter, we can adduce the strong connections between Rahner's Ignatian writings and his metaphysics: connections obvious from such ideas as 'transcendence becoming thematic', a transcendence in which God is present 'as the sustaining basis (*Woraufhin*) of this *Vorgriff*'.[6]

<hr/>

[3] 1978*b*, 11, *373–4*.   [4] 1978*b*, 16, *379–80*.   [5] 1956*a*, 125–6, *109–10*.

[6] 1956*a*, 148–9, *129*; 145, *126*: God is the pure and unrestricted *Woraufhin* of an unending movement (*unendliche Bewegung*), namely our supernatural transcendence. In normal German usage, *auf* can denote either a basis on which something occurs or a goal towards which something moves. However, *woraufhin*, despite the spatial connotation of *hin*, draws primarily on

This study, and in particular this chapter, adopts the latter inter-pretation. It argues that the 'first principle' of the 'supernatural logic' cannot be a particular, identifiable experience, but rather a regulative truth, which, though it is derived from revelation, applies universally. It draws on a suggestion put forward by Klaus Fischer. Discussing Rahner's 'transcendence becoming thematic' and its relationship to Christology, Fischer speculates that the former phrase represents not an experience in itself, but 'a methodologic-ally justified bracketing or abstraction'; the reality concerned never occurs purely or unambiguously.[7] Just as we never experience the principle of non-contradiction in isolation, so too the first principle of Ignatian discernment—the immediate presence of God in our experienced subjectivity—is to be understood, not as one empirical reality among others, but as a principle shaping all possible experience. Hence Rahner's apophatic rhetoric about the 'first principle' needs to be understood in terms of abstraction rather than exclusion.

Read at face value, Rahner's 1956 essay seems to centre on an experience which is without object, beyond language, and self-authenticating. These three claims can be accepted only with quali-fication. The remaining three sections of this chapter use both exegetical and speculative resources to explore each of these claims in turn. When Rahner says that the key Ignatian experience is 'without object', this cannot mean that it is somehow disembodied, but simply that our focus of attention shifts from categorical objects

the former; moreover, in the context of Rahner's philosophy it is this sense that should be given preference if serious misreading is to be avoided. Rahner resolutely avoids suggestions that the creature can move to the point of fusing with God. For Rahner, the attraction of Heidegger's 'ontological difference' lay in how it stressed the unbridgeable difference between creator and creature, how any finite creature must resist 'the mad and secret Hegelian dream of equality with God' ('The Concept of Existential Philosophy in Heidegger', 136). *Bewegung* has its roots in scholastic metaphysics, and perhaps might be translated as 'change'. If 'movement' occurs in a reality without the reality changing its identity, then there must be a mover distinct from the changed reality. The 'cosmological argument' for the existence of God depends on this principle, and on the impossibility of infinite regress. Whatever our judgement regarding the soundness of that argument, it clearly stresses the distinction between creator and creature.

[7] Fischer, *Der Mensch als Geheimnis*, 50. This present study, however, develops Fischer's sug-gestion rather more radically than he himself does. Cf. Fischer's later summary of how Ignatius shapes Rahner's theological anthropology, in which the Christological and categor-ical elements are very muted: 'Gott als das Geheimnis des Menschen. Karl Rahners theolo-gische Anthropologie—Aspekte und Anfragen', *Zeitschrift für katholische Theologie*, 113 (1991), 1–23, esp. 7.

as such to the conditions in ourselves enabling us to perceive the objects. 'Non-conceptual' is a highly problematic term, but it certainly cannot mean 'non-linguistic'. 'An experience which cannot deceive' does not imply that any one particular experience is necessarily authentic.

Objects and the Experience of God

At one point in the 1956 essay, Rahner speaks of how the key Ignatian experience is self-evident: 'that such an experience contains its grounding within itself, that—always provided we look at it in itself—it cannot deceive, that God's own self is there and just nothing else can be there—this is self-evident'.[8] The idiom of this sentence reflects in microcosm the general problems posed by the whole text. 'Such an experience—*eine solche Erfahrung*' suggests one particular experience; 'always provided we regard it in itself—*immer in sich selbst gesehen*' at least begins to suggest that the reality in question is an abstraction.

In this particular sentence, Rahner may be echoing one of the Ignatian Rules, which urges the need to distinguish between the pure 'consolation without preceding cause' and the period immediately after, 'when the soul remains warm' and where other thoughts can creep in.[9] But though the echo may be there, Rahner's 'always provided we regard it in itself' points towards a distinction between reality and concept, not towards the different temporal phases which preoccupy Ignatius. Immediately after the passage just quoted, Rahner begins to qualify:

But one must be careful. We are not dealing here with a conceptual representation of God, a conceptually articulated theorem concerning God.

However, Rahner's language here is in tension, not only with Ignatius, but also with his own mature theology. Elsewhere, Rahner speaks of how 'the aspect (*Moment*) of reflection', for all that it does not exhaust our self-awareness, is nevertheless integral to it.[10] Moreover, Rahner's account of existential ethics—within which the Exercises function as an epistemology—is explicitly restricted to the 'formal'. It deals with,

---

[8] 1956*a*, 148, *129*.   [9] *Exx*, n. 336.
[10] e.g. *Foundations of Christian Faith*, 16, 27 (*KRSW*, xxvi. 22).

the fact that such an existential ethics fundamentally exists, with its formal structures, and with the basic means through which such existential-ethical matters are known.[11]

Though the theory of existential ethics must abstract from particular situations—which, *ex hypothesi*, are unique and unrepeatable—it makes no sense to imagine the reality denoted by such a theory existing somewhere on its own, independent of particular situations.

Moreover, there are some passages in the 1956 essay, admittedly masked by Rahner's more extravagant rhetoric, which only make sense if the 'first principle' is understood as an abstraction. Early in the essay, Rahner stresses that he has not fallen victim to emotionalism. The experience is a rational one, not one of 'blind drives'. In a footnote, he then refers forward to how he will develop his argument:

The consolation which is genuinely of God, referred to in *Exx*, n. 330, is already synthesized with the apprehension of a genuine possible object of choice, which is amenable to a rational, objectifying (*gegenständlichen*) apprehension.[12]

Criticizing Suárez's interpretation of 'consolation without preceding cause', Rahner begins a sentence by referring to his own account in terms of 'an experience which occurs without sensory image', but then qualifies: 'or in which the imagery does not have what is otherwise the normal relation to its thought content'.[13] Later, he leaves it open whether 'the content standing over against the consciousness' must completely vanish in the key experience, or merely become 'more transparent' to supernatural transcendence.[14] Again, we are not, Rahner says, talking about a 'merely "transcendental subject" in metaphysical abstraction': the key Ignatian experience involves the person's commitment and engagement, 'their freedom, their distinctiveness, their history'.[15] Furthermore, only through such considerations can we make sense of the claim that the experience in question is pluriform and gradual.[16]

---

[11] 'On the Question of a Formal Existential Ethics', 229, *240*.

[12] 1956*a*, 103 n. 16, *90 n. 30*.   [13] 1956*a*, 139, *121*.   [14] 1956*a*, 147, *127–8*.

[15] 1956*a*, 148, *128–9*.

[16] 1956*a*, 144, *125*. Cf. Toner, *A Commentary*, 309–11, taking Rahner's rhetoric at face value, on the tension between this claim and the interpretation of the experience in question as exclusively of God: 'How can one be totally drawn into love of God in a slight degree?'

The unclarities and confusions in Rahner's rhetoric arise in part from his exegetical mistakes. In the 1956 essay, Rahner discusses two Ignatian texts—the rule about 'consolation without preceding cause', and a passage from an important early letter—and argues that they ground some kind of objectless consolation. In neither case is Rahner's exegesis of Ignatius plausible, let alone coercive.

Ignatius tells us that 'there is no deceit' in 'consolation without preceding cause' because 'it is only of God our Lord'. Further, as Ignatius grounds the latter statement, he talks of the creator entering, leaving, and making motion in the soul, 'drawing it totally in love of His Divine Majesty'.[17] Two points are important here. Firstly, the reference to a total drawing in love, whatever it means, does *not* distinguish consolations with and without preceding cause. Ignatius has already described consolation as such—any consolation—in terms of the soul being inflamed in the love of the 'Creator and Lord'.[18] Being drawn into God's love, for Ignatius, does not mean that we have ceased to deal with the realities of everyday experience. Secondly, 'without preceding cause' is not to be understood in any strong metaphysical sense, as 'without secondary cause'. Ignatius glosses 'without cause' as 'without any previous perception or understanding of any object such that through it consolation of this sort would come by the mediation of the person's own acts of understanding and will'.[19] Throughout the Exercises, consolation—and indeed desolation—are catalysed by various kinds of instruction and imaginative exercise. Ignatius here seems to be envisaging a consolation that arises without this kind of psychological stimulus.[20] He is not making what would be an indefensible speculative claim about the exclusion of *any* created causality whatever.

---

[17] *Exx*, nn. 330.1, 336.1. The issues raised by Ignatius's text demand expertise at once exegetical, speculative, and pastoral. Quite apart from their cultural diversity, the authors who have dealt with these matters vary widely in these different competences and in how they strike the balance between them. For a sense of the complexity, see Egan, *The Spiritual Exercises and the Ignatian Mystical Horizon*, 8–30. Particularly helpful are Bakker, *Freiheit und Erfahrung*; Gil, *La consolación*; Jean Gouvernaire, *Quand Dieu entre à l'improviste: L'énigme ignatienne de la 'consolation sans cause'* (Paris: Desclée, 1980).

[18] *Exx*, n. 316.1. Note, too, that this description has a practical corollary: 'consequently it cannot love any created thing on the surface of the earth in itself, but rather in the Creator of them all'.

[19] *Exx*, n. 330.2.

[20] Ignatius is here using scholastic terminology, but it is far from clear how much this fact should shape any interpretation. Drafts of the *Spiritual Exercises* suggested that the rule might be supported by citations from the *Summa theologiae* (I–II. ix. 1, 6; x. 4) about divine movement

The rule needs to be read in context. It is one of a series aiming at 'greater discrimination of spirits'. These are to be given to people whose spiritual struggle is subtle, involving temptation under the appearance of good. Ignatius is here envisaging people beset by conflicts between genuinely spiritual consolations, conflicts in which the promptings of 'the enemy' can no longer be distinguished in any straightforward or immediate way from those of the good spirit.[21] Far from being pivotal to any discernment process in the way Rahner suggests, the rule only applies in a particular class of difficult cases.[22] In such cases, Ignatius's second series of rules suggest that different strategies of discrimination are required, depending on whether or not the consolation is prompted by particular thoughts or impulses. If the consolation is *with* preceding cause, then the processes of discrimination and reflection need to centre on how the thoughts develop; if it is *without* preceding cause, then the discrimination required involves the careful separation of impulses arising out of the consolation itself from those developed in the consolation's aftermath.[23]

These formulations are clearly innocent of depth psychology; they need radical reformulation, if not replacement or abolition, if they are to be used by contemporary people. Equally, they also reflect a liberating conviction which is still valid: given a good and gracious God, and given good will on our part, our desires are to be taken as authentic unless there is reason to suppose otherwise.[24]

---

of the will, but in the manuscript he himself corrected, Ignatius deleted whatever was in the corresponding place so vigorously as to render it illegible. See MHSJ *Exx* (1969), 388–9. We can only conjecture why: perhaps Ignatius did not want to be interpreted as making a speculative statement at all (Gil, *La consolación*, 61–2); perhaps the underlying scholastic text was not the *Summa* itself (Bakker shows some impressive parallels between Ignatius's rule and a text on discernment by Denys the Carthusian: *Freiheit und Erfahrung*, 169–92, Appendix 3).

[21] *Exx*, nn. 328, 332, 9–10. Ignatius's elitism here is conditioned by a setting of cultural Christianity, in which it was effectively impossible to imagine God's action outside the Church. For contemporary Christians, Ignatius's teaching about subtle movements might apply also to unrecognized movements of grace among half-believers and non-believers as well as to the temptations of the committed.

[22] Gil, *La consolación*, 95.

[23] Contrast *Exx*, n. 336 with *Exx*, n. 333.1: 'We must pay very much attention to how thoughts carry on (*el discurso de los pensamientos*)'—the criterion of authenticity is whether or not the thoughts *continue* to provoke consolation.

[24] Cf. Toner's provocative and cogent discussion of the reliability of Ignatian discernment in *Discerning God's Will*, 274–86, here 286: 'To sum up . . . so long as the ground for certain assent to the conclusion of a discernment is sought in the evidence on which the conclusion rests, there is no ground for absolute or even for moral certainty . . . Nevertheless Ignatius sees a ground for genuine certitude which I have not found taken in full seriousness . . . except in

When such reason arises—because a consolation appears to have led a person astray—then this theological principle suggests different practical strategies depending on whether or not the consolation arose from particular thoughts or desires. The force of Ignatius's 'exclusively of God our Lord' is not metaphysical. This expression, rather, is functionally equivalent to 'it cannot deceive'.

Rahner's second Ignatian source is a passage from a letter of spiritual direction written in 1536 by Ignatius to Teresa Rejadell.[25] Rahner insists that we must have 'the courage' to take this text 'literally, without well-meaningly watering it down'. But here Karl Rahner is relying on a translation made by his brother Hugo. Once again, Hugo's translation is over-creative. Here is a close English translation of the original in parallel to one of Hugo Rahner's version, with the square brackets indicating a cut in Karl's quotation:

Original	**Hugo Rahner's Version**
It remains now to talk of what we feel as we learn (textual variant—as being) from God our Lord: how we are to understand it, and how, once it is understood, we can take advantage.	*Now it still remains for us to talk about what we are to make of those things the immediate origin of which from God our Lord we inwardly perceive and how we should use them.*
It happens that often Our Lord moves and forces our soul to one way or another of acting by opening our soul; i.e. speaking inside it without any noise of voices, raising the whole of it to his divine love; with us not being able, even if we wanted, to resist his purpose;	*For it happens sometimes that the Lord himself moves our soul, and as it were forces it to one action or another by making our soul wide open. That is, he begins to speak in our innerness without any noise of words, and he seizes the soul completely up to his love, and grants us a perception of himself, so that we, even if we wanted to, would be completely unable to resist it.*

the early directories.' Toner cites the official directory (*Dir*, n. 43.173): 'whenever anyone seeks God truthfully and wholeheartedly, God will never turn away from them, seeing that God's goodness and love for his creatures are so great that he often comes forth to meet even those who do not seek him'.

[25] 1956a, 132–4, *152–4*. For the letter itself, see MHSJ *EI*, i. 99–107, esp. 105 (Ignatius, *Personal Writings*, 129–35, esp. 133–4), and my translation, with commentary, of the most important parts in 'Discerning Behind the Rules'—though the latter argues for some positions which I am now persuaded are wrong.

and the purpose of his [that we take on must necessarily conform us with the commandments, the precepts of the Church, and obedience to our superiors, and it] is full of complete humility, because the same divine spirit is in everything.

Where quite often we can deceive ourselves is that, after the consolation or inbreathing of this kind, as the soul remains in delight, the enemy arrives[26]

This inner feeling [of which we become aware necessarily implies that we conform ourselves to his commandments, the precepts of the Church and obedience to our superiors. It] is filled with deep humility, because it is indeed God's own spirit which is at work in everything.

Nevertheless, we can sometimes deceive ourselves in this, in the following way: after such a consolation and inner enlightenment, the soul remains full of joy. Then the wicked enemy sneaks in[27]

Interpretation of such a complex and obscure text, particularly without Sor Rejadell's original letter requesting guidance, is obviously uncertain. But three points can safely be made. Firstly, the distinction between consolations with and without 'preceding cause' is not central to the advice Ignatius gives. Perhaps the experience being described here does count as a 'consolation without preceding cause', but Ignatius's main concern throughout the letter is to help Teresa have confidence simply in the fact that she is being consoled—by whatever means—and to avoid a misguided humility.

---

[26] '*Agora resta hablar, lo que sentimos leyendo* (textual variant—*seyendo*) *de Dios Nuestro Señor, cómo lo hemos de entender, y entendido sabernos aprovechar. Acaece que muchas veces el Señor nuestro mueve y fuerza a nuestra ánima a una operación o a otra abriendo nuestra ánima; es a saber, hablando dentro della sin ruido alguno de voces, alzando toda a su divino amor, y nosotros a su sentido, aunque quisiésemos, no pudiendo resistir, y el sentido [suyo que tomamos, necesario es conformarnos con los mandamientos, preceptos de la iglesia y obediencia de nuestros mayores, y] lleno de toda humildad porque el mismo espíritu divino es en todo. Donde hartas veces nos podemos engañar es, que después de la tal consolación o espiración, como el ánima queda gozosa, allégase el enemigo*'.

[27] '*Nun bleibt uns noch zu besprechen übrig, was wir von jenen Dingen zu halten haben, deren unmittelbaren Entsprung aus Gott unserem Herrn wir innerlich wahrnehmen, und wie wir sie benützen sollen. Da geschieht es manchmal, daß der Herr selbst unsere Seele bewegt und gleichsam zu diesem oder jenem Tun zwingt, indem er unsere Seele weit offen macht. Das heißt: er beginnt in unserem Innern zu sprechen, ohne jedes Geräusch von Worten, er reißt die Seele ganz zu seiner Liebe empor und schenkt uns ein Wahrnehmen seiner selbst, so daß wir, selbst wenn wir wollten, dem gar nicht widerstehen könnten. Dieses innere Gefühl, [dessen wir innewerden, besagt notwendig, daß wir uns seinen Geboten, den Vorschriften der Kirche und dem Gehorsam gegen unsere Oberen gleichförmig machen. Es] ist erfüllt von tiefer Demut, denn es ist ja Gottes eigener Geist, der in allem waltet. Dennoch können wir uns darin manchmal täuschen, so nämlich: nach einer solchen Tröstung und inneren Erleuchtung bleibt die Seele voll Freude zurück; da schleicht sich der böse Feind ein.*' I supply the part not quoted by Karl Rahner from the German (p. 387) of Hugo Rahner, *Saint Ignatius Loyola: Letters to Women* (the published ET drew directly from the original Spanish).

Secondly, even if the experience described here is a 'consolation without preceding cause' in some Ignatian sense of 'cause', it is not 'without cause' in Rahner's sense of being 'without object'. The experience does, *pace* Karl Rahner, seem to have a categorical object, namely the *operación* to which God 'forces' us, and indeed 'moves' us. Karl Rahner's theological claim may owe something to two options made in Hugo's translation, both of which, without justification, attenuate the link between God's action and a specific option. Whereas Ignatius says that 'Our Lord moves and forces our soul to one way or another of acting', Hugo detaches 'moves' from the reference to action, and introduces an 'as it were' to qualify 'forces'. Further, the Spanish *operación* seems synonymous here with the difficult Ignatian term *sentido*—hence my option to translate the latter as 'purpose', although Hugo Rahner's 'feeling' and 'perception' could be defended. Repeatedly, Hugo Rahner strengthens the language of interiority: *sentimos* is translated as 'we inwardly perceive', *sentido* as 'inner feeling', *espiración* as 'inner enlightenment', *hablando dentro della* as 'speaking in our innerness'. The effect is to suggest that the experience occurs in some kind of 'other' faculty, distinct from those which govern our normal living.

Thirdly, and more generally, Hugo Rahner's version comes across as principally a testimony *that* experience of God happens, and as bringing out how privileged and different such moments are. Ignatius, however, is probably taking the principle of God's presence in experience for granted, and is primarily concerned with how we can recognize, interpret, and thus profit from such experiences. The verbs in Ignatius's first sentence quoted—even if the variant is accepted—focus us on processes of reflection and discernment, in ways that Hugo's rendering, with its inflated talk of 'immediate origin', attenuates. Later, the evocative claim that 'the same divine spirit is in everything'—*pace* Hugo Rahner—appears not so much as a further statement of God's presence in the experience, as a ground for Sor Rejadell to trust its authenticity, and not give way to false humility. If it is of the Spirit, then it must necessarily be in tune with the Church—in other words, we might add, linked to the flesh-and-blood community of believers. Karl Rahner's cut—encouraged by Hugo's rearrangement of the syntax— only intensifies the distortion. Clearly, however, Ignatius's text refers to an experience of God all too compatible with everyday, ambiguous desires and conflicts.

Both speculative and exegetical argument, therefore, discredit any straightforward reading of Rahner's statement that in the key Ignatian experience, 'God's own self is present and nothing else at all can be'. This statement could be simply a mistake; it could also be an imprecise way simply of claiming that the experience is authentic. A more charitable option involves our drawing on the quite idiosyncratic account of *Erfahrung* offered by Rahner and Vorgrimler in the *Concise Theological Dictionary*. There, as we have already seen, *Erfahrung* is described as arising from 'the immediate reception of an impression' originating in a reality 'removed from our free disposing'. Moreover, religious *Erfahrung* only occurs in the context of a conceptual reflection: the two are distinct, but also inseparable. A more exact translation of *Erfahrung* would be 'passive element in experience'.[28] Such an account suggests that the Ignatian 'first principle' is not an experience in the normal sense at all, but the passive element abstracted from an event that always has an active side too, an active side remaining thoroughly fallible and worldly. Such a reading leads us to a more sober understanding of God's presence in Ignatian discernment than Rahner's rhetoric suggests. However, as we will discover, such an account of the matter provides all that a significant Rahnerian theology of the Ignatian Exercises requires.

Experience, Language, and Concepts

We turn now to what Rahner says about the absence of language from the key Ignatian experience. In a footnote early in the 1956 essay, Rahner stresses how our knowledge of individual imperatives from God does not depend on any kind of irrationalist illuminism, but remains within the sphere of the intellect—a faculty which, for the scholastic tradition, apprehends values as well as facts:

Only, we are not dealing with knowledge of a rationally discursive and conceptually objectifiable kind, but rather a knowledge, proper to the intellect, which is ultimately grounded in the simple self-presence of the inwardly enlightened subject. In the process of acting, the subject has self-awareness, without the one knowing and what is known being contrasted with each other in the way that is the case with those objects that are

[28] *Concise Theological Dictionary*, 164, *109*.

known by recourse to a sense-based imaginative model (*conversio ad phantasmata*).[29]

This passage invokes a quality of self-awareness in some sense independent of the objects experienced by the self, while implying that the mental state in question is thus not 'conceptual (*begrifflich*)'. A distinction is being made between the experience in itself and reflection on it. At the outset of *Foundations of Christian Faith*, Rahner stresses the importance of such a distinction for his whole theological project. No theology can be unconditionally valid,

> since it is obvious that reflection in general, and all the more so academic theological reflection, does not capture (*nicht einholt*) and cannot capture the whole of this reality which we make real through believing, loving, hoping, and praying. Precisely this permanent and insurmountable difference between basic Christian living and acting on the one hand, and reflection on this on the other, will be a constant preoccupation in this book. To see this difference constitutes a key insight, and represents a prerequisite for being led into the systematic understanding of Christianity.[30]

Clearly, Rahner is making a significant, meaningful distinction in such a statement. However, it is a mistake to describe 'the experience itself' as somehow beyond words. Obviously God's presence in our lives does not necessarily entail that we can name that presence or reflect on it. Moreover, this presence itself is far more important than any particular way in which we might articulate it. But nevertheless, if we claim, not just that God is present to us, but also that we can experience this presence, then we are also committed to saying that our language can somehow refer to the divine.

If I make the kind of simple existential claim from which Rahner's metaphysics of mind begins—for example 'Here is a table'—then, Rahner tells us, I already have the ability to abstract quiddities from particulars, and to transcend the particular cases before me. Indeed, I have a *Vorgriff* of reality as such, and hence of

---

[29] 1956a, 94–5 n. 9, *83 n. 23*: '*Nur handelt es sich nicht um eine Erkenntnis rational diskursiver und begrifflich gegenständlicher Art, sondern um eine intellektuelle Erkenntnis, die im letzten beruht auf dem schlichten Beisichsein des innerlich gelichteten Subjekts, das in seinem Aktvollzug um sich selber weiß, ohne daß der Wissende und das Gewußte sich in der Weise entgegengesetzt wären, wie dies hinsichtlich jener Objekte der Fall ist, die durch die Hinwendung zu einem sinnlichen Vorstellungsmodell* (conversio ad phantasmata) *gewußt werden.*'

[30] *Foundations of Christian Faith*, 2, *14* (*KRSW*, xxvi. 9). The rather complex expression, *Einführung in den Begriff des Christentums*, which constitutes the subtitle of *Foundations*, was Rahner's original title (*KRSW*, xxvi, p. xxvi).

God—a metaphysical awareness given only in and through aware-ness of physical reality. Further—and here we perhaps begin to go beyond Rahner—I have an interpersonally learned skill in the use of some word by which I can refer to the table (and, for that matter, command of the more complex idiom 'Here is' and of how to use the indefinite article).

The point is very important for the interpretation of Rahner's philosophy, for the development of any theology making central ref-erence to human experience, and for any theories about prayer or 'spirituality'. How does it affect our understanding of Rahner's 'transcendence becoming thematic'? The idea of God's action somehow transforming the subjectivity through which we experi-ence all phenomena, altering the self's sense of its own identity, seems unobjectionable, indeed helpful and suggestive. The suppos-ition that this process is 'non-conceptual' seems at best ambiguous and at worst wrong-headed. 'Non-conceptual' is admittedly not an exact translation of *unbegrifflich*, but Rahner nevertheless seldom dis-tinguishes the linguistic from the objectifiable and graspable, the *begrifflich* from the *begreifbar*. Obviously, God's otherness lies, as Hop-kins put it, 'past all grasp'; and the supernatural existential is a tran-scendental reality which as such cannot simply be read off from external historical data. But neither of those self-evident points commits us to the incoherence of *saying* that God's action lies beyond the realm of *language*.

At the end of a helpful demonstration of how Rahner's under-standing of Ignatius and Bonaventure lies behind his later Christ-ology, Joseph Wong writes the following sentence:

If the 'incarnate Word' is regarded as the proper object of the non-conceptual ecstatic love, here the expression, 'His Divine Majesty' (*su majestad divina*), should mean first of all Christ himself whose loving presence is directly experienced without any mental image or concept.

A footnote adduces similar thought-patterns in Teresa of Avila, John of the Cross, and *The Cloud of Unknowing*, at least as conven-tionally interpreted.[31] Such rhetoric—and the example is almost randomly chosen—stands at least in danger of falling into self-contradiction. The claim that the reality described is 'non-conceptual' sits ill with the elaborate theology built on this claim. If

[31] Wong, *Logos-Symbol*, 62.

the Word, indeed the incarnate Word, is the object of the experience in question, then the person reporting it (who may or may not be the person having it) must have some means of distinguishing this object. And any such means involves the use of language.

We have already referred to a famous passage in Ignatius's *Autobiography*, recounting a particularly important experience he had at Manresa, by the banks of the River Cardoner:

> as he was seated there, the eyes of his understanding began to be opened: not that he saw some vision, but understanding and knowing many things, spiritual things just as much as matters of faith and learning—and this with an enlightenment so strong that all things seemed new to him. One cannot set out the particular things he understood then, though they were many: rather, he received a great clarity in his understanding, such that in the whole course of his life, right up to the sixty-two years he has completed, he does not think, gathering together all the helps he has had from God and all the things he has come to know (even if he joins them into one), that he has ever attained so much as on that single occasion.[32]

Here if anywhere Ignatius was touched by God. Nothing happened to the river, but his whole being was transformed, and all things appeared new. Ignatius professes not to understand the process fully—a failure at once contrasting with and reflected by the luxuriant range of subsequent interpretation.[33] But he is still using linguistic resources to articulate, however incompletely, a distinction between this experience and other experiences, and on that basis to readjust his whole world-view. How can such distinctions be articulated except through some kind of language? Even in Rahner's theology, the difference made by the supernatural existential is not one that can simply be read off in categorical reality: it leads us, rather, to see the world in a new context, to reinterpret all our experience.

Rahner's frequent use of such terms as 'unsayable (*unsagbar*)' and 'nameless (*namenlos*)' is, strictly speaking, self-contradictory. The idiom sounds plausible only because we are captivated by a quite unnuanced understanding of language. In the 1956 discernment essay, Rahner takes up the phrase in the Rejadell letter describing

---

[32] *Aut*, n. 30.3–4.

[33] For example, Jesuits have disputed whether, and to what extent, Ignatius received in this experience some kind of premonition and divine charter regarding the Society of Jesus he was later to found; see Antonio Jiménez Oñate, *El origen de la Compañía de Jesús: Carisma fundacional y génesis histórica* (Rome: Jesuit Historical Institute, 1966). For a more Jungian approach, see Schwager, *Das dramatische Kirchenverständnis*, 52–7.

God's action as occurring 'without any noise of voices' (mistranslated by Hugo Rahner as 'without any noise of words'). Karl Rahner comments:

We may perfectly legitimately replace this by saying 'without concepts, without objectified individual realities over against us (*ohne objektivierte Einzelgegenstände*)'. For, assuming that what we think is not just something vague and unreliable, then, in inner experience, words and concepts, conceptually apprehended objects and the objects placed before oneself, are identical.[34]

This passage seems to contrast the Ignatian experience with an undifferentiated amalgam of the verbal, the conceptual, and that which objectively confronts us—the *gegenständlich*. Such a passage seems to presuppose, uncritically, an understanding of language whereby the naming of an object implies control over it. Given such an assumption, theologians will obviously be tempted to conceive the essence of faith as non-linguistic. Wittgenstein shows us, if nothing else, that our language in fact operates in an indefinite variety of ways:

Our language can be seen as an ancient city: a maze of little streets and squares, of old and new houses, and of houses with additions from various periods; and this surrounded by a multitude of new boroughs with straight regular streets and uniform houses.[35]

Straightforward ostensive definition is by no means the only mechanism through which language and reality relate.

An example from Shakespeare may be helpful here. Towards the end of *Hamlet*, the hero has two lines:

> There's a divinity that shapes our ends,
> Rough-hew them how we will.[36]

Despite the basic simplicity of the sense, the language is here being used with quite extraordinary density. The different sounds, the different meanings of 'divinity', 'end', and 'will', the interplay of Latinate and Anglo-Saxon vocabulary, the contrasting syntactic patterns of the two lines—all these contribute to the meaning of the

---

[34] 1956*a*, 153, *133*. With such a vague sentence, translation is more than normally debatable, but the details are not relevant here.

[35] Wittgenstein, *Philosophical Investigations*, § 18. See also §§ 23, 27.

[36] William Shakespeare, *Hamlet*, v. ii. 10–11.

sentence, a meaning which cannot be otherwise expressed. A competent piece of literary criticism on these lines will not seek to replace the lines with some simpler equivalent. Rather, its function will be to send the reader back to the lines themselves, to understand *them, their* particular pressures and tension, better—and *thus* to have an enriched experience of the reality expressed. Rahner made something like the same point when commenting on a line of the poet Brentano (even if, to an Anglo-Saxon ear, the line sounds eminently forgettable). Once one has done one's *Wissenschaft* on a literary text, 'would one not have to return to these words of the poet, to these primordial words, in order to understand, in order intimately and truly to grasp, what the long commentary "really" wanted to say?'[37] The climax of the Christian life may indeed be silence and abandonment before the mystery of God, but that mystery is given us in word and symbol.

Language's power to communicate meaning involves far more than the naming of particular objects. At one point in his *Spiritual Diary*, Ignatius experiences what he calls *loqüela*—some kind of gift of tongues, both interior and exterior.[38] He writes of a great harmony accompanying it, and of his feeling 'wholly moved to the divine love and to the *loqüela* divinely granted'. Then he adds 'but I cannot express it'. 'Express' here must mean something like 'describe accurately', not 'refer to', for the experience quite clearly has a meaning, a cognitive significance. Ignatius knows that it is wrong to be distracted by the mere sound. Through it, he tells us, 'I was being in the method I should follow. And I hoped for ever greater learning (*erudición*) in the future.'

Nevertheless, though Rahner may sometimes have laboured under an excessively crude theory of language, his theology was not dependent on it, and he could on occasion go beyond it. The title of *Hearer of the Word* is no redundancy: metaphysical truth is known on the basis of the sensory, supplemented by a discourse of negation,

---

[37] 'Priest and Poet', 298, *353*. 'Primordial word' (*Urwort*) is a technical term in some of Rahner's essays on poetry and on the Sacred Heart: see Fischer, *Der Mensch als Geheimnis*, 45–8; Wong, *Logos-Symbol*, 63–8.

[38] *Diary*, nn. 221–40, esp. 221–2, 234 (Ignatius, *Personal Writings*, 107–9). See also the discussion by John Futrell in an appendix, entitled 'The Vocabulary of "The Spiritual Diary"', to *Inigo: Discernment Log-Book: The Spiritual Diary of Saint Ignatius Loyola*, ed. and trans. Joseph A. Munitiz (London: Inigo Enterprises, 1987), 79–93, here 85–7.

First Principles

pointing us towards what is non-material.[39] Thus a claim about revelation is a claim about a 'twofold unity': that of 'supernatural reality
(*Sein*)' and of the word, implicitly a word indicating a meaning
beyond what meets the eye.[40] Moreover, this claim is of a piece with
Rahner's mature achievement.[41] Even in his writings on existential
ethics, Rahner distances himself from any unacceptably strong
account of 'non-conceptual experience'. In the essay 'Principles
and Prescriptions (Imperatives)', Rahner addresses an objection to
his theory. Surely the linguistic form of the imperative—so Rahner
imagines the objector speaking—committed as it is to general concepts, cannot express the kind of strictly individual obligation which
Rahner claims to exist. Rahner answers by invoking language's
power to express what cannot be generalized:

> a linguistic imperative does have its own characteristic relationship to the
> individual as such—just like a gesture, or someone pointing to what lies
> *here*, in front of them. (If God tells someone) 'you should be a doctor
> (although you could be a priest)', then this sentence in fact does not touch
> just on the general aspect of the concrete case which is this life and this
> vocation, but also on what is unique in this following of a vocation and in
> this life. It has expressed a reference to the concrete, and addressed this
> concrete reality to an *individuum ineffabile*.[42]

Once again, the paradox of talk about the 'ineffable' demands resolution. There is more to language than universal propositions.
Though the latter cannot express an individual moral imperative,

---

[39] *Hearer of the Word*, 129–36, *190–201* (*KRSW*, iv. 228–46), esp. 132, *193–4* (*KRSW*, iv. 234).
[40] 1937, 285, *339*.
[41] One important contribution of Mannermaa's was to discredit the view of the early
Rahner encouraged by Metz's re-edition of *Hearer of the Word*. Metz suggested that the first
edition advocated a crude, propositional account of revelation, which the mature Rahner
had abandoned for an account centred more on the imparting of supernatural reality as such
(*KRSW*, iv. 231–3 n. 104; ET of 2nd edn., 152–3 n. 2; Mannermaa, 'Eine falsche Interpretationstradition', 204). Confining his researches to the period before 1950, when Rahner published 'Concerning the Relationship between Nature and Grace', Mannermaa showed
conclusively that Metz's contrast was mistaken. Even in 'early' Rahnerian writings, the
'word' was correlated with the self-communication of God. Mannermaa's claims have led
many Rahner scholars to see Metz's revision as an unreliable curiosity and to work from the
first edition (*Hearer of the Word*, pp. vi–x). At the present stage of Rahnerian research, Mannermaa's findings can also be deployed tellingly against those who assert that Rahner's positions fail to give adequate weight to the categorical. Implicitly against Mannermaa, Metz
has recently supplied evidence that Rahner authorized the changes at least to the main text
of the second edition; at the same time Metz confirmed that he himself was responsible for
the footnotes (*KRSW*, vol. iv, pp. xvi–xvii).
[42] 'Principles and Prescriptions', 21, *20–21*.

these imperatives are still amenable to linguistic expression of some kind. Were that not the case, human beings could not be aware of them.

Rahner is not ultimately committed to the view that God's grace transcends language. The point, rather—adumbrated in the claim from *Hearer of the Word* that metaphysical language involves verbal negation—is that our language about God's grace can never be a discourse of control, of grasping. Two English words that are often synonymous point up the contrast: we cannot comprehend the divine, only 'under-stand' it. In English, 'concept' is a pluriform idea, often simply equivalent to 'word'.[43] By contrast, Rahner's claim that the experience of God is non-conceptual depends on a narrower understanding of 'concept' or *Begriff*, derived from Hegel, and within which the etymological links with the ideas of grasping and encompassing are still alive.[44] As Rahner's erstwhile colleague, Otto Muck, describes the matter, God's properties are 'incomprehensible (*unbegreiflich*)' only if *begreifen* implies that we can grasp the object in the sense of placing it 'within an ordered scheme of things known to us', or explain the object's existence causally. But there is no reason to suppose that this condition always applies, and in broader senses of *Begriff* our concepts not only can but also must be applied to God.[45]

Against Rahner's talk of the Ignatian 'first principle' being 'ineffable' or 'non-conceptual' we must insist that all human experience involves language. Rahner's denials can lead to his being misread, ironically, in terms of just the escapism that he seeks so laboriously to discredit in his metaphysical writings. Human experience can be pre-systematic, pre-theoretical,[46] but not non-linguistic. Three positive concerns, however, informing Rahner's use of such language must be affirmed and maintained. Firstly, the transformation that

---

[43] P. L. Heath, 'Concept', in Paul Edwards (ed.), *The Encyclopedia of Philosophy*, 8 vols. (London: Collier Macmillan, 1968), ii. 177–80, at 178, classifies six usages for the term, each of which depends on a permutation of two theoretical options, the first of these being threefold, the second twofold: 'The term "concept" is thus essentially a dummy expression or variable, whose meaning is assignable only in the context of a theory, and cannot be independently ascertained. Though a frequent source of confusion and controversy, it remains useful, precisely because of its ambiguity, as a kind of passkey through the labyrinths represented by the theory of meaning, the theory of thinking, and the theory of being.'

[44] See *Foundations of Christian Faith*, 1–2, *13–14* (*KRSW*, xxvi. 8–9).

[45] Muck, *Philosophische Gotteslehre*, 151.

[46] Rahner once wrote in a dictionary article—'Dreifaltigkeitsmystik'—of Ignatius's 'untheoretical experience'.

occurs when transcendence becomes thematic centres on the subject's identity: it is not directly caused by the objects which confront us. Secondly, the claim being made is a realist one: the reality in question is an independent given, one to which any of our theories or concepts are always responses. Thirdly, there is no question of our linguistic competence implying that we can manipulate or control the reality of grace.

Grace, Experience, and Certainty

So far in this chapter, then, we have established that what Rahner isolates as the key experience of Ignatian discernment is inseparable from experiences of a particular object, and that it is 'non-conceptual' only in restricted senses. We now need to consider directly its axiomatic status, its 'characteristic of underivability, of self-evidence'.[47]

If the key experience is always an abstraction, and never occurs on its own, it follows that it cannot give us axiomatic certainty regarding any particular judgement. Any existential-ethical judgement involves a synthesis between the discernment of God's call and other material judgements. It follows that even if the former of these is somehow infallible, the latter can always be questioned. In his discussion of Rahner's 1956 essay, Avery Dulles took issue with what he took to be Rahner's claims regarding an incontrovertible experience:

> In connection with the application of the Ignatian rules, it seems worthwhile to mention a rather obvious point too often overlooked, namely, that a prudent decision presupposes accurate information about what the decision involves . . . If I am convinced, for instance, that the Black Franciscans do what the Carthusians do in fact, my decision to join the former order, though otherwise thoroughly in accord with the rules of election, might well be a disaster. The technique of discernment, in its affective aspects, reveals only the harmony between my personal religious orientations and my *idea* of the object under consideration.[48]

For whatever reason, Rahner's reply ignored the issue. Perhaps he felt misread; perhaps he found the question just too boring and prosaic; perhaps he was working from a summary of Dulles's article

---

[47] 1956*a*, 143, *125*.   [48] Dulles, 'Finding God's Will', 150–1.

which omitted this point.[49] The answer becomes clear and straightforward, however, if we interpret the Ignatian first principle not as a particular experience but as a regulative truth. In that case, its axiomatic status centres not on a specific choice, but rather on the general claim that it *makes sense* to talk about a vocation being revealed by God in our experience.

For philosophical background to the 1956 essay, Rahner does little more than refer us back to his writing on the *intellectus agens* and on first principles in Aquinas: in other words, to *Spirit in the World* and associated writings.[50] Here, to put the point very minimally, Rahner draws on Maréchal, and no doubt through Maréchal on a longer tradition, to show that *systematic* scepticism, i.e. the claim that the gap between the phenomenal and the noumenal is intrinsically unbridgeable, involves a contradiction. As Rahner put the matter in a 1938 lecture, every claim about physical reality presupposes that the metaphysical question regarding knowledge of the external world has already been answered. For sceptics cannot intelligibly be taken to be sceptical about their own scepticism. *Physik*, everyday knowledge,

fundamentally presupposes, however critical it is of what meets the eye, an external world that is already known, and thus a knowledge that is always antecedently in the presence of the other. This still applies even when everyday knowledge believes itself to be experiencing merely a subjective feeling. For even this feeling still has an existence independent of the knowledge about it.[51]

Even a false statement depends on metaphysical and logical principles. The anti-sceptical position is not committed to the truth of any particular judgement. The claim is rather that there obtains a primordial correlation between knowledge and external reality, a correlation presupposed in the very making of a sceptical claim. Sceptics are not sceptical about their scepticism. Thus Rahner, immediately after claiming in the 1956 essay that the 'first principle' is incontrovertible, adds:

But one must be careful. We are not dealing here with a conceptual representation of God, a conceptually articulated theorem concerning God— not with a proposition concerning God, composed out of human concepts

---

[49] 1969, 290 n. 1 (original in English).
[50] 1956a, 139–140 n. 31, *121–122 n. 45*.
[51] 'Thomas Aquinas on Truth' (1938), 19, *27 (KRSW,* ii. 308).

which are necessarily, even when they refer to God, built out of the material of finite and inner-worldly concepts and representations through a *conversio ad phantasmata*. With that conceptual reality of God, and reference to God, there can, of course, be just as much error and misinterpretation as with any other proposition, or any other object of a free love.[52]

Rahner invoked a similar argument in the last of his Ignatian writings, the letter, found on his desk when he died, to a Jesuit enthused by the charismatic movement. While affirming the presence of grace in consciousness and lamenting Jesuit failure to theologize on this basis, he also makes some sharp comments on naive fideism and escapist piety. He refers his correspondent back to *Visions and Prophecies*.[53] Rahner's main hope seems to be that the young man read the sarcastic footnotes, but the central theological claim of that book is also relevant here. The 'mystical' touch of God occurs at a point deeper than sensibility. In terms of the 1956 essay, it is the self's *Transzendenz*, the conditions which enable it to be a human mind at all, that is transformed. One can believe unconditionally that God has acted at that level while remaining sceptical about particular visions, extraordinary phenomena, or judgements about what this divine touch might imply for our practice:

If the actual 'point' at which God primarily works lies deeper, 'behind' the sensory faculties of knowledge, if it opens up into a contact and union of the spirit in the human person with God, in other words to where the real event of *grace* has its place, then it becomes understandable and something automatically to be expected that the echo of this actual core-event in human sensibility will not only be governed by the event itself, but rather that all the other dispositions in the visionary will equally have an influence.[54]

In *Visions and Prophecies* itself, the point has two applications. Firstly, official ecclesiastical approval of apparitions at such places as Fatima commits no one to accepting all the claims associated with such cults. Secondly, explanations of the events in terms of the natural or human sciences do not necessarily discredit them theologically. In our more general context, we can make a distinction between general conviction and particular event. We may know through revelation that God is at work in us always and everywhere, and in that sense transcendentally. But this implies just nothing

[52] 1956a, 148, *129*.   [53] 1984, 132, *2*.   [54] *Visions and Prophecies*, 62–3, *59–60*.

about the incorrigibility of a particular experience or a particular religious statement.

In his reply to Dulles's criticisms of the 1956 essay, Rahner made a comparison between Ignatius and Aristotle. Both formulated principles implicit in everyday reasoning. Aristotle's covered knowledge in general; Ignatius's covered knowledge under grace:

I still think that in this respect Ignatius Loyola has the same kind of significance for the Church as Aristotle does for secular logic. In the realm of the secular, Aristotelian logic has always been used, even before Aristotle; and, even before Ignatius, people used a logic of existential decisions with regard to salvation unreflectively, yet in the light of grace (i.e. conditioned by the grace-laden orientation of human identity, unreflectively but really present in consciousness). But nevertheless it was only through Aristotle that the one logic became a reflective and ordered body of knowledge (*Wissenschaft*), and through Ignatius that the other did: the philosophers' discipline regarding their own method, the saints' discipline regarding the lived Christian life.[55]

Rahner finds in Ignatius an analogue to Aristotelian first principles of logic and ontology.[56] But such 'first principles' are clearly not equivalent to some particular privileged experience. We have no experience of the principle of non-contradiction 'neat', independent of its disclosure in our language and our judgements, including our wrong judgements. We extrapolate such principles from our ongoing experience, through cumulative reflection. To use the distinction standard in modern German, our experience of such principles is an *Erfahrung*, not an *Erlebnis*: we may experientially realize (*erfahren*) a principle like the law of gravity, but what we actually experience (*erleben*) are bodies falling to the ground.

As we saw in Chapter 3, Rahner's philosophy grounds a weak sense in which human consciousness presupposes a knowledge of God. Our minds are correlated with reality, and we necessarily

[55] 1969, 291, *243*.

[56] Since Rahner wrote, it has become fashionable for historical studies of Ignatius to find Aristotelian influences in his texts. Ignatius would have picked up Aristotelian idiom both in Paris, and, perhaps more significantly, in his courtly training prior to conversion. See, for example, Boyle, 'Angels Black and White'; Georg Eickhoff, 'Iñigo de Loyola, die Reichen und die Armen. Der Begriff der "Gerechtigkeit" in Spanien um 1500', *Geist und Leben*, 63 (1990), 324–44; Rogelio García-Mateo, 'Los estudios filosóficos de Ignacio de Loyola y su espiritualidad', *Manresa*, 62 (1990), 73–86. For a reading of Ignatian discernment (and to some extent of Rahner) in the light of Aristotelian moral philosophy, see Hughes, 'Ignatian Discernment'.

adopt, however unreflectively, a *Weltanschauung*. We must therefore
have epistemic contact with the reality which that *Weltanschauung*
expresses. In that sense, we are necessarily *beim Sein im ganzen*—in
contact with reality as a whole and its ground, in contact with that
to which a true *Weltanschauung* would conform. Equally, such knowledge is quite compatible with our *Weltanschauung* being wrong: the
axiomatic principle is merely that *Weltanschauung* questions are
meaningful.

Once again, inadequate Ignatian exegesis may be contributing
to the misleading impression Rahner's rhetoric gives, in particular
as regards the three Ignatian 'times' of election: the first 'time' of
irresistible attraction, the second of discrimination between spirits,
the third of reflecting on pros and cons.[57] Rahner's account depends
on an assumption that is quite widespread, yet which requires at
least serious qualification if not outright rejection. He rather
assumes that Ignatius is listing these three alternatives in order of
desirability, as if God is somehow more, or more certainly, operative
in the first than in the third. Rahner, as we have already noted at the
outset of Chapter 5, rehabilitates the second 'time' against an anti-
illuminist tradition of regarding the third as safer and more rational.[58] There are structural links between Rahner's position here
and his argumentation regarding the supernatural formal object—
argumentation which in its turn reflects patterns in Rahner's reading of Bonaventure. 'The immediate experience of God' in the
graced self is different from—although it presupposes—the inferential experience of God as creator: similarly, the third, 'rational'
mode of election exists only as a deficient, partial form of the second.[59] 'Rapture' and the first 'time' become limit cases, privileged
moments essential to a theory, but which no one will normally
experience. There are parallels, too, with Rahner's moral
epistemology: the first 'time' corresponds to divine command; the
second to 'existential' ethics and discerned obligations; the third to
'essential' ethics and universal rules.

There is, admittedly, some basis in the Ignatian texts for seeing
the three 'times' of election as presented in order of preference. The

---

[57] *Exx*, nn. 175–89.
[58] For documentation, see Jacques Roy, 'L'election d'après Saint Ignace: interpretations
diverses', *Revue d'ascétique et de mystique*, 38 (1962), 305–23, an essay that re-explores the primary
sources under Rahner's influence.
[59] 1956a, 169, *147*; 103, *90–1*.

Exercises themselves tell us that the third 'time' is to be used only if the first and second 'times' have not yielded a result,[60] while Ignatius's own Directory—a kind of practical commentary— repeatedly echoed by his successors, indicates that the three 'times' are to be tried in the order listed.[61] The official Directory of 1599 sees the first 'time' as 'miraculous', 'quite out of the ordinary', and 'not subject to any rule'; it also says that the first two 'times' are to be preferred to the third, because they involve the will rather than the intellect. By implication, therefore, the second is the preferred 'time'.[62]

However, there are at least three reasons why this interpretation of the matter should be rejected. Firstly, Ignatius's heading for the listing of the three 'times' stresses that *any* of them can lead to a good decision: 'three times for making—in any one of them—a good and sound election'.[63] Ignatius's own practice, and his recommend- ations in the *Constitutions*, seem to have depended much more on third-time procedures, albeit of more varied and differentiated forms than the *Exercises* themselves would suggest.[64] Though the early sources may indicate a preference for the *use* of the second- time over against the third, this is not a presumption in favour of second-time *results*. Rather, the fruits of either method can in principle, depending on circumstances, override those of the other.[65] In particular, the recommendation that a third-time elec- tion be 'confirmed' in prayer is not, *pace* Rahner, to be read as an implicit transition back to the second 'time'.[66]

Secondly, the disjunction between heart and head, or will and intellect, informing both what the *Directory* and Rahner say about the second and third 'times', is not Ignatian. Both the second and third Ignatian 'times' involve both the cognitive and the affective faculties. The second 'time' involves not just consolations and deso- lations, but also a process of experimental reflection. Conversely, the third-time process of reflection is influenced and shaped by the prayer which has preceded: exposure to the gospel message

[60] *Exx*, n. 178.   [61] *Dir*, n. 1.18–19.   [62] *Dir*, nn. 43.187, 43.190.

[63] *Exx*, n. 175.1: '*tres tiempos para hacer sana y buena elección en cada uno dellos*'.

[64] See Meures, 'The Ministry of Facilitation', n. 18, and my 'The Draughthorse's Bloodlines'.

[65] e.g. *Dir*, n. 43.207. Toner, *Discerning God's Will*, 249–50, rather overstates the case in sug- gesting that there was a presumption in favour of the third 'time'.

[66] *Exx*, nn. 183, 188; 1956*a*, 96, *84*; Toner, *Discerning God's Will*, 191–232, 249–50.

modifies standards of rationality. The reflection characteristic of the third 'time' depends not only on deductive reasoning, but also on intuitive and emotional considerations. Knauer tellingly cites a passage from Ignatius's own list of pros and cons in connection with the process recounted in his *Spiritual Diary*. First in Ignatius's list of reasons for not accepting sacristy endowments arose from a desire for imitation of Christ's poverty: 'the Society gains greater spiritual strength, and increased devotion, the more it contemplates and imitates the Son of the Blessed Virgin, our Creator and Lord, so poor and so afflicted'. The object of an election process is always a personal reality; the election implies a judgement that a certain course of action is appropriate to a particular individual or group. The second-time process approaches the issue through reflection on how an individual is consoled, on their sense of identity under God; the third through reflection on the particular options under consideration.[67] Though either can be used autonomously, it is normal for them to be used together, with the result of one 'time' being used to confirm the other.[68] Ignatius is certainly aware of something like the Rahnerian distinction between essential and existential ethics, but he uses it to distinguish candidates for his full process from those whom it would overburden and whose needs are simple enough for rules to satisfy. By contrast, both the second and third 'times' put forward alternative methods for Ignatian decision in the full sense.[69]

Thirdly, the sense of compulsion in the first 'time'—'without doubting nor being able to doubt'—may indicate not a properly theological certainty, but simply a subjective psychological state. A curious passage from Ignatius's *Autobiography* shows clear parallels with Ignatius's first 'time':

He was continuing in his abstinence from eating meat, and was firm on that—in no way was he thinking of making a change—when one day, in the morning when he had got up, there appeared to him meat for the eating, as if he could see it with his bodily eyes, without any desire for it having been there before. And together with this there also came upon him a great assent of the will that, from then on, he should eat meat. And although he could still remember his intention from earlier, he was

[67] Knauer, 'Die Wahl', 326: The second and third 'times' of election 'are best distinguished as the method of "objectivation" and "subjectivation"'.

[68] Ignatius's *Spiritual Diary* here serves as an impressive model. See Toner, *Discerning God's Will*, 236–54, esp. conclusion on 254.

[69] *Exx*, n. 18; Knauer, 'Die Wahl', 329.

incapable of being doubtful about this: rather he could not but make up his mind that he had to eat meat. And when he recounted this afterwards to his confessor, the confessor was telling him he should consider whether perhaps this was a temptation. But he, examining the matter well, was incapable of ever being doubtful about it.[70]

The will is shown an option, and drawn to it, in a way that cannot be resisted; on this ground one can conclude that the option represents God's will. Such a claim is open to obvious objection, particularly once one allows for the findings of depth psychology. But it is at least historically plausible to imagine Ignatius's first 'time' as centring on an experience of rooted conviction, a conviction to be distinguished, not only from a sense of having worked through a valid argument (third 'time'), but also from the affective attraction which he called spiritual consolation (second 'time').[71] Moreover, granted Christian premises about divine beneficence, and granted the kind of conscientiousness Ignatius shows here, the substantive claim begins to appear less absurd.

Taken together, these points show that Ignatius's three 'times' for election have important features in common. All three 'times' presuppose that God's grace is present in human consciousness and decision-making; even in the third 'time', God is asked to 'put into my soul what I should desire'.[72] All, too, involve cumulative and fallible processes of reasoning; even the first 'time', if Ignatius's decision to resume eating meat is indeed an example of it, involves reflection and scrutiny. The difference lies not in different strikings of the balance between divine and human agency, but in the kind of evidence and argumentation involved.[73] In all three cases the divine action can be relied on, axiomatically; but we can only discuss it in abstraction. It can never be isolated.

As we have seen, Rahner's 1956 essay on discernment is heavily dependent on what he makes of Ignatius's 'consolation without preceding cause'. According to Rahner, this is 'a divine motion in regard to which it is indubitable that it comes from God'. Ignatius puts it forward, 'not as an object to be tested but as the

[70] *Aut*, n. 27.1–3; see Knauer 'Die Wahl', 331–2; Toner, *Discerning God's Will*, 108–10.
[71] For further discussion, see the provocatively original chapter on the first 'time' in Toner, *Discerning God's Will*, 107–29.
[72] *Exx*, n. 180, see n. 184; Toner, *Discerning God's Will*, 170–1.
[73] Toner, *Discerning God's Will*, 233–54; his *What is Your Will, O God?*, 12, offers a useful chart. See also Knauer, 'Die Wahl', 332.

starting-point and criterion of the test'.[74] Whatever we make of the claim about divine origin, we must note the complete lack of textual evidence for the view that Ignatius sees a *particular* experience of this kind as foundational or necessary to any discernment process. Toner's discussion of the point is brief and devastating:

> What is it that leads Rahner to propose that consolation without previous cause is for Ignatius the first principle of all discernments of spirits and of God's will? . . . Is there some particular text or texts of Ignatius which he sees as clearly and cogently pointing to consolation without preceding cause as the first principle? If so, after many readings of Rahner's essay I have been unable to find any. Neither have I been able to find such texts in any of those writers who profess to follow Rahner in this matter. Rather, Rahner seems to begin from his own premise that all discernment has to be founded on some *indubitably* divine motion within our experience.[75]

Rahner's services to Ignatian exegesis, particularly regarding 'consolation without preceding cause', have consisted more in the questions he opened up than in the answers he gave. Nevertheless, however dubious his handling of Ignatius's texts, Rahner identified an important theological issue: how to articulate the 'supernatural logic' and 'first principles' involved in the discernment of God's will.[76] Though Ignatius's 'consolation without preceding cause' has

---

[74] 1956*a*, 131, *114*.

[75] Toner, *A Commentary*, 303. See the whole section (pp. 301–13), and Toner, *Discerning God's Will*, esp. 316–22.

[76] One of Rahner's critics at this point echoes Claudel: 'Rahner has drawn theologically straight . . . with exegetically crooked lines' (Bakker, *Freiheit und Erfahrung*, 53 n. 34). See also Gil, *La consolación*, 90: 'Although I agree with Rahner's theory regarding the appropriate kind of a priori, his attempt to discover this model in Exx 330 gives rise to major reservations.' By contrast, most previous discussions of Rahner and Ignatius take one of two broad positions: either they accept Rahner's Ignatian exegesis uncritically (e.g. Fischer, Egan, Schwerdtfeger, Zahlauer), or else they see its flaws as discrediting his whole theory (e.g. Bakker, Toner). Rahner may not have been strongly committed to his exegesis; at one point he contrasts the 'stimulus (*Anstoß*)' he is claiming to provide with what might emerge from a full historical study of Ignatius's life and teaching. He tells us that he is only asking a question, 'even where, in order not to become too boring, it takes the form of a firm statement' (1956*a*, 89 n. 3, *78 n. 17*). Only in the 1956 essay does Rahner's discussion of these Ignatian texts figure large, and he was later prepared to concede to his opponents on the strictly exegetical issues. He may have been influenced, more or less consciously, by the strictures in Knauer's 1959 letter (see Appendix for text). After 1956, there are only a few perfunctory references to 'consolation without preceding cause' (1972, 163*, *206*; 'Dialogue with God?', 130, *157*; 1976, pp. xv–xvi). Moreover, in 1972 he acknowledged serious differences of opinion among specialists on this point (1972, 161, *205*), an acknowledgment which the typescript confirms as coming from Rahner himself, rather than from Neufeld, who supplied the essay in question with copious and helpful footnotes.

a more restricted reference than Rahner supposes, Ignatius certainly believes that in the Exercises God and the creature can deal with each other immediately, and that this interplay should make a difference to our choices. 'The decisive, the crucial, the radically Ignatian element in the Exercises' is 'the immediacy of creator and creature'. This immediacy, 'of its nature decisively goes beyond what is merely a matter of essence, the generally valid, what is always the case'. The Ignatian choice cannot happen without this immediacy, and only makes sense when seen as its fruit.[77]

Francis Thompson, a Victorian Roman Catholic poet, once wrote movingly of how the human soul, in need and distress, could cry to God, and then see,

> Christ walking on the water,
> Not of Gennesareth but Thames![78]

Given a Christian doctrine of God, this quotation is a poetic equivalent to what Rahner puts on Ignatius's lips—'I encountered God'—and can help us summarize the issues at stake in this chapter. Thompson's claim raises two kinds of question. The first is biographical. Did Thompson really have this experience as he slept rough in London? Or was it a hallucination caused by laudanum? Did he just 'make it up'? But even sceptical answers to such questions presuppose a positive judgement about issues of another kind: whether it *makes sense* to talk about Christ appearing in our contemporary experience *at all*. Conversely, whatever the truth-status of his particular experience-claim, Thompson's poem stands or falls chiefly with the theology it expresses.

Rahner's 'immediate experience of God' and 'transcendence becoming thematic' are best understood, not in terms of the particular events which may have led to their formulation, but rather with reference to the theological claims, applicable to all possible experience, which they imply. If God is present in the self, then any growth in self-awareness, any experience of transcendence becoming thematic, is necessarily a growth in awareness of God. The claim is not the absurd one that every occasion of self-reflection is somehow guaranteed as true, but simply that such processes are fundamentally oriented towards truth—*systematic* scepticism

---

[77] 1961, 266, *289*—cf. *Exx*, n. 15.3–6.
[78] Francis Thompson, 'In No Strange Land', cited from *The New Oxford Book of English Verse*, ed. Helen Gardner (Oxford: Oxford University Press, 1972), 802.

regarding such experiences implies a contradiction. Moreover, given this interpretation, there is no requirement that our growth in grace be smooth or constant: on the contrary, it may be chaotic, and is as liable to regress as progress.

If we interpret the 'first principle' of supernatural logic as a regulative truth, then it appears as a logical consequence of four more basic intuitions. Firstly, human beings are created by God as distinctive individuals, not just as numerically distinct examples of a natural kind. Secondly, ethics is naturalist, derived from a consideration of the way things are, rather than from strict principles or from divine commands as such. Thirdly, God's grace is universally offered. Fourthly, reality and awareness are correlated. Together these entail that it makes sense to interpret our experience as the ongoing history of grace, involving calls from God addressed to us—both as individuals and as groups—in our specificity, and to take decisions accordingly. But just nothing follows regarding the success of any specific attempt on our part to do so.

In its interpretation of the 'first principle' of Ignatian discernment, this chapter has gone beyond Rahner's own account in clarifying the nature of that key experiential reality. It has also detached Rahner's substantive theology from his dubious handling of Ignatian texts. Rahner's vision of 'spirit in world' implies that human experience of the spiritual and the 'transcendent' is shaped by language and tradition. If God's grace is uniquely significant, it must correlate with a uniquely significant pattern of language use identifying it. We have also seen that the grounding of Rahner's 'I encountered God' turns, not so much on particular mental states at particular times, but on the validity of the tradition enabling such a claim to be made in the first place.

However, this chapter has not addressed fully the concerns which led Rahner, sometimes, to invest the key Ignatian experience with a stronger level of certainty than this account of the matter would allow. Perhaps Rahner's concern to establish how the key Ignatian experience is incontrovertible can be satisfied if we explore further what is now appearing more clearly as its dependence on the collection of events and texts we call New Testament revelation. Perhaps, as the elderly Rahner began to suggest, the certainty of the Ignatian experience of God derives from, and clarifies, the certainty available to believers regarding the Christian tradition as a whole. The next chapters explore these suggestions further.

8

The Standard of Christ

Rahner's 'immediate experience of God' does not occur in isolation. 'Immediate' means only that we cannot *infer* God's gracious, supernatural presence to the world as self-giver merely from the world's existence. But God's spiritual touch is compatible with, and indeed requires, mediation of other kinds. Because our identity and awareness are primordially relational, primordially dependent on data from outside, our transformation in grace must correlate with a gracious presence in the external world.

A specifically Christian theology, however, needs to say more. Christianity claims that certain historical realities, centring on the person of Jesus Christ, mediate the presence of God in unique and decisive ways. Moreover, Rahner's own theology of Ignatian discernment implies that particular options exercise a similar function, albeit derivatively, for the individual or community concerned. In other words, Rahner's general claim that the spiritual is always worldly needs to be supplemented by an account of how some particular worldly realities have a special function in the Christian economy. Further, this supplementary account needs to be twofold: one part of it, centring on Jesus Christ and canonical tradition, must be universal in scope; another part must be pluralist, respecting the indefinitely diverse ways in which particular people find God through their choices. This chapter and the next explore how such an account might be constructed. The present chapter focuses on Christ and the Church; the following one deals with particular discernments.

Rahner, Jesus Christ, and the Experience of God

Critics of Rahner's account of Ignatian discernment have understandably concentrated on the 1956 essay, and regularly noted the almost total absence therein of any reference to

Christ.[1] For Michael Schneider, Rahner's account is excessively introspective, failing to express how God's action in Christ involves something more than the unfolding of human potential:

> For Ignatius the encounter with the Lord occurs neither through the unthematic becoming thematic, nor through a 'core experience' of a transcendental contact between consciousness and God (*'Kernerlebnis' einer transzendentalen Gotteserfahrung*), but rather through a confrontation with the divine call, impelling the person through their perceptions of their own inner movements . . . God's call goes out to the individual, not through transcendental experience but in the concrete encounter with the historical Jesus of Nazareth—a call to decision, and to the ultimate, radical discipleship which is always also a discipleship of the cross.[2]

For Josef Sudbrack, Rahner's account offends against the logic of practical reason. Ignatius's rules and election procedures are extrapolations from a personal, historical process of confrontation with the gospel, and can only be understood correctly from within such a context.[3]

Rahner often seems to invite such criticism. In the 1955 Canisianum conferences, for example, Rahner seems to suggest that an Ignatian devotion to the heart of Christ serves merely to forestall the decadent excesses of what is truly and distinctively Ignatian. It prevents indifference from degenerating into uncommitted functionalism, self-control from sliding into heartlessness, and an authentic devotion to the Church as God's instrument from becoming an ecclesiastical fanaticism, for which the Church is 'an end in itself'.[4] For von Balthasar, such a statement shows up the theological nullity latent in Rahner's philosophy. It is absurd, he implies, to see the heart of Christ as merely a categorical supplement to a transcendental piety: Christ's heart, rather, is the definitive revelation of a love transcending Kantianism.[5] With this particular text, the issue is partly one of literary genre: Rahner is here expressing a kind of

---

[1] According to Spohn, 'The Reasoning Heart', 47 n. 32, there are but four references to Christ in 1956*a*. This paragraph draws on the much fuller account of the secondary literature on this topic given by Zahlauer, *Karl Rahner und sein 'produktives Vorbild'*, 235–41.

[2] Schneider, *'Unterscheidung der Geister'*, 128–9. The translation may seem cumbersome, but it would be equally inelegant, as well as misleading, to render both *Erlebnis* and *Erfahrung* as 'experience'.

[3] Josef Sudbrack, 'Fragestellung und Infragestellung der ignatianischen Exerzitien', *Geist und Leben*, 43 (1970), 206–26, esp. 219.

[4] 1955, 188–90, 525–7. Cf. 1956*b*.

[5] von Balthasar, *The Moment of Christian Witness*, 65–6.

Hegelian antithesis to his original thesis, and the language about Ignatius as a man primarily of transcendental piety should be read within the synthesis Rahner ultimately constructs. Nevertheless, a substantive point remains to be answered, one that has been well put by the American scholar, Bruce D. Marshall. Throughout his theology, Rahner seems to begin by developing a general speculative account of human fullness under God, and then to introduce Jesus Christ as an illustration of this account. But, for Christians, Christ is constitutive, not just illustrative, of God's dealings with humanity: 'because the Christian belief in redemption is necessarily tied to Jesus Christ, it cannot be regarded as a paraphrase of some more basic belief, from which Jesus Christ is absent, that the world is redeemed. Jesus Christ . . . is not . . . an optional enrichment of the Christian belief in redemption.'[6]

In their discussions of Rahner's Ignatian writings, Schwerdtfeger and Miggelbrink have rightly insisted that what Rahner means by 'transcendence' is always historically mediated. They have then invoked that principle to clarify Christ's role in Ignatian discernment as presented by Rahner, admittedly through a process of constructive interpretation.[7] Neither, however, has directly faced the full force of the objections. In any Christian account of the experience of God, we require not just any mediation of the transcendence that becomes thematic, but rather a quite specific and decisive mediation through Jesus Christ.[8]

Zahlauer, by contrast, for whom such constructive interpretation is methodologically suspect,[9] is content simply to admit that in Rahner's theology, and in particular in Rahner's account of

---

[6] Bruce D. Marshall, *Christology in Conflict: The Identity of a Saviour in Rahner and Barth* (Oxford: Blackwell, 1987), 54. For an attempt to refute this cogent, well-argued attack, see my 'Rahner, Christology, and Grace', esp. 292–4.

[7] Miggelbrink, *Ekstatische Liebe im tätigen Weltbezug*, 31–5, may, however, be over-severe in his refutation of Schneider, whose view surely has some exegetical foundation. Drawing on Rahner's study of Bonaventure, where 'spiritual touch' and 'ecstasy' are synonymous, Miggelbrink argues that the key Ignatian experience can be described as an 'ecstasy'. As such, it is an *akthafter Vollzug* (something which happens through activity), and thus, 'as a matter of epistemological and metaphysical necessity only possible for human beings, "spirits in world", in the *conversio ad phantasmata*' (p. 32).

[8] Fairness requires us to add that neither Schwerdtfeger nor Miggelbrink are directly concerned with the Ignatian writings, and use them only as illustrations supporting the central themes of their studies.

[9] Zahlauer, *Karl Rahner und sein 'produktives Vorbild'*, 244. In a footnote on the same page, my own dissertation is said uncritically to presuppose the legitimacy of such a method.

Ignatian discernment, 'the "Jesus-pole" is missing'.[10] For Zahlauer, Rahner's reading of Ignatius always, throughout his career, reflected the fresh discovery of the 'spiritual, mystical Ignatius' in the 1920s, and the liberation this discovery represented in a situation where Ignatian spirituality had appeared as merely 'ascetical' meditation.[11] Such one-sidedness in theology is not necessarily a vice: it is inevitable, and can, when properly acknowledged, be fruitful.[12] Here, however, a distinction needs to be made. Within Christian theology, 'mystical' writing may legitimately leave what is specifically Christian understated or even unexpressed, providing that such writing does not contradict, even if only implicitly, Christianity's claim that Jesus Christ in some sense specifies any valid account of the 'spiritual' or the 'transcendent'. If we accept Zahlauer's judgement, for all its biographical plausibility, as the last word, then we concede that Rahner's contribution is at best of marginal significance for Christian theology, and at worst seductively heretical.

Some points, admittedly, can be made straightaway in Rahner's defence. The index of Joseph de Guibert's *The Theology of the Spiritual Life*, a distinguished and intelligent example of early twentieth-century spiritual theology, contains no entry at all for Jesus Christ within the sections of the book dealing with mystical prayer. By contrast, the original version of Rahner's 1937 essay on Ignatian spirituality and world-affirmation starts from an account of mysticism

[10] Zahlauer, *Karl Rahner und sein 'produktives Vorbild'*, 316, cf. 247.

[11] Ibid., 329: 'The form of Ignatian spirituality is marked by a fascinating, although occasionally fragile, *polarity*, with the poles conditioning each other. However, the weight of Rahner's Ignatian interpretation lay, from the beginning of his theological thought, on one pole: that of the possibility of an immediate experience of God, an experience that fascinated Ignatius. This led, as I have shown, to a *one-sidedness as Rahner's work emerged (werkgenetischen Einseitigkeit)*, which became especially manifest in "The Logic of Concrete Individual Knowledge" and is clearly shown up by a criticism such as Sudbrack's. What Rahner took on board was principally *the mystical, spiritual Ignatius*. A key theoretical indication of this was the fact that he could call the founder of his order a *"man of transcendental piety"*' (emphases original).

[12] Zahlauer, *Karl Rahner und sein 'produktives Vorbild'*, 332. Zahlauer is prepared to accept what von Balthasar excoriates: the use of Christ, in particular his heart, as an 'antidote' to a mere transcendental piety (1955, 190, 520). He admits both that this use of Christ in theology may be in principle questionable, and that Rahner may not in practice have achieved the balance he sought. 'But on the other hand, the question arises . . . as to whether mere coherence can be an ultimate criterion. Is it not rather that a theology becomes in any special way fruitful only when it has the courage to concentrate on one dimension? The one-sidedness . . . can unleash great theological creativity, precisely because it is aware of its specific constitution and orientation.'

as 'the experience, based on the grace of Christ, of the immediate dealing between the personal God and the human person . . . We find Christian mysticism where the living God of Jesus Christ deals immediately in his own self with the soul.'[13] Rahner toned this passage down when the essay was reprinted,[14] and we have already seen how, in both versions, the opening of the essay is theologically hesitant. Nevertheless, the fact that the young Rahner, unlike the standard textbooks of his day, could talk of Jesus Christ and mysticism in the same breath is significant.

It should also be noted that the problem is one which most of Rahner's predecessors simply failed to address. In Ignatius himself, for example, we find motifs of intense devotion to Christ, normally linked to the Cross, together with evocations of God's presence in all creation, but without any sense of the tensions between such statements. In the first of the First Week Exercises on sin, Ignatius bids us consider the general history of sinfulness, personal and corporate, only to move us, abruptly and dramatically, into imaginative dialogue with the crucified Christ.[15] Modern practitioners often supplement Ignatius with Christological material in parts of the *Exercises* where this is lacking; commentators, if they have been aware of the problem at all, have sought to legitimate this practice, linking it to early Jesuit tradition,[16] and perhaps vaguely invoking the cosmic Christ. Ignatius himself was uninterested in speculative issues: his concern, rather, was simply to keep us wondering about and wondering at the fact that 'the Creator made himself human, and from eternal life came to temporal death'.[17] Nevertheless, some

---

[13] *Zeitschrift für Aszese und Mystik*, 12 (1937), 123. Zahlauer, *Karl Rahner und sein 'produktives Vorbild'*, 203, may be right to claim that the reference to God's 'dealing immediately' with the soul echoes *Exx*, n. 15.6.

[14] The *SzT* version (1937, 279–80, *351–2*), dating from the mid-1950s, perhaps arises from a sharpened sense of the need, in the wake of *Humani generis*, not to exclude the possibility of natural mysticism. Contrast 1969, 291, *243*, where Rahner, having set out his theory of the supernatural existential, continues: 'I believe, therefore, that there is no place at which a purely natural mysticism exists.'

[15] *Exx*, nn. 46–54, esp. 53.

[16] Spanish authors seem to preponderate among those who discuss this issue. A thorough, recent contribution, referring abundantly to earlier studies, is Manuel Gesteira Garza, 'Cristo ¿"principio y fundamento" de los Ejercicios Espirituales?', *Miscelánea Comillas*, 49 (1991), 327–67. Gesteira's opening review contrasts 'theocentric' and 'Christocentric' interpretations of the texts, echoing an unhelpful commonplace in work on Christianity and other 'religions'. More accessible is Hugo Rahner, 'The Christology of the Exercises' (1962), in *Ignatius the Theologian*, 53–135.

[17] *Exx*, n. 53.1.

kind of answer has to be possible. How can we reconcile Rahner's 'immediate experience of God' with a conviction that such experience must be, in Ignatian terms, under the 'standard' of Christ?[18] If God is truly creator of all that exists, what is the place for a unique, saving Jesus Christ who seems to divide the world into those for him and against him, and who, in Augustinian fashion, appears to override the creation's original goodness? Conversely, if God's own self has been revealed in the life, death, and resurrection of Jesus, surely we can no longer accept, without qualification, a speculative understanding of God which seems to preclude incarnation and grace.[19]

In 1978, Rahner's Ignatius insists that 'there is no Christianity which can find the God past all grasp while bypassing Jesus'.[20] Equally, he is not simply being modest when he tells us, 'I know that with what I have said I have not clarified the mystery of how history and God are united.'[21] Can we find resources in Rahner's theology that enable us to make that clarification? We will begin by looking at some fragmentary hints on this issue from Rahner's answers to questions about the 1956 essay. These texts suggest that there were, in Rahner's mind, closer links between his Christology and his theology of death than commentators have recognized. The main body of the chapter draws on these connections to offer an account of Rahner's Ignatian Christology, before passing on to the question of how Rahner understands the Church's role in Ignatian discernment.

---

[18] A key moment in the Exercises is the meditation on Two Standards, one Christ's, one Lucifer's, encouraging the retreatant to become aware of insidious temptations to egoism, and to pray to be received in poverty under the standard of Christ (*Exx*, nn. 136–47). 'Standard' is the established translation for *bandera*. In the original, the connotations are purely military, but the suggestion that Christ provides a standard, or norm, for our choice is surely in keeping with Ignatius's wider concerns, whereas the military imagery has become embarrassing. A recent study of this mediation, tracing the ideas back to Augustine's *City of God*, is Stefan Kiechle, 'Die ignatianische Meditation der "Zwei Banner": Zu ihrer Traditionsgeschichte von Augustinus bis Ignatius von Loyola', *Geist und Leben*, 66 (1993), 188–201.

[19] One Jesuit commentator who did appreciate the issues at stake here, advocating an extreme position, was Juan Luis Segundo. For him, historical revelation discredited a metaphysical, ideologically loaded theology deriving from Greek philosophy. In *The Christ of the Ignatian Exercises*, trans. John Drury (London: Sheed and Ward, 1988 [orig. pub. 1982]), 41–3, he complains of how Ignatius's conception of the creator–creature relationship in such passages as the Principle and Foundation (*Exx*, n. 23) is 'wholly unaffected by any christology', and 'in open opposition to christological data such as those offered by Paul to the Romans and Galatians'.

[20] 1978*b*, 20, *385*.   [21] 1978*b*, 21, *385*.

Ignatian Discernment and the Death of Christ

Rahner's accounts of Christ's role in Ignatian discernment are few and fragmentary. He once used the analogy of Aristotelian form and matter as a metaphor for how the transcendental and Christological aspects of Ignatian discernment interrelate.[22] When Peter Knauer wrote to Rahner in 1959, suggesting that the 'first principle' of Ignatian discernment lay not in 'consolation without preceding cause' but with a Christological text, the Third Manner of Humility, Rahner replied that this idea was 'well worth considering'.[23] But it was only in a reply to a review essay, written by Avery Dulles to mark the English translation of the 1956 essay, that Rahner even begins to develop the point.

Christology was one of the issues highlighted by Dulles. Ignatius's meditations on the life of Christ are important, suggested Dulles, because they protect us from making decisions based purely on the basis of temperament. Reference to Christ keeps open the possibility that we might be called to holiness not through 'developing . . . natural talents . . . but perhaps by sacrificing certain natural possibilities'. 'The discernment of spirits, then, is not simply a matter of viewing the object of the election in the light of my own spiritual inclinations; even more importantly, it demands reference to Christ as the living concrete norm.'[24]

Rahner's answer under this heading fell into two parts.[25] The first amounted to an admission that Dulles had put his finger on a serious lacuna in his account, although a lacuna shared by all the conventional theologies of grace. All grace is the grace of Christ, as Ignatius's gospel meditations imply. But to say that much was not enough. The second part of the answer offered 'a particular aspect' in terms of which the Christological dimension of the choice could be seen 'perhaps most clearly':

The choice or rejection of a particular object is possible only when a person has, by the grace of God, freed themselves from an immediate fixation (*von einem unmittelbaren Verfallensein*) on this object and thus attained their openness to God's immediacy as the only fixed point of their actual living. This distancing—which I do not mean just as something theoretical but also as something actually lived (*existentielle*)—from a particular, finite value or

---

[22] 1954/5, 8–9, *12–13*.   [23] The text is reproduced in the Appendix.
[24] Dulles, 'Finding God's Will', 152.   [25] 1969, 292, *244–5*.

good in the sphere of the person's actual living is, however, in all truth, whether one reflects on this or not, a participation in Christ's death. Only from Christ, crucified and risen, does it have the guarantee that such a dying is possible, and that dying is not at root after all just a falling into absurd emptiness. The only person who can really choose freely (*sourverän*) is one who, through the grace of God (which is that of Christ crucified), has been liberated from the enslaving tyranny of inner-worldly 'principalities and powers'—i.e. from the illusion of unbelief, the illusion that there is something in the world of human lived experience out of which a person must make an absolute if they are to survive. The death of this illusion, this 'dying', which is part of the fundamental structure of every act of Christian choice, is a dying which happens in the grace of Christ together with Christ, whether one knows this reflectively or not—a dying which in actual death, if this takes place 'in the Lord', reaches its climax and perfect victory, just as it was begun in the person's being baptized into the death of Christ.

At first sight, this and similar passages in Rahner's late Ignatian writings[26] seem simply to be saying that Jesus is important as an example of indifference and spiritual freedom. If so, they are unsatisfactory: such a position fails to distinguish between Jesus Christ and any saint, whether within or outside the visible Church.[27] But Rahner's reply to Dulles echoes major themes in his speculative work, notably regarding the theme of death. By interpreting what Rahner says here in the light of these echoes, we can develop a more interesting and adequate theological position.

The Significances of Death

For Rahner, death was more than a biological fact, and a good or heroic death more than a sign of moral virtue. Death, rather, epitomized the reality of the human.[28] What it is to be a bodily spirit, to

---

[26] Cf. 1975, 9–10; 1978*b*, 20–1, *385–6*.

[27] See Zahlauer, *Karl Rahner und sein 'produktives Vorbild'*, 242: 'even if his Heideggerian training enables Rahner to open up an important depth-dimension of the human person, it remains a question whether the election is really given a christological grounding just by a reference to the parallel between every human being's susceptibility to death and the exemplary death of Jesus on the cross'.

[28] Earlier accounts of Rahner's theology of death have now been superseded by Carlos Federico Schickendantz, *Autotrascendencia radicalizada en extrema impotencia: la comprehensión de la muerte en Karl Rahner* (Santiago: Pontificial Universidad Católica de Chile, 1999)—German summary available in KRA. In English, see Peter C. Phan, *Eternity in Time: A Study of Karl Rahner's Eschatology* (London: Associated University Presses, 1988), 79–115.

find one's identity and fulfilment through interaction with what lies outside the self—all this finds its fulfilment only in death. When, therefore, Rahner invokes the fact of Christ's death in his interpretation of Ignatius, his primary concern is neither to present us with a model of generosity and heroism, nor to evoke a satisfaction theology of the atonement. Rather, Rahner is stressing how Christ's death demonstrates his full and unreserved sharing in the human condition, in all its vulnerability, and how his resurrection symbolizes God's irrevocable vindication of broken humanity. It is on this basis that we can have, as Rahner puts it to Dulles, a guarantee empowering us to be 'indifferent', and to find our security in the mystery of God rather than in any created value. Whereas there are many saints whose example we can profitably imitate, it is only in Jesus risen that we have a *guarantee* of how human life, in all its threatenedness, stands permanently and irrevocably, through grace, in immediate contact with God.

In this understanding of death in general, and of Christ's death in particular, Rahner more or less consciously echoes Ignatius's *Exercises*, where the Incarnation appears as a process culminating in the Cross. For prayer on Christ's birth, Ignatius encourages the exercitant to focus on the people in the scene: 'look and consider what they are doing, the way the journeying and struggling is, so that the Lord may be born in the utmost poverty and, after so many struggles of hunger, of thirst, of heat, of cold, of injuries and insults, die on a cross'.[29] Though Ignatius encourages us to make choices out of prayer over the life of Christ, no particular episodes between the infancy and the Passion are laid down. Ignatius implies that such material should be chosen in line with the person's particular situation.[30] But all his own more original and more essential material for the period of election—the consideration of the Kingdom, the Two Standards, the Three Classes of Person and the Three Manners of Humility—centres on Christ's death.

Rahner's account of death emerges from his highly developed philosophy of mind, and indeed brings that vision into sharpest relief.[31] Death represents a paradox. It is, in both senses of the word, the end of human life:

[29] *Exx*, n. 116.1–2.   [30] *Exx*, n. 162.
[31] See Mannermaa, '*Lumen fidei*', especially the last section (pp. 102–13) on continuities between Rahner's accounts of death and faith, and ch. 3 (pp. 43–71), partially reproduced in 'Eine falsche Interpretationstradition', on the categorical element in revelation. Useful

The end of a human being—as a self-conscious person—is an active consummation from within, an act of self-completion, a moment of growth and expression that preserves life's fruit, the person's total self-possession, an accomplishment of one's full self, the culmination of what it is to be a person. And at the same time, indissolubly and in a way that affects the whole human being, a human being's death—the end of a material and biological living being—is a breaking off from outside, a destruction, an accident, happening to the human being from without and unpredictably, without its being guaranteed that this death meets the person at the moment in which they have interiorly come to terms with their life.

This end is 'both fulfilled and empty, active and suffered'; it involves both 'having taken possession of oneself and having had one's being taken away from oneself'.[32] Interpreted thus, death radicalizes the pattern of human knowing and willing. Human identity is achieved only in and through receptivity, and human freedom through the personal integration of a reality which, ultimately, is just given to us. Death exhibits how the personal, for all its dependence on the material, is not exhausted by it.

The same principle informs Rahner's spiritual theology and his ethics. Ignatian indifference, writes Rahner in reply to Dulles, amounts to a freedom from 'the illusion of unbelief, the illusion that there is something in the world of human lived experience out of which a person must make an absolute if they are to survive'. Ethics must respect human transcendence, a point that was all too relevant at the outset of Rahner's career:

any philosophical account of the religious is fundamentally wrong if it declares that the object of religion corresponds to any finite aspect of human nature. No objectified projection of racial characteristics, of blood or nation, of the world or of anything else, not even the conception of absolute humanity, can be considered as the 'divine'. For, as a self-conscious being, the human person has always already transcended this finite reality, and is directed towards something that is fundamentally—not just as a matter of degree—more than all this.[33]

---

summaries can be found by consulting the index to Schwerdtfeger, *Gnade und Welt*. Schickendantz, drawing on important early material left unpublished by Rahner (KRA, I. B. 7), has confirmed Mannermaa's interpretation. The published text in which the continuities are made most explicit is 'The Passion and Asceticism'.

[32] *On the Theology of Death*, 48, 37–8.
[33] *Hearer of the Word*, 54, 87 (*KRSW*, iv. 104).

We are free to integrate (or not) whatever we are given into our conscious decision; 'nature' is, at least in principle, subject to the freedom of the 'person'.[34] Moreover, the detachment, or 'indifference', characteristic of the good moral life anticipates the ultimate dispossession of death.

Bodily, material reality, therefore, always contributes to Rahner's transcendental experience, but in such a way as to point towards something beyond itself. The point applies also to the mediation offered by Christ. In 1978, Rahner's Ignatius is dismissive about what were then the fashionable 'death-of-God' theologies, 'your modern Jesuanity, in which you think you can only find humanity when you pompously and one-sidedly proclaim the death of God, instead of realizing that precisely in this human being as a human being God has expressed and promised himself'.[35] In any tenable Christology, Christ's humanity is not simply humanity: it also has the function of pointing beyond itself to a reality about God. The consequences are austere. Even in Christ, God is present within history only in two modes, both of which point to something more than the historical:

in the mode of *promise*—the promise of the ongoing transcendence of the categorical, which affirms absolutely hope's starting point and categorical goal, but only as a mere stage in hope—and in the mode of *death*—death as the most radical event of that negation which belongs to the very nature of every historically mediated revelation, and which becomes absolute in death because nothing categorical can any longer be hoped for.[36]

When, therefore, Rahner replies to challenges about Christ's role in his interpretation of Ignatius by evoking Calvary, Rahner must be understood as invoking two theological convictions: Christ's unreserved sharing in the human condition, and death as the paradigm moment in which earthly reality, through promise and negation, can mediate the transcendent.[37] How do these hints clarify

---

[34] The *locus classicus* for this idea is 'The Theological Concept of Concupiscentia'.
[35] 1978*b*, 20*, *384*.   [36] *Foundations of Christian Faith*, 210, *210* (*KRSW*, xxvi. 203).
[37] Rahner's critics have regularly attacked his subordination of Christ's death to the salvific will of God, as evoked below. In the context of such attacks, Rahner's own criticism of sub-Anselmian satisfaction theories is ironically telling. Such theories do not clarify why it was precisely Christ's *death* that redeemed us. The conventional concept of Christ's satisfaction—once articulated outside the feudal context in which Anselm's text originally made sense—depends on the principle that *any* moral act of Christ is of infinite value 'in consequence of the infinite dignity of his divine person' (*On the Theology of Death*, 66, *57*). But from this it follows, in clear tension with the biblical witness, that just any moral act on Christ's part would have sufficed.

Christ's unique and distinctive role in our ongoing experience of God, and particularly in the experience that leads to discernment?

Christ's Mediation

In *On the Theology of Death*, Rahner presents the conventional satisfaction theology of atonement as incomplete. He is concerned to rehabilitate a 'physical' theory of how Calvary and Easter affect us—though 'physical' here, as he is quick to remind us, has nothing to do with modern physics. According to such a view, Christ's bringing about grace in us is not a matter merely of 'juridical and moral causality'. On the contrary, Christ has 'a direct connection, even if only as an instrument' with the grace God gives human beings at large.[38] Thus, Christ's death has transformed the reality and experience of death for all of us,

> not just in the sense that death brought about . . . (this transformation) . . . objectively through a moral causality, but rather in the sense that in Christ, through his deed done in grace, death encompasses what could of itself have been only the experience of sin, and thus became something quite different from what it appeared to be.[39]

The reality and experience of our death—and in this theology what is said about death applies in lesser measure to the whole of human life—is transformed by Christ's death.

In this 1957 text, Rahner is characteristically cautious. His account of the Cross's 'physical' effect supplements rather than replaces the rhetoric of satisfaction. By the 1970s, Rahner was expressing his disagreement with satisfaction theologies much more openly. In their conventional form, satisfaction theories of the atonement implied a change in the divine mind wrought by the bloody death of Christ.[40] Such a conception could not be reconciled with the doctrine of divine simplicity. More generally, Christ's uniqueness could only be coherently understood as a moment within an all-embracing reality of divine self-gift:

> A special 'intervention' of God . . . can only be understood as the historical concreteness of God's transcendental self-communication, which is

---

[38] *On the Theology of Death*, 74, *61*.   [39] Ibid., 78*, *64*.

[40] *Foundations of Christian Faith*, 282–3, *277* (*KRSW*, xxvi. 269–70). For an explicit reference to Anselm in this regard, see 'The One Christ and the Universality of Salvation', 208, *262*.

always intrinsic to the concrete world . . . every operative intervention of God in his world, for all that it is free and underivable, is always only the becoming historical and becoming concrete of that 'intervention' in which God, as the transcendental ground of the world, has from the outset embedded himself in this world as its self-communicating ground.[41]

What makes Christ's death different from other deaths, therefore, is not an 'objective' change, but rather its power to reveal what is latent in all death, and indeed in all that is human even at its most vulnerable and fragile. Christ is the irrevocable *expression* of a divine saving will encompassing *the whole* of humanity. In order to respect tradition, Rahner describes the causal relationship between the saving will of God and the death of Christ as reciprocal. But the death itself has causal force only in a transferred sense:

The salvific will of God, which is pure initiative, posits this life of Jesus consummating in death, and thus makes itself real and manifest as something irrevocable. In this, the life and death of Jesus (taken together) are 'causes' of God's salvific will (to the extent that these two realities are seen as different), in so far as in precisely this life and death this salvific will establishes itself as something real and irreversible.[42]

It might be thought that such an approach fails to do justice to traditional teaching about Christ's uniqueness. But this traditional teaching was itself inconsistent, in that it compromised God's immutability. A theology of salvation respecting this principle must see the 'unsaved' not as really existing but as a counterfactual abstraction, as what in some sense could have been, but never, mercifully, actually has been.

It could also be objected that such an account of the atonement confuses the subjective and the objective, the true-for-us with the true-in-itself. Here the reply must be that such a distinction does not apply to personal realities. How we experience the grace of God just *is* an aspect of its reality. This consideration then yields a sense, albeit a properly secondary one, in which, at least for believers, Christ's death does make a real difference to human experience of God. Though it may be pagan to say that Christ's death transforms God from an angry God to a gracious one, nevertheless the fact that Christ has died and has risen transforms how Christians understand fragility and death, both their own and that of non-believers

[41] *Foundations of Christian Faith*, 87, *94* (*KRSW*, xxvi. 87–8).
[42] Ibid., 284, *278* (*KRSW*, xxvi. 271).

and misbelievers. And if the resurrection transforms how Christians *understand* the experience of death, then there is a sense in which it also transforms the experience *itself*.

In his discussion of anonymous and explicit Christianity during the 1978 testament, Rahner's Ignatius implies a similar distinction. Grace and the Incarnation specify the very reality of God. On this basis, he can affirm that 'there is no Christianity that can find the God past all grasp while bypassing Jesus', a principle that applies even to an anonymous Christian. But what this means is simply that they share the human condition, vulnerable yet graced, with Jesus of Nazareth, who is the definitive exemplar of a reality embracing all. In their deaths, they find all that ultimately matters about Jesus:

> God has willed that many, unspeakably many, find him because they are merely *seeking for* Jesus. And when they fall into the abyss of death, then after all they are dying with Jesus in his Godforsakenness, even if they cannot name this fate of theirs by this blessed name. For God has allowed this darkness of finitude and guilt into the world only because he wanted to make it his own in Jesus.[43]

Yet, even as Rahner's Ignatius accepts that God calls the majority of the human race to fulfilment in some other way, he can also stress, starkly, the importance of Jesus's life and death for his own reflective decision-making:

> one has only found Jesus fully, and in him God's own self, when one has died with him. But when you realize that this dying with Jesus must happen all the way through life, then certain characteristics of Jesus's life do after all, despite their seeming fortuitousness and their dependence on historical and social circumstance, take on a terrifying significance. I don't know if the characteristics of the specific ways of Jesus's prosaic life, the characteristics under whose law I fell, clearly have an especially insistent weight for all who—whether expressly or anonymously—find God and are saved. It seems not to be so.[44]

Though Jesus does not objectively change the reality which we experience, he does disclose a potential in this reality and thus enables believers to appropriate it with an assurance that is transformative. His death does not affect the objective reality of God's grace which we experience, but it does change the interactive reality which our experience actually is. Thus it is that something like

---

[43] 1978*b*, 20, *385*.   [44] 1978*b*, 21, *386*.

Ignatian imaginative contemplation, prayerful appropriation of the story of Jesus, is a normative, though not exclusive, means through which we can appropriate our graced identity under God, and make decisions accordingly.

In his reply to Dulles, Rahner spoke of the Ignatian choice as a *Partizipation* in Christ's death. The term evokes Plato, and Rahner's brief dictionary article on its indigenous German equivalent, *Teilhabe*, suggests a significant connotation.[45] The article evokes Rahner's theology of grace and the concept of quasi-formal causality. In theology, it is not that an object, by virtue of its creation,

is similar to God, and *thus* represents God and *thus* a participation in God is bestowed. Rather God as himself is the one who bestows himself immediately in participation, and co-sustains, in himself through quasi-formal causality, the created act in which this self-communication of God is received.

Participation in Christ implies that we appropriate his reality, in the multiple and diverse ways in which our 'matter' differs from that of Jesus of Nazareth. Incarnation and grace are two aspects of one all-embracing mystery:

although the hypostatic union is also a once-and-for-all event in its own essence, and viewed in itself it is the highest conceivable event, it is nevertheless a moment within the whole, the whole which is the gracing of the self-conscious creation in general (*der Begnadigung der geistigen Kreatur überhaupt*) . . . Grace in all of us and hypostatic union in the one Jesus Christ can only be considered together, and as one reality they signify the one free decision of God for the supernatural order of salvation, for his self-communication.[46]

Earlier in this study, when we were considering Rahner's theology of grace and his interpretation of Bonaventure, we noted a general pattern. Rahner seeks middle courses between extrinsicist and intrinsicist positions, and renegotiates inherited conceptions of the unity and distinction between God and the creation. The Christology and soteriology just outlined are a further illustration of this pattern. Here too, Rahner attenuates conventional extrinsicist accounts of the distinction between creator and creature, thereby making room for a new and fuller articulation of the unity. Traditional Alexandrian Christology had always stressed that Jesus is

[45] 'Teilhabe'.   [46] *Foundations of Christian Faith*, 201, *201* (*KRSW*, xxvi. 194).

not just one among other 'prophets, religious geniuses, and reformers'.[47] Rahner articulates this conviction, not in terms of a different
metaphysical constitution (a road which all too easily leads to
Docetism), but rather in terms of a particular relational function
within the whole economy of grace. This move then enables Rahner to retrieve more Antiochene approaches to Christology, and to
articulate more boldly the Chalcedonian 'consubstantial with us as
regards his humanity'.[48] Jesus remains an exemplar, but an exemplar of a qualitatively different kind. In him, in his resurrection, we
have a guarantee that the ambiguities of our human existence,
culminating as they do in death, nevertheless can find a positive
resolution. The hypostatic union in Jesus,

is distinguished from our grace not by what has been offered in it, which in
both instances, including that of Jesus, is grace. It is distinguished rather
by the fact that Jesus is the pledge (*Zusage*) for us; we ourselves are not the
repetition of the pledge (*wir nicht selber wieder die Zusage*), but those who
receive God's pledge to us.[49]

Such a Christology articulates Jesus's uniqueness, while also
affirming that human beings as such are also daughters and sons of
God. Indeed, Jesus's uniqueness consists precisely in his power to
guarantee that status, and to empower our realization of it—a realization which occurs in the event of 'transcendence becoming
thematic', in Ignatian choice. Thus the event of Christmas, Rahner
tells us in his 1974 homily, is the 'highest, obviously one-off, unsurpassable and model case' of Ignatian discernment.[50] The unique-

[47] Ibid., 288–9, *282* (*KRSW*, xxvi. 275).

[48] Rahner never wrote a full systematic Christology; even chapter 6 of *Foundations of Christian Faith* is a compilation of earlier writings, with little attempt to create an overall structure
of argument. There are certainly places—for example in the seminal 'Some Implications'
(345, *374*)—where a more Alexandrian conception seems to be uncritically assumed. A full
study of how Rahner's Christology developed remains to be written, and obviously goes far
beyond the scope of this present study. More extensive discussions can be found in a number
of recent works: Wong, *Logos-Symbol*; Farrugia, *Aussage und Zusage*; John M. McDermott, 'The
Christologies of Karl Rahner', *Gregorianum*, 67 (1986), 87–123, 297–327; Ignacy Bokwa, *Christologie als Anfang und Ende der Anthropologie* (Frankfurt: Peter Lang, 1990); Evelyne Maurice,
La Christologie de Karl Rahner (Paris: Desclée, 1995). For further elaboration of the approach put
forward here, see my 'Grace and the Unfolding of Revelation: The Approach of Karl
Rahner', *Epworth Review*, 22/1 (January 1995), 63–73; 'Rahner, Christology, and Grace'; and
'Karl Rahner and the Heart of Christ'.

[49] *Foundations of Christian Faith*, 202, *202* (*KRSW*, xxvi. 195).

[50] 1974*c*, 6*, *332*: '*Weihnachten ist der höchste, natürlich einmalige, unüberbietbare und exemplarische
Fall dieser Einheit von Transzendenz und konkreter Freiheit.*'

ness of Jesus Christ consists in the 'effective promise' he represents, in his guarantee that our otherwise ambiguous experiences are also potential instances of that union. Thus this promise, this guarantee, decisively determines how Christian believers find God in their experience.

Discernment, Tradition, and the Church

Rahner's 'immediate experience of God', therefore, allows, indeed requires, a decisive role for Jesus Christ. But this is only part of this chapter's task. We must also reckon with the fact that Christ's standard comes to us through human, historical means, through a tradition. For all Christian theology, this tradition is embodied in the Scriptures; for a Roman Catholic theologian such as Rahner, the structures of Church authority, at their 'hardest and bitterest' in the Roman Catholic Church,[51] are also privileged mediations of grace. Yet, at first sight, Rahner's account of the experience of God seems to imply emancipation from such unattractive realities. At the beginning of the 1956 essay, Rahner clearly recognizes a tension between what he is about to say and Ignatius's well-known readiness to defer to a command from higher authority. He asks,

how is this *a priori* delimitation of the possible field of God's will consistent with that unmediated utterance of that will by God's own self, where God works directly with his creature? Why, if this utterance exists, is this external norm not thereby basically superseded, or reduced to the level of a purely secondary auxiliary means which God just happens to use?[52]

Rahner's answer to his own rhetorical question is evasive: 'but at this initial stage this problem should not yet occupy us'. He never, however, fully addresses the question he raises here.

There are many pages, sometimes quite eloquent ones, on the Church in Rahner's Ignatian writings. In the 1955 Canisianum conferences, for example, Rahner highlights devotion to the Church as one of the three major characteristics of Ignatian spirituality, and gives a whole section to it in each of the three talks.[53] But again it is the reply to Dulles that provides the most helpful starting-point. Dulles's review article on the 1956 essay had included a throwaway

---

[51] 1978*b*, 38, *408*.   [52] 1956*a*, 90, *79*.
[53] 1955, 186–7, *517–18*; 197–9, *524–5*; 207–9, *531–3*.

line towards the end: Rahner's account could 'advantageously incorporate much that Rahner himself has said in other articles concerning . . . the ecclesial dimension of all authentic spirituality'.[54] This became one of the three issues on which Rahner commented. Rahner's answer, professedly incomplete, simply named two conditions that any Ignatian theology should satisfy. On the one hand, a valid choice must be made 'in the context of the hierarchically constituted Church'. On the other hand, the will of God cannot simply be deduced from Church law and from the directives of Church leaders—such a position would make Ignatius's elaborate process superfluous. The Ignatian experience proceeds from the Church's charismatic dimension. As such it at once forms 'part of the Church's essence', and yet 'stands beyond the control of ecclesiastical institutions'.[55]

The form of this answer—the naming of two conditions which an adequate theology must satisfy—points us once again to a central theme in Rahner's theology: the rearticulation of the difference made by Christianity. Neither intrinsicism nor extrinsicism are sustainable. On the one hand, the Church has a real significance for the choices we make; Ignatian discernment is more than a pious name for common sense. On the other hand, however, Church authority may not be conceived simply as supplying the truth of God to an otherwise benighted, graceless humanity. In Christology, Rahner's mediating position leads us to see Christ as a uniquely significant model, empowering us to realize our own distinctiveness under God: we are his companions rather than his clones. In ecclesiology similarly, Church authority offers us an indispensable relational context for working out our discipleship: we are in permanent dependence on the Church's word, but not necessarily obedient to it. A Christian ethics must always be decisively shaped by Christian tradition, but will not necessarily repeat that tradition in its inherited or prevailing form.

To pursue this issue fully would draw this study into wide-ranging current discussions within moral theology. Here we must confine ourselves to the idiom in which Rahner himself pursued it, simply accepting his assumption that canonical tradition is embodied, not just in normative words and symbols, but also in authorized speakers who can require the obedience of believers at large.

---

[54] Dulles, 'Finding God's Will', 152.   [55] 1969, 293, *246*.

How can Rahner's theology of the 'immediate experience of God' incorporate his ecclesial commitments? Within the Roman Catholic tradition, such issues often arise in dramatic, conflictive form. All too easily, a more or less formal discernment process can point towards a course of action which Church authority forbids or prevents. Examples come readily to mind: Roman Catholic women who feel called to ordained ministry; liberationist theologians and pastoral workers clashing with cautious bishops in Latin America; untold numbers of individuals who cannot in conscience accept official pronouncements on sexual morality. This discussion is not concerned with the rights and wrongs of any particular case or issue. The focus is rather on an assumption latent in Catholic consciousness—and perhaps, *mutuatis mutandis*, in Christian awareness as a whole—that there is some kind of presumption in favour of authority, or of received tradition. Can one articulate this intuition without rendering it either theologically trivial or ethically outrageous?

Rahner's general position, as we have already seen, seems to be that such conflicts are inevitable but provisional. Rahner reminds the Germanicum seminarians that the attitude which led his own people to reject Jesus can also appear in the Church and its clergy:

Even if the Church as a whole—in contrast to the Synagogue—is so seized by God's love that it is absolutely incapable of escaping his grace, still the individual Christian, the individual priest and whole social groups within the Church can act just as the Jewish people did when they rejected the Son of God in front of Pilate and demanded another Messiah who would be to their liking.[56]

However, it is only faith, and hope in divine providence, that can lead us to the conviction that such rejection will never be absolute, and that the potential conflicts between obedience and fidelity to conscience will never be definitively irreconcilable.[57]

Though the issues raised here regarding authority and infallibility are obviously massive,[58] Rahner's account may be ultimately

---

[56] 1954/5, 230, *231*.   [57] 1978*b*, 27, *394*.

[58] For a good and reliable guide to Rahner's ecclesiology, see Lennan, *The Ecclesiology of Karl Rahner*. On the particular issue raised here, see Medard Kehl, *Kirche als Institution: Zur theologischen Begründung des instituionellen Charakters der Kirche in der neueren deutschsprachigen katholischen Ekklesiologie* (Frankfurt: Knecht, 1976), 204–19; Manuel Alcalá, 'La tensión theologia–magisterio en la vida y obra de Karl Rahner', *Estudios eclesiásticos*, 54 (1979), 3–17 (German trans. in Vorgrimler [ed.], *Wagnis Theologie*, 355–69); Georg Rheinbay, *Das ordentliche Lehramt in der*

defensible as far as it goes. If Christ represents God's guarantee that salvation is possible for all, then the guarantee must extend to the means through which it is received and appropriated, even though we are in no position to see how this guarantee is verified. What the mature Rahner wrote about the hypostatic union applies here too:

The clarity and ultimate definitiveness of Christian truth is the irrevocability of humanity's having been consigned into the mystery (*die unerbittliche Überantwortetheit des Menschen in das Geheimnis hinein*), and not the clarity that comes from comprehending a partial element of humanity and its world.[59]

However, questions remain about how we are to conduct ourselves penultimately. What of the respect due to the so-called 'ordinary magisterium'? Vatican II spoke of the *obsequium animi religiosum* due to local bishops and to the Pope, even when there was no question of infallibility being invoked.[60] Commenting on this passage, Rahner noted its roots in the traditional manuals, and pointed up the distinction between this *obsequium* and the 'absolute assent of faith' (*assensus fidei—absolute Glaubenszustimmung*). There are, and must be, 'lesser degrees of religious obedience in the sphere of faith', and the complexity these imply is rooted 'in the nature of human knowledge and the historical way in which revelation and tradition occur'.[61] The guarantee constituted by Christian revelation, which has binding ethical force, is somehow, to some degree, at work even in situations where unconditional obedience is out of the question.

As we have already seen, this account of Church authority stands in some tension with what Rahner is prepared to say about the charismatic element in the Church. In the 1978 testament, to be an ecclesial Christian is to stand in 'critical relationship' to the Church,

because the Church, by virtue of God's inclination to it, remains ultimately always open and subject to God's Spirit, who is always more than institution, law, the letter of the tradition, etc.

Kirche: Die Konzeption Papst Pius' XII. und das Modell Karl Rahners in Vergleich (Trier: Paulinus, 1988).

[59] *Foundations of Christian Faith*, 181, *183* (*KRSW*, xxvi. 177).
[60] *Lumen gentium*, n. 25 (Tanner, *Decrees of the Ecumenical Councils*, 869). On the general issues here, see Ladislas Örsy, *The Church: Learning and Teaching. Magisterium—Assent—Dissent—Academic Freedom* (Leominster: Fowler Wright, 1987); Richard R. Gaillardetz, *Witnesses to the Faith: Community, Infallibility, and the Ordinary Magisterium of Bishops* (New York: Paulist, 1992).
[61] 'Kommentar zum III. Kapitel', 235–6.

There are no 'complete guidelines or institutional mechanisms' ready to hand for resolving the conflicts that may thus arise.[62] True though this may all be, Rahner's position remains incomplete. Unless *obsequium religiosum* is a mere velleity, we still need some account of how an individual Christian's disagreement with a representative of Church authority has a different status from a disagreement between Christians at large. We need to avoid ecclesiastical fascism; equally, what a representative of Church authority says has some kind of status above that of their personal opinion. How can we articulate a tenable middle position?

An answer is provided by the refined theology of 'the immediate experience of God' developed in this study. Both philosophical and Christological considerations have led us to suggest that Rahner's own formulations need to be extended in such a way that they include reference to language, tradition, and history. Historical events, mediated by memory, shape our self-experience. One cannot, therefore, have what one claims to be an experience of God's grace, or identify such an experience in a non-believer, without implicitly affirming the axiomatic status of Christian tradition. The resurrection, in other words, guarantees a frame of reference. Moreover, commitment to that frame of reference, far from conflicting with 'the immediate experience of God' as is often suggested, constitutes a necessary condition for identifying that experience, and indeed, in one sense, for having it at all. This insight may enable us to resolve some of the conflicts in Rahner's ecclesiological writing.

When individual Christians find themselves clashing with office-holders, even their dissent is rooted in a fundamental acceptance of shared assumptions, a fundamental shared contact with the reality of grace—a reality which the inherited tradition and its official bearers symbolize, but do not exhaust. Thus dissent *can* be ecclesial: unconditional acceptance of Christian revelation does not commit us to totalitarian ideologies of obedience. A meaningful argument about, for example, the ordination of women or the political commitments of the Church presupposes an agreement on canons of truth and meaning. If the gospel is true, the reality to which we refer in such arguments, however mistaken our claims about it may be, is somehow more than what is presupposed in rational argument as

---

[62] 1978*b*, 27, *394*.

such. Further, our only access to this 'more' comes through the Christian tradition and its particular patterns of language use. In these terms, we can meet Dulles's concern, and articulate 'the ecclesial dimension of all authentic spirituality'. No one can claim to have 'the immediate experience of God' except with reference to Church tradition and the body of believers.

Such an approach articulates a special assistance of the Holy Spirit within the particularity of the Christian tradition, without committing us to a crudely interventionist understanding of divine action. Talk of the unconditional and infallible applies primarily to the faith-conviction that God has acted in the world definitively and irrevocably in Jesus Christ, and to the validity of the particular tradition and frame of reference stemming from that event. Any particular statement *within* that frame of reference, however, including those of legitimate Church leaders, may be conditioned by a failure to accept God's grace fully or to formulate the reality in question with proper reference to all relevant factors. It is primarily the generative power of Christian tradition, and only derivatively the authority of any office-holder, that is the proper and most central focus of unconditional assent. There can therefore be circumstances in which a hierarchical directive is conditioned by the sinfulness of the office-holder, and which the individual may, perhaps must, conscientiously disobey. Such a course of action may be painful and conflictive, but it is most misleading to refer to it as 'a break with the Church'.

Rahner's 'immediate experience of God' is emancipated from hierarchical control: it is 'not simply mediated through the ecclesiastical machinery'.[63] But such statements are not to be understood in terms of 'private judgement' prevailing over against the Church. It is rather that a Christian's identity and judgement, however intimate or idiosyncratic, are already shaped by ecclesial mediation. When Rahner asserts the individual's experience of grace, seemingly over against the Church, the real contrast being made is between the ecclesial reality of grace and the hierarchically sanctioned.

Admittedly, these last pages have been an exercise in constructive interpretation rather than strict exegesis. In a very late prayer, expressing exasperation at Church leadership, Rahner made a

---

[63] 1978*b*, 27, *394*.

revealing admission: 'perhaps my eyes are cloudy, and I'm emo-
tionally biased against "authority" and "power"'.[64] His own theology generates a distinction between the hierarchical and the
ecclesial which he often failed to recognize. One striking example
comes from a moving piece in which Rahner spoke of various Jesuit
friends, each seeking unobtrusively to serve God and God's people.
Nevertheless, Rahner describes the spirit inspiring such people as
having 'a priority above every kind of social—even ecclesiastical—
factor'.[65] Such formulations reveal an instinctive tendency to con-
fuse the social reality of the Church and of Christian discipleship
with what can only ever be a part of that reality: the institutional
structures.

More generally, it must be admitted that Rahner often sounds
committed to unacceptable sub-Cartesian assumptions, almost as if
he were an old-fashioned Liberal Protestant with a biretta. At the
end of an interview given on the Exercises in 1978, Rahner made a
contrast between Ignatian and liturgical prayer. It is obviously a
meaningful and noble thing for Christians to pray the Lord's Prayer
together, says Rahner, 'but one can't seriously claim, no matter how
devoutly and earnestly we pray this Our Father together, that the
immediacy to God which Ignatius talks about in the Exercises is
thereby attained and realized'. Liturgy serves to support the immediate experience of God, but does not of itself attain the radicality of
the Ignatian experience.[66] Such a statement resonates with modern
instincts, and clearly contains grains of truth. Liturgical prayer and
personal prayer are clearly different kinds of experience. But it is
both a philosophical and theological mistake to suppose that personal prayer attains God directly whereas the liturgy puts something in the way.[67] Both forms of prayer are social practices aimed at
fostering awareness of God's omnipresent immediacy. And both,
not just public prayer, can be spiritually dysfunctional.

Walter Kasper criticizes Rahner for taking 'too little notice of the
fact that the content of historical reality implies a specification of
the transcendental conditions of understanding: a specification

[64] 'Prayer for the Church', 116, *143*.
[65] 'Why I remain a Jesuit', 33, *28*.   [66] 1978*c*, 180, *40*.
[67] See e.g. Peter E. Fink, 'Public and Private Moments in Christian Prayer', *Worship*, 58
(1984), 482–99; Rowan Williams, 'The Suspicion of Suspicion: Wittgenstein and Bonhoeffer',
in Richard H. Bell (ed.), *The Grammar of the Heart: New Essays in Moral Philosophy and
Theology* (San Francisco: Harper and Row, 1988), 36–54.

which can neither be derived from these conditions as such, nor be fully understood in their terms'.[68] This judgement, however, is plausible only if it is directed at Rahner's actual achievement. It does not apply to Rahner's method and project as such.[69] A fairer assessment is offered by James Bacik:

although Rahner's deepest instincts remain individualistic, his fundamental theological approach is definitely open to the interpersonal and institutional dimensions of human existence, and thus has enabled him to make important contributions to social questions.[70]

Rahner's transcendental theology can and should be extended. When this is done, this theology not only allows but positively requires reference to the decisive, irreplaceable role of Christ and of the tradition stemming from him. 'The immediate experience of God' is intrinsically connected to 'the standard of Christ', conveyed to us through tradition, and beheld from within the body of believers.

[68] Walter Kasper, *Jesus the Christ*, trans. V. Green (London: Burns and Oates, 1977), 50*.
[69] Muck, 'Heidegger und Karl Rahner', 269: 'These objections take into account only the result, not the nature of the method.'
[70] Bacik, *Apologetics*, 53–4.

9

Decisions and Discipleship

The previous two chapters have been exercises in clarification. In Rahner's writing, 'the immediate experience of God' is an integral—if often unacknowledged—aspect of ordinary human living, not some kind of escape into disembodiment. Moreover, Christianity tells us that God exists as a gracious God, as self-giver, a truth demonstrated by the resurrection of Jesus. The Church's witness to this fact empowers believers to accept their fragmentariness, the ambiguity of their everyday experience, in the faith that resurrection life is God's purpose for the whole creation. In that sense, Christian tradition decisively shapes both how believers experience God, and how they can construe human experience universally. It is time now to revisit Rahner's accounts of how particular Ignatian decisions happen. This present chapter concentrates on Ignatian discernment in the conventional sense, on how the experience of grace can govern choices about how to live the Christian life. The following chapter will focus on how Rahner's theology of Ignatian choice applies also to the process of accepting Christian faith as such.

The general principle underlying Rahner's account of Ignatian discernment is simple. The moment of 'transcendence becoming thematic' is a moment when, under God, we appropriate our 'nature', our graced identity, more fully. Given Rahner's naturalist assumptions about ethics, such moments of insight have implications for our actions. Ignatian discernment involves a synthesis between a particular object and 'rightly understood supernatural transcendence'.[1] In what follows, we will begin by seeing how the ideas developed in the previous two chapters can help us describe more fully the kind of change which comes about when 'transcendence becomes thematic'. We will then pass on to the question of

---

[1] The phrase comes from Rahner's 1959 letter replying to Peter Knauer's criticisms of the 1956 essay. The text is reproduced in the Appendix.

how, theologically, to interpret the desires and projects that emerge from a discernment process.

Reorienting the Self

It is only in and through the material that we apprehend what transcends the material. Our *Geist*—mind or spirit—is always *in Welt*, 'in world'. The previous chapters have argued the need to extend this key Rahnerian conviction. Our specifically human identity, our transcendence, is shaped not only by what Rahner called 'matter', but also by interpersonal and cultural factors: language, tradition, and history. For Christian theology, chief among these factors are the events of canonical revelation. If we modify our understanding of Rahnerian 'transcendence' in the light of these latter claims, can we say more about the key Ignatian moment?

A good starting-point for answering this question is Part III of *Hearer of the Word*, a text which brings out clearly the close links in Rahner's thought between epistemology and ethics, between theoretical and practical reason. We have already seen how Rahner claims here that all human knowing and willing is somehow responsive to an absolute creative initiative from God. Towards the end of his argument, Rahner makes a further claim: this responsiveness is shaped through a history of concrete, finite choices. It is not simply that the human person is free to affirm or reject the basic orientation towards God given in human existence as such. Everyday decisions, rather, have a cumulative effect: they shape what some moral theologians now call 'character'. Each choice conditions the next:

> And because the human person does not therefore simply string out individual deeds one after the other without any connection, but rather in every deed sets down a law governing his or her whole activity and life, it follows that human beings do not simply act in ways that are good or bad: they themselves become good or bad.[2]

Thus each human being synthesizes their basic orientation to God with their own 'order of love', an attitudinal structure shaped by a history of decision.

It follows that the 'love', the affective attitude towards God,

[2] *Hearer of the Word*, 85–6, *131–2* (*KRSW*, iv. 156–8).

necessarily given with human consciousness as such 'is never given "neat" simply on its own, but always and only with an overlay, determined in either a similar or a contrary way by the order of love freely set up by the actual person concerned'.[3] This ethical attitude shaping human identity informs our knowledge, in particular the knowledge of God implicit in our self-awareness:

> The truth in any knowledge of God—speaking now of how an individual understands their God—is always also a function of the orderedness or disorderedness of their love. It is not the case that a person initially knows God 'neutrally', and then wonders about whether to adopt a position of love or hatred towards this God. Such a neutral knowledge, such 'objectivity' is a philosophers' abstraction.[4]

Metaphysical knowledge is self-involving, and thus our ability to apprehend truth depends on our moral state. Growth in metaphysical awareness is a matter of 'conversion' quite as much as of intellectual insight or new research findings.[5] Our awareness of ourselves and God is shaped by our personal history.

This passage from *Hearer of the Word*—anticipating contemporary retrievals of virtue ethics—brings out how the key Ignatian experience, the moment of 'transcendence becoming thematic', is always a moment of conversion and reinterpretation: a moment when our self-awareness and values somehow change. It also confirms the logical status of Rahnerian 'transcendence'. No more than the sparse text of Ignatius's *Exercises* does Rahner's 'transcendence becoming thematic' offer a full description of a discernment process. Both Rahner and Ignatius seek to articulate patterns of meaning and significance that are always embedded in individual lives, in all their particularities, vicissitudes, and indeed ambiguities.

However, the idiom of individual choice may lead to misunderstanding. Its immediate implication is that we start at birth with a clean slate, and make our own way through our life-history. But in fact—as Rahner well knew from Church teaching on original sin and on concupiscence—we do not start life unmarked by what our ancestors have made of the world. We receive our initial sense of identity through inheritance and socialization. The 'overlay' of 'love', the attitudinal filter through which we appropriate our self-awareness, is there from the start, and our knowledge of God in

---

[3] Ibid., 86, *133* (*KRSW*, iv. 156–8).   [4] Ibid., 86*, *133* (*KRSW*, iv. 160).
[5] Ibid., 87, *134* (*KRSW*, iv. 160)—quotation marks Rahner's.

self-awareness never occurs except through this filter. Indeed, the process of maturing is largely one of acquiring the capacity to make one's own choices, rather than uncritically taking over inherited conventions. In one sense, then, all theology is liberation theology, arising from critical scrutiny of inherited plausibility structures.

A similar pattern—of individualist idiom obscuring the interpersonal nature of human identity—occurs in an important footnote to Rahner's 1956 discernment essay.[6] Rahner is defending his interpretation of Ignatius's 'consolation without preceding cause', arguing that it should be construed as 'consolation without object (*Gegenstand*)'. He notes how the self-awareness in any everyday mental act is not in itself directed to an object, and thus specifies the question:

> The question thus can only be: is there this kind of non-objective awareness with respect to other realities as well as with respect to one's own 'I'? If the answer to that question in the case of God is yes, then the idea of a 'non-objective' experiential knowledge of God (*eine 'gegenstandslose' Erfahrung Gottes*) occurring through being taken up completely into God's love . . . becomes conceivable.

Moreover, Rahner believes that he has already provisionally established, from the tradition, the possibility of such non-objective awareness of God. Earlier in the note, he has referred us to the French version of his account of spiritual touch in Bonaventure, reminding us of the claim therein that 'here on earth there is an experience of the love of God which occurs without the intellect having any share in it'.

Rahner is here working with an individualist account of transcendence, and arguing that individuals nevertheless affirm God in affirming themselves. But once we allow a historically shaped concept of human transcendence and identity, the claim about 'non-objective' awareness of realities other than one's own self no longer needs argument. Our relationships with others, for good or ill, condition our whole identity, the whole ensemble of our engagements with external reality. When we grow in awareness of that identity, the experience is always non-objective. It may be triggered by a particular object, but the point at issue is always an interpretation of our situation which cannot simply be read off from the object. The

---

[6] 1956*a*, 134–5 n. 28, *117 n. 42*. Though the ET of the passages here quoted is acceptable, there are some serious mistakes elsewhere in the note.

prodigal son may look at the pigswill, but he comes 'to himself' and realizes—to put it minimally—that his life could be different. We have already noted Rahner's reading of the spiritual senses in Bonaventure: his insistence that spiritual senses are not a parallel set of faculties but our normal senses, purified and used rightly.[7] Something like that contrast applies here: as we appropriate in the light of the gospel the truth of who we are, our 'immediate' experience, our spontaneous perceptions and responses to the world, are transformed.[8]

Rahner's concept of 'transcendence' is therefore a formal one; it is always embedded in specific life histories, and its 'becoming thematic' is always a developmental process. When Rahner's account of Ignatius is read in these terms, many of the criticisms raised against it appear misplaced.

William Spohn, for example, comparing Rahner with American theologians such as Jonathan Edwards and H. Richard Niebuhr, is concerned at Rahner's concentration 'on radical freedom and "transcendence" as the core of the self'. By contrast, Niebuhr points towards 'the unique history which has formed the individual':

Whatever answer I give to the moral question, 'What ought I to do?' will be profoundly affected by my answer to the question of identity, 'Who am I?' . . . For example, if I feel myself to be a victim, I am likely to inject weariness and fear into even innocent relationships. My defensiveness may be all the more powerful if this image of being a victim remains unconscious. My spontaneous reactions will be defensive or even hostile, leading me to actions which are more appropriate to my fear of being violated again than to the actual situation, which may contain nothing objectively threatening. Discernment will be operating but it will be neurotic discernment, skewed by my inadequate self-image.[9]

However, on the reading of Rahner proposed in this study, Spohn's Niebuhrian account of the matter specifies rather than replaces Rahner's.[10] The first sentence quoted here merely repeats the

---

[7] 'The Doctrine', 110 ('La doctrine', 269).
[8] For further development, see my 'The Ignatian Prayer of the Senses', esp. 410–12.
[9] Spohn, 'The Reasoning Heart', 35. One may conjecture that 'weariness' is a misprint for 'wariness'.
[10] Spohn's general tone suggests that he is criticizing Rahner, even if some formulations (e.g. 'Karl Rahner tests possible responses against a basic sense of the self. Niebuhr *clarifies* this by analysing the basic symbols which shape the individual's self-understanding' [p. 33, emphasis mine]) might support an alternative reading of Spohn.

ethical vision of *Hearer of the Word*. God's grace is not a gift to some separated inner self, but rather an invitation and an empowerment to shape one's whole life. What Spohn presents as an alternative to Rahner in fact vividly describes how one instance of the process might feel:

> Christian conversion involves moral transformation precisely because it challenges the central images of the self. *Metanoia* means rethinking my personal history through a new set of images which the community proposes as normative. If I have previously conceived of myself as victim, I no longer can remember the past as a series of undeserved injuries and fear a future which will contain more of the same. Viewing myself as one who has been forgiven and empowered to forgive others, I need to reinterpret that history of injuries. Because I now believe that the cross and resurrection of Jesus will be part of my own experience, my attitude towards injury cannot be simply resentment and wariness. The events are not changed, but their meaning must be if I am to be a Christian. If the God I now believe in brought life precisely where death had seemed invincible in the experience of Christ, then I am enabled to look for life in the most threatening memories of my own past. Reinterpreted in light of the normative images of faith, my past can issue in compassion for the suffering and a new capacity for service.[11]

Rahner's more abstract, metaphysical idiom, however, articulates some dimensions of the reality more satisfactorily than Spohn's 'American approach'. Firstly, Rahner's avoidance of specific historical or personal reference leaves greater room for pluralism. Spohn's example remains one among alternatives; the dynamic can occur in an indefinitely wide range of situations and personalities, some of which lie beyond the range of our descriptive sympathy. The writing in Spohn's article appeals to modern English-speaking readers because it draws on prevailing cultural and religious values; Rahner's more austere account leaves room for the process to occur also in ways we Westerners would not spontaneously imagine. Secondly, Rahner's account brings out that it is not the symbol or word alone which enables the change in identity, but also the divine reality which the symbol expresses. Spohn's replacement of theological metaphysics with narrative makes it unclear why it should be specifically the gospel, and not some perhaps more edifying or beautiful alternative, that should resource

[11] Spohn, 'The Reasoning Heart', 35–6.

our discovery of identity under God. Paradoxically, Rahner's realist metaphysics enables him to be more generous than Spohn in recognizing God's grace, and indeed the dynamics of Ignatian discernment, among non-believers.[12] The truth of Christian symbolism depends not on its aesthetic qualities alone, but on the validity of its metaphysical reference.

'Transcendence becoming thematic', therefore, is always a matter of conversion, and of growth in authentic relationship with the created world as a whole. Hence the process organically involves specific choices. Thus, in 1978, Rahner's Ignatius presents specific life-options as mediations of God's grace:

When I used to envisage and play out to myself my freedom's possibilities, and set them before my freedom's emerging decision, I experienced (*erlebte*) that, on the one hand, one alternative shone through itself, fitted into the open freedom which leads to God's own self and remained transparent to him, whereas this was not the case with the other—though, in themselves, all such possibilities, which, each in their own way, derive from him, could have been small tokens of the infinite God. In some way like this (it's difficult to make it clear) I learnt to make further distinctions within what was already seen as objectively and rationally possible and as ecclesiastically permissible: distinctions between that bounded reality in which the incomprehensibility of the boundless God willed to be near me, and that in which, although a matter of empirical fact and in itself also quite sensible, remained in a certain way dark and an obstruction to God. It would, after all, be crazy just to say that everything in reality—on the ground that it is real and originates in God—must offer equal access to God for every human individual. For then no decision of our freedom, even unavoidable ones, would have any special significance.[13]

---

[12] See 1956*a*, 165, *143–4*. Spohn's criteria for adjudicating between different purportedly Christian visions are not fully developed. He criticizes the use of promised-land symbolism to legitimate apartheid on both biblical and ethical grounds: the land symbolism is 'canonically minor', and its use here contravenes the New Testament, while the behaviour thus generated violates 'ordinary moral standards' ('The Reasoning Heart', 43). The first of these arguments is fideist: on what basis are priorities within the canon decided, and who decides what conforms to the New Testament? The second seems to involve a retreat to some pre-Christian account of 'ethical standards', in a way that seems both to be rationalist and to undermine Spohn's own project of establishing a distinctively Christian ethics. For further criticism of Spohn on this point, with reference to Aristotle, see Hughes, 'Ignatian Discernment', 424–6.

[13] 1978*b*, 17*, *381*.

Responsive Choice and the Emergence of Desire

A further question arises here, however. The object of choice is a mediation of grace in some special sense—it is not simply that any created reality reflects the action of God. At the same time, it must also be somehow subordinate to the canonical symbols of Jesus Christ and official tradition. How can the necessary distinctions be articulated? We have already noted Nikolaus Schwerdtfeger's suggestion: in the key Ignatian experience, God's own reality is immediately present, expressed in a categorical *Realsymbol*.[14] Just as Jesus is the symbol, the definitive and necessary categorical expression, of God's self-gift generally, so our choice of action embodies our transcendental 'immediacy to God'. This suggestion is a helpful beginning, but the concept of *Realsymbol* needs to be refined and extended.[15]

To begin with, we must distinguish canonical and non-canonical symbolization. Jesus is a canonical symbol of God's grace; our life-choices may, like his life, death, and resurrection, truly symbolize the gracious presence of God, but in a derivative, responsive mode. Schwerdtfeger is right to draw on Rahner's Christology in order to interpret Rahner's reading of Ignatius, but the strategy needs to be pursued further. In particular, we must exploit Rahner's insistence that the Incarnation, for all its uniqueness, is a key point in an all-pervasive process. In the redemption, God wills '*one and the same* grace, that brings forth Christ, *and* gives us the possibility of turning freely to God'.[16] The second of the Münster lecture theses states simply that our relationship to Jesus Christ, the foundation of all Christology, refers to Christ 'in a primordial unity of what he is "in himself" and his "significance for us", without this unity being fully dissoluble'.[17] Ignatius's discernment guidelines, on this account, merely express a dynamic given in Christianity as such:

---

[14] Schwerdtfeger, *Gnade und Welt*, 318.

[15] In *Gnade und Welt*, 322–4, Schwerdtfeger struggles valiantly, though ultimately unsuccessfully, with what he admits is a 'tension' in Rahner's position between two claims: firstly, that only consolation without *Gegenstand*, the perception of God 'in the heart', is absolutely certain; secondly, that human beings only have this pure consolation in the context of an inclination towards a particular object.

[16] *Foundations of Christian Faith*, 283, 277 (*KRSW*, xxvi. 270).

[17] 'Grundlinien einer systematischen Christologie', 18. Compare *Foundations of Christian Faith*, 204, *204* (*KRSW*, xxvi. 197), where the strikingly stark syntax of the original has been modified.

Christianity in its explicit and full form is not merely an abstract theory, a reality that is thought of, ultimately, as objective and thing-like, and towards which one subsequently, as something extra, takes a position personally. Christianity really does understand itself, in its most distinctive essence, as an existential event: what we call a personal relationship to Jesus Christ.[18]

Theology can only operate in 'pale abstraction' from this lived relationship.[19] Similarly, the 1978 testament speaks of how the narration of Jesus's story cannot reduce to a theory: 'above and beyond theory, the story must also be renarrated over and over again, and thereby its story itself continued'.[20] The convergence with the 1955 retreat conference on discipleship, on *Nachfolge Christi*, will be obvious. The offer of grace as irrevocably expressed in Christ, and our responses, however fickle or fragile, are complementary aspects of one and the same reality. In particular, the 'transcendence' which 'becomes thematic' is different in each individual case. As we appropriate, anonymously or explicitly, the event of Christ, with the all-pervasive grace this event symbolizes, we appropriate also not some uniform 'transcendence', but a unique individuality created for graced intimacy with God. Our choices under God's grace build up the *pleroma* of Christ, responding to and continuing what God has already begun.

The object of Ignatian choice, therefore, serves as a *Realsymbol* of God's grace for the person concerned, but in a way secondary to, and derivative from, the primary mediation of grace: Jesus Christ. This distinction, helpful though it is, nevertheless needs to be developed further. The decisions emerging from Ignatian discernment are liable to go wrong, in ways that mainstream Christianity would not want to attribute either to Jesus or to the Bible. Whereas the pledge embodied in Jesus has been given us once and for all, our response is a cumulative, lifelong affair, occurring 'perhaps painfully and with failures'.[21] Making the Exercises might lead a person, for example, to opt for a career as a pianist, only for them to lose their hands in an accident. A young woman may decide, through Ignatian discernment, to join a religious order, only to be refused—perhaps on quite inadequate grounds—by the

---

[18] *Foundations of Christian Faith*, 306, *298 (KRSW*, xxvi. 290–1).
[19] Ibid., 307, *299 (KRSW*, xxvi. 292).   [20] 1978*b*, 20*, *385*.
[21] *Foundations of Christian Faith*, 307, *299 (KRSW*, xxvi. 292).

responsible superior. By contrast, what has been said so far seems to ascribe a kind of divinely guaranteed certainty to the process. Even in 1972, when he had moderated his earlier claims about the certainty of the Ignatian experience, Rahner could still claim that an Ignatian choice was 'certain' on the ground that it arose from 'the experience of grace'—and contrast this with the objective reasons supporting such a choice, grounds which would always be less than conclusive.[22] Surely, however, the everyday Christian quest for God's will is fraught with fallibility. To say that the fruit of Ignatian discernment is the *Realsymbol*, even in an attenuated sense, of God's grace still seems unrealistic. As the elderly Rahner, at least, saw, it can all too easily 'turn out later . . . to be inadequate, provisional, replaceable, and even detrimental'.[23]

Ignatius himself must be our initial source for tackling this question, which is one that Rahner never directly faced. Ignatian discernment is reliable, provided we understand its object appropriately. The fruit of Ignatius's process consists primarily in the specification and purification of a *desire*, and only secondarily in the actions or events to which these desires may lead.[24] Ignatian imaginative prayer typically ends with a 'colloquy': an imaginative conversation between the retreatant and either God or one or more of the persons in the scene being contemplated. Ignatius does not here intend primarily a pious reflection, but rather an honest dialogue aimed at the clarification of attitudes. A version of the *Exercises* written prior to 1541 brings out the point particularly clearly:

And here you should set out what you want, not in order to teach God—who knows what you desire before you come to prayer—but in order to inflame your own mind with a greater desire of this gift as you name it and explain it verbally.[25]

Ignatian prayer fosters the surfacing of desire, as raw material for discernment.[26]

[22] 1972, 162*, 206.   [23] 'Dialogue with God?', 130, 157.
[24] On the role of desires in Ignatian spirituality, see E. Edward Kinerk, 'Eliciting Great Desires: Their Place in the Spirituality of the Society of Jesus', *Studies in the Spirituality of Jesuits*, 16/5 (November 1984), 1–29; Michael Ivens, 'Desire and Discernment', *The Way Supplement*, 95 (Summer 1999), 31–43.
[25] MHSJ *Exx* (1969), 576; see also *Exx*, nn. 54, 109, 199. For further information on this and similar texts, and for powerful arguments against the marginal status they have hitherto been ascribed, see Rogelio García-Mateo, 'Importancia de los "textus accomodati" para el estudio e interpretación de los "Ejercicios espirituales"', *Estudios eclesiásticos*, 69 (1994), 367–85.
[26] See my 'To Reflect and Draw Profit'.

One intense moment recorded in Ignatius's *Spiritual Diary* shows a keen respect for the limits of discernment. Ignatius feels intense confirmation of his sense that the Society's legislation on poverty should be made stricter than the original agreement between the companions had envisaged:

During mass, there were different feelings in confirmation . . . when I held the Blessed Sacrament in my hands, there came to me from within words, and intense movement, of never leaving Him, not for all heaven or earth or etc., feeling new impulses, devotion, and spiritual joy.

But Ignatius was not being carried away totally. He added a proviso: 'I was adding, "for my part", "doing what in me lay": this latter referred to the companions who had signed.'[27] The general principle has been well articulated by Jules Toner: 'discernment is limited to finding God's will regarding the discerner's *own* free and responsible choice . . . What God actually wills to happen as consequences of the discerner's decision and free choice is beyond the limits of discernment.'[28]

Two biblical examples illustrate the point. When the prodigal son looks at the pigswill and comes to himself, he resolves to go home. But the happy and straightforward outcome of that desire is secondary to the desire itself. The prodigal's resolve would still have been a valid and necessary expression of his change of heart, even had his father then turned up on the spot, or alternatively had the father been dead when the son returned. It is not the going home as such which matters, but rather the change of attitude which informs it. Integral to growth in grace is a renewed symbolic self-understanding, issuing in desires and projects which become real in some way or other. But the *particular* ways in which they become real are not in themselves integral to the process of conversion in the way that the desires as such are. In 1549, Ignatius himself—or his assistants—made the point in terms of Jonah, who is commanded by God to announce Nineveh's impending destruction, but whose motivations are then purified through God's sparing the city:

[27] *Diary*, n. 69.2, 23 February 1544 (Ignatius, *Personal Writings*, 85*). Given the fragmentary nature of the original, translation is more than normally disputable.
[28] Toner, *Discerning God's Will*, 50, 62. Toner, who conclusively discredits any Rahnerian account of Ignatian discernment drawing solely on the 1956 essay, has been very influential on what follows.

even the prophets themselves do not always see everything in the prophetic lights as clearly and without qualification as their expressions can indicate. Thus it happened that Jonah said without qualification, 'Yet forty days and Nineveh shall be overthrown!' and it did not happen, or at least he did not express the condition which God Our Lord's eternal disposition had attached to that statement, namely, 'unless they did penance'.[29]

As Rahner himself put it in 1959, our choices always fit into a wider pattern of divinely sustained contingency, over which we have no control. Our desires as inspired by the Jesuit motto, 'for the greater glory of God', must respect God's other dispositions, which might well have us act 'for his lesser glory':

Humanity's being at the disposal of God has an impermanent quality. Obedience precisely does not mean making a magnificent plan once and for all according to some abstract principle. Rather it means essentially that obedience must exist in the historical dimension of our human existence—obedience always conditioned by the new, the unforeseen and the incalculable.[30]

Rahner's 1956 essay, as we have seen, draws on two main Ignatian sources: the discernment rules about 'consolation without preceding cause', and the first letter to Teresa Rejadell. Both sources stress the need to distinguish between the immediately given divine consolation itself and what may happen afterwards. Here the soul often, 'through one's own course of habits and the consequences of the concepts and judgements, or through the good spirit or through the bad, forms various resolutions and opinions which are not immediately given by God our Lord'.[31] In both texts, particularly in the letter, Ignatius contrasts the absolute confidence we may have in the divinely given consolation with the healthy scepticism appropriate for what we might add to that experience. In particular, painful experiences arising from these additional cogitations do not discredit the consolation in itself.

Implicit in the Ignatian writings, therefore, is a distinction between the desires stimulated by the gospel and the outcomes to which such desires may lead. Ignatian discernment involves more

[29] MHSJ *EI*, xii. 634 (Ignatius, *Personal Writings*, 211–12), quoting Jonah 3: 4. The source is a report evaluating claims made by two Jesuits and a Franciscan, allegedly under prophetic inspiration. See Manuel Ruiz Jurado, 'Un caso de profetismo reformista en la Compañía de Jesús: Gandía 1547–1549', *Archivum historicum Societatis Iesu*, 43 (1974), 217–66.
[30] 1959, 35–6, 42–3.   [31] *Exx*, nn. 336.4–5.

than a simple growth in openness to God: the surfacing of desires is integral to the process. The point of the distinction is to secure a sense in which the Ignatian process has some clear and reliable practical significance, while at the same time allowing for the fact that good Ignatian decisions may not work out as planned.

Rahner's one attempt at formulating such a distinction himself comes in a passage we have already encountered from the 1956 essay. Rahner is commenting on what he sees as the key experience:

> Now, that such an experience contains its grounding within itself, that—always provided we look at it in itself—it cannot deceive, that God's own self is there and just nothing else can be there—this is self-evident. But one must be careful. We are not dealing here with a conceptual representation of God. . . . With that conceptual reality of God, and reference to God, there can, of course, be just as much error and misinterpretation as with any other proposition, or any other object of a free love.[32]

Under pressure, indeed, Rahner insists the object to be chosen can never be the 'immediate, and, in the full sense, proper object' of the key Ignatian experience;[33] the question of choice actually arises only when the fundamental consolation has been 'overlaid by and combined with impulses that have finite causes and objects'.[34] This attempt to articulate the distinction not only distorts Ignatius's own texts, which clearly do link particular projects to the experience of consolation,[35] but is also theologically inconsistent. The disjunction between 'God's own self' and a categorical representation of God cannot be sustained if God's own self is, through grace, expressed in the world of space and time. The distinction we need is not that between transcendental and categorical, or between experience itself and the words we use to articulate experience, but rather that between desire and its outcome. Ignatian discernment yields a puri-fied desire. If one avoids any temptation to look for more than that, and if Ignatius's process is followed competently and conscien-tiously, there is no reason why it should not be regarded as reliable.[36] Our desires act-after and act-with God's gift of self to the creation.

Even if our attempts to act on the desires God's self-gift evokes in us are quite misguided, or meet with frustration, this does not dis-credit the Christian interpretation of our experience that led us to

---

[32] 1956a, 148, *129*. [33] 1956a, 158, *137*: '*unmittelbares und eigentlichstes Objekt*'.
[34] 1956a, 160, *139*. [35] See Toner, *A Commentary*, 246–8.
[36] Toner, *Discerning God's Will*, 274–315, is provocatively cogent on this point.

embark on the attempts in the first place. The two examples cited
above—that of the injured pianist and the young woman frustrated
in a religious vocation—do not need to be interpreted as cases of
botched or inauthentic discernment. They can be seen as instances
where desires inspired by God, and properly discerned, come,
under God's providence, to be used for a purpose different from
what the people concerned first imagined.

Once again, the account of Rahner given in this chapter builds
on foundations laid by him rather than simply reporting what he
actually wrote. Even in the 1978 testament, Rahner's own account
of the Ignatian choice is couched in an individualist, abstract idiom.
Rahner's Ignatius speaks of God's self-giving love enabling something created to appear 'as the thing loved and preferred, as the
thing chosen to be from among many other possibilities remaining
empty':

And the human person, standing in God's modeless light, acts-with this
inclining of God towards a particular, finite creature; this creature is for
the person lovable, beautiful, ultimately of eternal validity, because God's
own self can accomplish and does accomplish the past all grasp miracle of
his love, that of giving himself.[37]

We become aware, says Rahner, of the fullness of God's love only
when it leads us towards specific courses of action, towards something willed by God in another sense:

This experience of acting-with God's inclination to what is not God, and
yet which, without there being any confusion, can no longer, as a result of
this inclination, be separated from God, is first had when one thing is experienced as willed by God in contrast to another.

Only then does Rahner remind us that this object of God's inclination is, properly speaking, a person rather than a thing, and thus
identifies this action-with as Christian love of neighbour.

As elsewhere in Rahner's Ignatian writings, the interpersonal is
acknowledged, but later and less fully than is necessary. Erhard
Kunz's overall judgement on this matter is a fair one:

In the form in which it is often levelled, the charge that Rahner does not
take history in its uniqueness sufficiently seriously is certainly unjustified.
The fact that it comes up repeatedly, despite Rahner's protests, is

<hr />

[37] 1978*b*, 18*, *382*.

probably due to the fact that the principle of dialogue and of intercommunication does not have sufficient effect on Rahner's work, given the nature of the approach from which he started.[38]

The enigmatic passage just quoted from the 1978 testament needs to be developed, bringing out how our choices are never simply individual affairs, but are always conditioned by other human beings, indeed by the rest of creation. Thus this chapter has insisted on how our transcendental experience is socially constructed; it has also drawn, more fully than the others, on Ignatian material in order to bring out that the central object of Ignatian choice is a desire—a desire always subject to contingencies and to the desires of others. We discern not in order to assuage anxiety about the future, but in order to undergo 'the purification of the motive | In the ground of our beseeching'.[39] With such provisos, however, Rahner's general vision can be endorsed and confirmed. The graced desires which we choose, discerningly, to affirm stand in responsive continuum with God's self-giving love for the creation, made irrevocably manifest in Jesus Christ—a love moving, however meanderingly and darkly, towards an end where God will be all in all.

[38] Kunz, 'Glaubwürdigkeitserkenntnis und Glaube', 440.
[39] 'Little Gidding', in *The Complete Poems and Plays of T. S. Eliot*, 196.

10

The Decision of Faith

'Such a conviction . . . is basically outrageous.'[1] What grounds Karl Rahner's claims about the human experience of divine grace, and about Ignatius Loyola? The 1956 essay suggests that Rahner is appealing to some kind of self-evident experience in order to ground claims going beyond what theology alone might deliver. Rahner's doctrines of the supernatural existential and of the supernatural formal object lead to an account of God's grace as something which can indeed be experienced, but which we cannot clearly distinguish from the 'purely natural'. For Rahner in 1956, the conclusion is clear: '*this* kind of awareness is of no account as regards the possibility of the discernment of spirits'.[2] Ignatius's Exercises involve a certainty 'that must lie deeper' than empirical evidence, and that cannot be translated into abstract statements.[3] This conviction passes over, at least in tone, to the 1978 testament. The idiom at times is that of simple experiential testimony, as though anything that tradition, dogma, or theology can offer is but a pale shadow of what really matters: 'God's own self. God's own self I experienced, not human words about God.'[4]

If the claims of this study so far are correct, the relationship between the Ignatian experience and everyday Christianity must be much closer. To say this, however, does not of itself undermine the claim that the Ignatian experience is self-evident, because, for Rahner, Christian revelation too 'cannot be grounded starting from humanity—neither that it happens, nor that it must happen, nor its intrinsic nature'.[5] Christology involves 'an ontological ultimate which a merely rational ontology would perhaps never suspect'.[6] What we can say, however, is that the two appeals to self-evidence— in Christian revelation generally and in the Ignatian experience

[1] 1978b, 12, 374.   [2] 1956a, 126, 110.   [3] 1956a, 150 n. 35, 131 n. 49.
[4] 1978b, 12, 375.   [5] Hearer of the Word, 5, 17 (KRSW, iv. 17).
[6] Foundations of Christian Faith, 222, 220 (KRSW, xxvi. 213).

more specifically—are ultimately the same appeal. The Ignatian experience and the decision to believe in Christianity at all involve the same kind of process. In a weak sense at least, they can be said to legitimate each other. This conclusion emerges from a constructive interpretation applied to what Rahner wrote on Ignatius in his youth and in his middle age. It also converges with claims in two later pieces: a talk given on how Jesuits should understand the Church, and a piece published in 1972. Entitled 'Reflections on a New Task for Fundamental Theology', this latter formed part of a *Festschrift* for the noted Spanish Jesuit theologian, Joaquín Salaverri (1892–1979).[7] The 'new task' consisted in exploring how Ignatian discernment could clarify the problem known as the *analysis fidei*: the relationship between the absolute commitment of faith and what can only be the relative certainty of any grounds given for it.[8] Whereas in 1956, Rahner had stressed the difference between the Ignatian experience and the ordinary life of grace, here he brings out the structural parallels. Fundamental theology must involve 'a logic of the practical reason involved in faith, a logic of existential decision', a topic 'substantively identical with the rules for Election in Ignatius of Loyola'.[9] By implication, both Christian tradition and what Rahner takes to be the key Ignatian 'first principle' have a foundational role in Christian epistemology, and their relationship is one of mutual confirmation.

This chapter, therefore, explores the relationship between Ignatian discernment and fundamental theology, taking up unfinished business about the grounding of the Ignatian experience. Certainly against the Rahner of 1956, we must insist that Ignatian discernment is trustworthy only because its basic presuppositions follow analytically from New Testament revelation. Nevertheless, Rahner is not wholly wrong in his 1956 claim that our ongoing experience of

---

[7] For biographical information, see the opening article of the *Festschrift*: 'Introducción bibliográfica', *Estudios eclesiásticos*, 47 (1972), 319–29. Fuller bibliographies of Salaverri's work can be found in *Miscelánea Comillas*, 34–5 (1960), 11–16; 70 (1979), 97–9.

[8] This formulation is based on 1972, 164, *209*. For a clear historical account of the problem, see Kunz, 'Glaubwürdigkeitserkenntnis und Glaube', or, more briefly and generally accessibly, 'Analysis fidei'. Fernando Manresa, *Ejercicios Espirituales y teología fundamental: 'Una tarea nueva para la teología fundamental' (Karl Rahner)* (Barcelona: Cristianisme i Justicia, 1991) offers a Spanish summary of Rahner's text, some helpful explanation of the background issues, and a critical discussion of the issues raised.

[9] 1972, 164, *208*.

grace has a distinctive foundational role. As Christians continue to 'find God's will' in ever new and surprising ways, the process serves to confirm, albeit in a relatively weak and informal sense, the claims of Christian revelation.

Grace, Experience, and Warrants

Despite what Rahner may sometimes have written, claims about the Ignatian experience of God stand or fall with claims about Christian revelation as such. Indeed, Rahner himself wrote in 1974 of how the Ignatian Exercises 'presuppose, and *exercise* people in, what belongs to the basic substance of Christianity'.[10] Reference to the gospel is both necessary and sufficient to ground claims about the Ignatian 'first principle', the immediacy of God to our ongoing experience.

Our question here is not about particular instances of discernment, but about the validity of the practice as a whole. What allows us to interpret our ongoing experience in terms of God's continuing self-gift? When Rahner's Ignatius tells us that he experienced God immediately, what leads us—if we are Christians in sympathy with Rahner—to take the claim seriously? Why do we not reject it out of hand, as we would sentences such as 'I saw a square circle yesterday', or 'In 1940 I had a wonderful holiday touring a peaceful, tranquil Europe'? A part of the answer must surely be a belief that an immediate experience of God involves neither a logical contradiction—such as the idea of a square circle—nor an actual falsehood—such as the idea of a peaceful continental holiday in 1940. Given Rahner's understanding of 'the immediate experience of God', we can only hold this belief on the basis of Christian revelation, the guarantee offered us in Christ. The truth of Christian tradition as a whole is at least a presupposition for claims about God's presence in our ongoing experience.

But we can go further. The truth of Christian tradition is not only a necessary condition for the validity of Rahner's 'first principle', but also a sufficient one. Rahner's 'first principle' amounts to a logical consequence of mainstream Christian belief. We do not have to invoke any further, 'experiential' grounding. Crucial here are the

[10] 1974*b*, 70, *96* (emphasis original).

clarifications developed in previous chapters. Rahner's 'first principle' must be understood in less extravagant terms than his rhetoric may suggest, as a regulative truth, applicable to all experience, and Christologically specified. 'The immediate experience of God' is not given to us as a categorical, bounded reality; Rahner's point does not depend on any one particular experience that we may have. The point, rather, is that it must make sense, indeed the fullest and most comprehensive sense possible, to interpret our ongoing reality in terms of the Christian credal commitment, of the mystery of grace made irrevocably manifest in Christ. Such interpretations always involve both divine and human freedom, and hence they can never be simply deduced from the gospel or from Christian tradition. Ongoing experience of God, therefore, retains a distinctive foundational role, but one remaining secondary to, and derivative from, the primary, generative guarantee which is the resurrection of Christ.

Rahner's 'first principle' of supernatural practical reason can thus be reformulated in something like the following terms: our reality is such that it can be appropriately and authentically interpreted, indeed fully experienced, only with reference to Christian tradition. Christianity offers distinctive, uniquely disclosive, criteria of significance and truth. To talk of reality without reference to Christian tradition is like talking of sexual love in purely physiological terms, without reference to emotion. Such discourse is not false; indeed in some situations (for example, a medical investigation) it is helpful; but in the normal case it is clearly inappropriate. It overlooks important aspects of the reality, and is ethically degrading, however true it is that no instance of human love exists in independence from physiology. So here with Rahner's 'immediate experience of God'. It is not that created objects play no part, but rather that more is involved. If Christianity is true, then human realities and experiences can only be understood, ultimately, in terms of the kind of relationship with God that Christianity proclaims to be possible; only with reference to Christian concepts can we fully appropriate reality, or 'come to ourselves'. This does not commit us to the view that any particular use of this tradition to interpret our experience is guaranteed. We are simply accepting the guarantee offered by the resurrection of Jesus, a guarantee that the tradition as a whole is in principle reliable. Moreover, not even in Jesus's case is the axiomatic truth of Christianity given 'neat', independently of uncertain contingencies.

When Rahner's Ignatius says, 'I experienced God immediately', he is not doing what his tone —especially when heard from an Anglo-Saxon context—might suggest. He is not offering experiential testimony as an alternative or supplement to what we already know from the Scriptures. Such statements are best interpreted as stressing, not the grammatical object—'God'—but rather the verbs: 'encountered', 'experienced'. A gloss might run as follows: 'I came to realize that the conventional statements of a Christian culture are making claims about me and about my experience.'[11] Rahner's positions were developed in reaction to what was in his youth a standard Roman Catholic view: that grace was real, but in principle inaccessible to human awareness. There was a rooted hostility to the idea that experience could be theologically significant.[12] The effect, through Vatican II, of the kind of approach Rahner developed has been far-reaching—so much so that it may be difficult to appreciate how it was once revolutionary. Without the theological rehabilitation of history and experience which theologians of Rahner's generation brought about, today's liberation theologies—at least within Roman Catholicism—could never have arisen.[13]

Revisioning Fundamental Theology

In the 1972 essay, Rahner presents it as a 'new task' that fundamental theology should draw on Ignatian resources. 'New' it may have been for the kind of fundamental theology pursued by Salaverri, but even in *Hearer of the Word* Rahner had parted company decisively with this approach. The allegedly new elements in the 1972 essay build on some of Rahner's long-standing convictions. Rahner's talk of novelty may have been a matter of mere tact and courtesy;

[11] Cf. *Foundations of Christian Faith*, 16–17, 27–8; 306–7, 298–9 (*KRSW*, xxvi. 22–3, 290–1).

[12] The Irish Ignatian commentator, Joseph Veale, discussing changes in the understanding of Ignatius during the twentieth century, suggests that 'the change with the most revolutionary consequences was the discovery that it was respectable to use the word "experience" . . . In my four years of studying theology between 1949 and 1953 I never heard the word. It was not imagined that it might have anything to say to the dreadful theological aridities of those days. The dominant orthodoxy at the time frowned on it.' 'Dominant Orthodoxies', *Milltown Studies*, 30 (1992), 43–65.

[13] See Klaus P. Fischer, *Gotteserfahrung: Mystagogie in der theologie Karl Rahners und in der Theologie der Befreiung* (Mainz: Grünewald, 1986); Jon Sobrino, 'Karl Rahner and Liberation Theology', *Theology Digest*, 32 (1985), 257–60.

alternatively, he may himself have only just begun to perceive the connections between his Ignatian writings and his convictions on nature and grace.

Whatever we make of the newness rhetoric in Rahner's writings on this topic, we need to explore the substantive connections between the grounding of faith and the Ignatian choice. We can begin from the 1972 essay itself. Rahner begins by reflecting on Roman Catholic 'fundamental theology' since the Enlightenment. The subdiscipline has always worked with the material and the intellectual problems of its time. By using the scholarly methods current in philosophy, history, and the social sciences, fundamental theologians have traditionally sought 'to vindicate the objective credibility of faith and the subjective obligation to believe', as a form of apologetics directed towards at least the more educated of their contemporaries.[14] But now, says Rahner, such an approach is no longer possible, given the complexity of the issues involved:

Which fundamental theologian could still seriously imagine that they have simultaneously a full grasp of existentialism, linguistic philosophy, Anglo-Saxon positivism, and structuralism? In this area, who could still believe that they have such a precise knowledge of Jewish theology at the time of Jesus that they could provide with scholarly exactitude an exegesis of, say, Matthew 16 that will serve as fundamental theology—unless they become a specialist in a very narrow field and thus no longer have any idea regarding a thousand other problems in fundamental theology? . . . Many further such questions could be asked.[15]

A traditional 'direct method' in fundamental theology, establishing the rational basis for faith conclusively, is no longer a practical possibility. Rahner therefore proposes an alternative, an 'indirect method'.[16] Major personal decisions of all kinds need to be taken without the agent being able to mount a fully comprehensive analysis of all the factors involved. By teaching that we could never be certain of our state of grace, the Council of Trent at least hinted at a recognition of the point.[17] Such decisions happen in every context,

---

[14] 1972, 157, *199*.   [15] 1972, 158–9, *201–2*.

[16] Nicholas P. Healy, 'Indirect Methods: Karl Rahner as an *ad hoc* Apologist', *The Thomist*, 56 (1992), 613–33, offers a useful overview of this concept in Rahner's theology, situating Rahner's contribution against contemporary North American discussions. See also Farrugia, *Aussage und Zusage*, which, as its subtitle indicates, explores the 'indirectness' of Rahner's theological method as exemplified in his Christology.

[17] *Decree on Justification*, n. 12 (Tanner, *Decrees of the Ecumenical Councils*, 676).

and such must be the decision of faith. But we need to articulate the distinctive kind of rationality involved in this case. The various conventional theories of the *analysis fidei* are unsatisfactory: either they fail to recognize 'the radical difference' between the absolute commitment of faith and the at best conditionally certain rationale offered by fundamental theology, or else they make a lame, unspecified appeal to 'the decision of "the will" '. An appeal to the enlightenment of the Holy Spirit and to the grace of faith is certainly legitimate, but more has to be done: 'one must give some clearer indication of what this actually is, how it works, and how it can overcome this discrepancy in a legitimate way'.[18] The indirect approach required, Rahner then says, is exemplified by Ignatius's account of Christian decision, and can be applied to the more fundamental question under discussion here.

Rahner's references here to how fundamental theology might develop are probably disingenuous. He had developed such an 'indirect method' at the outset of his career, more than thirty years previously. When Rahner wrote *Hearer of the Word*, he was probably preparing to succeed to the chair of fundamental theology in Innsbruck.[19] Yet even so, in this work he was distancing himself very clearly from that subdiscipline as conventionally practised. The work is a study in *Wissenschaftstheorie*—not 'the philosophy of science' but the theory of how academic disciplines interrelate.[20] In it, Rahner is working out a relationship between philosophy and revealed theology radically different from that implicit in the then standard fundamental theology.[21]

Without appealing directly to revelation, conventional fundamental theology sought to demonstrate 'certain knowledge of the fact of divine revelation' and to establish faith as reasonable and credible.[22] That framework established, revelation then appeared as 'a mystery in the strict sense':

[18] 1972, 160–1, *204*. Compare Kunz, 'Analysis fidei', 584–5.
[19] Neufeld, *Die Brüder Rahner*, 131–2.
[20] *Hearer of the Word*, 1, *9–10* (*KRSW*, iv. 8).
[21] To situate Rahner's claims in historical context, two helpful reference works are: Walter Kern, Hermann J. Pottmeyer, and Max Seckler (edd.), *Handbuch der Fundamentaltheologie* (Freiburg: Herder, 1985–8); René Latourelle and Rino Fisichella (edd.), *Dictionary of Fundamental Theology* (London: St Paul's, 1994), esp. Fisichella's own article on 'Credibility', 193–209.
[22] Miguel Nicolau and Joaquín Salaverri, *Sacra theologiae summa*, vol. 1 (Madrid: Biblioteca de autores cristianos, 1958), n. 38.

a state of affairs so inaccessible to human knowledge that, firstly, its actually being the case can only be known by means of a communication from God in the word, and, secondly, even after this communication, the fact that such a thing is intrinsically possible cannot be made positively perspicuous.[23]

This account of revealed mystery, and of its relationship to the rest of our knowledge, is unsatisfactory. At one level, it reduces the divine mystery to one object of knowledge among others: from revelation we simply acquire additional instances of the kind of truth normally available to us. At another, the discontinuities between the mystery and other objects of knowledge make it unclear how a finite mind can appropriate the mystery at all:

In other words, standard fundamental theology clarifies only very deficiently how, on the one hand, humanity, by virtue of its essence as a self-conscious reality, can be capable of receiving such an extension of its knowledge, how room for this possible knowledge could be part of the human person's natural state of existence, without, on the other hand, this knowledge itself thereby, at root, being the necessary fulfilment of this natural human constitution.[24]

As has already been implied, the version of fundamental theology which Rahner rejects can be abundantly documented from Salaverri's own work, including a major book which Salaverri co-authored with, of all people, the pioneer Nadal scholar, Miguel Nicolau. Moreover, not even Vatican II, let alone the short essay Rahner wrote for Salaverri's eightieth birthday, brought about conversion.[25] In 1972, Rahner understates his disagreement with Salaverri's approach; as with his oft-repeated statement about tomorrow's believers necessarily being mystics, Rahner disguises his criticism of conventional accounts, and presents their incoherence as mere obsolescence. But his advocacy of the indirect method emerges from a powerfully felt and long-standing sense of how the manualist approach involved contradictions.

---

[23] *Hearer of the Word*, 13, 28 (*KRSW*, iv. 32).
[24] Ibid., 13, 28–9 (*KRSW*, iv. 32).
[25] See his 'Teología fundamental', *Miscelánea Comillas*, 33 (1975), 43–67. This text, purporting to describe the discipline in the light of Vatican II, shows no awareness of the objections raised against such an approach, and criticizes strongly the tendency to interweave fundamental and dogmatic theology. Major figures such as Rousselot and Rahner are simply not mentioned. Moreover, the published extracts from Rahner's correspondence during the Council contain disparaging references to Salaverri (Vorgrimler, *Understanding Karl Rahner*, 180, 199).

Rahner's position in *Hearer of the Word* is a descendant of that developed by the French Jesuit, Pierre Rousselot (1878–1915) in *The Eyes of Faith*. Previous approaches had seen,

the relationship between faith and the knowledge of faith as credible as a one-way, linear succession, and they tried to present the process of faith as a strict, logical succession of individual acts (even if they knew that real life very often did not conform to this logical order). Rousselot sees faith, from the outset, as a personal, living act, aroused by the revelation-reality from without, and sustained by grace within. Here there is no one-way, linear succession, nor any one-way relationship of dependence. The individual elements stand within a richly tense unity, in a relationship of mutual conditioning and sustenance.[26]

Rahner's account of faith stands in this tradition. Vatican I had reaffirmed that Catholic faith must in some sense be accessible to all through natural reason.[27] Manualist fundamental theology, exemplified by a figure such as Salaverri, attempted to meet this requirement by grounding the mysteries of faith on deductive foundations supposedly accessible to 'unaided human reason'. Rahner, following Rousselot, adopts a different strategy. He insists on the universality of grace, at least as offer, and on the isomorphism that must obtain between what is known and the agent who knows. As Rahner put the matter in 1966:

Fundamental theology can no longer . . . remain just a preliminary construction, in which, formally, the abstract facts of there being a revelation and of its representation by the Church are just presented. All Christian dogmas require, in their material content, a fundamental-theological interpretation as to how they can be understood and assimilated by a human person today, setting them alongside all that rightly or wrongly counts as self-evident for this person. Dogmatic and fundamental theology must thus interpenetrate in a quite new way.[28]

The task of apologetics is not to justify the truths of faith by the standards of some neutral reason, but to show up the connections between Christian proclamation and everyday human existence. As a recent commentator puts the matter:

---

[26] Kunz, 'Glaubwürdigkeitserkenntnis und Glaube', 429. Raffelt and Verweyen, *Karl Rahner*, 17–21, suggest that the ultimate source for Rahner's 'indirect method' may be the work of Maurice Blondel (1861–1949).

[27] Vatican I, *Dogmatic Constitution on the Catholic Faith*, n. 4 (Tanner, *Decrees of the Ecumenical Councils*, 808).

[28] *Handbuch der Pastoraltheologie*, ii/1. 268 (*KRSW*, xix. 308).

Karl Rahner was unwilling to be satisfied with an attitude of 'take it or leave it' ('it' being the dogmas of the Church). He wanted, rather, to point up for people of today how the central truths of Christian faith, and faith itself as an attitude, still had something to offer—this something also being a challenge—for humanity today.[29]

The key distinction here is between two senses of 'natural'. The manualist tradition sees 'natural' as 'what is or would be the case abstracting from grace': Rahner sees it as 'that which, in the factual order, universally obtains'. The doctrine of grace as a supernatural existential amounts to the claim that grace is supernatural in the first sense, and natural in the second.

By thus putting the idea of a 'natural knowledge of God' on a new footing, this approach can make some classically Barthian assertions. A Christian relationship to Jesus Christ is self-validating, and 'cannot be produced or constructed "from without"'; there can be no question of proving the validity of supernatural revelation from 'purely natural' premises. Nevertheless, it still makes sense to argue for the truth of Christianity, and to preach it to a non-believer. Christianity's mutual interconnections can be demonstrated, and an appeal can be made to the reality of grace which Christianity claims already to be present within the human person.[30] Rahner describes the process as follows:

Fundamentally, the Christian can only do the following: presuppose that there is already present within the person who hears, in the root of their being, an understanding offered to the freedom of faith, and tell this person, through an objectifying articulation, the understanding they have already been given. If the hearer also accepts the Christological statement explicitly, the speaker in this case has not in any proper sense brought forth this understanding of faith, in its primordial unity, but only brought it to itself in objectifying concepts. If this reflective statement . . . is not accepted in an express confession of faith, then the one who speaks must recognise that one of two things is true. Either the one hearing, in freedom, has closed themselves to an understanding that was, in itself, there for them in a unity of grace and the historical message brought to them; or the grace of Christ, previously present within the person in any case, has not yet, in the saving providence of God, set up the *kairos* for this inner light of grace to find its historical objectification in an explicit faith in Jesus the Christ.[31]

[29] Hilberath, *Karl Rahner*, 27.
[30] *Foundations of Christian Faith*, 206, *205–6* (*KRSW*, xxvi. 199).
[31] Ibid., 231–2, *229* (*KRSW*, xxvi. 222–3).

No one can judge how far each of these alternatives applies to any particular case.

On a Rahnerian reading of the Exercises, the Ignatian choice happens when a particular option stimulates a person or a group to appropriate more fully their identity as creatures of God and temples of grace. There are obvious parallels with what Rahner is here saying about the choice to believe in the first place. In both cases, the external object correlates with a reality of grace already present in the believer. In both cases too, the decision is a free one, but its legitimacy is grounded in a realist claim about the nature of things.

However, in 1972, Rahner can still claim that this Ignatian approach is somehow new. For his own positions in fundamental theology, Rahner acknowledges a debt to Rousselot, and also points back to Newman's concept of the 'illative sense'. Fairly or not, Rahner sees their accounts as incomplete. Rousselot and his descendants, though rightly invoking the grace of faith, fail to specify it adequately, or to integrate it within a convincing description of the human person. They also fail to show how our supernatural transcendence 'enters into a synthesis with the categorical object of revelation, in a basically "verifiable" way, endowing this latter with the credibility that empowers the human person to make an absolute, though always of course also free, assent of faith.[32] For its part, Newman's theory of the illative sense seems merely to assert of how practical reason, in any sphere of activity, can never be reduced to a theoretical deduction.[33] But such an account fails to recognize the uniqueness of the decision at stake. If we try to extend either Rousselot's or Newman's approach, says Rahner, we find ourselves dealing, explicitly or not, with Ignatius.[34]

A recent American attempt to address the problem is that of George A. Lindbeck. For Lindbeck it is an illusion to suggest that universal norms of reasonableness will yield criteria for adjudicating between systems of belief and language. No such norms can be formulated without implying a commitment to one particular system:

Yet this does not reduce the choice between different frameworks to whim or chance . . . reasonableness in religion and theology, as in other domains,

[32] 1972, 165*, *209*.

[33] For a comparison of Rahner and Newman, see Heinrich Fries, 'Theologische Methode bei John Henry Newman und Karl Rahner', *Newman Studien*, 11 (1980), 191–210, followed by Rahner's reply, 'Stellungnahme und Diskussion', 211–15.

[34] 1972, 165, *209–10*.

has something of that aesthetic character, that quality of unformalizable skill, which we usually associate with the artist or the linguistically competent . . . Reason places constraints on religious as well as on scientific options even though these constraints are too flexible and informal to be spelled out in either foundational theology or a general theory of science.[35]

'Instinct' and 'aesthetic sense' are surely useful concepts in this connection. Rahner, however, reminds us that Christian belief is nevertheless grounded in the world that is the case, and yields truth about that world not yielded by other, perhaps more impressive and beautiful, ideologies. The 'right instinct' in question here is 'right' because it responds to the reality of God's creation, independently of any decision we make about that reality. It must be distinguishable from human projection, either arising from our personal self-indulgence, or from the power-relations within Church and society operative at any given time. Moreover, perhaps *pace* von Balthasar, much deeply authentic Christianity fails to meet the standards of *haute culture*. The skill and beauty in question here reflect the reach of a God who holds nothing created in abhorrence. Rahner invokes Ignatius's rules in this context because he sees in them a means of guaranteeing the realism of Christian faith. The discovery of attunement between the object of revelation and our sense of self under God will always be intuitive and tentative, but it rests on a correlation independent of our choice.

Christian belief involves the claim that the world, however we might like it to be, is in fact such that it only yields full sense when the language of Christian tradition is applied. The justification both of academic theology and of the spirituality industry lies precisely in this orientation to the real implicit in the religious claim, and the consequent perennial need for believers to be freed from their projections, illusions, and superstitions.

Ignatian discernment, therefore, and the assent of faith involve the same kind of process: the discovery of a congruence between a particular historical option and our sense of self under God. The making of a specific choice becomes the condition for our being able to find God's grace in all our reality and experience. The process requires what Rahner, in a striking late essay, called 'a nameless virtue': the acquired facility for justifying one's decisions

---

[35] George A. Lindbeck, *The Nature of Doctrine: Religion and Theology in a Postliberal Age* (London: SPCK, 1984), 130–1.

rationally while at the same time recognizing the limits of any justification.[36] Rahner's thought may be difficult to follow here because
his underlying models of truth and knowledge are not those of, say,
the natural sciences; paradoxically, a thinker such as Salaverri
adopts the latter much more uncritically. Grace, the divine self-gift,
is not a datum for us to look at and observe. If it were, then we could
not reconcile its omnipresence and its guaranteed triumph with the
claim that certain particular options on our part are decisive for its
unfolding. Grace, rather, denotes the deepest principle of our identity. Its unavoidable presence and the promise it represents do not
depend on our appropriation, but nevertheless demand it. As we
grow we 'come to ourselves'. This process occurs through specific
choices, through acknowledgements that certain definite commitments correspond to our deepest nature, and free us for authentic
relationship with all that exists. Yet these choices are not fixed
points, but rather crucial transitions in a lifelong process. In Christ,
we see God's pattern and promise for the *whole* of creation; in a
properly made vocational choice, we shape our life, as far as within
us lies, in such a way as to open us most fully to God's ongoing self-
gift in and through *all* our experience.

The Witness of Holiness

At the risk of impertinence, this study suggests that Rahner's interpretation of Ignatius improved with age. In 1972, he moderated
decisively a tendency, above all in the long 1956 essay, to present
Ignatian mystical experience as a source of knowledge of God somehow independent of doctrine. Even so, the tone of some later pieces,
notably the 1978 testament, still echoes the earlier understanding,
and this chapter concludes by highlighting a truth hidden in that
earlier view. Though Ignatian discernment, whether conscious or
anonymous, can only be justified and grounded with reference to
Christian tradition, there remains a subordinate, weaker sense in
which the reverse is true: successful Ignatian discernment reinforces
and confirms the credibility of the wider Christian tradition.

   In Rahner's Christology, our response to Christ is an aspect of
Christology itself, because Christ's relationship with us is part of his

---

[36] 'Plea for a Nameless Virtue', esp. 36–7, *301–2*.

identity. The tradition thus represents a beginning. It offers us indispensable resources for discovering the truth of God, but it does not embody the whole truth. Moreover, the particular form in which that tradition comes to us will also be shaped by corruption as well as by sanctity. 'The immediate experience of God' is a constant to be verified in ever new ways.

What Rahner once wrote about the development of dogma can be extended here:

The unfolding of God's ultimate revelation is a process. As the process of God's revelation, it is unique, and therefore has no *a priori*, distinct from and really *superior* to it, which at the same time exhaustively determines it. Unlike the events of natural science, it cannot be comprised under such formal laws as would enable us actually to predict any later phase.[37]

There is a principle of coherence, even if our only knowledge of it takes the form of surrender. Already in *Hearer of the Word* we had been told of how we can only act-with the divine initiative in love and darkness, without comprehending what occurs.[38] There is a haunting, if very obscure passage at the end of Rahner's 1955 Canisianum conferences on Ignatian spirituality and devotion to the Sacred Heart. The process of discovering our vocation also involves the discovery of our call to individuality under God:

Though this does indeed come from one's inmost centre, it is precisely as such not one's own in the sense of coming from one's own resources, but one's own in the sense of being given: that which is most one's own, because it is of God. In other words, we discover the personal only as we go out to encounter that image of ourselves which God has made for himself, the image of us which he holds before us and which always both humiliates and delights us, imperfect as we are, because we recognise in it both ourselves and our God. We can do no more than move towards it; it is only slowly revealed, and never wholly in this life. While we are still pilgrims, it is not only God but also ourselves that we can know only in reflections and parables; it is ourselves too that we shall know only *some day*—even as we are known.[39]

As, therefore, Christian tradition develops, as we discover our own identity in Christ under God, things happen which cannot simply be deduced from the tradition itself. Our continuation of the divine self-gift is conditioned by the distinctiveness of our identity

[37] 'Considerations on the Development of Dogma', 7–8, *16*.
[38] *Hearer of the Word*, 79, *122* (*KRSW*, iv. 146).   [39] 1955, 205–6, *537*.

and of our circumstances. To this extent, therefore, the continuation is self-authenticating, or rather it authenticates, in unpredictable, unprecedented, and unrepeatable ways, the gospel which animated us, and generated our response. Though what happens under grace remains grounded in gospel truth, the relationship is one of charismatic continuation rather than deductive dependence. For Rahner, as we have seen, Jesus causes the grace worked immediately in us, not or not merely through moral or juridical imputation, but as an instrument used by God to bring about something new. If such grace manifestly occurs, it redounds to the credit of the instrument, of the whole tradition in which it stands.

The point being made is a commonplace in Catholic piety: the existence and witness of saints serves to manifest the glory of God, and to confirm the authenticity of Christian tradition. Here, however, we have a proper theological grounding for it. This feedback effect of holiness and good works is clearly secondary: the tradition itself is the primary source. If the Christian tradition did not yield saints, this would not necessarily be a sign that the tradition was bogus, for whole cultures could be deficient in their response. Conversely, a professedly Christian resister such as Franz Jägerstätter,[40] or indeed a more ambiguous figure such as Oskar Schindler, can strengthen our sense of Christian tradition, even though such figures represent only a tiny minority of people in their predicaments. The pastoral method of the *Exercises* fosters precisely the discovery of new and unprecedented responses to the gospel, rooted in the unique life-history of individuals. This creative diversity of response authenticates and renders more credible the tradition generating it.

This section imitates Ignatius himself by alluding to personal, perhaps quite intimate, experiences of Christianity, while refraining from direct description. People need to discover their own truth, and find their own style of witness. We can end by quoting one of Ignatius's characteristically open-ended statements. Near the end of the *Constitutions* he compiled for the Society of Jesus, Ignatius wrote the following:

---

[40] On this figure (1907–43), a sacristan and farmer executed for his refusal to accept conscription into the Nazi forces, and on the theological issues he raises, see the collection *Franz Jägerstätter: Christlicher Glaube und politisches Gewissen*, edd. Alfons Riedl and Josef Schwabeneder (Thaur: Thaur Verlag, 1997), esp. Severin Renoldner, 'Jägerstätters Widerstand gegen den Nationalsozialismus', 251–72.

It will help to use with discernment and moderation the favours conceded by the Apostolic See, seeking only the help of souls, with complete sincerity. For thus God our Lord will carry forward what he has begun; and the fragrance, grounded in truth, of good works will increase people's devotion, so that they come to be helped by the Society and to help it towards the end which it seeks: the glory and service of His Divine Majesty.[41]

This is obviously a specifically Jesuit text, but it illustrates many of the points at issue in this chapter. Ignatius envisages that his followers will be given canonical privileges—their ministry on mission may require, for example, that they be given prerogatives normally reserved to bishops. Such privileges are ambivalent. On the one hand, they represent continuity with gospel tradition. Rightly used, they open people to the divine freedom. But they also come freighted with a political and social significance that might be oppressive. Ignatius shows realism about this, encouraging his followers to use discrimination—another possible translation for *discreción*—and to use the privileges only to the extent that they are constructive. One might compare what Rahner said in his 1978 testament: 'your theology and your canon law must serve, in the first place, the papacy specifically in the form it will have to take in the future if it is to be a help, not a hinderance, to the unity of Christianity'.[42]

Through authentic gospel living and ministry, God carries forward what God has begun. The tradition is what Ignatius calls an *instituto*—a beginning to be completed, not a fixed possession. Ultimately the continuation 'can be taught only by the unction of the Holy Spirit and by the prudence which God our Lord communicates to those who trust in His Divine Majesty'.[43] This divine teaching nevertheless works through human freedom. In doing so it yields a fragrance, grounded in the truth of things, and fosters a growth and nourishment that are reciprocal. Thus, as it generates and grounds new forms of holiness, the tradition is also renewing itself, and displaying its credibility.

[41] *Const*, x. 12 [825].   [42] 1978*b*, 32, *400*.   [43] *Const*, IV. viii. 8 [414.3].

11

Ignatius, Rahner, and Theology

At the end of his 1972 essay for the Salaverri *Festschrift*, Rahner wrote of how Jesuit thinkers had underestimated Ignatius:

> It seems as though the Jesuits have certainly regarded him as a devout and holy man, and one who has acquired, through his work, great significance in the history of the Church. But, it is fair to say, so far they have hardly seen him, in his own right, as one of the great and central figures in the history of ideas (*Geistesgeschichte*) at the beginning of modernity (*der Neuzeit*).[1]

Rahner was not in any strict sense a theologian of the Ignatian Exercises, nor was he a specialist in 'spirituality'. His early essays on historical figures, and his involvement with the kerygmatic theology movement, may suggest that he was once tempted to move in that direction; ultimately, however, Rahner chose a different path. He drew on the spiritual tradition, both in Ignatius and more generally, as a resource for renewing theology and faith *as a whole*. 'Spirituality' was too important to be left as a mere branch of theology.

This study has reviewed central aspects of this renewal: Rahner's use of Ignatian material to rework dogmatic, fundamental, and pastoral theology, and to articulate in new, more coherent ways, the difference which Christianity makes to the human condition. It has also attempted to fill out connections which Rahner left implicit, in the hope of rendering Rahner's underlying project both clearer and more credible than it might at first sight appear. One final, overall issue remains. It has become a commonplace among Rahner's admirers that Ignatian spirituality is central to his achievement. This claim, however, needs to be interpreted and specified with some care, a task that will occupy the first part of this concluding chapter. We will then go on to explore some implications that Rahner's Ignatian approach has for theology as a whole: the interconnections between experience and doctrine; the relationship in

[1] 1972, 165–6*, *210*.

the academy between theology and spirituality; and how tradition should function in the Christian life.

Rahner and Ignatian Sources

Rahner himself claimed that Ignatius was the most significant source of his theology, and this evidence must obviously be respected. Nevertheless, there are several good grounds for questioning it. In the first place, Rahner wrote relatively little on Ignatius. An early essay on Ignatian imaginative prayer, attributed in typescript to Karl Rahner, now appears to be by his brother Hugo;[2] if that is so, Karl wrote only one major independent piece on Ignatian spirituality before the 1950s, namely 'The Ignatian Mysticism of Joy in the World' (1937). From his mature period we only have two sets of eight-day retreat conferences, and some occasional essays. Many of these latter were occasioned by the quatercentenary of Ignatius's death in 1956.[3] In making the judgement that Ignatius was central to his achievement, the elderly Rahner, perhaps prompted by his disciples, was extrapolating.

We must also acknowledge that Rahner's attempts at serious Ignatian exegesis are both few and flawed. Outside his retreat conferences, which are largely conventional in their use of Ignatius's text, there are only three significant examples: his account of

---

[2] In 1928, the Rahner brothers prepared a *Festschrift* for their father's sixtieth birthday, consisting of essays which the two of them had written (KRA, I. A. 7–11). In it there is a piece entitled 'Die Anwendung der Sinne in den geistlichen Übungen des heiligen Ignatius'; and a second typescript version tells us that its date is 1926. The Application of the Senses is a form of imaginative prayer prescribed by Ignatius for the end of most days after the First Week of the Exercises. The essay exists in two typescripts, both of which attribute it to Karl. However, in the archive copy of the *Festschrift*, the attribution has been corrected to 'Hugo', seemingly by Karl himself. The typescripts may be based on the manuscript now in the Karl-Rahner-Archiv. The text itself is in Hugo's hand, but Karl's name, in Karl's writing, appears at the top—presumably an indication of ownership. Two late texts of Hugo's confirm his own authorship: 'Eucharisticon Fraternitatis' (1964), in Kustermann and Neufeld (edd.), *'Gemeinsame Arbeit in brüderlicher Liebe'*, 65; and a footnote in the book version of his own later essay on the Application (1957), in *Ignatius the Theologian*, 208 n. 30. The early essay broadly follows the standard interpretation established by Joseph Maréchal, on which see my 'The Ignatian Prayer of the Senses', 393–8. For fuller discussion of the authorship issue, see Zahlauer, *Karl Rahner und sein 'produktives Vorbild'*, 98–100.

[3] One important text produced for this anniversary, which has not been mentioned in this study because of its narrowly Jesuit focus, is an essay on Jesuit obedience, radically discrediting authoritarian models previously in vogue: 'A Basic Ignatian Concept'.

'consolation without preceding cause', his reading of the first letter to Sor Rejadell, and his interpretation of Ignatius's mystical states at the end of his life. None of these, as we have seen, are defensible as exegesis. Moreover, his concept of 'the immediate experience of God' derives not from Ignatius so much as from Gregory of Nyssa, from Evagrius, and above all from Bonaventure. The Ignatian support Rahner adduces is perfunctory and underdeveloped: he merely gestures towards Ignatius's phrase about the creator dealing immediately with the creature, while overlooking Ignatius's total reticence on the theology he is presupposing. Again, Rahner's accounts of Ignatian indifference often tend towards an overinterpretation in terms of transcendental philosophy.

Much that is often presented as distinctively Ignatian in fact amounts to no more than an expression of Christianity as such. It is quite clear that Jesuits of Rahner's generation were inspired to speculative innovation by the discovery of Jesuit source material.[4] But there is nothing distinctively Jesuit about 'finding God in all things'. In any vocation, the quest for God must pervade one's whole existence; in another sense, the Jesuit vocation depends, like any other vocation, on making certain options and excluding others. Similar movements can be documented from other spiritual traditions. Though, as we have seen, the official Jesuit interpretation of Nadal's 'contemplative in action' depends in part on a misreading of Aquinas, there are striking parallels between this interpretation and attempts by modern Dominicans to recover the apostolic nature of their charism.[5] Furthermore, the accounts of Carmelite or Dionysian mysticism, against which Jesuit authors, in various ways, have contrasted their own tradition, are often sub-Christian, and a travesty of what Teresa of Avila, or John of the Cross, or Denys actually taught.[6] There is nothing specifically Ignatian or Jesuit about a 'mysticism of world-affirmation', because there is nothing Christian at all about a 'mysticism of world-negation'.

The study of Jesuit sources undeniably provoked a renewal of the theology done by Jesuits. However, this renewal centred not on

---

[4] The clearest illustration of this kind of discovery is perhaps Coreth's splendid, if unconsciously triumphalistic, 'Contemplation in Action'.

[5] See e.g. Simon Tugwell, *The Way of the Preacher* (London: Darton, Longman, and Todd, 1979).

[6] See e.g. Denys Turner, *The Darkness of God: Negativity in Christian Mysticism* (Cambridge: Cambridge University Press, 1995).

the specifically or distinctively Ignatian, but rather on the lived experience of Christianity as such to which the Ignatian sources bore witness. The discovery that God could be found in all things was not a discovery about Ignatius, but rather a liberation from a sub-Christian world-view. The modern study of spirituality, both inside and outside Christianity, is bedevilled by alienating, and sub-Christian, accounts of the self and its experience. Once these are filtered out, the differences between Ignatian spirituality and other forms of spirituality appear relatively small, at least as regards the effect any spirituality can or should have on theology.

Purely biographically, therefore, there are grounds for doubting the elderly Rahner's assertions about how Ignatius was the most significant influence on his theology. The central insight reflected in the 1978 testament is that 'mystical' vocabulary applies to Christian existence as such. Implicitly, Rahner attributes this insight to Ignatius: Ignatius, so to speak, 'de-cloistered God'.[7] It would be false, however, to claim that Ignatius himself made such a move, for Ignatius was no speculative thinker; moreover, other spiritual traditions, properly studied and meditated upon, might also have led Rahner to this claim. However, for better or worse, the community in which Rahner came to maturity and lived out his Christian life was one shaped by Ignatian tradition. Hugo Rahner was a key figure in the rethinking of that heritage, a reassessment prompted by a huge wealth of newly edited source material. It is only natural to suppose that this rediscovery, with all the untidinesses, misconceptions, and inaccuracies involved, nevertheless gave decisive psychological and spiritual impetus to Karl Rahner's creativity. In that relatively weak sense, the biographical claim about Ignatian influence on Karl Rahner can certainly be accepted.

Moreover, the links between Rahner's theology and Ignatian spirituality are genuine and distinctive, although the key Ignatian text for establishing this claim is dealt with only once in Rahner's Ignatian writings, in the Germanicum retreat conferences, and then only implicitly. In 1974, Rahner named an important methodological principle for the interpretation of the *Exercises*:

A commentary on the text of the *Exercises* must be equally concerned with the substantive assertions and the practical instructions. The two

---

[7] The phrase is taken from Joseph Veale, 'The Unique Elements in Ignatian Spirituality', *Milltown Studies*, 30 (1992), 97–101, here 100.

condition each other. There are not merely psychological issues lurking behind the seemingly how-to-do-it, psychological instructions in the text. Rather, these latter often imply a whole theology, and therefore to comment on them is *also* a genuinely theological task.[8]

It is illuminating to apply this principle to Ignatius's presentation of the Incarnation:

how the Three Divine Persons were looking at the whole flatness or roundness of the whole world filled with human beings, and how, seeing that all were going down to hell, it is determined in their eternity that the Second Person should become human to save the human race.[9]

Although the 'substantive assertions' here suggest that the Incarnation arises simply as God's reaction to human sinfulness, these have to be offset against the theology implicit in the prayer process. The point of the meditations, and of the divine action, is not simply to restore the human person to some state of happiness, or to instil some truth into the mind. Nor does Ignatius's vision centre on any penal-substitutionary view of the Cross. The real goal is the shaping of the exercitant's freedom in responsiveness to Christ.

Ignatius's suggestions for prayer on the Incarnation encourage us 'to ask for a knowledge of the Lord from inside (*conocimiento interno del Señor*), who for me has become human, that I may love him and follow him more',[10] and this prayer has its counterparts throughout the latter three Weeks of the Exercises. The Incarnation thus appears, not as a propositional truth to be learnt, or as a comfortable datum gratifying our complacency, but rather as a pattern to be reproduced and re-enacted through our free choices. As John O'Malley has put the matter, Ignatius's *Exercises* was not,

a book of dogma, but a dogmatic book—that is, it assumes that its basic message is the common Christian heritage and that that message, therefore, need not be argued. What was needed was personal appropriation, a clinging to the message with all one's heart and then a translation of it with all one's heart into one's life.[11]

Thus, as we saw, the 'colloquy' ending the Exercise is an occasion for articulating desires. The truth of the gospel is there not only to be 'reflected on', but also to be 'reflected', as in a mirror; in Ignatius's Spanish, the one word may have both significances.

[8] 1974*b*, 73, *100*.   [9] *Exx*, n. 102.1–2.   [10] *Exx*, n. 104.
[11] O'Malley, *The First Jesuits*, 42.

Moreover, the reflecting takes place through our *action*; the gospel story is not just a story about the Trinity and Mary, but also a drama in which we take part, in our prayer experience and in the subsequent ordering of our lives.[12] However inchoately, this style of prayer implies a vision of the compassionate God who invites us into the triune life—an invitation to which we respond through a life-history of choice. The canonical narrative evokes a potential within us.

Ignatius's presentation of the Incarnation sidesteps theological speculation, and confines itself to the dogmatic unnegotiables. The event is both a human and a divine reality, even if we cannot see how these two aspects can be connected. This does not mean that Ignatius was hostile to theology, but only that any systematic theology must be relative to different situations. But Ignatius's presentation nevertheless extends the Chalcedonian formula in one important respect. Implicit in the exercitant's prayer to 'follow' this reality is a third dogmatic unnegotiable: whatever exists objectively also exists subjectively. Reality and experience are correlated. If this history is true, it must find an echo in the awareness of any human being—a point cryptically implicit in Ignatius's claim that the creator deals 'immediately' with the creature.[13] But here too, Ignatius leaves elaboration open. Like Rahner after him, Ignatius confines himself to formal principles, setting out a framework within which Christian discipleship can take on an indefinite variety of forms. Grace is mediated through different symbolic expressions. The distinction between canonical and non-canonical symbols appears here as that between the story of Jesus, the irrevocable norm, and the variety of ways in which human beings can 'draw profit' from it. As Rahner's Ignatius says at the outset of the 1978 testament, his message was, in content, the constant message of the Church: 'and yet I thought—and this opinion was true—that I could say what was old in a new way'.[14] Rahner and Ignatius share, and share distinctively, two features in common: firstly, a sense of how any Christian truth is also a truth of human experience; secondly, the art of distinguishing between a general pattern and its different, indeed unpredictable, ongoing expressions.

---

[12] See further my 'To Reflect and Draw Profit', and contrast the pre-Ignatian tradition recorded in Margot Schmidt, 'Miroir' (1980), in *Dictionnaire de Spiritualité*, x. 1290–1303, esp. 1299–1301; here, mirroring the divine connotes purity of heart and cognitive awareness.
[13] *Exx*, n. 15.6.   [14] 1978*b*, 11, *373*.

If theological truth is experiential, it follows that it is always unfinished. We can never grasp it directly, but only move towards it. It is given us, not as something to be grasped, in a *Griff,* but as something calling us ever forward, a *Vorgriff*.[15] Perhaps many other Christian writers have made that point, but arguably only Ignatius has made it the structural principle of his major texts. Both the *Exercises* and the *Constitutions* are open-ended works, works to be used, works in which what really matters is not described because it cannot be predicted: the preservation and increase which comes only 'through the almighty hand of Christ our God and Lord'.[16] The same applies to *Foundations of Christian Faith*. Prompted by the pluralism and complexity of contemporary theology, and by the impossibility of a 'direct method' in fundamental theology, Rahner claims that theology's object is such that the discipline must always be, in a certain sense, 'unscholarly'—although this unscholarliness can nevertheless be the object of a disciplined reflection.[17] Rahner had stated the principle rather better at the outset of his first major essay in Christology:

The clearest and most transparent formulation, the most hallowed formula, the classic crystallization of the centuries-long work of the praying, thinking, and struggling Church regarding the mysteries of God—this lives . . . precisely out of the fact that it is the beginning and not the end, the means and not the goal, *one* truth which makes freedom for *the*—ever greater—Truth.[18]

To repeat: nothing here has been said which does not apply to Christianity as a whole, and neither Rahner nor Ignatius would have wanted to preach any gospel other than that of Jesus Christ. But they enrich our appreciation of that gospel by interpreting it in a creative fashion, and this reinterpretation represents a decisive, irrevocable step in Christian self-awareness. Both concentrate on articulating the formal principles of how the divine freedom, in its own, perhaps scandalous, logic, works among us in ever new ways. And both exhibit a rare talent: the humble wisdom not to make

[15] Otto Muck, 'Heidegger und Karl Rahner', 269, defending Rahner's philosophy against the objection that it leaves out the historical, interpersonal, and linguistic, points out that its basis lies, not 'in a premise which leads to nothing other than what is latent within it, but in a point of entry that leads further'.

[16] *Const*, x. 1 [812.2].

[17] *Foundations of Christian Faith*, 8–10, *20–2* (*KRSW*, xxvi. 15–17).

[18] 'Current Problems in Christology', 149, *169*.

their own experience a norm, but rather to abstract from that experience only what applies universally. Austere and unattractive though their written expression may be, such an approach to the gospel is uniquely suited to empower free response.[19] At various points in this study we have noted the coexistence in Rahner's thought of Christological and transcendental idioms, and we have explored the relationship between them. From this present perspective, however, we can also see why Rahner's vision—and Ignatius's—requires both idioms, and why there are some advantages in their relative disconnection. The Christological idiom stresses that, for Christian theology, any experience of God must also involve the Christ who is consubstantial with the Father, even if the person concerned cannot articulate it in those terms. The more abstract idiom reminds us that such experience will be in conformity to Christ himself, under the freedom of the Spirit, but not necessarily in conformity to Christian expectation or convention. Fidelity to Christ's standard entails a freedom not simply to repeat Christian precedent. Because the mystery symbolized in Christ affects 'the whole history of the human race', our knowledge of God comes through various sources: there is a knowledge of God—the God of Jesus Christ—which is 'more than what the encounter with Jesus Christ provides'.[20] Thus the transcendental terminology serves to protect the subversiveness proper to authentic Christology. The divine self-gift generates an incalculable variety of responses. 'Faith comes from what is heard and what is heard comes by the

---

[19] Two recent, fuller attempts to develop an Ignatian theology on the basis suggested are: Christoph Théobald, 'Une manière ignatienne de faire de la théologie', *Nouvelle revue théologique*, 119 (1997), 375–96; Barbara Hallensleben, *Theologie der Sendung: Die Ursprünge bei Ignatius von Loyola und Mary Ward* (Frankfurt: Knecht, 1994). This latter, massive study, besides retrieving for theology the figure of Mary Ward (1585–1645), an Englishwoman who founded an Ignatian institute for women, argues impressively that the concept of *Sendung* (mission) should not merely ground a rethinking of consecrated life, but should also be made a central theme in Christian theology. The book suffers from trying to do too much, but it remains immensely stimulating and a valuable source of reference.

[20] *Foundations of Christian Faith*, 13*, 25 (*KRSW*, xxvi. 19): '*Es gibt eine Erkenntnis Gottes, die nicht adäquat durch die Begegnung mit Jesus Christus vermittelt wird.*' *Adäquat* has a technical resonance, and *vermittelt* an informal one, which their English cognates lack. If one reads the sentence without these resonances in mind, the misinterpretation can be disastrous. For example, Harvey D. Egan, 'Christian Apophatic and Kataphatic Mysticisms', *Theological Studies*, 39 (1978), 399–426, at 422, reads this sentence as a justification for 'apophatic' mysticism, in such a way as to encourage the all too frequent tendency to read Rahner as a neo-Gnostic. The point is not that Rahner is postulating some alternative route to God besides the incarnate Christ, but rather that this Christ has to be understood in relationship to the whole creation.

preaching of Christ.'[21] Yet steps need to be taken so that what is heard is not some merely human word, but 'what it really is, the word of God'.[22] In the world as we know it, these steps involve purification and correction, the overcoming of sinfulness. But even in an unfallen world, God's self-gift to changing humanity, humanity as spirit in world, would imply a tradition in permanent expansion, constantly expressing itself in new ways.

'The Knowledge Derived from Experience'

In the critical section of this study, we noted Peter Eicher's reaction against the first studies of Rahner to highlight the importance of spirituality. Eicher was concerned that such readings of Rahner could legitimate mindless piety, and lead to the abandonment of disciplined theological thinking.[23] If the claims of this study are correct, however, Rahner's theology meets Eicher's legitimate concerns.

To understand the issues at stake, we need to abandon any easy distinction between 'subjective' and 'objective' reality. Rahner's account of experience is realist: for him, truth is independent of human decision. However, our apprehension of the real and of the true is itself an element within the real and the true; hence no clear distinction can be drawn between the true-in-itself and the true-for-us. Rahner's Ignatius tells us that 'the awakening of . . . divine experience' is 'the acceptance of a constitution in the human person'.[24] In the realm of the personal, 'experience' is a constitutive feature of 'essence'. The *reality* of the human consists in its dependence on 'experience', on *Erfahrung*: 'the immediate reception of an impression from a reality (inner or outer) that is outside our free disposal'.[25] Human identity is realized, therefore, in unpredictable dependence. Thus if doctrine and theology are to refer to fully human realities, and express human identity adequately, they must be permanently open to new experiential continuation. Indeed, only so are they rightly understood.[26]

---

[21] Romans 10: 17.   [22] 1 Thessalonians 2: 13.
[23] Eicher, 'Erfahren und Denken', 142–3.   [24] 1978*b*, 15, *378*.
[25] *Concise Theological Dictionary*, 164–5, *107–8*.
[26] A significant recent dissertation impressively correlates Rahner's Christology and his theology of prayer, bringing out 'the distinctive union between the faith-*knowledge* directed

Conversely, these continuations remain intrinsically dependent on doctrine. One of Rahner's more vivid examples illustrates the point. At the outset of *The Church and the Sacraments*, Rahner reflects on the difference between a simple prayer for forgiveness and sacramental reconciliation. Against a vulgar Catholic view that only the latter of these events is truly an event of grace, Rahner insists that both can be. The difference is rather that the latter is linked explicitly to the guaranteed sacramental sign:

In the first case, the *sign* (i.e. the prayer, the contrition, in other words what the individual person as such 'privately' does) to which God has attached God's grace is *in itself* inwardly 'under threat'—that is, it could become, of itself, invalid, and become, of itself, deprived of the characteristic whereby it is the tangibility of God's gracious address. In the second case, the sign has an irrevocable, eschatological validity. Of itself it is the sign of the covenant of God with human beings, established eternally and unrepentantly by God—a sign which is a very part of this eternal, unrepentant aspect of God's will for salvation, a very part in such a way that it can never itself lose this quality of being this tangibility of God's yes to human beings.[27]

Rahner's account acknowledges the real presence of God's grace outside official sacramental channels, and thereby represents a liberation which Catholic awareness still needs to appropriate. At the same time, however, it itself retains traces of vulgar cultural Catholicism. For the 'mere' prayer for forgiveness, which Rahner presents as a non-sacramental event, is non-sacramental only in a narrow, juridical sense. In a broader sense, it depends on explicit reference to the guarantee mediated by the Bible. In the 'private' event, a suitably contrite person can know 'with absolute certainty, on the basis of the trustworthy and irrevocable word of the divine promise, that God really forgives them their guilt'. The difference between the two cases lies merely in *how* Christian symbols, with the guarantee they embody, are configured and invoked. The claim that experience—whether inside or outside the Church—is sustained by God's grace depends on an acceptance of a Christian interpretation of reality, a commitment to Christian axioms. Rahner's

towards the self-communication of God, and the faith-*experience* which receives it. These two shape each other; they are equally fundamental, and cannot be reduced one to the other': Ralf Stolina, *Die Theologie Karl Rahners: Inkarnatorische Spiritualität—Menschwerdung Gottes und Gebet* (Innsbruck: Tyrolia, 1996), here 251.

[27] *The Church and the Sacraments*, 28, 26.

'immediate experience of God' and Christian traditional doctrine stand in mutual dependence. To adapt a dictum of Kant's: doctrine without experience is empty; experience without doctrine is blind. The claim that the experience of grace plays a foundational role in Rahner's theology is only secondarily, if at all, a biographical one. Admittedly, one of Rahner's most perceptive commentators, Klaus Fischer, once wrote—perhaps in an unguarded moment—of how Rahner's theology of experience and grace is grounded in his own life-history: Rahner, says Fischer, can describe the mystical experience that is so central to his theology 'because he has himself originally had it'.[28] But an appeal to experience, however interesting it may be biographically, cannot of itself establish the *truth* of a theological claim. Such a strategy leaves no means for distinguishing authentic insight from the ravings of a fanatic.

The experience which matters for Christian theology is that which involves insight into the tradition's meaning, facilitating thus the continuation of that tradition. At Emmaus, the disciples experience a transformation of identity and self-awareness accomplished through creative reinterpretation of tradition, an experience which is *both* a warm, personal encounter, *and* a process of learning to reread the Scriptures. We can take, almost at random, another example from a spiritual text, from the diary of Pierre Favre, the first of Ignatius's companions to remain with him permanently:

As I was making my communion at Mass, I had another desire: I wished with great devotion and asked accordingly that this most holy Sacrament would see fit to make me in some way its obedient instrument, and likewise of his mother, of each and every angel, and of all the saints, of all the souls in purgatory and of all the living. And that through this instrument each one of these could work as they wished. In this way today I offered myself to them all.[29]

This text, like countless others of its kind, at once recounts the author's experience, and also expresses and develops Christian tradition. Readers will differ in their assessment of its value. But such differences depend on how authentically we see such a passage as

[28] Fischer, *Der Mensch als Geheimnis*, 22–3: '*weil er sie ursprünglich selber gemacht hat*'. Cf. Vorgrimler, *Understanding Karl Rahner*, 11.
[29] *The Spiritual Writings of Pierre Favre*, ed. and trans. Edmond C. Murphy, John W. Padberg, and Martin E. Palmer (St Louis: Institute of Jesuit Sources, 1996), n. 142 (12 October 1542).

developing the tradition we share, not on how far it corresponds to Favre's actual experience. Our assessment would not be affected were we somehow to discover that he did not 'have' the experiences in question at all, and that some secretary in Ignatius's office sat down and forged the document.

When we say that experience is foundational to Rahner's theology, we are not making any claim about his having received private revelations. Rahner may well have been led to theologize creatively by events in his spiritual life, but the truth of his theology depends on the cogency of his arguments. His claims about experience in theology stand or fall, not on how accurately they report his biography, but rather on the skill and comprehensiveness with which they enable us to systematize Christian truth. The theology of the supernatural existential demands our attention ultimately because it resolves problems which disable other theologies of nature and grace, not because of any prayer-experience which might have led Rahner to develop it.

Theologically significant experience just is that experience in which 'transcendence becomes thematic', in whatever way and to whatever degree: the moment when the self's gracious reality is appropriated and realized—in both the cognitive and objective senses—anew. Through the experience, one reinterprets tradition, and thus learns to see oneself and the world in new ways—a process which may well lead to new forms of action. Psychologically, this process will be varied in form. It might be like Hopkins's delighted and seemingly sudden recognition in 'Hurrahing in Harvest':

> I wálk, I líft up, Í lift úp heart, éyes,
> Down all that glory in the heavens to glean our Saviour;[30]

Equally, the process can be much more sombre, as when Hopkins in his 1883 retreat meditated on the Emmaus narrative. The meditation

was made in a desolate frame of mind; but towards the end I was able to rejoice in the comfort our Lord gave those two men, taking that for a sample of his comfort and them for representatives of all men comforted, and that it was meant to be of universal comfort to men and therefore to me and that this was all I really needed; also that it was better for me to be

---

[30] Hopkins, *Poetical Works*, 149.

accompanying our Lord in his comfort of them than to want him to come
my way to comfort me.[31]

There is no lawlike correspondence between the biographical
and theological realities. On the contrary, God's immediate dealing
with the creature happens in ever new ways.[32] As Rahner puts the
matter, 'the clarity and persuasiveness of the many different kinds of
experience of this sort . . . varies greatly in individual human beings,
matching the diversity of their historical modes of existence'.[33]
Thus the one who mediates the tradition, 'the one who gives the
Exercises', should not show a preference, but merely allow this
immediate dealing to happen, letting 'joy size | at God knows when
to God knows what'.[34] Or, as Rahner put it, through the persona of
Ignatius:

> it is a matter of the ultimate essence of these Exercises, however ecclesial
> they are, that the retreat director (as you called him or her later) does not
> mediate the Church's word as such, in an official fashion. Rather they just
> give (if they can) supervision, very cautiously and from a distance, to help
> God and humanity really meet each other, immediately.[35]

Willibald Sandler neatly makes the necessary distinction
required to understand the foundational role of experience in
Rahner's theology. Rahner did not make his own experience the
norm of Christian truth, but he did insist that Christian dogma was
rightly understood only as a matrix for the interpretation of human
experience in general, in all its unfinishedness and unpredictability.
One may not speak of a theologically relevant and foundational
experience,

> in the sense that Rahner's theology would be understood as the self-
> presentation, exclusively, of a favoured mystic. It is rather that Rahner's
> theology can only be understood on the basis of a fundamental orientation
> to experience. Rahner developed his theological ideas not from the intrinsic
> dynamism of philosophical speculation, but from reflection on his own,
> unspectacular, lived experience of doing things (*Taterfahrung*). Its aim . . . is

[31] Gerard Manley Hopkins, *Sermons and Devotional Writings*, ed. Christopher Devlin
(Oxford: Oxford University Press, 1959), 254.
[32] Kues intriguingly compares Rahner's handling of general law and individual vocation
with speculations in Jung about experiences which the people concerned interpret as religious, but in ways conflicting with conventional imagery and dogma: *Werde, der du sein sollst!*,
223–7.
[33] *Foundations of Christian Faith*, 59, 68 (*KRSW*, xxvi. 62).
[34] *Exx*, n. 15.4–6; Hopkins, 'My own heart' (*Poetical Works*, 186).   [35] 1978*b*, 13*, 376.

to show its interlocutor the appropriate consequences of their own experience of doing things, and thus to enjoin upon them new decisions, decisions deepening their yes to God.[36]

Theology and Spirituality

This account of doctrine and experience can illuminate what it means to study 'spirituality', and, moreover, clarify how this study relates to the activity called 'theology'.[37] At the outset of his 1956 essay on Ignatian discernment, Rahner stresses that a spiritual text, even one whose formulations seem sometimes naive and archaic, can and must serve as a source for academic theology.[38] Rahner devotes much space to defending this claim, and is conscious of diverging from many of his theological colleagues.

For Rahner, the truth of Christianity involves our ongoing self-transformation. In naming the truth of the world as it is, we situate ourselves and, at least implicitly, name our obligations. We cannot step outside the process, as it were, and take an overview. Such is the force of a recurring formula in Rahner that might otherwise appear a meaningless incantation: the unity of being and knowing. Applied to theology, this principle implies that our acceptance of the gospel word, and its transformative effects on us, are an intrinsic aspect of the gospel itself.

Significant consequences follow for the relationships between the various branches of theology. The so-called 'pastoral' or 'practical' disciplines are no longer secondary to more 'neutral' studies such as those of systematics or Scripture. No longer will it do to define pastoral theology as 'the doctrine of how the truth, once it is recognized, is to be applied and appropriated', or as ' "the technical theory" through which historical and systematic theology are applied to the life of the Church'.[39] Such accounts imply that everything we really need is already available, established in the

---

[36] Sandler, *Bekehrung des Denkens*, 65–6.

[37] For a fuller discussion of these issues, see Declan Marmion, *A Spirituality of Everyday Faith: A Theological Investigation of the Notion of Spirituality in Karl Rahner* (Leuven: Peeters, 1998).

[38] 1956a, 84–9, 74–8.

[39] James A. Whyte, 'Practical Theology', in Alastair V. Campbell (ed.), *A Dictionary of Pastoral Care* (London: SPCK, 1987), 212–13, here 212. Whyte attributes these accounts, without giving sources, to Häring and Tillich.

tradition. The most a practical discipline can do is to convey this established truth to the present situation. Rahner opts decisively against such a position. The truth of God remains to be discovered and fashioned, through our acceptance of the ongoing process of grace. What we make of that truth is integral to its identity. We only discover God indirectly, through our engagement in the human process, and never attain, even in the beatific vision, a complete grasp. Indeed, if we are made to know God, then 'grasp' is an inappropriate metaphor for the fullness of knowledge.[40]

It might seem that such a view leads to the abolition of any distinction between theoretical and practical disciplines, between, say, the theology of grace and the study of spirituality. Rahner, however, did not go that far. He did, nevertheless, reformulate the identity of the practical disciplines. In 1967, he offered the following as a definition of practical theology:

> Practical Theology is the particular theological discipline concerned with how the Church actualizes itself here and now (both as this in fact is and as it should be), on the basis of the *theological* elucidation of each particular situation in which the Church, in all its dimensions, must actualize itself.[41]

Rahner's stress on 'theological' is important here. The practical theological disciplines deal with human experience from a quite specific point of view, determined by Christian tradition. Underlying the definition is a view of the world as a permanent dialogue between divine initiative and creaturely response. Practical theology focuses primarily on our response, whereas other branches focus on the structures common to all possible responses.

On first reading, such an account of practical theology may look hardly distinguishable from 'applied theology'. But there is an important difference. Underlying 'applied theology' is a model of knowledge as propositional: to know is to grasp correct sentences. In Rahner's practical theology, the knowledge of God consists in a relationship, generative of new forms of life. We look back to the

---

[40] 'The Concept of Mystery in Catholic Theology', esp. 56, 78: 'As long as we measure the loftiness of knowledge by its perspicuity . . . as long as we think that analytical and co-ordinating, deductive and controlling insight is more, not less, than the experience of the divine past-all-graspness, then we have understood nothing about mystery and nothing about the true nature of grace and glory.'
[41] 'Practical Theology Within the Range of Theological Disciplines', 102, *134* (*KRSW*, xix. 504).

past of Jesus, and are led, in Hopkins's phrase already quoted, to 'admire and do otherwise'; doctrine exists to empower new forms of response. The specific forms our discipleship should take cannot simply be deduced from reflection on Christian origins. In the proclaimed word, the Spirit continues to work, and this kerygma 'cannot itself just be a merely simplified version of academic theology, even if this theology is correct'.[42]

Rahner developed such theories in a situation where Catholic theology faculties were well established at state universities. The student body was composed overwhelmingly of seminarians, and the professors were generally, if not universally, priests. He was reacting against a tendency, within that world, for the practical subdisciplines to be marginalized, and indeed often despised for their lack—whether real or imaginary—of substance and rigour. Rahner is insisting that our ongoing experience, schooled by Christian tradition, constitutes an integral element in that tradition. By implication, dogmatics and spirituality study complementary, and not cleanly distinguishable, aspects of one and the same reality.

A generation after Rahner's retirement, the debates about the nature of 'spirituality' have changed. 'Spirituality', a word with a complex history, has come to be applied in contexts far beyond the conventionally ecclesial or religious. 'Spirituality' extends more widely than theology, and at least in some sense beyond Christianity. Thus Sandra Schneiders insists:

> theology does not contain or control spirituality . . . spirituality is not a subdivision of either dogmatic or moral theology . . . I find most convincing and clarifying the position that regards spirituality as an autonomous discipline which functions in partnership and mutuality with theology.[43]

A 'theological approach',

rules out, or at least prescinds from, the study of some of the most interesting phenomena on the current spirituality scene such as the integration into Christian spirituality of elements from non-Christian sources, e.g. native spiritualities, the other world religions, or feminism in a way that goes well beyond classical ecumenical or inter-religious dialogue. Furthermore, the theological approach has a strong tendency to apply normative

---

[42] 'Kerygmatische Theologie', 126.
[43] Sandra M. Schneiders, 'Spirituality in the Academy', *Theological Studies*, 50 (1989), 676–97, here 687, 689. The discussion has been continued in the recently founded *Christian Spirituality Bulletin*. I attempt to review the issues in 'Spirituality and the University', *The Way Supplement*, 84 (Autumn 1995), 87–99.

criteria of acceptability, which is not equivalent to the deductive and derivative approach of the nineteenth century manuals but which nevertheless does make spirituality subject to dogmatic and moral theology in a way I consider far too restrictive given the enormous variety and latitude of contemporary Christian spirituality.[44]

The question of whether spirituality should be a theological discipline or not is ultimately a faith question. The answer depends on whether any theology can still offer, in any sense, an account of all possible experience, and in particular on whether the universal claims of Christianity can still, in any form, be sustained.[45] As our consciousness of human diversity expands, the question becomes more acute.

If the answer to that question is negative, then it follows, logically but also trivially, that there are aspects of human experience where Christian theology is inapplicable. The only issue to be settled then is whether it is possible to find a definition of 'spirituality' that is not dependent on Christian assumptions, that is coherent, and that is suitably inclusive.[46] If, however, students of spirituality still wish to accept that Christian tradition has a universal, definitive status, then Rahner's theological approach offers an approach to Christian truth which may be helpful. Underlying Schneiders's insistence that spirituality be emancipated from theology is a sense that theologians might try to control and restrict the diversity of phenomena now investigated by students of spirituality. The spiritual, as these scholars remind us, should not be 'hampered by narrow, institutionally-defined conceptions of what is religiosity', nor confined

[44] Sandra M. Schneiders, 'A Hermeneutical Approach to the Study of Christian Spirituality', *Christian Spirituality Bulletin*, 2/1 (Spring 1994), 9–14, here 12.

[45] Schneiders defines 'spirituality' as 'the experience of conscious involvement in the project of life-integration towards the ultimate value one perceives' ('The Study of Christian Spirituality: Contours and Dynamics of a Discipline', *Christian Spirituality Bulletin*, 6/1 [Spring 1998], 1, 3–12, here 1–3). In a Christian spirituality, 'these formal categories are specified by Christian content'; by implication Hinduism or feminism, say, could supply alternative contents. Such an approach marginalizes issues regarding the truth of religious beliefs, as well as any claim that one's religion could be a unique source of universally valid truth. What appears as a debate about how systematic theology relates to other academic disciplines in the study of spirituality may be masking deeper issues about how the Christian relates to the human.

[46] For example, is it possible to speak of Buddhist spirituality, given that Buddhism is reticent regarding affirmations about a transcendent being, without rendering the term 'spirituality' so broad as to be useless? Or should we content ourselves with acknowledging the Christian roots of the concept of 'spirituality', and see the study of what we call 'Buddhist spirituality' as part of a Christian interpretation of Buddhism?

to the behaviours recognized and approved by mainstream churches.[47] In terms of this discussion, Rahner's work implies an important distinction. The spiritual interpenetrates the human: it exists beyond the official Church and theological dogmas do not fully determine it. But, on Christian assumptions, the spiritual remains co-extensive with the grace of God made manifest in Christ. Thus, while insisting that Christian theology must shape any ultimate interpretation of human experience, this Rahnerian position does not involve a claim that theology controls or restricts what other sources of knowledge may contribute. Rahnerian theology exists as a set of regulative principles in partnership. Ongoing experience or research may subvert, radically, prevailing conceptions as to how these principles might be specified.

The Uses of Tradition

Rahner's earliest essays on 'the immediate experience of God' are redolent of a narrow clerical culture. It is hard for contemporary readers to grasp why Roman Catholic theologians in the early decades of the twentieth century argued so bitterly about the issues. It was Rahner's achievement to bring his own positions within these debates into a broader context. Within this narrow world of spirituality, of asceticism and mysticism, Rahner found in Bonaventure and others convictions about 'the immediate experience of God'. He saw—perhaps with Ignatius's help—that these convictions applied, not primarily to privileged people and situations, but to the human condition as a whole. Everyday human experience became an indispensable source for theology.

On this basis, Rahner renegotiated for Catholic theology the relationship between nature and grace, between the word of Christianity and human reality at large. While not abandoning the Augustinian stress on God's free, gratuitous initiative, Rahner insisted that such gratuitousness must be within the divine dispensation from the beginning. Thus he created new space in Catholic theology for concerns conventionally repressed and held in

[47] Meredith B. McGuire, 'Mapping Contemporary American Spirituality: A Sociological Perspective', *Christian Spirituality Bulletin*, 5/1 (Spring 1997), 1, 3–8, here 1. This article cogently exemplifies the strengths of an approach less defined by theology.

suspicion: Pelagius's insistence on the inherent goodness of human freedom; an Antiochene stress on the full humanity of Jesus; Protestantism's recognition of authority within the whole Church. The revealed Word, Christ and the tradition he inaugurates, neither smothers the human as such (the heresy of extrinsicism), nor does it reduce to what we know of the human anyway (the heresy of intrinsicism). Rather it constitutes a uniquely necessary instrument, irrevocably deployed by God in order to bring the whole creation to gracious fulfilment.

The revolutionary changes in Roman Catholicism marked by Vatican II cannot, obviously, be ascribed to any one theologian or prelate. Nevertheless, the convergence between these changes and Rahner's theology is striking. In a profound essay, the historian John O'Malley has pointed to how the call to read the 'signs of the times' represented a revolutionary departure from precedent: 'Vatican II took greater note of the world around it than any previous council, and it assumed as one of its principal tasks "colloquies"and conversations with that world'. *Aggiornamento* was a new concept in the history of Roman Catholic thought, marking a profound shift in thinking:

> Given the incomplete state of studies on the idea of reform, it is precarious to generalize. Nevertheless, two distinguished historians of religious reform, Hubert Jedin and the late Delio Cantimori, have independently ventured the opinion that the perennial spirit of Catholic reform was accurately epitomized by . . . Giles of Viterbo (1469–1532), in his inaugural address at the Fifth Lateran Council: 'Men must be changed by religion, not religion by men'. What Vatican II's *aggiornamento* called for was precisely the opposite. It determined that religion should be changed by men, in order to meet the needs of men (*sic*).[48]

Rahner himself made a similar point when claiming that Vatican II marked the emergence of a 'world Church', as opposed simply to a Church reflecting European and perhaps North American culture.[49] One aspect of his position turned on how the Council marked a transformation in consciousness regarding the world

[48] O'Malley, 'Reform, Historical Consciousness, and Vatican II's Aggiornamento' (1971), in *Tradition and Transition*, 46–7.
[49] Here I refer to two 1979 essays: 'Basic Theological Interpretation of the Second Vatican Council', and 'The Abiding Significance of the Second Vatican Council'. But Rahner was making this point as early as 1966: *Handbuch der Pastoraltheologie*, ii/1 259–61 (*KRSW*, xix. 300).

outside institutional Christianity: non-Roman Catholic Christians were no longer simply benighted heretics, pagans no longer simply in error. Rather, if the Churches ever are reunited, the non-Catholic Christians will bring something positive; and even the institutional forms of paganism can be of salvific significance. Prior to the Council 'none of this was actually explicit in the Church's awareness, but it is present there now and cannot now be removed, since it is understood, not as a modern liberal trendiness but as an element of Christian conviction as such'.[50]

The idea of God's presence in history, in other words, has implied profound changes in Roman Catholic self-understanding. If Rahner's testimony is to be trusted, his own contribution to that change is rooted in what he learnt from Ignatian spirituality. Ultimately, therefore, in interpreting, defending, and developing Rahner's writings on Ignatian spirituality, we are dealing with something central to Christian theology as a whole. Rightly understood, commitment to tradition and openness to the historical process—in particular to what as yet lies outside the visible Church—vary in direct, not inverse proportion.

Christian truth and Christian language are essentially symbolic, permanently open to new unfolding. They make only the austerely formal claim that, in Jesus and in the tradition stemming from him, God has made a complete gift of self. It can be left entirely open how that claim is further to be specified, even if we can never disinvent past contingencies. The exegetes, the social scientists, the feminists or whoever are permanently liable to call into question any particular opinions we hold on the relevant material issues. Christian tradition is not the only source we need in order to interpret reality fully and deduce our obligations. We must use it, rather, as one indispensable resource, in indefinite interaction with a plurality of others.

Shortly after Vatican II, Rahner speculated on the nature of theology in a pluralist world, and suggested that we might have to envisage 'two forms of theology running parallel'. The one,

would try—as far as this is possible—to undergird and contain this pluralism of mindsets today. As far as possible—even if never in complete purity—it would try to call on, to bring into play, and to answer in faith ('redeem') only that experience of existence which is nevertheless still common, and permanently so.

---

[50] 'The Abiding Significance of the Second Vatican Council', 99, *314*.

The other kind of theology would 'courageously let itself disintegrate into a plurality of theologies'.[51] It was Rahner's achievement to show us that such pluralism was no disaster, rather a reflection of the deepest sense of Catholicity, a mirror of God's creative freedom. In this achievement, Rahner at least resembles Ignatius.

'Ignatius is a person of transcendental rather than categorical piety.'[52] As we have seen, Hans Urs von Balthasar took exception to this statement, on the ground that it discounted historical revelation. But in fact there are deep affinities between transcendental theology and the pedagogy of the Exercises. Neither Ignatius nor transcendental theology takes us away from the historical, but they do recognize that the formal truths of Christian revelation are susceptible to indefinitely many continuations. Life under Christ's standard is pluriform. Fidelity to Christian tradition, the following of Christ's standard, simply means flexibility and openness before the ongoing action of God. Rahner shows us how we can hold to the absoluteness of Christianity while renouncing the dishonest fetish of a comprehensive explanation of all that occurs. The tradition furnishes, rather, a framework empowering response to the multiple disclosures of God's mystery.

Von Balthasar's work certainly allows for pluralist perspectives on the reality of Christ, but he seems to believe that the tradition should guarantee our ability straightforwardly to distinguish the authentic from the distorted. In an interview given in 1976, Balthasar commented on Rahner's theology as follows:

I have tried to see Christianity or the figure (*Gestalt*) of Christ in the first place as a figure, and his Church together with Christ. One can walk round a figure and see it from all sides. Again and again one sees something different and yet one sees always the same thing. Thus I do not believe in the pluralism of which Rahner's pessimism is so convinced. Rather I believe in catholicity . . . because we—or at least we Christians— always look towards the same thing, even if we also cast glances towards only parts of it.[53]

---

[51] 'Philosophy and Philosophizing in Theology', 59, *82*.   [52] 1955, 183, *515*.

[53] ' "Geist und Feuer": Ein Gespräch mit Hans Urs von Balthasar', *Herder Korrespondenz*, 30 (1976), 72–82, here 76. I have developed this account of von Balthasar's criticisms of Rahner in 'Von Balthasar, Rahner, and the Commissar', *New Blackfriars*, 79 (1998), 26–33; see also Williams, 'Balthasar and Rahner', and Eamonn Conway, *The Anonymous Christian—a Relativised Christianity?: An Evaluation of Hans Urs von Balthasar's Criticisms of Karl Rahner's Theory of the Anonymous Christian* (Frankfurt: Peter Lang, 1993).

Rahner rarely reacted in public to von Balthasar's criticisms of his work, but a comment made to a Jesuit audience in 1973 can serve as a rejoinder:

> If we were to behave as if our being Christian gave us a 'world-view' in which everything fits together harmonically, we would, in the end, be setting ourselves up to be God. This is because the whole of reality is a symphony only for him. To make pluralism into a symphony—as good old Balthasar does—a symphony which we can hear as such: this is fundamentally impossible.[54]

As Rahner's Ignatius put the matter to his modern disciple in 1978:

> People have often accused your theology of being cheaply eclectic. There is of course something right about that charge. But if God is the 'ever greater God', who outstrips every system within which humanity seeks to bring reality under its control, then your 'eclecticism' can also perfectly well be an expression of how God is too much for humanity and of how humanity willingly accepts that divine being-too-much. After all, in the end there is no system within which a person, from the one point at which they stand, could take in the whole. Your theology should not operate lazily, in cheap compromises. But a thoroughly elaborated, transparent system in theology would be a false system. In theology too you are the pilgrims seeking the eternal homeland of truth, in an Exodus ever new.[55]

In the chapel of the house in Innsbruck where Rahner lived during his most productive years, a visitor is confronted by a large wall mosaic. At the centre stands Christ, dressed in priestly vestments and carrying the cross, with his heart openly displayed. On the right is Thomas Aquinas, holding the *Summa theologiae*; on the left we find Ignatius, with his *Constitutions* leaning against his cloak.

Rahner was not the sort of theologian who took works of art as a starting-point, but this mosaic can nevertheless stand as an illustration of Rahner's approach to Christianity. Rahner's writings on the Sacred Heart depend relatively little on the idea of reparation so strongly emphasized in the mainstream devotional tradition.[56] For Rahner, the term 'heart' points, rather, to a metaphysical truth

[54] 'Leben in Veränderungen', 8.   [55] 1978*b*, 32*, *400*.
[56] For further development, see my 'Karl Rahner and the Heart of Christ'. For more comprehensive studies of Rahner's writings on the Sacred Heart, see Annice Callahan, *Karl Rahner's Spirituality of the Pierced Heart* (Lanham: University Press of America, 1985), and Michael J. Walsh, *The Heart of Christ in the Writings of Karl Rahner: An Investigation of its Christological Foundation as an Example of the Relationship between Theology and Spirituality* (Rome: Gregorian University Press, 1977).

about human identity, about being a 'spirit in world'. Our access to our own 'hearts', our self-presence, comes only in and through our interactions, through our presence to others. When devotion to Christ centres on the symbol of his heart, this reminds us that Christ's revelation occurs only in and through his relationships with us. The Jesus we read of in the gospel must become the cosmic Christ who incorporates us. Thus Christian tradition remains permanently to be continued.

Thomas Aquinas and Ignatius have their place in the picture, because both developed articulations of Christianity particularly respectful of this fundamental principle. If the word of God is proclaimed in terms of Thomas's austere scholasticism or of Ignatius's terse requests 'to reflect and draw profit', then the event is completed only when the hearer responds, participating in the mystery in ways that we cannot predict in advance. In 1956, Rahner had written of how Ignatius's qualities had still not been fully appropriated or appreciated. 'In regard to what is most his own, his day seems . . . still to come.'[57] In context, this remark refers to Ignatius's role in the history of ideas; it could, however, also stand as an emblem of how Rahner took from Ignatius the sense of a God who is ever greater, of Christian revelation as constantly generating new forms of life.

This study can end as it began: by evoking how the idea of Rahner writing a *Dogmatik der Exerzitien* issued only in a few jottings and in an empty notebook. As Ignatius said in another context, it is God's own supreme wisdom and goodness which must 'preserve, direct, and carry forward' what God has begun.[58] Seen in themselves, our efforts are only fragments: mere attempts to clear space so that God's grace can be disclosed.

---

[57] 1956a, 87 n. 1, 76 n. 15: '*scheint er uns noch in seinem Eigentlichsten noch am Kommen zu sein*'.
[58] The allusion is to Ignatius's statement of purpose in his Preamble to the *Constitutions* (n. 135).

APPENDIX

Peter Knauer, Karl Rahner, and the First Ignatian 'Time'

In 1959, Peter Knauer wrote to Rahner, raising critical questions about Rahner's large 1956 essay on Ignatian discernment. Though still in his early twenties, Knauer had already produced what has become a seminal translation of Ignatius's *Spiritual Diary*.[1] Knauer argued for two main positions. Firstly, the fundamental principle underlying second-time discernment was articulated by Ignatius not in the rule about 'consolation without preceding cause', but in the description of the Third Manner of Humility—a claim already noted in Chapter 8 of the present study. Secondly, Knauer argued that 'consolation without preceding cause' was linked, not to the second Ignatian 'time' but to the first. Knauer supported these claims with a set of exegetical arguments connected to the complex textual issues handled in Chapter 7 above, largely anticipating ideas which he later published.[2]

Rahner's answer ran as follows:

Dear Companion,
Since tomorrow I begin three weeks of travelling, and moreover at other times am pressed for time, I'm afraid it's not possible for me to answer your letter—for which I thank you—thoroughly (and that is what one must do if the answer is to have any

---

[1] Knauer's subsequent work has been in three main areas. Firstly, he has continued to translate Ignatian texts, culminating in two major volumes: Ignatius von Loyola, *Briefe und Unterweisungen* and *Gründungstexte der Gesellschaft Jesu* (Würzburg: Echter, 1993–8)—though note that this edition does not include all the valuable commentary from his earlier versions of some of the works, notably the *Diary* and the *Exercises*. A phrase from Knauer's 1959 letter foreshadows his characteristic approach: 'In my . . . textual studies of St Ignatius . . . I have always had the impression that Ignatius expresses himself admittedly very inelegantly, but nevertheless with astounding precision.' Secondly, he has published regularly in the field of ethics, most famously his seminal article of 1965, 'The Hermeneutic Function of the Principle of Double Effect', to be found in Charles E. Curran and Richard A. McCormick (edd.), *Readings in Moral Theology No. 1: Moral Norms and Catholic Tradition* (New York: Paulist, 1979), 1–39. Thirdly, as professor of fundamental theology at the Jesuit *Hochschule* in Frankfurt, he has made distinctive contributions in this field, the most substantial of which is his book, *Der Glaube kommt vom Hören*; here the subtitle, 'ecumenical fundamental theology', is significant. Needless to say, these three concerns cross-fertilize: for a bibliography, see his home page: http://www.st-georgen.uni-frankfurt.de/bibliogr/knauer.htm.

[2] Knauer, 'Die Wahl'; *Der Glaube*, 391 n. 613.

point). Your thesis is certainly something to think about. The link with the Third
Degree of Humility seems to me well worth considering. It could certainly also
very well be that Ignatius, in the actual first time of election, thought to himself of
the link between a specific object of choice and the actual fundamental consolation
as so suddenly, and yet clearly, worked by God, that the first time comes about just
when that link occurs. But what would still remain true in what I say, something
which seems to me very important, is that there is no question of the pure suddenness, in itself alone, of a specific object or decision being a criterion. Ignatius certainly, explicitly or implicitly (for he was thinking of people making the Exercises),
thought of a decision arising suddenly as something standing in open, *super*natural
transcendence—a transcendence *remaining* open with the object there. Now,
whether this convergence between this object and rightly understood transcendence is apprehended through some kind of evidence that suddenly arises and is
immediately clear (which alone you would call the first time, and perhaps would be
right in so doing—I can't check it now), or whether the knowledge of this convergence requires a longer time and a certain testing—this seems to me to be perhaps
not unimportant, but nevertheless a secondary question. For the main thing is still
that a 'grounding' for the individual decision is being worked out that does not just
depend on the suddenness or puzzling quality with which a thought or impulse
arises. If one just wanted to say, as a justification for this, that with such an experience (*Erlebnis*!) it is just obvious to a person that it's been caused by God, then
one has put forward a thesis, but not given any justification. To that extent, the
real concern of my essay still seems to me both important and right. Nor do you
refute it. Nor either am I able or willing to refute your researches—if only
because at the moment, as I said, with the best of intentions I do not have the time
to go into these questions. I wish you much success, happiness, and personal
profit in your Ignatian studies and researches. With best wishes, Yours sincerely.
Karl Rahner.[3]

---

[3] Original text (typing mistakes silently corrected): *Lieber Mitbruder, da ich morgen für drei
Wochen verreisen muss und auch sonst knapp bei Zeit bin, so ist es mir leider nicht möglich, ausführlich (und
das müsste man, wenn die Antwort überhaupt einen Sinn haben soll) auf Ihren Brief zu antworten, für den ich
Ihnen danke. Ihre These ist sicher beachtlich. Die Verbindung mit dem 3. Grad der Demut scheint mir durchaus
erwägenswert. Es kann ja ganz gut sein, daß Ignatius in der eigentlich ersten Wahlzeit sich die Verbindung
eines bestimmten Wahlobjekts und des eigentlich Grundtrostes so plötzlich und doch deutlich durch Gott
gewirkt gedacht hat, daß erst diese Verbindung die eigentlich erste Wahlzeit darstellt. Richtig bliebe bei mir
immer noch und scheint mir sehr wichtig, daß die reine Plötzlichkeit eines bestimmten Objektes oder
Entschlusses für sich allein ernsthaft nicht als Kriterium in Frage kommt. Ignatius hat sicher ausdrücklich oder
implizit (weil er an Leute in den Exerzitien denkt) den plötzlich auftauchenden Entschluß als einen in der
offenen, übernatürlichen und mit dem Objekt offen bleibenden Transzendenz stehenden gedacht. Ob nun
das Zusammenpassen dieses Objekts und der richtig zu verstehenden Transzendenz in einer Art plötzlich
auftretenden und sofort klar seienden Evidenz erfaßt wird (was Sie allein 1. Wahlzeit nennen würden und
worin Sie vielleicht recht haben; das kann ich jetzt nicht prüfen) oder ob die Erkenntnis dieses Zusammen-
passens längere Zeit und ein gewisses Prüfen erfordert, das scheint mir vielleicht nicht unwichtig, aber doch eine
sekundäre Frage zu sein. Denn die Hauptsache ist doch, daß eine 'Evidenz' der individuellen Entscheidung
herausgearbeitet wird, die sich nicht bloß stützt auf der Plötzlichkeit und Rätselhaftigkeit des Auftauchens eines
Gedankens und Antriebs. Wenn man dazu nur noch sagen würde, bei einem solchen Erlebnis sei einem eben
evident, daß das von Gott gewirkt wird, dann hat man eine These aufgestellt, aber keine Begründung gegeben.
Und insofern scheint mir das eigentliche Anliegen meines Aufsatzes immer noch wichtig und richtig zu*

As already noted, Rahner could easily accept Knauer's claim about
how the 'supernatural logic' of second-time election might be formulated
Christologically. He had himself already done the job, in retreat conferences in 1954–5—though the text had not yet entered the public domain
and hence was unknown to Knauer at this point. However, Rahner rather
misunderstands Knauer's claims about 'consolation without preceding
cause' and the first 'time'.[4] Drawing on a position already hinted at in the
1956 essay, Rahner speculates that the first 'time' need not be considered
as an exceptional case, to be discounted in any generally applicable theology, but rather as an accelerated version of the second.[5] Knauer was,
however, saying something different. Though he was departing from a
tradition which saw the first 'time' as exceptional, he was reformulating,
rather than denying, the claim that it represented an epistemology different from that of the other two 'times'.

In his published writings on this theme, Knauer sees a distinctive theological significance in the fact that the first-time conviction arises uncaused
by prior acts of the understanding or will. Knauer connects this feature of
first-time experience with the requirement for any adequate account of
the *analysis fidei*, of how faith is grounded: faith occurs neither 'rationalist-
ically, through rational argument, nor fideistically, through a leap of the
will (*Willensaufschwung*)'. The first 'time', therefore, is privileged, in so far as
it deals with the unconditional assent proper to matters of faith, and with
'the liberating view of created reality as it presents itself when it is recog-
nised as loved by God'.[6] By contrast, the second and third 'times' represent
complementary strategies for discovering the duties arising from a naturalist ethics. When Ignatius abandons vegetarianism,[7] what he is recognizing is that Christian faith frees us from quasi-idolatrous anxiety about
what we should do.

Any discussion of the first 'time' must be tentative: Ignatius's indications
are scanty and ambiguous.[8] That said, Knauer's position rests on exegetical claims that are questionable. Firstly, neither of the key source texts for
the first 'time' mentions consolation; indeed, Ignatius's decision to resume
eating meat is marked by a striking absence of the affective.[9] Secondly, as

---

*sein. Dem widersprechen Sie auch nicht. Und ich kann und will auch Ihren Untersuchungen nicht widerspre-
chen. Schon weil ich zur Zeit, wie gesagt, beim besten Willen die Zeit nicht habe, diesen Fragen nachzugehen.
Ich wünsche Ihnen in Ihren ignatianischen Studien und Untersuchungen viel Erfolg, Freude und Gewinn
für Sie selbst. Mit freundlichen Grüssen Ihr ergebener Karl Rahner.*

[4] At various points in the gestation of this study, Knauer has kindly and patiently replied
to queries of mine in conversation and by letter. In May 1990 he wrote to me, 'I didn't actually, at the time, find Rahner's answer to my letter met the point (*zutreffend*)'.

[5] Compare 1956a, 159, *138–9* with 1956a, 105, *92*.   [6] 'Die Wahl', 334.
[7] *Aut*, n. 27, discussed in Chapter 7.   [8] Toner, *Discerning God's Will*, 126.
[9] Ibid., 114–18. A Knauerian counter-argument would adduce the description of consolation in the Rejadell letter discussed in Chapter 7. There, second-time discernment is being

argued in Chapter 7, the claim that 'consolation without preceding cause' involves neither intellect nor will need not be given the theological weight that Knauer attributes to it. It could simply refer to how the consolation arises without (conscious) connection to the material over which the exercitant has been praying (see the discussion above). Thirdly, Knauer sees a first-time election as referring primarily to the conviction of faith, rather than to particular options: 'Ignatius is simply recognising that the issue of "eating meat" or "not eating meat" is not a matter of faith.'[10] But the two texts describing the first 'time', the description in the *Spiritual Exercises* and the account of Ignatius abandoning vegetarianism in the *Autobiography*, do not seem concerned with whether or not simply to believe in Christianity, but rather with how such belief should be lived out and expressed. The account in the *Autobiography* is striking precisely because Christians at different times have understood vegetarianism as expressing both spiritual anxiety and spiritual freedom.

In its published form, however, Knauer's interpretation of the first 'time' is linked to his distinctive and original project of an 'ecumenical fundamental theology', and needs to be interpreted and evaluated in this context.[11] For Rahner, and also for Toner, Ignatius's three 'times' represent three different ways in which the same reality—God's will for a person's life—can be discovered; Knauer sees the three methods on opposite sides of a sharp distinction between faith and reason. For Knauer, the second and third of Ignatius's 'times' are complementary methods for discovering the duties arising from a naturalist ethics: the second 'time' focuses on the subject's dispositions, while the third considers the pros and cons of particular options. The first, is quite different. Ignatius's abandonment of vegetarianism represents an emancipation from fear, 'an experience of the freedom which comes from faith', a corollary of the message that God's own self is communicated to us.[12] The will of God is a twofold reality of

---

applied in the context of a consolation which cannot be resisted. It would also note Ignatius's third description of consolation: 'every increase in hope, faith, and charity' (*Exx*, n. 316.4). Both of these arguments are weighty. If, however, we accept the second, then 'consolation' covers any good motion stirred in us by God. This makes it difficult to interpret Ignatius's account of the third 'time', when there is no movement of spirits (*Exx*, n. 177.3), but where nevertheless God is asked to 'move my will and put in my soul what I ought to do' (*Exx*, n. 180.1). As for the first consideration, Bakker, *Freiheit und Erfahrung*, plausibly suggests that Ignatius's teaching on discernment developed gradually. If so, we might well speculate that the Rejadell letter antedates the two distinctions between first and second 'times' and between consolations with and without 'preceding cause'.

[10] Private communication, autumn 1998.

[11] A recent comparative study brings out more generally how different Jesuit thinkers have interpreted Ignatius in the light of their particular philosophical concerns: Karlheinz Ruhstorfer, 'Das moderne und das postmoderne Interesse an den Geistlichen Übungen des Ignatius von Loyola', *Theologie und Philosophie*, 73 (1998), 334–63.

[12] Knauer, 'Die Wahl', 334.

grace and law: the word heard in faith (first 'time') frees us to engage appropriately in the ethics built into nature (second and third 'times').
The differences between Knauer and Rahner turn on ways of conceiving revelation. Though both have more in common with each other than with a thinker like Salaverri, Knauer's footnotes[13] nevertheless suggest that Rahner, as—to use a current smear-word—an 'onto-theologian', is forced by an ontology of substance into the error of confusing the divine and the created in the order of grace. By contrast, an adequate fundamental theology would insist, with the Protestant tradition, that 'no created quality can ground *communio* with God'.[14] Hence Rahner's expression, the 'supernatural existential', is acceptable only if it is understood relationally:

It is true that one can designate 'being created in Christ' as the 'supernatural existential'. But we are not talking here about an additional created reality or about an intrinsic change in the ontological status of the creature, but rather about a relational change: that of having been taken up into the relationship the Son has with the Father.

But Rahner's idiom fails to respect this distinction:

In Karl Rahner's theology the hiddenness (*Verborgenheit*) of what is to be revealed seems not sufficiently respected: the hiddenness which consists in the fact that God's love for us cannot take its measure from anything created, and therefore cannot be read off from anything created.[15]

Particularly if the kind of constructive interpretation used in this study is legitimate, some defence of Rahner may be possible. Rahner's theology can be read in terms of a purely formal use of the language of *Sein*, leaving it open for the content to be specified in terms of relationship.[16] The

---

[13] The most important of these references in *Der Glaube* are: n. 12 (p. 24, on *Hörer des Wortes*); n. 169 (p. 134, on Christology); n. 228 (p. 170, on the supernatural existential); n. 241 (p. 179, on 'pure nature').

[14] Knauer, *Der Glaube*, 17 n. 1: '*keine geschaffene Qualität Gemeinschaft mit Gott begründen kann*'.

[15] Ibid., 170–1 n. 228.

[16] 'Nature and Grace' (itself written for ecumenical purposes), 177, 223–4: 'grace, right from the outset, cannot be thought of in separation from the personal love of God and its answer in humanity. One is not thinking in a "thing-like" way with such grace; we are not dealing with something which is put at human beings' 'disposal' except in the context of that letting oneself be disposed of which is proper to precisely the freest of grace, the miracle of love. The only reason why people (this applies to Roman Catholics as well) still think in ontic categories here, is that for a Catholic philosophy it simply is the case that what has real effects (and what could be more real and effective than the love of God?) must be thought of as "real", as "being", and that the highest must be expressed in the most abstract words. And therefore the deed of God's love, which precedes our activity . . . and must be thought of as the ground of that activity, can only be expressed by using "essential" categories (state, accident, *habitus*, infusion etc.) as well as those like "deed" and "love".'

Rahnerian counter-objection to Knauer is obvious: grace, even relationally conceived, makes a difference to created reality, to the being of things. Though there is no question of justifying revelation on the basis of some 'neutral' philosophy, the Christian message is interwoven in a distinctive way with 'presuppositions' in the hearer, 'that are there inescapably and necessarily . . . in the ultimate ground of human existence', even though 'the message of Christianity through its call at the same time creates these presuppositions'.[17]

Knauer at one point tells us that God's love does not entail,

> a change in the world in its own subsistence regarded in itself (*in ihrem Eigenbestand für sich betrachtet*). Rather what is at stake is a real relationship of God's in regard to the world, a relationship that brings with it a change in the world. This change consists in *communio* with God, but it can never be spoken of as something detached from that *communio*.[18]

The Rahnerian approach developed in this study would not deny this statement, but it does insist on a corollary: God's love makes a difference to the nature of the creation, and hence, given a naturalist approach to ethics, to the duties and obligations implicit in creation's order.[19] The mystery of faith, therefore, which Knauer presents as peculiar to the first Ignatian 'time', must be present—even if only incipiently or implicitly, even indeed if it is being rejected—in any human decision process.[20] Its contribution to Christian practical reasoning is not that of a counterpart, essentially in contrast with a denuminized naturalism, but rather as a leaven, transforming and enriching nature from within, and hence at least sometimes specifying the obligations arising from a naturalist ethics. God's grace may be wholly other, but it is an other shaping the whole of creation. Whereas Knauer sees a sharp disjunction between the epistemologies of faith and reason, Rahner presents them as integrated. If faith as such

---

[17] *Foundations of Christian Faith*, 24, *35* (*KRSW*, xxvi. 29).

[18] Knauer, *Der Glaube*, 179–80.

[19] Compare Lash, *Easter in Ordinary*, 230: 'Being in relation . . . does not explain any event in the world that was previously puzzling. It does not solve any particular problem . . . being in relation does not, in itself, rearrange the furniture of the world or make any particular difference . . . And yet, it does seem correct to say that being in relation . . . makes all the difference in the world. It may even change the world (and, in that sense, come to make particular differences) because people in relation . . . may find that they are newly enabled to *cope*, with fresh energy and clear-sightedness, with all the particular problems that engage their attention and responsibility.'

[20] See, for example, Knauer, *Der Glaube*, 171 n. 228: our creation in Christ 'remains hidden (*verborgen*) prior to the proclamation of faith, and cannot even be experienced "unthematically" (*läßt sich auch nicht "unthematisch" erfahren*)'. The issue here is how far Rahner's distinctive use of the term 'experience'—compatible with the object being 'hidden'—is a legitimate, indeed necessary, extrapolation from Christian proclamation.

involves a trust that is not fideist, and a rationality that is not rationalist, the principle must apply also to any instance of Christian practical reasoning. The Christian economy of unity-in-relationship generates theologies both of dramatic interchange and of graced being. There are long-standing disputes about which of these is more fundamental, and about how far the two are compatible. These disputes, regarding which Knauer's position differs both from Rahner's and from mine, require another book. This one ends simply with two comments.

Firstly, Rahner's transcendental approach to theology, rightly understood, is not an alternative to a more historical theology of the Word. Rather, it articulates the general, abstract conditions which must obtain if any proclamation of the Word is to be intelligible.

Secondly, these conditions allow for pluralism, even conflict, in the manner of their fulfilment. Perhaps one of Rahner's most important lessons is that God's truth can be expressed by both parties to a dispute, even when their statements and languages are in a real sense contradictory. In terms of Rahner's Ignatian writings, the process of 'transcendence becoming thematic' can occur among different people in conflicting ways, leading to tensions between different styles of *Nachfolge*—discipleship, or 'following-after'. As the elderly Rahner's Ignatius puts the point:

> There seem to be many ways of following after Jesus. There's not much point in bringing these different ways under one heading, and distilling out of the different concrete forms of such discipleship one unitary essence of this discipleship, by saying that they're all one 'in spirit'. That may be quite true . . . But there are concrete forms of this discipleship that are different, that remain frighteningly different, that even seem to threaten and negate each other.[21]

---

[21] 1978*b*, 21, *386*.

BIBLIOGRAPHY

This bibliography falls into three sections. The first lists Rahner's most significant writings on Ignatian and Jesuit topics, adding background information where appropriate. The second offers, alphabetically by title, other works written or edited by Rahner referred to in this study. The third gives a list of other sources repeatedly used.

Full bibliographies of Rahner's texts in German and of Rahnerian secondary material in all languages can be found on the Freiburg University library website (www.ub.uni-freiburg.de/referate/04). A useful list of English-language material up till Rahner's death is C. J. Pedley, 'An English Bibliographical Aid to Karl Rahner', *Heythrop Journal*, 25 (1984), 319–65.

For help with various queries, I am especially grateful, once again, to Dr Roman Siebenrock at the Karl-Rahner-Archiv. I also thank Mr Frank Oveis of the Crossroad–Continuum Publishing Group, New York, and the following Jesuits: Kenneth Baker (New York); Andreas Batlogg (Innsbruck); Erwin Bücken (Cologne); Joseph Conwell (Spokane); Emerich Coreth (Innsbruck); William Dych† (New York); Hans Grünewald (Munich); Walter Kerber (Munich); Fridolin Marxer (Basel); Laszló Polgár (Rome); Alfonso Salas (Santiago); Gustav Schörghofer (Vienna); and Hermann Zeller (Innsbruck).

I Rahner's Chief Writings on Ignatian and Jesuit Spirituality

The following list gives all Rahner's major Ignatian texts known to date, together with any minor pieces used significantly in this study. It does not include material on narrowly Jesuit topics—these are, however, listed in the bibliography to the dissertation on which this study is based: 'The Direct Experience of God and The Standard of Christ: A Critical and Constructive Study of Karl Rahner's Writings on the *Spiritual Exercises* of Ignatius Loyola', D.Phil. thesis (Oxford, 1990). The dates given are those of the earliest known continuous version of any given piece. With unpublished material, the dating is sometimes based on Rahner's appointments diary (KRA, III. E. 1), which gives a very full list of his non-university activities from the time of his ordination in 1932 until 1964. The editions and translations listed are those from which I normally work. Where they are not the earliest, I have noted that fact, and given an appropriate reference. Conventions regarding cross-references are the same as in the main body of the study.

1922/5 ' "Die aszetischen Schriften in den Monumenta Historica S.J." verfaßt von Hugo Rahner SJ 1922—erweitert von Karl Rahner SJ 1925', ed. Karl H. Neufeld, *Zeitschrift für katholische Theologie*, 108 (1986), 422–33. Archive: KRA, I. A. 5.

A *catalogue raisonée* of such *Monumenta* volumes as were then available. Copies of this text were made and distributed for private circulation among Jesuits, and the work was at least once further revised in 1937. The published version is based on a copy found in the Jesuit novitiate in Nuremberg, and contains minor corrections of detail and style as well as editorial footnotes.

1935 'Über die Gnade des Gebets in der Gesellschaft Jesu—Nach P. Hieronymus Nadal S.J.', *Mitteilungen aus den deutschen Provinzen*, 13 (1935), 399–411.

A German translation of a 1562 Nadal text on prayer, together with an introduction, published in the German-speaking provinces' in-house journal. Again a piece on which Karl and Hugo Rahner collaborated. The Spanish original is in MHSJ *MN*, iv. 672–81. There is an English translation of the full text by L. Schillebeeckx in *Woodstock Letters*, 89 (1960), 285–94, and of extracts by Martin Palmer in *Studies in the Spirituality of Jesuits*, 22/5 (November 1990), 51–3.

1936 *Dogmatik der Exerzitien* (title editorial). Archive: KRA, I. B. 308.

An empty notebook with the title in Karl Rahner's handwriting. Inside are two loose pages of manuscript jottings and a postcard from Fr. Emmerich Raitz von Frentz. Some of the material has been transcribed in a footnote to Andreas Batlogg, 'Karl Rahner: Jesus lieben?—Zum Schicksal einer Veröffentlichung aus den 80er Jahren', *Geist und Leben*, 67 (1994), 90–101, at 93–4.

1937 'The Ignatian Mysticism of Joy in the World', *TI*, iii. 277–93. 'Die ignatianische Mystik der Weltfreudigkeit', *SzT*, iii. 329–48.

A talk given in Vienna in February 1937 to an adult education group entitled the Logos-Verein, and first published in *Zeitschrift für Aszese und Mystik*, 12 (1937), 121–37. The footnotes were updated before publication in *Schriften zur Theologie* in 1956, and one paragraph completely re-written.

1954/5   *Spiritual Exercises*, trans. Kenneth Baker (London: Sheed and
         Ward, 1967).
         Betrachtungen zum ignatianischen Exerzitienbuch (Munich: Kösel,
         1965). Archive: KRA, i. a. 88, 134, 241.

This text originates mainly from an eight-day retreat which Rahner gave
in the autumn of 1955 for students at the Germanicum, a German-
language seminary in Rome under Jesuit direction. The retreat took place
in the college's holiday house, San Pastore. The recipients of the retreat
worked together to transcribe the conferences and duplicate them. However, for the first four conferences they used a similar document produced
by Jesuit scholastics at Pullach, where Rahner had given a retreat the year
previously.

The codex produced went through three further editions, all made by
students at the Canisianum, the international seminary in Innsbruck, in
the years 1958–9. Before the second edition was made, Rahner supplied
corrections, some of which were illegible to the editors. He also substituted
an essay on the Incarnation (later published in *TI*, iv. 105–20 and then in
Foundations of Christian Faith, 212–28) for the twelfth of the original conferences. For publication in 1965, Rahner did nothing except write a foreword: the text was in fact subjected to further slight corrections by Fr Hans
Wulf and by Dr Paul Neuenzeit, a publisher's editor. Note therefore that
Rahner's contribution to the written text is in fact minimal.

There is a further duplicated version of these conferences which claims
to originate from the 1955 retreat, but which seems in detail quite different
from both the original text and the Innsbruck reworkings—though it does
incorporate the article Rahner substituted for the twelfth of the original
conferences. There is no indication of when or where this further version
was prepared.

The English translation was made on the basis of the penultimate and
final Innsbruck typescripts. Some of the changes made for the published
German text were incorporated into the English version at the proof
stage. For the purposes of this study, I take the published German text as
finally authoritative, but occasionally refer to variants when they are of
interest.

1955   'Ignatian Spirituality and Devotion to the Heart of Jesus', in
       Mission and Grace, iii. 176–210.
       'Ignatianische Frömmigkeit und Herz-Jesu-Verehrung', in *Sendung
       und Gnade*, 510–33.

Three conferences given for seminarians at the Canisianum in Innsbruck
in preparation for the feast of the Sacred Heart, 1955, first published in
Korrespondenzblatt des PGV im Canisianum zu Innsbruck, 90 (1955–6), 5–17.

1956*a* 'The Logic of Concrete Individual Knowledge in Ignatius Loyola', in *The Dynamic Element in the Church*, 84–170.
'Die Logik der existentiellen Erkenntnis bei Ignatius v. Loyola', in *Das Dynamische in der Kirche*, 74–148.

First published as 'Die ignatianische Logik der existentiellen Erkenntnis: Über einige theologische Probleme in den Wahlregeln der Exerzitien des Heiligen Ignatius', in Friedrich Wulf (ed.), *Ignatius von Loyola: Seine geistliche Gestalt und sein Vermächtnis (1556–1956)* (Würzburg: Echter, 1956), 343–405.

1956*b* 'Ignatius von Loyola: Zur Aktualität des Heiligen', *Geist und Leben*, 57 (1984), 337–40. Archive: KRA, I. A. 101.

Originally written for a celebratory volume, as 'Der hl. Ignatius und die Englischen Fräulein', in *250 Jahre Institut BMV der Englischen Fräulein, St. Pölten 1706–1956* (privately published), 69–71. The 1984 version omits the purely celebratory paragraphs and makes small stylistic corrections.

1956*c* 'Hausexhorte zum Ignatiusjubiläum Juni 1956' (title corrected). Archive: KRA, I. A. 110.

A talk given to the Jesuit community in Innsbruck on the vigil of the feast of the Sacred Heart, 7 June 1956. A translation was published in Spanish to mark Rahner's death and his eightieth birthday: 'Una orden antigua en una nueva época: La Compañía de Jesús y su devoción al Corazón de Cristo', *Estudios eclesiásticos*, 59 (1984), 131–8.

1959 'Being Open to God as Ever Greater: On the Significance of the Aphorism "Ad majorem Dei gloriam"', *TI*, vii. 25–46.
'Vom Offensein für den je größeren Gott: Zur Sinndeutung des Wahlspruches "Ad maiorem Dei gloriam"', *SzT*, vii. 32–53. Archive: KRA, I. A. 328.

An address given to a private Jesuit meeting held at Rottmanshöhe in Easter week 1959, taped, transcribed, and slightly shortened for original publication in *Geist und Leben*, 39 (1966), 183–201.

1961 *Meditations on Priestly Life*, trans. Edward Quinn (London: Sheed and Ward, 1973).
Einübung priestlicher Existenz (Freiburg: Herder, 1970). Archive: KRA, I. A. 173.

From archive evidence, this book appears to be based on a transcription of retreat conferences given in July 1961 to Jesuit scholastics in Innsbruck immediately prior to their priestly ordination. The text was stylistically reworked before publication, and some passages were omitted, including a version of the 'Prayer on the Eve of Ordination' (*Prayers for a Lifetime*, 117–23, *146–55*), which Rahner says he wrote originally for Jesuit ordinands twenty years previously.

1968 'Die gewandelte Ekklesiologie und die Jesuiten heute'. Archive: KRA, I. B. 184.

A duplicated typescript of a talk given at a Jesuit meeting in October 1968.

1969 'Comments by Karl Rahner on Questions Raised by Avery Dulles', trans. James M. Quigley, in Friedrich Wulf (ed.), *Ignatius of Loyola: His Personality and Spiritual Heritage (1556–1956)*, trans. ed. George E. Ganss (St Louis: Institute of Jesuit Sources, 1977), 290–3.
'Im Anspruch Gottes: Bemerkungen zur Logik der existentiellen Erkenntnis', *Geist und Leben*, 59 (1986), 241–7. Archive: KRA, I. A. 583.

Rahner here answers Dulles's 1965 article in *Woodstock Letters*. According to a note on one of the typescripts in the archive, the text arrived in the United States in January 1969. Fr. William Dych, who was involved in the commissioning of Rahner's reply, suggested privately to me that the true date may be 1967 or 1968. The book in which this response appears is otherwise a translation of the collection in which 1956*a* appears, but with only a summary of Karl Rahner's original essay.

1972 'Reflections on a New Task for Fundamental Theology', *TI*, xvi. 156–66.
'Einige Bemerkungen zu einer neuen Aufgabe der Fundamentaltheologie', *SzT*, xii. 198–211. Archive: KRA, I. A. 763.

A *Festschrift* essay in honour of Joaquín Salaverri, first published in *Estudios eclesiásticos*, 47 (1972), 397–408. The notes are editorial.

1974*a* 'Modern Piety and the Experience of Retreats', *TI*, xvi. 35–55.
'Moderne Frömmigkeit und Exerzitienerfahrung', *SzT*, xii. 173–97. Archive: KRA, I. A. 859.

Originally a talk at a meeting of retreat-givers in Vienna held in October 1974, published in three parts as 'Die Bedeutung der ignatianischen Exerzitien für eine Frömmigkeit von heute', *Experiment*, Winter 1974, 7–11; Spring 1975, 6–16; Summer 1975, 7–16. The *Schriften* version is a stylistically tidied version of this text. There were also two different summaries published: in German, 'Über den geistesgeschichtlichen Ort der ignatianischen Exerzitien heute', *Geist und Leben*, 47 (1974), 430–49; in English (as well as French and Spanish), 'The Significance of the Ignatian Exercises for Modern Spirituality', *Centrum Ignatianum Spiritualitatis*, 6/2 (1975), 70–83.

1974*b* 'The Ignatian Exercises', in *The Practice of Faith*, 100–3.
'Wesensbestimmung und Darbietung der Exerzitien heute', in *Wagnis der Christen*, 95–101.

1974*c* 'Christmas in the Light of the Ignatian *Exercises*', *TI*, xvii. 3–7.
'Weihnacht im Licht der Exerzitien', *SzT*, xii. 329–34. Archive: KRA, I. A. 877.

A Christmas homily for the community at the Berchmanskolleg, Munich, printed with some stylistic corrections and footnotes.

1975 Foreword to Ignatius Loyola, *Geistliche Übungen*, translated and annotated by Adolf Haas, 2nd edn. (Freiburg: Herder, 1967), 9–10. Archive: KRA, I. A. 887.

1976 Foreword to Harvey D. Egan, *The Spiritual Exercises and the Ignatian Mystical Horizon* (St Louis: Institute of Jesuit Sources, 1976), xiii–xvii. Archive: KRA, I. A. 923.

Egan's book originates in a doctorate done under Rahner's direction at Münster. The preface contains some material from 1975. KRA has only fragments of the original.

1978*a* Foreword to Peter Köster, *Ich gebe euch ein neues Herz* (Stuttgart: Katholisches Bibelwerk, 1978), 13–14.

The book is a popular presentation of the Ignatian process, written by a German Jesuit.

1978*b* 'Ignatius of Loyola Speaks to a Modern Jesuit', in *Ignatius of Loyola*, ed. Paul Imhof, trans. Rosaleen Ockenden (London: Collins, 1979), 11–38.
'Rede des Ignatius von Loyola an einen Jesuiten von heute', *SzT*, xv. 373–408. Archive: KRA, I. A. 980.

Original German publication in *Ignatius von Loyola*, co-produced with Paul Imhof and Helmut Nils Loose (Freiburg: Herder, 1978). This has a preface not incorporated in the *SzT* edition.

1978*c*   'The Immediate Experience of God in the Spiritual Exercises of
         Saint Ignatius of Loyola', trans. John M. McDermott, in *Karl
         Rahner in Dialogue*, 174–81.
         'Unmittelbare Gotteserfahrung in den Exerzitien', in *Karl Rahner
         Im Gespräch*, 2.31–41.

Interview with Wolfgang Feneberg, first published in *Entschluß*, 33/5 (May
1978), 8–11.

1978*d*   'Mystik—Weg des Glaubens zu Gott', in *Horizonte der Religiosität*,
         11–24.

First published in *Entschluß*, 33/6 (June 1978), 6–11.

1978*e*   'Ignatius of Loyola', trans. Frederick G. Lawrence, in *The Great
         Church Year*, 329–40.
         'Ignatius von Loyola', in *Das große Kirchenjahr*, 475–91. Archive:
         KRA, I. C. 214.

A talk given to a Jesuit community for the vigil (30 July) of the feast of
St Ignatius.

1984   'A Letter to a Young Jesuit in the Charismatic Renewal', *Centrum
         Ignatianum Spiritualitatis*, 15/2 (1984), 131–4.
         'Brief an einen jungen Jesuit in der charismatischen Bewegung'.
         Archive: KRA, I. A. 1191.

According to the journal editors, the English version of this text, which was
also published in French and Spanish, was lying on Rahner's desk at the
time of his death in March 1984.

II   Other Texts by Karl Rahner

The dates in brackets immediately following the title give, where applicable, the date at which the first complete form of the text can be shown to
have been ready.

'The Abiding Significance of the Second Vatican Council' (1979), *TI*, xx.
    90–102; 'Die bleibende Bedeutung des II. Vatikanischen Konzils', *SzT*,
    xiv. 303–18.
'Ansprache zur Bedeutung des Studiums in der Gesellschaft Jesu' (1940?,
    title editorial) (KRA, I. C. 211).

'Der Anspruch Gottes und der Einzelne' (1959), *SzT*, vi. 521–36.

'The Appeal to Conscience' (1950), in *Nature and Grace and Other Essays*, 84–111; 'Situationsethik und Sündenmystik', *Stimmen der Zeit*, 145 (1950), 329–42.

Aszese und Mystik in der Väterzeit: Ein Abriß der frühchristlichen Spiritualität (1939), ed. Karl Heinz Neufeld (Freiburg: Herder, 1989). Expanded German trans. of Marcel Viller, *La spiritualité des premiers siècles chrétiens* (Paris: Bloud & Gay, 1930). Also available in *KRSW*, iii. 123–390.

'A Basic Ignatian Concept' (1956), in *Mission and Grace*, iii. 144–75; 'Marginalien über den Gehorsam', in *Sendung und Gnade*, 487–509.

'Basic Theological Interpretation of the Second Vatican Council' (1979), *TI*, xx. 77–89; 'Theologische Grundinterpretation des II. Vatikanischen Konzils', *SzT*, xiv. 287–302.

'Der Begriff der Ecstasis bei Bonaventura' (1934), *Zeitschrift für Aszese und Mystik*, 9 (1934), 1–19 (orig. of part of 'The Doctrine of the "Spiritual Senses"').

'Begleittext zu *Geist in Welt*' (1939? 1957?), *KRSW*, ii. 431–7.

Bekenntnisse: Rückblick auf 80 Jahre, ed. Georg Sporschill (Vienna: Herold, 1984).

'Bemerkungen über das Naturgesetz und seine Erkennbarkeit' (1955), *Orientierung*, 19 (1955), 239–43.

'Bin ich berufen? Kriterien für eine Lebensentscheidung' (1980), in *Horizonte der Religiosität*, 41–50.

'Ein Brief von P. Karl Rahner' (1973), in Fischer, *Der Mensch als Geheimnis*, 400–10.

'Ein brüderlicher Geburtstagsbrief' (1965), in Kustermann and Neufeld (edd.), *'Gemeinsame Arbeit in brüderlicher Liebe'*, 69–74.

'Christian Living Formerly and Today' (1966), *TI*, vii. 3–24; 'Frömmigkeit früher und heute', *SzT*, vii. 11–31.

The Church and the Sacraments (1961 [based on 1955 article]), trans. W. J. O'Hara (London: Burns and Oates, 1963); *Kirche und Sakramente* (Freiburg: Herder, 1961).

'Concerning the Relationship Between Nature and Grace' (1950), *TI*, i. 297–317; 'Über das Verhältnis zwischen Natur und Gnade', *SzT*, i. 323–45.

Concise Theological Dictionary (1961, rev. 1976), co-authored with Herbert Vorgrimler, trans. Richard Strachan et al. (London: Burns and Oates, 1983); *Kleines theologisches Wörterbuch* (Freiburg: Herder, 1985).

'The Concept of Mystery in Catholic Theology' (1959), *TI*, iv. 36–73; 'Über den Begriff des Geheimnisses in der katholischen Theologie', *SzT*, iv. 51–99.

'The Concept of Existential Philosophy in Heidegger' (1940), *Philosophy Today*, 13 (1969), 126–37. (Orig. lost; this ET by Andrew Tallon depends on a French translation by Renatus Celle and first published under the name of Hugo Rahner. See *KRSW*, vol. ii, pp. xxxi, 317–46, 488.)

'Considerations on the Development of Dogma' (1958), *TI*, iv. 3–35; 'Überlegungen zur Dogmenentwicklung, *SzT*, iv. 11–50.

The Content of Faith: The Best of Karl Rahner's Theological Writings, edd. Karl Lehmann and Albert Raffelt, trans. ed. Harvey D. Egan (New York: Crossroad, 1994); *Rechenschaft des Glaubens: Karl-Rahner-Lesebuch* (Freiburg: Herder, 1977).

'Current Problems in Christology' (1954), *TI*, i. 149–200; 'Probleme der Christologie von heute', *SzT*, i. 169–222.

'Dialogue with God?' (1973), *TI*, xviii. 122–31; 'Zwiegespräch mit Gott?', *SzT*, xiii. 148–58.

'La Doctrine des "Sens Spirituels" au moyen-age', *Revue d'ascétique et de mystique*, 14 (1933), 263–99.

'The Doctrine of the "Spiritual Senses" in the Middle Ages' (1933), *TI*, xvi. 104–34; 'Die Lehre von den "Geistlichen Sinnen" im Mittelalter', *SzT*, xii. 137–72 (orig. generally cited from 'La doctrine des "Sens Spirituels"', or 'Der Begriff der Ecstasis').

'Dreifaltigkeitsmystik' (1959), *LTK*, iii. 563–4.

The Dynamic Element in the Church, trans.W. J. O'Hara (London: Burns and Oates, 1964); *Das dynamische in der Kirche* (Freiburg: Herder, 1958).

'*E latere Christi*: Der Ursprung der Kirche als zweiter Eva aus der Seite Christi des zweiten Adam—Eine Untersuchung über den typologischen Sinn von Joh 19.34', *KRSW*, iii. 1–84.

Encounters with Silence (1937), trans. James M. Demske (Westminster, Md.: Newman Press, 1966); *Worte ins Schweigen* (Innsbruck: Rauch, 1938).

'Erfahrungen eines katholischen Theologen' (1984), in *Karl Rahner in Erinnerung*, ed. Albert Raffelt (Düsseldorf: Patmos, 1994), 134–48.

'The Eternal Significance of the Humanity of Jesus for our Relationship with God' (1953), *TI*, iii. 35–46; 'Die ewige Bedeutung der Menschheit Jesu für unser Gottesverhältnis', *SzT*, iii. 47–60.

'Ethik und Mystik' (1941), KRA, I. B. 8.

Faith in a Wintry Season: Conversations and Interviews with Karl Rahner in the Last Years of his Life, edd. Paul Imhof and Hubert Biallowons, trans. ed. Harvey D. Egan (New York: Crossroad, 1990); *Glaube in winterlicher Zeit: Gespräche mit Karl Rahner aus den letzten Lebensjahren* (Düsseldorf: Patmos, 1986). (The English version includes a translation of 'Gnade als Mitte menschlicher Existenz', while omitting some of the pieces in the original.)

Foreword to Hugo Rahner, *Worte die Licht sind* (Freiburg: Herder, 1981), 7–16.

Foundations of Christian Faith: An Introduction to the Idea of Christianity, trans. William V. Dych (London: Darton, Longman, and Todd, 1978); *Grund-*

kurs des Glaubens: Einführung in den Begriff des Christentums (Freiburg: Herder, 1976). Also available in *KRSW*, xxvi. 1–446.

'Die geistliche Lehre des Evagrius Pontikus', *Zeitschrift für Aszese und Mystik*, 8 (1933), 21–38.

'*Gemeinsame Arbeit in brüderlicher Liebe*': *Hugo und Karl Rahner. Dokumente und Würdigung ihrer Weggemeinschaft*, edd. Abraham Peter Kustermann and Karl H. Neufeld (Stuttgart: Akademie der Diözese Rottenburg-Stuttgart, 1993).

'Die Geschichte der Lehre von den geistlichen Sinnen' (1928), KRA, I. A. 7.

'Gnadenerfahrung' (1960), *LTK*, iv. 1001–2.

'Gnade als Mitte menschlicher Existenz: Ein Gespräch mit und über Karl Rahner aus Anlaß seines 70. Geburtstages' (1974), *Herder Korrespondenz*, 28 (1974), 77–92; ET in *Faith in a Wintry Season*, 13–38.

'Grace B: Systematic' (1968), *SM*, ii. 415–22; 'Gnade III: Zur Theologie der Gnade' *SM*, ii. 450–65. This text reworks material from 1960 in *LTK*, iv. 991–1000.

'De gratia Christi' (1938), 1st edn. (Innsbruck: unpublished lecture codex).

The Great Church Year: The Best of Karl Rahner's Homilies, Sermons, and Meditations, ed. Albert Raffelt, trans. ed. Harvey D. Egan (New York: Crossroad, 1994); *Das große Kirchenjahr: Geistliche Texte* (Freiburg: Herder, 1987).

'Grundlinien einer systematischen Christologie' (1972), in *Christologie—systematisch und exegetisch: Arbeitsgrundlagen für einer interdisziplinäre Vorlesung*, co-authored with Wilhelm Thusing (Freiburg: Herder, 1972), 15–78.

Handbuch der Pastoraltheologie, 5 vols., co-edited with Franz X. Arnold, V. Schnurr, and L. Weber (Freiburg: Herder, 1964–72). (Rahner's contributions have been re-edited by Karl Heinz Neufeld in *KRSW*, xix.)

Hearer of the Word: Laying the Foundation for a Philosophy of Religion (1937), trans. Joseph Donceel, ed. Andrew Tallon (New York: Continuum, 1994); *Hörer des Wortes: Zur Grundlegung einer Religionsphilosophie* (Munich: Kösel-Pustet, 1941). (2nd edn., of disputed authenticity, ed. J. B. Metz [Munich: Kösel, 1963], trans. R. Walls [London: Sheed and Ward, 1969] under the title *Hearers of the Word*. Both editions of the original can be compared in *KRSW*, iv.)

Homily for St Stanislaus (1942?, title editorial), KRA, I. C. 48.

Horizonte der Religiosität, ed. Georg Sporschill (Vienna: Herold, 1984).

'Im Jesuitennoviziat des Jahres 1919: "Ein Tag im Exerzitienhaus Feldkirch"' (1919), *Geist und Leben*, 58 (1985), 81–2.

'"The Intermediate State"' (1975), *TI*, xvii. 114–24; 'Über den "Zwischenzustand"', *SzT*, xii. 455–66.

I Remember: An Autobiographical Interview with Meinold Krauss (1984), trans. Harvey D. Egan (London: SCM, 1985); *Erinnerungen: im Gespräch mit Meinold Krauss* (Freiburg: Herder, 1984).

Is Christian Life Possible Today?: Questions and Answers on the Fundamentals of Christian Life (1982), trans. Salvator Attanasio (Denville, N.J.: Dimension Books, 1984); *Mein Problem: Karl Rahner antwortet jungen Menschen* (Freiburg: Herder, 1982).

Karl Rahner in Dialogue: Conversations and Interviews 1965–1982, edd. Paul Imhof and Hubert Biallowons, trans. ed. Harvey D. Egan (New York: Crossroad, 1986); *Karl Rahner Im Gespräch*, 2 vols. (Munich: Kösel, 1982–3).

'Kerygmatische Theologie' (1961), *LTK*, vi. 126.

'Kommentar zum III. Kapitel der dogmatischen Konstitution über die Kirche' (1966), *LTK*, Supp. i. 210–47.

'Konsequenzen und Ergebnisse', unpublished draft material (KRA, I. A. 723ƒ) for W. Kerber, K. Rahner, and H. Zwiefelhofer, *Glaube und Gerechtigkeit: Überlegungen zur theologischen Begründung von Dekret 4 der 32. Generalkongregation* (Munich: private Jesuit publication, 1976).

'Leben in Veränderungen: Perspektiven der Hoffnung für die Gesellschaft Jesu' (1973), KRA, I. B. 46.

Mission and Grace: Essays in Pastoral Theology, 3 vols., trans. Cecily Hastings et al. (London: Sheed and Ward, 1963–6); *Sendung und Gnade: Beiträge zur Pastoraltheologie*, 5th edn., ed. Karl H. Neufeld (Innsbruck: Tyrolia, 1988).

'Mystical Experience and Mystical Theology' (1974), *TI*, xvii. 90–9; 'Mystische Erfahrung und mystische Theologie', *SzT*, xii. 428–38. (This text was re-edited more conservatively by Josef Sudbrack, as an appendix to the 1989 edition of *Visionen und Prophezeiungen*.)

'Mystik VI: Theologisch' (1962), *LTK*, vii. 743–5.

'Nature and Grace' (1960), *TI*, iv. 165–88; 'Natur und Gnade', *SzT*, iv. 209–36.

Nature and Grace and Other Essays, trans. Dinah Wharton (London: Sheed and Ward, 1963).

'Naturrecht IV: Heutige Aufgaben hinsichtlich des Naturrechts' (1962), *LTK*, vii. 827–8.

'Das Noviziat heute: Aus einem Gespräch Karl Rahners mit Novizenmeistern' (1983), *Ordensnachrichten*, Suppl. 3 (1986), 10–34.

'The One Christ and the Universality of Salvation' (1975), *TI*, xvi. 199–204; 'Der eine Jesus Christus und die Universalität des Heils', *SzT*, xii. 251–82.

'The Passion and Asceticism' (1949), *TI*, iii. 58–85; 'Passion und Aszese', *SzT*, iii. 73–104.

'Philosophy and Philosophising in Theology' (1967), *TI*, ix. 46–63; 'Philosophie und Philosophieren in der Theologie', *SzT*, viii. 66–87.

'Plea for a Nameless Virtue' (1980), *TI*, xiii. 33–7; 'Plädoyer für eine namenlose Tugend', *SzT*, xv. 298–302.

'Practical Theology Within the Totality of Theological Disciplines' (1967), *TI*, ix. 101–14; 'Die praktische Theologie im Ganzen der theologischen Disziplinen', *SzT*, viii. 133–49 (*KRSW*, xix. 503–15).

The Practice of Faith: A Handbook of Contemporary Spirituality, edd. Karl Lehmann and Albert Raffelt (London: SCM, 1985); *Praxis des Glaubens: Geistliches Lesebuch* (Freiburg: Herder, 1982).

'Prayer for the Church' (1984), in *Prayers for a Lifetime*, 114–17; 'Für die Kirche', in *Gebete des Lebens*, 141–4.

Prayers for a Lifetime, ed. Albert Raffelt (Edinburgh: T. and T. Clark, 1986); *Gebete des Lebens* (Freiburg: Herder, 1984).

'Priest and Poet' (1956), *TI*, iii. 294–317; 'Priester und Dichter', *SzT*, iii. 349–75.

'Principles and Prescriptions' (1957), in *The Dynamic Element in the Church*, 13–41; 'Prinzipien und Imperative', in *Das dynamische in der Kirche*, 14–37.

'The Prospects for a Dogmatic Theology' (1954), *TI*, i. 1–18; 'Über den Versuch eines Aufrisses einer Dogmatik', *SzT*, i. 9–28.

'On the Question of a Formal Existential Ethics' (1955), *TI*, ii. 217–34; 'Über die Frage einer formalen Existentialethik', *SzT*, ii. 227–46.

'Reflections on the Experience of Grace' (1954), *TI*, iii. 86–90; 'Über die Erfahrung der Gnade', *SzT*, iii. 105–9.

'Reflections on Methodology in Theology' (1969), *TI*, xi. 68–114; 'Überlegungen zur Methode der Theologie', *SzT*, ix. 79–126.

'Reflections on the Problem of the Gradual Ascent to Christian Perfection' (1944), *TI*, iii. 3–23; 'Über das Problem des Stufenweges zur christlichen Vollendung', *SzT*, iii. 11–34.

'Reflections on the Unity of the Love of Neighbour and the Love of God' (1965), *TI*, vi. 231–49; 'Über die Einheit von Nächsten- und Gottesliebe', *SzT*, vi. 277–98.

'Remarks on the Dogmatic Treatise "De Trinitate"' (1960), *TI*, iv. 77–102; 'Bemerkungen zum dogmatischen Traktat "De Trinitate"', *SzT*, iv. 103–33.

Sehnsucht nach dem Geheimnisvollen Gott: Profil—Bilder—Texte, ed. Herbert Vorgrimler (Freiburg: Herder, 1990).

'Situation Ethics in an Ecumenical Perspective' (1965), in *The Christian of the Future*, trans. W. J. O'Hara (London: Burns and Oates, 1967), 39–48; 'Zur "Situationsethik" aus ökumenischer Sicht', *SzT*, vi. 537–45.

'Some Implications of the Scholastic Concept of Uncreated Grace' (1939), *TI*, i. 321–46; 'Zur scholastischen Begrifflichkeit der ungeschaffenen Gnade', *SzT*, i. 347–75. (The final section of this essay does not appear in the 1939 version, and was presumably added for the 1954 publication of *Schriften zur Theologie*, i.)

Spirit in the World (1936), trans. William V. Dych (London: Sheed and Ward, 1968); *Geist in Welt: Zur Metaphysik der endlichen Erkenntnis bei Thomas von Aquin* (Innsbruck: Rauch, 1939). (Now available as *KRSW*, ii, with cross-references to pages in both earlier editions. Dych worked from Johannes B. Metz's expanded 2nd edn. [Munich: Kösel, 1957].)

'The "Spiritual Senses" according to Origen' (1932), *TI*, xvi. 81–103; 'Le Début d'une doctrine des cinq sens spirituels chez Origène', *Revue d'ascetique et de mystique*, 13 (1932), 113–45.

'The Spirituality of the Church of the Future' (1977), *TI*, xx. 143–53; 'Elemente der Spiritualität in der Kirche der Zukunft', *SzT*, xiv. 368–81.

'Teilhabe' (1964), *LTK*, ix. 1340–1.

'The Theological Concept of Concupiscentia' (1941), *TI*, i. 347–82; 'Zum theologischen Begriff der Konkupiszenz', *SzT*, i. 377–414 (*KRSW*, viii. 3–32).

'Theology and Anthropology' (1966), *TI*, ix. 28–45; 'Theologie und Anthropologie', *SzT*, viii. 43–65.

On the Theology of Death (1957), trans. Charles H. Henkey (London: Nelson, 1961); *Zur Theologie des Todes: Mit einem Exkurs über das Martyrium* (Freiburg: Herder, 1958).

'The Theology of the Symbol' (1959), *TI*, iv. 221–52; 'Zur Theologie des Symbols', *SzT*, iv. 275–311.

'Thomas Aquinas on Truth' (1938), *TI*, xiii. 13–31; 'Die Wahrheit bei Thomas von Aquin', *SzT*, x. 21–40 (*KRSW*, ii. 301–16). (1st pub. in Portuguese; the German text has been edited by Karl Heinz Neufeld.)

The Trinity (1965), trans. Joseph Donceel (London: Burns and Oates, 1967); taken from chapters in *Mysterium Salutis*, edd. Johannes Feiner and Magnus Löhrer, 5 vols. (Einsiedeln: Benziger, 1965), ii. 317–401.

'Über die Verkündigungstheologie: Eine kritisch-systematische Literaturübersicht' (1941), *KRSW*, iv. 337–45.

Visions and Prophecies (1958, earlier version 1952), trans. Charles Henkey and Richard Strachan (London: Burns and Oates, 1963); *Visionen und Prophezeiungen: Zur Mystik und Transzendenzerfahrung*, 3rd edn., ed. Josef Sudbrack (Freiburg: Herder, 1989).

Wagnis des Christen: Geistliche Texte (Freiburg: Herder, 1974).

'Warum uns das Beten nottut' (1924), in *Sehnsucht nach dem Geheimnisvollen Gott*, 77–80.

'Why am I a Christian Today?' (1972), in *The Practice of Faith*, 3–17; 'Warum bin ich heute ein Christ?', in *Wagnis des Christen*, 27–40. Also in *KRSW*, xxvi. 489–97.

'Why I Remain a Jesuit' (1973, title supplied P.E.), in *The Jesuits: Year-Book of the Society of Jesus* (1974–5), 30–3; 'Die Jesuiten und Die Zukunft. Anläßlich eines historischen Datums', *Frankfurter Allgemeine Zeitung*, 31 August 1973, 28. ET 1st pub. in a series of articles each headed 'And what do you think?'. The 'historical fact' in the title of the orig. was the bicentenary of the Society's suppression.

'Zu einer Theologie der Mystik' (1974), in *Visionen und Prophezeiungen*, 99–108.

III   Other Texts Cited

This list contains only texts that are particularly important or which are quoted repeatedly above. Texts referred to only once are referenced fully in the footnotes. The Freiburg University Library website now has a full bibliography of secondary literature on Rahner: readers interested in pursuing specific topics can download this bibliography, and use the 'find' function on their browsers.

ALFARO, JUAN, 'Formalobjekt, übernatürliches', in *LTK*, iv. 207–8 (1960).

ASHLEY, JAMES MATTHEW, *Interruptions: Mysticism, Politics, and Theology in the work of Johann Baptist Metz* (Notre Dame: University of Notre Dame Press, 1998).

BACIK, JAMES J., *Apologetics and the Eclipse of Mystery: Mystagogy according to Karl Rahner* (Notre Dame: University of Notre Dame Press, 1980).

BAKKER, LEO, *Freiheit und Erfahrung: Redaktionsgeschichtliche Untersuchungen über die Unterscheidung der Geister bie Ignatius von Loyola* (Würzburg: Echter, 1970).

BALTHASAR, HANS URS VON, *The Moment of Christian Witness*, trans. Richard Beckley (San Francisco: Ignatius Press, 1994 [orig. 1st pub. 1966]); *Cordula oder der Ernstfall* (Einsiedeln: Johannes Verlag, 1987).

BONAVENTURE, *Opera omnia*, 10 vols. (Quaracchi: St Bonaventure Press, 1882–1902).

BOYLE, MARJORIE O'ROURKE, 'Angels Black and White: Loyola's Spiritual Discernment in Historical Perspective', *Theological Studies*, 44 (1983), 241–57.

BRUGGER, WALTER (ed.), *Philosophisches Wörterbuch*, 18th edn. (Freiburg: Herder, 1990 [1st pub. 1947]).

CORETH, EMERICH, 'Contemplation in Action', in Robert W. Gleason (ed.), *Contemporary Spirituality* (New York: Macmillan, 1968), 184–211; '*In actione contemplativus*', *Zeitschrift für katholische Theologie*, 76 (1954), 55–82.

—— *Metaphysik: Eine methodisch-systematische Grundlegung*, 3rd edn. (Innsbruck: Tyrolia, 1980 [1st pub. 1961]).

Dictionnaire de Spiritualité: Ascétique et Mystique, Doctrine et Histoire, 16 vols. (Paris: Beauschesne, 1937–94).

DULLES, AVERY, 'Finding God's Will: Rahner's Interpretation of the Ignatian Election', *Woodstock Letters*, 94 (1965), 130–52.

EGAN, HARVEY D., *The Spiritual Exercises and the Ignatian Mystical Horizon* (St Louis: Institute of Jesuit Sources, 1976).

EGAN, HARVEY D., '"The Devout Christian of Tomorrow will be a Mystic": Mysticism and Karl Rahner's Theology', in William J. Kelly (ed.), *Theology and Discovery: Essays in Honor of Karl Rahner SJ* (Milwaukee: Marquette University Press, 1980), 99–112.

EICHER, PETER, 'Erfahren und Denken: Ein nota bene zur Flucht in meditative Unschuld', *Theologische Quartalschrift*, 157 (1977), 142–3.

The Complete Poems and Plays of T. S. Eliot (London: Faber, 1969).

ENDEAN, PHILIP, 'Discerning Behind the Rules: Ignatius' First Letter to Teresa Rejadell', *The Way Supplement*, 64 (Spring 1989), 37–50.

—— 'The Ignatian Prayer of the Senses', *Heythrop Journal*, 31 (1990), 391–418.

—— 'Ignatius and Church Authority', *The Way Supplement*, 70 (Spring 1990), 76–90.

—— 'To Reflect and Draw Profit', *The Way Supplement*, 82 (Spring 1995), 84–95.

—— 'The Draughthorse's Bloodlines: Discerning Together in the Ignatian *Constitutions*', *The Way Supplement*, 85 (Spring 1996), 73–83.

—— 'Rahner, Christology, and Grace', *Heythrop Journal*, 37 (1996), 284–97.

—— 'Karl Rahner and the Heart of Christ', *The Month*, 30 (1997), 357–63.

FARRUGIA, EDWARD G., *Aussage und Zusage: Zur Indirektheit der Methode K. Rahners, veranschaulicht an seiner Christologie* (Rome: Gregorian University Press, 1985).

FISCHER, KLAUS P., *Der Mensch als Geheimnis: Die Anthropologie Karl Rahners. Mit einem Brief von Karl Rahner* (Freiburg: Herder, 1974).

—— *Gotteserfahrung: Mystagogie in der Theologie Karl Rahners und in der Theologie der Befreiung* (Mainz: Grünewald, 1986).

GIL, DANIEL, *La consolación sin causa precedente: Estudio hermenéutico-teológico sobre los nn. 330, 331, y 336 de los Ejercicios Espirituales de San Ignacio de Loyola y sus principales comentaristas* (Rome: CIS, 1971).

GUIBERT, JOSEPH DE, *The Theology of the Spiritual Life*, trans. from 4th edn. Paul Barrett (London: Sheed and Ward, 1954).

—— *The Jesuits: Their Spiritual Doctrine and Practice: A Historical Study*, trans. William J. Young, ed. George E. Ganss (St Louis: Institute of Jesuit Sources, 1986 [orig. written by 1942]).

HILBERATH, BERND JOCHEN, *Karl Rahner: Gottgeheimnis Mensch* (Mainz: Grünewald, 1995).

The Poetical Works of Gerard Manley Hopkins, ed. Norman H. MacKenzie (Oxford: Clarendon Press, 1990).

HUGHES, GERARD J., 'Ignatian Discernment: A Philosophical Analysis', *Heythrop Journal*, 31 (1990), 419–38.

IGNATIUS LOYOLA (*Autobiography [Reminiscences]*, *Diary*, and selected letters) *Personal Writings*, trans. and ed. Joseph A. Munitiz and Philip Endean (London: Penguin, 1996).

—— (Constitutions) The Constitutions of the Society of Jesus, trans. George E. Ganss (St Louis: Institute of Jesuit Sources, 1970).

—— (Directories, written also by followers) On Giving the Spiritual Exercises: The Early Jesuit Manuscript Directories and the Official Directory of 1599, trans. and ed. Martin E. Palmer (St Louis: Institute of Jesuit Sources, 1996). MHSJ Directoria Exercitiorum Spiritualium (1540–1599), ed. Ignacio Iparraguirre (Rome, 1955).

—— (Spiritual Exercises) 'The Literal Version', trans. Elder Mullan, in David L. Fleming (ed.), Draw me into your Friendship: A Literal Translation and a Contemporary Reading of the Spiritual Exercises (St Louis: Institute of Jesuit Sources, 1996); MHSJ Sancti Ignatii de Loyola Exercitia Spiritualia, edd. José Calveras and Cándido de Dalmases (Rome, 1969).

—— (other original source material) MHSJ Sancti Ignatii de Loyola epistulae et instructiones, 12 vols., edd. M. Lecina, V. Agusti, F. Cervós, and D. Restrepo (Madrid: 1903–11); MHSJ Fontes Narrativi de S.Ignatio de Loyola et de Societatis Jesu initiis, edd. D. Fernández Zápico, C. de Dalmases, and P. Leturia, 4 vols. (Rome, 1943–60).

—— (Spanish manual edition) Obras completas, 5th edn., ed. Ignacio Iparraguirre, Cándido de Dalmases, and Manuel Ruiz Jurado (Madrid: BAC, 1991).

IMHOF, PAUL, and BIALLOWONS, HUBERT (edd.), Karl Rahner: Bilder eines Lebens (Zurich: Benziger, 1985).

The Collected Works of St. John of the Cross, trans. Kieran Kavanaugh and Otilio Rodríguez (Washington: Institute of Carmelite Studies, 1979).

KNAUER, PETER, Der Glaube kommt vom Hören: Ökumenische Fundamentaltheologie, 6th edn. (Freiburg: Herder, 1991 [1st pub. 1978]).

—— 'Die Wahl in den Exerzitien des Ignatius von Loyola: Vom Geistlichen Tagebuch und anderen ignatianischen Schriften her gesehen', Theologie und Philosophie, 66 (1991 [written 1967]), 321–37.

KUES, WOLFGANG, Werde, der du sein sollst!: Impulse für religiös gedeutete Entscheidungen von Karl Rahner und C. G. Jung (Frankfurt: Peter Lang, 1996).

KUNZ, ERHARD, 'Glaubwürdigkeitserkenntnis und Glaube (analysis fidei)', in Walter Kern, Hermann J. Pottmeyer, and Max Seckler (edd.), Handbuch der Fundamentaltheologie, iv (Freiburg: Herder, 1988), 414–49.

—— 'Analysis fidei', in Lexikon für Theologie und Kirche, 3rd edn. (Freiburg: Herder, 1993–), i. 583–6.

KUSTERMANN, ABRAHAM PETER, and NEUFELD, KARL H. (edd.), 'Gemeinsame Arbeit in brüderlicher Liebe': Hugo und Karl Rahner. Dokumente und Würdigung ihrer Weggemeinschaft (Stuttgart: Akademie der Diözese Rottenburg-Stuttgart, 1993).

LAHITTON, JOSEPH, La vocation sacerdotale: traité théologique et pratique, 1st edn. (Paris: Lethielleux, 1909).

LANGE, HERMANN, *De gratia: Tractatus dogmaticus* (Freiburg: Herder, 1929).

LASH, NICHOLAS, *Easter in Ordinary: Reflections on Human Experience and the Knowledge of God* (London: SCM, 1988).

LEHMANN, KARL, 'Introduction', in Rahner, *The Content of Faith*, 1–42.

LENNAN, RICHARD, *The Ecclesiology of Karl Rahner* (Oxford: Clarendon Press, 1995).

LONSDALE, DAVID, *Eyes to See, Ears to Hear: An Introduction to Ignatian Spirituality* (London: Darton, Longman and Todd, 1990).

McINTOSH, MARK A., *Mystical Theology* (Oxford: Blackwell, 1998).

MACQUARRIE, JOHN, and CHILDRESS, JAMES F. (edd.), *A New Dictionary of Christian Ethics* (London: SCM, 1986).

MAIER, MARTIN, 'La Théologie des Exercices de Karl Rahner', *Recherches de science réligieuse*, 79 (1991), 535–60.

MANNERMAA, TUOMO, 'Eine falsche Interpretationstradition von Karl Rahners *Hörer des Wortes*', *Zeitschrift für katholische Theologie*, 96 (1970), 204–9.

—— '*Lumen fidei et obiectum fidei adventicium: Die Spontaneität und Rezeptivität der Glaubenserkenntnis im frühen Denken Karl Rahners*' (typescript in KRA, deposited by Bishop Karl Lehmann; orig. in Finnish, subtitled *Uskontiedon spontaanisuus ja reseptiivisyys Karl Rahnerin varhaisessa ajattelussa* [Helsinki: Missiologian ja Ekumeniikan Seura R. Y., 1970]).

METZ, JOHANN BAPTIST, *Faith in History and Society: Toward a Practical Fundamental Theology*, trans. David Smith (London: Burns and Oates, 1980 [orig. 1st pub. 1977]).

MEURES, FRANZ, 'The Ministry of Facilitation', *The Way Supplement*, 85 (Spring 1996), 62–72.

MIGGELBRINK, RALF, *Ekstatische Gottesliebe im tätigen Weltbezug: Der Beitrag Karl Rahners zur zeitgenössischen Gotteslehre* (Altenberg: Telos, 1989).

MUCK, OTTO, *Philosophische Gotteslehre* (Düsseldorf: Patmos, 1983).

—— 'Heidegger und Karl Rahner', *Zeitschrift für katholische Theologie*, 116 (1994), 257–69.

NADAL, JERÓNIMO, works cited according to MHSJ *Epistolae (Monumenta) P. Hieronymi Nadal*, edd. F. Cervós and Miguel Nicolau, 6 vols. (Madrid and Rome, 1898–1964).

NEUFELD, KARL H., 'Unter Brüdern: Zur Frühgeschichte der Theologie Karl Rahners aus der Zusammenarbeit mit Hugo Rahner' (1st pub. 1979), in Kustermann and Neufeld (edd.), *'Gemeinsame Arbeit in brüderlicher Liebe'*, 11–31.

—— *Geschichte und Mensch: A. Delps Idee der Geschichte—Ihr Werden und Ihre Grundzüge* (Rome: Gregorian University Press, 1983).

—— *Die Brüder Rahner: Eine Biographie* (Freiburg: Herder, 1994).

NICOLAU, MIGUEL, *Jerónimo Nadal S. I. (1507–1580): Sus obras y doctrinas espirituales* (Madrid: Consejo superior de investigaciones científicas, 1949).

—— 'Nadal, Jerónimo', in *Dictionnaire de Spiritualité*, xi (Paris: Beauchesne, 1981), 3–15.

O'MALLEY, JOHN W., *Tradition and Transition: Historical Perspectives on Vatican II* (Wilmington: Michael Glazier, 1989).

—— *The First Jesuits* (Cambridge, Mass.: Harvard University Press, 1993).

RAFFELT, ALBERT, and VERWEYEN, HANSJÜRGEN, *Karl Rahner* (Munich: Beck, 1997).

RAHNER, HUGO, *Saint Ignatius Loyola: Letters to Women*, trans. Kathleen Pond and S. A. H. Weetman (Edinburgh: Herder, 1960); *Ignatius von Loyola: Briefwechsel mit Frauen* (Freiburg: Herder, 1956).

—— *Ignatius the Theologian*, trans. Michael Barry (London: Geoffrey Chapman, 1968); chapters of *Ignatius von Loyola als Mensch und Theologe* (Freiburg: Herder, 1964).

—— *The Vision of St. Ignatius in the Chapel of La Storta*, 2nd edn., trans. Robert O. Brennan (Rome: CIS, 1979 [orig. 1st pub. 1935]); a chapter in *Ignatius von Loyola als Mensch und Theologe* (Freiburg: Herder, 1964).

RENO, R. R., *The Ordinary Transformed: Karl Rahner and the Christian Vision of Transcendence* (Grand Rapids: Eerdmans, 1995).

ROUSSELOT, PIERRE, *The Eyes of Faith*, trans. Joseph Donceel, ed. John M. McDermott (New York: Fordham University Press, 1990); 'Les yeux de la foi', *Recherches de science réligieuse*, 1 (1910), 241–59, 444–75.

SANDLER, WILLIBALD, *Bekehrung des Denkens: Karl Rahners Anthropologie und Soteriologie als formal-offenes System in triadischer Perspektive* (Frankfurt: Peter Lang, 1996).

SCHNEIDER, MICHAEL, *'Unterscheidung der Geister': Die ignatianischen Exerzitien in der Deutung von E. Przywara, K. Rahner und G. Fessard* (Innsbruck: Tyrolia, 1983).

SCHWAGER, RAYMUND, *Das dramatische Kirchenverständis bei Ignatius von Loyola* (Zurich: Benziger, 1970).

SCHWERDTFEGER, NIKOLAUS, *Gnade und Welt: Zum Grundgefüge von Karl Rahners Theorie der 'anonymen Christen'* (Freiburg: Herder, 1982).

SPOHN, WILLIAM C., 'The Reasoning Heart: An American Approach to Christian Discernment', *Theological Studies*, 44 (1983), 30–52.

TANNER, NORMAN P. (ed.), *Decrees of the Ecumenical Councils* (London: Sheed and Ward, 1990).

TONER, JULES J., *A Commentary on Saint Ignatius' Rules for the Discernment of Spirits: A Guide to the Principles and Practice* (St Louis: Institute of Jesuit Sources, 1982).

—— *Discerning God's Will: Ignatius of Loyola's Teaching on Christian Decision Making* (St Louis: Institute of Jesuit Sources, 1991).

—— *What is Your Will, O God?* (St Louis: Institute of Jesuit Sources, 1995).

TRÜTSCH, JOSEF, SS. *Trinitatis inhabitatio apud theologos recentiores* (Trent, 1949).

VORGRIMLER, HERBERT (ed.), *Wagnis Theologie: Erfahrungen mit der Theologie Karl Rahners* (Freiburg: Herder, 1979).

—— *Understanding Karl Rahner: An Introduction to his Life and Thought*, trans. John Bowden (London: SCM Press, 1986 [orig. 2nd edn. 1985]).

WONG, JOSEPH H. P., *Logos-Symbol in the Christology of Karl Rahner* (Rome: Libreria Ateneo Salesiano, 1984).

WILLIAMS, ROWAN, 'Balthasar and Rahner', in John Riches (ed.), *The Analogy of Beauty* (Edinburgh: T. and T. Clark, 1986), 11–34.

WISEMAN, JAMES A., '"I Have Experienced God": Religious Experience in the Theology of Karl Rahner', *American Benedictine Review*, 44/1 (March 1993), 22–57.

WITTGENSTEIN, LUDWIG, *Philosophical Investigations*, 3rd edn., trans. G. E. M. Anscombe (Oxford: Blackwell, 1967 [written by 1949]).

ZAHLAUER, ARNO, *Karl Rahner und sein 'produktives Vorbild' Ignatius von Loyola* (Innsbruck: Tyrolia, 1996).

Index

Themes in the work of Ignatius and Rahner are referenced under the headings in their names.

Printed in the United States
R3139400002B